(Photograph by Milford B. Newhouse)

JOHN HUMPHREY NOYES

(From the bust by Bergman)

A YANKEE SAINT

John Humphrey Noyes and the Oneida Community BY

ROBERT ALLERTON PARKER

NEW YORK
G. P. PUTNAM'S SONS
1935

Printed in the United States of America
by the Van Rees Press

CONTENTS

PART ONE: PUTNEY

PART TWO: ONEIDA

PART THREE: RETREAT

LIST OF ILLUSTRATIONS

PART ONE

PUTNEY

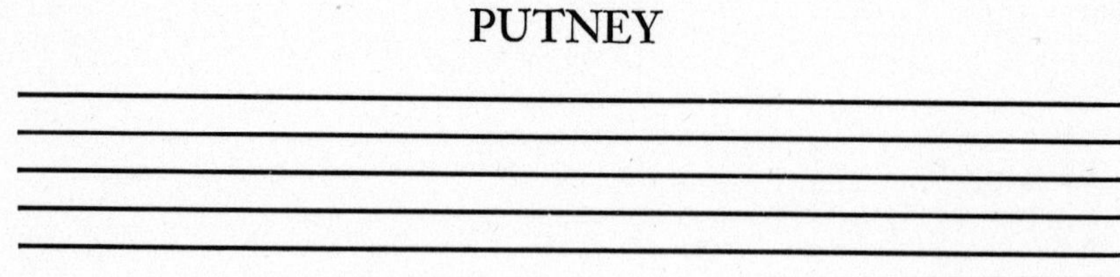

Chapter I: POLLY HAYES

From dust I rise,
And out of nothing now awake;
These brighter regions which salute mine eyes,
A gift from God I take.
The earth, the seas, the light, the lofty skies,
The sun and stars are mine, if these I prize.

A stranger here
Strange things doth meet, strange glory see;
Strange treasures lodged in this fair world appear,
Strange all and new to me;
But that they mine should be, who nothing was,
That strangest is of all, yet brought to pass.

—Traherne.

I

Captain Blakesley of New Haven bought the meadowland west of Brattleboro. His four sons sent a letter south, urging their friend Rutherford Hayes to come up for a visit. One bitter day in February, 1778, this lanky, raw-boned youth of twenty-one arrived at the little frontier settlement.

The Blakesleys and their neighbors hailed the coming of this muscular young man, who had some training in blacksmithing; Brattleboro was in sore need of a smith. The Blakesley boys described to the newcomer the delights and excitement of life in the Green Mountains—hunting, fishing, trapping, sledding. He was not going to spend the rest of his life in the backwoods, Rutherford retorted. But the men of Brattleboro paid little attention to his protest. Before young Hayes fully realized what was happening, they had organized a "bee." All the men of the little community gathered with their pikepoles. They cleared away the deep snow, and soon the young giant from New Haven was taking an active part in the "raising" of a smithy. Skillfully they framed and fitted the hewn parts together. Then, with a great shout, they lifted the ponderous bents into the air. Tenons slipped into their places in the mortises. Sturdy young men shinned up the newly hoisted bents. Deep draughts from stone jugs seemed to double their agility and daring, as they handled the newly-cut rafters and drove pins into the braces. If, toward the conclusion of the "bee," tongues grew a bit thick, no one doubted the necessity of good liquor and joviality for the successful and rapid accomplishment of a "raising." At last, the whole structure stood solidly and steadily upright.

The frame of Rutherford Hayes's shop had been pinned, not spiked together—for nails were still a scarcity. That was one reason Brattleboro needed a blacksmith. Less than a month after his arrival, sparks were flying from his anvil. "A dirty, black business!" he used to cry, half-apologetically, "but it does bring in white money!"

Young Hayes found lodging with the Smiths, a family which had come to the wilderness from Hadley, Massachusetts. The eldest of the nine Smith children was Chloe, a girl of sixteen. Hard-working, obedient, cheerful, she was already inured to the hardships of frontier life. Her grave, appealing countenance drove all thoughts of returning to New Haven from the mind of Rutherford Hayes. They were married the following year—in 1779. Chloe was eighteen when their first child was born. It was a little girl, and they named her Polly.

In physical endurance Chloe Hayes was a fitting companion for her brawny husband. In will-power, neighbors testified, she was even more indomitable. Not long after the birth of Polly, an opportunity to take over the management of a tavern near West Brattleboro, at a point where the pike turned west over the green hills to Marlboro, was offered to the young couple. They named it the Hayes Tavern; but soon it was known in the neighborhood of Brattleboro as the Big House. How proud the young Hayeses were of its fourteen great fireplaces! The largest of them all, with its long, blackened crane, and its spacious Dutch ovens for roasting meat and fowls, roared in the cellar. There, under the rafters of a low-beamed ceiling, Mrs. Hayes established an undisputed reputation as the first cook in southern Vermont.

A noisy brood of little Hayeses, as the years passed, gathered like chicks about her busy petticoats. Upstairs to bed they were sent before the crowd in the great taproom to the right of the wide hallway became noisy. How merry was the ballroom on the second floor of the Big House, when the whole countryside gathered to celebrate the admission of Vermont as the fourteenth State of the Union! A bar-cupboard opened off this ballroom, and, there, on such festive occasions, Chloe Hayes officiated. She could wait on the guests of these tavern balls all night, and start out the next morning on horseback, with her husband, on a two-hundred mile trip to Bainbridge, in Chenango County, New York, to visit the elder Smiths.

Late every Saturday afternoon, Mrs. Hayes pushed her work-basket as far as she could under the high, four-poster bed, so that she might not be tempted by it over the Sabbath. Every Saturday

evening at sunset, the wooden shutters of the public rooms were drawn. No refreshments were served again until Monday morning. Like the rest of the good folk of Brattleboro and its countryside, the Hayeses obeyed the Sabbath laws with unflinching rigidity. They recognized their need for the protection of God. The loneliness of the wilderness, the rigors of frontier life, the wolves that howled in the forests—had not Catherine Mason of Bennington been eaten by a pack of wolves on her way home from an evening of merry-making?—such menaces as these taught the imminence of death and the necessity for an assured and divine protector.

2

Little Polly Hayes could never forget the long succession of parsons who called at the Big House. The best-behaved child was rewarded by the high privilege of serving the reverend gentleman a glass of wine in the parlor. Since she was the eldest of the brood, that honor most often fell to Polly.

When darkness fell, the children were promptly packed up the steep stairs to the big bedroom reserved for them. Four beds were set up in that chilly room—one in each corner. They were filled with the entire second generation of Hayeses—according to size and sex. Then, as Polly grew into a tall, awkward girl—they noted her resemblance to her father—she was given the duties of caring for the smaller children. Winter was perhaps the busiest time of year, even for a growing girl. Early in December pigs, fat bullocks and heifers were led to the block. Then followed the making of sausages and head-cheese, the trying out of lard and tallow. Candles were molded and dipped, brine barrels filled for the pork. This arduous labor lasted until February. Then girls and boys crowded into the great sled and drove away to the singing-school, to quaver "China" and sound the harmonies of "Mear." It was a time of courtship; when the moon rose, the young men escorted the maidens home.

Polly Hayes, too, had her share of the swains; but her parents agreed that none of the young men could hold a candle to John Noyes, even though he was thirty-six years old.

John Noyes was directly descended from a strongly marked, clannish family which had emigrated to the colonies from England in 1634 and settled at Newbury, Massachusetts. A Noyes was the first minister of that town. John Noyes was a descendant of this cleric's brother Nicholas, and was fifth in line from the emigration. These Noyeses spread over New England. Joseph, grand-

father of John, moved in 1740 to Atkinson, a small town fifteen miles west of Newbury. There his descendants remained and multiplied; there John Noyes was born, April 2, 1764.

The Atkinson Noyeses were steady, God-fearing, able and stodgy. They were taciturn, shy, hesitant to mix their blood with that of outsiders. But, to their consternation and dismay, some "sport" would crop out in every generation.

John Noyes was one of five brothers. Humphrey married Judith Noyes; Joseph married Anna Noyes; Samuel married Lydia Noyes; Peter married Sarah Noyes. Each of the four had married a cousin or kin of some degree. This "breeding in and in" was the incubus on the latent genius of the Atkinson clan. The hidden cause of these consanguineous marriage was bashfulness—general bashfulness toward mankind, and special bashfulness toward the opposite sex. The Atkinson Noyeses were said to be so bashful they could not pop the question to anybody but cousins. This trait became known as "the Atkinson difficulty."

In youth John Noyes was not much inured to hardships; his constitution was never very firm. From the age of seventeen, and for ten years, he taught in eighteen district schools of New England. "Probable earnings in ten years, allowing for loss of time and medical expenses, $500. Average per year, $50." Despite such handicaps, John Noyes fitted himself for college while teaching and in the summer of 1791 entered Dartmouth. He had what he had saved from his earnings and $600 left him by his father, who had died the year before. He was twenty-seven years old—probably the oldest in his class. His maturity, philosophical turn of mind, social disposition, and conversational felicity made John Noyes something of a popular oracle. From 1791 to 1799 he was a student and tutor at Dartmouth, and was in contact with all of the students of that decade, including Daniel Webster.

Tired of teaching, aged thirty-five, John Noyes decided to seek his fortune in Vermont, then a new country. He settled in Brattleboro, glad of the chance to "clerk" in a store and learn the elements of business. Soon, in association with General Jonas Mann, he was conducting a busy trading-post. It was not a store in our modern sense: it was a clearing house where backwoodsmen and country folk gathered to barter their products—exchanging potash for tea, coffee and plainstuffs, and sealing the bargain with the customary mug of flip. From magistrates and ministers downward, all classes drank liquor at the general store. Business prospered and increased. Like other New England merchants of the period, John Noyes made at least two trips a year to Boston.

By horseback and stage coach the journey took three or four days each way; each merchant carried pistols for self-protection.

Noyes found lodging at the Big House of the Hayeses. This residence brought him in friendly, neighborly touch with the teamsters, woodsmen and potash-makers of the whole district. On winter evenings they gathered in the public room of the Hayes Tavern. With oxen teams secure in the stables, sledges heavily loaded for an early start next morning, the teamsters lounged before the great roaring fire, industriously greasing their home-tanned boots. Hard cider and Medford rum set tongues wagging. Chilled bodies relaxed into a mellow glow. And John Noyes, the silent man, the educated man, the ex-headmaster, was too adroit in business to hold himself aloof from wholesome, primitive mirth or to refrain from tippling. It was all a part of sound trading.

Noyes soon became aware of Polly Hayes, the tall, radiant girl of nineteen who kept discreetly in the background. He began to escape from the tavern turmoil into her company; then he learned that she was already betrothed.

He turned to Mrs. Hayes (she was but one year his senior), and unburdened his problem to her sympathetic ear. Polly, the mother confided, had given her word to some backwoods swain and her conscience—a fine young flower of New England conscience—would not release her from this promise. Moreover, that Atkinson difficulty stood in Noyes's way.

What chance had an ex-schoolmaster in his waning thirties to attract this downright, outspoken girl of nineteen? John Noyes proffered great, wordy, floral pieces of theology, philosophy, literature. Never had Polly listened to such information on all subjects—never had she met any one so intimately familiar with matters so far above the comprehension of a Windham County girl. Never had John Noyes been encouraged by such an appreciative listener. But then it was almost impossible to descend from such high levels to the delightful, inarticulate absurdities of love-making, to kisses and caresses. As for impulsive gestures, Polly Hayes found Mr. Noyes as close and guarded as a chestnut in its burr. Moreover, he was just commencing business with little capital, and the timorous ex-schoolmaster could hardly gather courage to go off into the uncertainty and expense of matrimony. The courtship lingered till 1804, and was brought to a conclusion, Polly always said, by her demand for a practical decision. At the ripe age of forty, John Noyes freed himself from the Atkinson difficulty. With a sigh of relief, Polly at last heard the first, tongue-tied expression of love from those small, pursed, pedantic

lips. And in the same year, 1804, marriage vows were exchanged.

Little Mary was born in September, 1806; a year later another girl was born, named Joanna; and two years later, also in September, still another girl, named Elizabeth. If John Noyes had any misgivings concerning the advent of a son, he concealed them from his adoring wife.

Mrs. Noyes was proud of his increasing prominence in the growing community. The sign in front of the store now read, "Noyes, Mann & Hayes" (Polly's brother had been made a partner). In the intricacies of backwoods business and frontier finance, Squire Noyes was looked upon as the village Solomon. With undivided respect, Brattleboro listened to his genial stories and was duly impressed with his homely counsel. Here was a man with a college education, a graduate of Dartmouth, a scholar who had been headmaster at Chesterfield Academy, a sage who understood Greek and Hebrew—a vigorous moralist, a thoughtful philospher. Just the man, in truth, to represent Brattleboro in the Vermont Legislature!

3

Polly Noyes sat listening to her husband's Fourth of July address in Brattleboro in 1811. Vermont, only nineteen years old as a state of the Union, was proud of its achievements. Jonas Galusha was governor; James Madison was President of the United States; and the miracle of steam transit had been successfully inaugurated on Lake Champlain these three years. Her husband's words came to Polly Noyes's ears with increasing emphasis. "All things beneath the sun are permanent in nothing but vicissitude. This is the peculiar characteristic of all human projects. They can never bear the stamp of perfection, for they are the work of an imperfect hand.... Far be it from us to damp the joys of the present occasion by fearful forebodings." Were they on the verge of war?—of revolution, change, destruction? John Noyes's Tory voice was denouncing the excesses of the French Revolution.

On September 11, "Freeman's Meeting Day," John Noyes learned that his fellow-citizens had chosen him their representative in the State Legislature. Some one hurried into the election meeting and whispered that he was needed at home immediately. Mrs. Noyes was bearing him a son at last. When Polly Noyes looked upon her little boy, she sighed with relief, and prayed that he might beome a "minister of the Everlasting Gospel." She resolved to bring him up in the ways of the Lord—to teach him

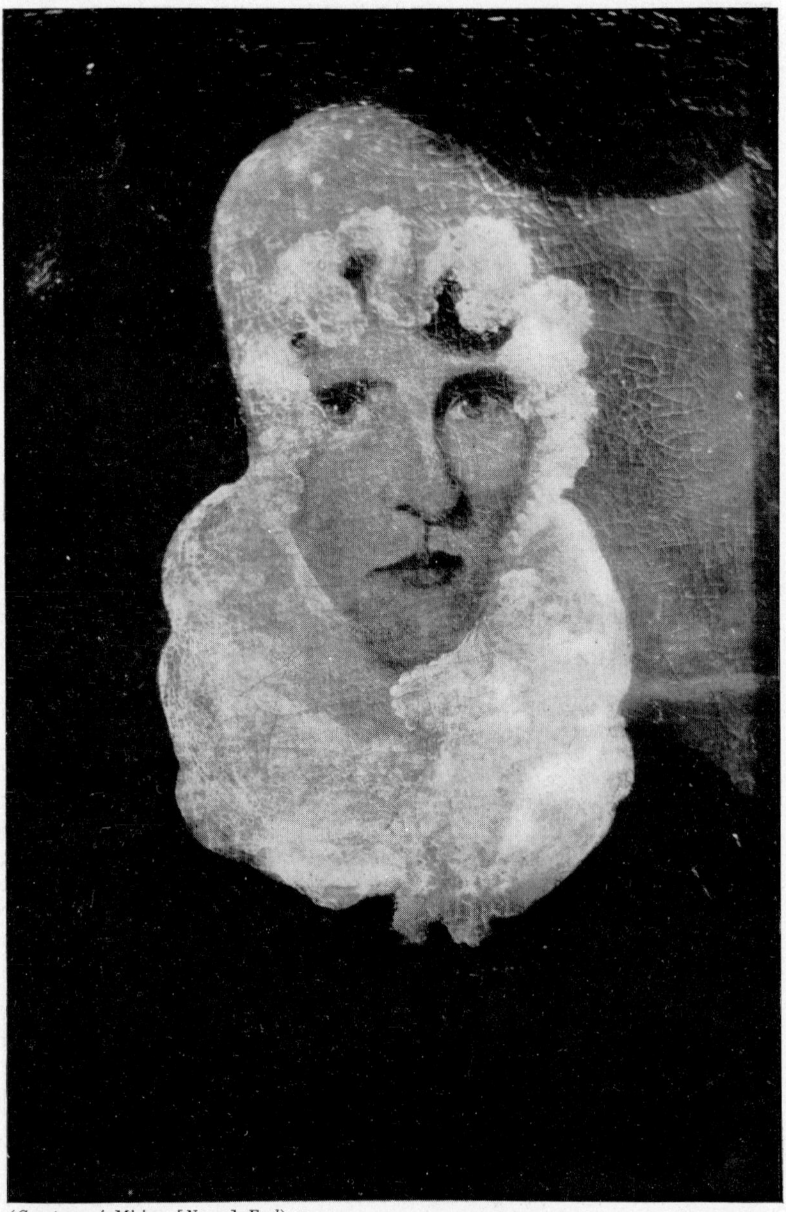

(*Courtesy of Miriam* [*Noyes*] *Earl*)

POLLY HAYES NOYES

(From an old portrait in oil)

(*Courtesy of Miriam* [*Noyes*] *Earl*)

HON. JOHN NOYES

(From an old portrait in oil)

never to seek material advantage at a sacrifice of the spirit. She could not foresee—merciful provision of Providence—that years later, his challenge to Vermont respectability would bring the High Sheriff to their door; that for generations to come the name of her firstborn son would be whispered throughout Vermont with derisive leers—and mentioned not at all in the presence of children.

The Noyeses named their first son John Humphrey—the middle name in honor of Mr. Noyes's father and eldest brother. The boy seemed to bring good luck. In the years that followed, John Noyes advanced in prosperity. It was common gossip that the Squire had made a great deal of money out of the War of 1812, and that he knew how to make that money work for him to the best advantage. In 1815 John Noyes was elected to the House of Representatives from southern Vermont. It was a great honor, but it was quite impossible to carry the family to Washington, for there were now six children: two more sons, George and Horatio had been born in 1813 and 1815.

Steamboats were gradually coming into use; but fifteen years or more were to pass before the advent of the railroad. It was a long and dangerous journey from Brattleboro to Washington. John Noyes spent eleven days in noisome stage coaches and steamboats, which might explode at any moment. His itinerary took him from East Brattleboro to Hartford, New Haven, New York, Trenton, Philadelphia, and Baltimore. Through New Jersey he was warned to protect his baggage against highwaymen.

Philadelphia vastly impressed the Congressman-elect; certainly, in his opinion, it was the most cultured city of the whole continent. But Washington—a dreary place, indeed! The British had burned the public buildings the year before, and the ruins remained. In the autumn chill the avenues and thoroughfares, though laid out on a majestic scale, passed through swamps and wilderness. John Noyes was impressed by the great buildings which had escaped destruction, and he possessed foresight enough to picture a Washington "when it will be famed for its elegance and splendor." He occupied a large chamber on Pennsylvania Avenue, from which he viewed the carriages, the bustle, the show, the jostle of great folk from all over the country and foreign lands. The little girls at home wondered if their father wore knee breeches—or "small clothes"—at the great receptions. Boots were frowned upon at Mrs. Madison's Wednesday evening levees—because boots and muslins did not mix. Lacking small clothes, the gentlemen from the less urbane states—John Noyes seemed to be

one of them—tied their pantaloons down to shoes or boots. A laborious session during the first three months in 1816, when representatives entered the House at nine and continued "in great exertion and agitation of mind till five and six o'clock, without drinking anything but water," convinced John Noyes that a Congressman's career was "a dog's life and worse.... After all this fatigue we return to our quarters almost totally exhausted in body and mind; and if we are not beyond eating, we eat like dogs whatever is set before us...."

His children crowed their delight when the Hon. John Noyes returned to Brattleboro that summer, but he encouraged no outward demonstrations of affection. The younger children were puzzled by this silent, graying man past fifty, who happened to be their father—a chilling contrast to their impulsive, warm-hearted, romping mother, whose sympathies radiated in all directions. Despite the difference in temperament and ages, each exhibited a deference toward the other. And though Mrs. Noyes grew gradually accustomed to a faint odor of alcohol about her husband, she made no remonstrance.

The very day after the Fourth of July, in 1817, the Noyes children were told that a new little sister had been sent by the Lord. The name of Harriet Hayes Noyes was chosen for her. On March 2, 1819, eighteen months later, another daughter was born, Charlotte Augusta. The last child—a son—was born on December 4, 1822. When little George died, this youngest was given the same name—George Washington Noyes. About that time belated news from distant Ohio came, news of the death of Polly's younger brother, Rutherford, and of the birth of a posthumous son, Rutherford Birchard Hayes. Some six decades later, this Rutherford Hayes was to be chosen, by a hair's breadth, President of the United States.

In 1817 John Noyes retired from public life and prepared to close his business. No trace of his sickly, delicate youth remained. He had become a healthy, stalwart squire, a model of Shakespeare's "Justice, In fair round belly, with good capon lined." He had accumulated a fortune sufficient for his own purposes, a safe competency for himself and a good start for his children. Meanwhile he was looking about for a place suitable for a final residence. New Haven seemed to offer entrancing possibilities. It was not, however, Mrs. Noyes insisted, merely a matter of the intellectual welfare of the children; religion was even more important. For three months she gave herself up to special prayer before making this momentous decision. "She was ready to spoil

our chances for worldly advantages," one of her daughters wrote later, "rather than that we should forget God."

They were attracted to Putney, a little town ten miles north of Brattleboro. Sheltered by hills descending from the Green Mountain range on the west, just across the blue Connecticut River from a New Hampshire town on the east, Putney promised peace, comfort, isolation. Then, and for years after, there was no railway within forty miles of it. The Noyeses moved there in 1821, and settled down to their final work, the education of their children.

The Noyes house, spacious and dignified as became the Squire's exalted position, became known as Locust Grove. It stood on a pretty eminence overlooking the secluded little village to the south, a great white, boxlike mansion majestically silhouetted against a background of vibrating green.

Mrs. Noyes soon became a familiar and commanding figure in the village activities. To Putney children she was like a queen out of a story-book. Her frame was large almost to the point of gauntness. Her imperious head, high above the ears, was surmounted by a crown of rebellious red hair. She strode through the paths and byways of Putney with a stately walk. Her mercurial temperament enlivened the tradespeople and neighbors, and rescued many a church meeting from the blight of dullness. Her silvery voice rang out loudly and clearly, always persuasively and usually joyously. Her hospitality was prompt and unbounded.

Already prominent in Brattleboro, the Noyeses took their place in the aristocracy of Putney. Judge White, who had also been in Congress, and Squire Noyes became fast friends. Their lands adjoined; both boasted large families; both had three accomplished daughters, just back from boarding schools, dazzling less favored females with their fresh accomplishments. Captain Green's daughters had been educated at Miss Willard's academy for young ladies, in Troy; and his only son had been sent away to college—accepted gesture of aristocracy. The Putney minister, learned, urbane, a rotund, genial gentleman of the old school, was an enthusiast for the laboratory rather than the pulpit. And General Leavitt, with his notorious love of ostentation and luxury, exhibited all the instincts of a Southern nabob.

4

John Noyes the younger was growing fast. He was a thoughtful lad, but, as Mrs. Noyes soon perceived, violent and passionate

when provoked to anger. At an early age, he became a natural leader amongst his Brattleboro companions. "I can see him now," Polly Noyes mused in after years, "marching off at the head of a company of his playmates, all armed with mullein stalks."

She had little cause to complain of John's conduct. When he was eight, Mrs. Noyes took the children across country to a revival. John was promptly "converted," but the experience was soon erased by growing interests. Polly taught the children to read daily from the Testament. Their religious education fell to her. Though Squire Noyes respected his wife's piety, he himself was indifferent to Gospel teachings.

By the time he was nine, little John had made such astounding progress in his studies that it was decided to send him away to the school at Amherst. Mrs. Noyes accompanied the lad to the town, and left him there in a proper boarding place. As he sat alone in his bedroom, and the wind whistled mournfully around the house, John succumbed to a paroxysm of homesickness; then went to the bookstore, bought ink and paper, and resolutely began to keep a journal.

After the family had moved to Putney, John was transferred at the age of eleven to a school nearer home—the Academy in Brattleboro, for which Squire Noyes had donated the land. In 1826, young John was ready to enter college. Yale seemed to be first choice. With the impulsiveness of his age—his fifteenth birthday was approaching—John Noyes made the premature purchase of that high-standing "Yale" collar affected by all loyal students at New Haven. But when Mrs. Noyes insisted that Dartmouth was a safer place for the morals of young men, Squire Noyes was pleased, and in September, the two John Noyeses, senior and junior, set off for Hanover. Mr. Noyes arranged for his son to board with Madam Brown, impoverished widow of a former president of the college. Uncomplainingly, the youth was up at five on chill winter mornings; to prayers at quarter after; then recitations; and not until afterward, with hunger gnawing, to breakfast; after that, study until eleven, and then a class in *Græca Majora*, which consumed an hour. Then dinner at one; study until four; then an hour of grammar; prayers at quarter before six; then supper, after which tomorrow's lesson in Livy must be prepared. Such was John's busy day and with characteristic defiance of student opinion, taunted by freshmen for wearing a "standing joke," he persisted in flaunting that "Yale" collar.

During John's sophomore year, in 1828, the students at Dartmouth College noted, with excitement, the arrival of a tall,

thin man of forty-six, with high cheek bones, dark skin, and impressive, deep-set dark eyes. The almost funereal tones of the low voice, the almost languid manner, conveyed a sense of leonine pride. Daniel Webster had graduated from Dartmouth at the beginning of the century; now he was one of the famous figures of the nation. On the evening of that eventful day, this distinguished alumnus held a levee (so it was named) at his hotel. Professors and outstanding students were presented to the great man. John was introduced by Professor Chamberlain as "the son of Tutor Noyes."

The great black eyes seemed to pierce those of the trembling youth. "I wish I could do you as much good as your father did me!" Memorable words to receive from Daniel Webster—words to be quoted verbatim, words to be written home immediately, words to be preserved for the annals of the Noyes family.

At seventeen, in his junior year, John began a new journal. He saw himself as a budding author, and called this daybook "Fugitive Pieces, by the author of etc., etc." He was uncommonly penetrating in probing the characters of his classmates. Of one he wrote: "He is niggardly of his own, but liberal of other people's money, and in proof of this I may truly say that I have frequently seen him engage heart and hand in a *jolly scrape*, but never knew him to have his wallet about him when the bills were to be paid." Young Noyes began to rebel against the stiff, cold reserve which passed as good breeding, and expressed his indignation in doggerel. He resolved to overcome the inborn bashfulness that made him seem to himself such a stupid dunce. He cried for a brazen front and nerves of steel. "I swear by Jove, I will be impudent! So unreasonable and excessive is my bashfulness that I fully believe I could face a battery of cannon with less trepidation than I could a room full of ladies with whom I was unacquainted." John's cheeks burned with shame at nettling memories of the mortification produced by "the Atkinson difficulty." Sometimes he even wished himself a hermit or a savage.

What conversations they indulged in, those scholars of eighteen and nineteen! Philosophy, religion, literature, politics, the daring verses of Lord Byron! Long walks of three miles before breakfast, checkers (every one beat John Noyes),—all delightful diversions. But John awoke, as well, to the "necessity of a person having resources of enjoyment within himself," and to the ultimate misery of those who depend wholly upon social excitement.

The year of graduation came, and John Noyes's name was on the list of "Junior Appointees"; he won the distinction of deliver-

ing an oration on graduation day; he was elected to Phi Beta Kappa. How swiftly he had passed through childhood, youth, to manhood! The changes in his life seemed so tumultuous to him that he asked himself if he were lacking in stability. He had been simple and credulous, averse to society—especially that of the opposite sex—preoccupied with hunting and fishing. Then, of a sudden, blossomed an ambition for popularity, an interest in his fellow-men; later, a passion for learning. Then he had found consolation in philosophic stoicism. Then the "mazes of dissipation," followed by another revolution, with "virtue, honor and the dictates of conscience" ruling supreme.

His face was still freckled; his hair was sorrel; his sloping shoulders accented the length of his neck. In despair, this awkward, ungainly youth confessed to himself that looks had a vast deal to do with attraction and success in the world, particularly in the matter of girls. In love, as in everything else, we must bring what we have to offer into the marketplace, at least where it can be seen and appreciated. Girls, he knew, would not take the trouble to hunt for hidden virtues. Still, it was well to remind oneself every five minutes that faint heart never won fair lady.

A year later John began to exhibit more confidence. Social ambition began to sprout. His new self-esteem was fortified by the purchase of bell-bottomed pantaloons, a pair of square-toed boots, patent leather stock, and pyramid-shaped hat. Thus accoutered, he strode down the village street—a man of fashion!

After his graduation, he went to study law in the office of Larkin G. Mead—who, in 1829, had become the husband of John's eldest sister, Mary—in the village of Chesterfield, New Hampshire. Despite his great self-consciousness and an intense conviction of his own inferiority in looks, John Noyes loved the fun of the boys and girls of the village. A singing school was started and he realized that in order to retain his place in the "flirtation ring" he must join that school. But he could not distinguish one note from another, nor reognize a discord. Then he discovered an old fiddle in a closet of the law-office. It had been the favorite instrument of poor old Leach, a blind fiddler who once wandered over the countryside about Chesterfield, and, not unlike an old Scottish bard, had been revered in all the villages he visited. John now set himself the task of picking out the notes in an old book of psalm tunes. When every one had left the office, Noyes extracted the fiddle from its hiding place and often persisted in his practice until midnight. From that fiddle he acquired all the confidence he

needed to hold his place among the young men in the singing school and to "carry on" with the girls during intermissions.

As the winter of 1830 set in, John Noyes found it more difficult to keep his mind on Blackstone. He was bewitched by thoughts of another nature. Unnamed desires pounded like breakers in his imagination. He was excited—happy in anticipation of encounters which rarely eventuated. He was smolderingly jealous of his competitors in gallantry. The school at Chesterfield would close in thirteen weeks and all its young ladies would flutter away like thistledown to their homes. Caroline would go too. Such was the state of John's mind when, on November 8, 1830, he made his début as an advocate. He stammered, he trembled, he tangled himself in the web of his own verbiage. "You did not plead worth a damn!" exclaimed Squire Spaulding afterward.

To Caroline, John composed poems ending with such phrases as "love shall light us home." But love did not light Caroline home. Prosaically and unromantically she was preparing to depart, and John was thown into deep distress. Should he propose marriage? He gave the matter hard, close thought, and finally, in characteristic Atkinson Noyes fashion solved the problem by flight to home and mother in Putney. He was not yet twenty.

5

Revivals swept the country like prairie fires. Strange, uncouth evangelists scattered the pollen of myths and harsh doctrines in remote villages, backwoods settlements, forest clearings. They were gifted with rudimentary dramatic power and showmanship, and they tapped an almost bottomless reservoir of credulity. They organized protracted religious meetings, often in the open air. With shrewd intuition they upset the daily routine of the settlers and sharpened the edge of their unappeased hunger for deliverance.

Generations schooled in today's myths hardly realize how completely, how unreservedly, how uncritically the American masses of the early nineteenth century accepted the reality of Biblical characters, the actuality of Scriptural prophecy, as they were expounded by itinerant revivalists. These unscrupulous, even sinister, showmen suffused all with a warm, breathing, personal immediacy. To establish verisimilitude, to transmute illusion into accepted "fact," to clinch belief—such was their object. To this

end they cast their spell over gatherings of all sorts and conditions of men, women, and children, all athirst for superhuman deliverance from mundane hardships.

The message was inevitably Messianic and catastrophic. These apostles of the wilderness could compute the chronology of the Second Coming. They asserted that, beyond peradventure of doubt, the conversion of the world must be completed within their time. The Day of Judgment was fast approaching; all despotisms of the earth were to crumble at the advent of the Prince Emmanuel! In scorching, demoniac wrath they demanded immediate and unconditional repentance of all sin. Such, they reiterated, with the relentless insistence of a savage tom-tom, was the first and last condition of forgiveness and salvation. They took their cue from Jonathan Edwards, who had inaugurated the first revival one hundred years before. Endlessly repeated, and corrupted beyond recognition in the telling and retelling, the itinerant evangelists copied his sensational sermon on "Sinners in the Hands of an Angry God."

The impact of such exhortations upon the overwrought emotions of the credulous has often been described and deplored. Some of these manifestations survive in primitive Negro churches today. Even repressed New England witnessed such extraordinary phenomena as the "jerks," common in the Great Revival in Kentucky. "Protracted" meetings often produced a chaos of electric emotion, sometimes accompanied and sometimes followed by sexual irregularities. Unscrupulous persons of both sexes loitered about, quick to exploit the unguarded emotions of the repentant. The low level of the culture of the human beings upon whom these revivals worked cannot fully account for this curious convergence of religious and sexual impulses. The revival districts afterward seemed like territory over which lightning had raged, scorching and withering every green thing. Often the trail of the more unsrupulous revivalists could be traced by the generosity with which they scattered their seed. Earlier, Pierrepont Edwards, son of Jonathan, had acquired under-cover notoriety for this foible. "It is with pain that I refer to the evangelists of that era. Among them all (with exception of Finney and Nash) I cannot recall a single man who did not after a few years lose his unction, and become equally disqualified for the office of evangelist and that of pastor," wrote Asa Mahan in his autobiography.

The great revival that swept the country in 1830 was a terrifying revelation of that undying desire for salvation reborn with each generation. Nothing more sharply reveals man's uncon-

scious trepidation than this passion for freedom from sin, for perfection, for life everlasting. Ardent young men set out to evangelize the world; they determined to free the slaves of the South; they organized Bible, Tract and Education Societies; they initiated the temperance movement; they firmly resolved to furnish every family on earth with copies of the Bible. To be up and doing was the watchword of these youthful zealots.

6

Distress and humiliation following the financial crash of 1827 also prepared Putney for the great revival. At the "protracted" meetings, old castes were abolished; the low were raised up, the proud humbled. Vain shows of silks and satins were now frowned upon. Prayer meetings supplanted the frivolity of dances. Religion even took precedence over business—and the finer theological points of conversion and salvation were discussed in bar-rooms and the village stores. Abby White came back to Putney from Mrs. Grant's seminary at Ipswich with only one thought—the salvation of souls. She was an accomplished singer and musician, and her voice was now lifted only in sacred song. Abby and other young Putney converts were strongly attracted to Mrs. Noyes, because she had always led a life of prayer and devotion.

John, too, returned, having finished his year in the law-office in Chesterfield. His twentieth birthday came and went. He looked forward to another year of study and practice in Brattleboro. Religion did not trouble this aristocratic young man of the world, as he considered himself. He was firmly resolved, for the present at least, to indulge the lust of the eye and the pride of life—and to risk the consequences. The voice of desire was never stilled, day or night. Religion, he expostulated, was another form of intoxication, a frenzy to which all, indeed, were liable. Be careful, he warned himself, not to be caught in this snare. The young man did not suspect that such soliloquies were sensitizing his psyche for the internal revolution.

A four-day "protracted" meeting began in Putney, on September 14, 1831. John announced to his mother that he would attend the opening session. His love of the world and its pleasures, he said, was so strong, that he could trust the strength of his own mind to resist the evangelist's assault.

"Why then do you go?" Mrs. Noyes asked.

"To please you," John replied.

For two days young Noyes resisted a mounting flood of ex-

citement sharpened by vague suggestions of sin troubling to young folk who stood at the threshold of life. The inner conflict mounted to its climax. John Noyes resisted. The call to the anxious on the final day of the revival was not strong enough to humble his pride. In his spirit reigned an ominous calm—the calm that precedes battle. After this crisis was passed, he took to his bed with a cold. Suddenly the idea of the uncertainty of life obsessed his mind. It was but a step to the idea of the necessity of submitting to God.

John's first impulse was to confide these secret thoughts to his mother. He turned to the Bible; he prayed and meditated. In a paroxysm of fear, he began to sweat. Next day he read to his mother from the New Testament. Now, almost miraculously, the Scriptures glowed with a new fire. Only God and the life eternal were worthy of his consideration. The worldly values of men no longer seemed of the slightest importance. New light gleamed, at first dim and barely perceptible, then increasing until it seemed to attain the glory of the sun at dawn.

"But these are the evidences of conversion," exclaimed Mrs. Noyes. Before the end of that day John Noyes resolved to consecrate his life to the service of God's truth. When he believed, it was his nature to put conviction into action.

Four weeks after this inner revolution, the excited youth set off for Andover and entered its celebrated theological seminary. He naïvely assumed that Christians everywhere were full of zeal and love, that this seminary would gather the very flower of all the churches, and was therefore little less heavenly than a habitation of angels. Fresh from the "world," from the study of mundane law, he had some misgivings as to the reception which such a Saul would receive. His insight soon penetrated the mealy-mouthed hypocrisy of his fellow-students and aroused misgivings of another sort. Learning was of far greater account with theological students generally, he discovered, than true spirituality. A discouraging place for one who had vowed to live in the "revival spirit" and be a "young convert" forever!

The letters and journals of that period contain sharp vignettes of undernourished, clammy-handed divinity students clad in somber black, debating the more minute implications of eschatology and hermeneutics (the staple diet of the Andover curriculum). Religion seemed debased into an ignoble profession, the first step toward a tame, safe livelihood—a means of genteel, unmanly subsistence. Noyes discovered little or no occasion for any special education of the heart.

"What would the churches, with their glowing zeal and their glorious revivals, think, if they could look in upon us and see how lifeless and worldly we are?" John asked in his journal. He believed that not only was there less fervor and simplicity of devotion at Andover than in ordinary, unregenerate society, but, on the whole, considerably more levity, bickering, jealousy, intrigue, and sensuality than in any equal gathering of young men. His first doubts concerning professional religion were born.

With all the fire of his newly awakened conscience, he began to fight the spiritual blight hanging over Andover. And to make matters worse, John suffered more from the temptations of sensuality during that year than he was ever to suffer during any other part of his life. Floods of sin seemed ready to engulf him; but he rejoiced finally in "bringing into captivity every thought to the obedience of Christ."

Larkin G. Mead, his sister Mary's husband, cautioned him against becoming infected with the missionary spirit, but without effect. John fell immediately into fellowship with those who exhibited the most reckless zeal—converts who pledged themselves to the most remote and hazardous fields. He, too, decided to go, and sent his pledge to the American Board of Missions. At that callow age, despite what he witnessed at Andover, he innocently believed that Christianity was permanently established and was already in full operation in his own country! The spirit which animated the Apostles would send every man who was able to serve Christ into heathen lands. He wrote: "Suppose an angel were hovering over the earth, surveying all nations at once, with a view to selecting his field of labor in the gospel. Where would he alight? In the midst of Asia." Thither he determined to go.

This resolution led him into an inner circle of young men who were preparing to go out as missionaries to the far corners of the earth. They called themselves "The Brethren." They confided to their new member that their society had been in existence at Andover since the days of Newell and Fisk.

In order to purify their souls, to prepare themselves for the arduous tasks and adventures awaiting them on islands of the Antipodes, in the jungles of the dark continent, this little band met once a week for the purpose of telling each other their faults. One by one, in the alphabetical order of their names, each submitted to the criticism of the whole group. In the plainest, most unvarnished manner, these Brethren recited the breadth and extent of their comrade's defects. Silently, without verbal protest,

each was compelled to submit. No retorts, no protests, no explanations—and especially, no backbiting, no revenge.

They were to scatter soon, these Brethren, never to meet again. Lyman and Munson were to carry the message of the gospel to the islands of the East Indies; to meet Death undismayed at the hands of cannibals. Tracy was to penetrate, unharmed, into the heart of China; Champion to carry the Word into African jungles; and Justin Perkins to become a Nestorian in Asia Minor.

Yet in daring and in incredibility, the life adventure of none of "The Brethren" ever matched that of John Humphrey Noyes. Though destined to remain in his own native land, he was to come into collision with taboos even more rigidly enforced than those of any tribe of equatorial Africa, to suffer tortures more prolonged than those inflicted upon Lyman and Munson in Sumatra; finally to be driven into exile for his attempt to establish the Kingdom of Heaven in the United States of America.

Chapter II: ABIGAIL MERWIN

Except a man be born anew, he cannot see the Kingdom of God. JOHN 3:3.

I

"TAKE care! That is heresy! If you get out of the traces, the ministers will whip you in!" cried Squire Noyes.

Young John was home from his year at Andover, and had been airing his own views concerning certain theological doctrines. Already there was evident a distinct note of rebellion against cut-and-dried, professional religion. He was not yet twenty-one, but he was in revolt against authority.

"Never!" retorted the young man. "Never will I be compelled by ministers or any one else to accept any doctrine that does not commend itself to my mind and conscience."

Yale seemed to him to be more enlightened than Andover, and so young Noyes decided to pursue his studies in the middle class of the seminary in New Haven. A few days after his twenty-first birthday he left Putney once more. With his comrade McLain he found lodgings in the home of a "pious sea-captain, preparing to labor among the sailors." New Haven, he discovered, was a hothouse of stimulating ideas and new impulses. "Hardware" Dwight awakened John's conscience to the crying injustice of slavery, and threw himself into religious work among the Negroes of New Haven. That winter he helped Mr. Dwight and a little group of indignant students and citizens to organize the New Haven Anti-Slavery Society, one of the first Abolitionist groups to raise its voice in protest. At the seminary, John became head of a small coterie to whom even the professors seemed pedestrian and unenlightened.

With this group, and elsewhere, John developed all the implications of Dr. Nathaniel W. Taylor's doctrine that men can and must live to the full extent of their moral ability—that sinless perfection is, and must be, attainable in this life. Such a theory was in direct opposition to the "miserable sinner" Christianity. The timid were shocked. They began to suspect heresy. Only one or two dared express open sympathy with Noyes.

At that period so-called "free churches," fertilized by revival hysteria, were springing up everywhere. These churches attracted those whose cravings could no longer be appeased by the orthodox denominations. They reveled in the intoxicating ecstasies of the "New Measures"—which the sober conformists denounced.

The nucleus of such a Free Church came into being in New Haven in 1831, and John Noyes was inevitably drawn into this group, which met in the Orange Street Chapel. The heterogeneous little congregation of eleven or twelve welcomed the adherence of this eager, impatient, brilliant student from the seminary, and his amazing familiarity with the Testament and his glorious hopes for the future.

They lacked a meeting-house and their combined financial resources could not support a regularly employed pastor. They found consolation in the conviction that they were primitive Christians of a new apostolic era. Protracted gatherings in the cozy parlor of Mr. Everard Benjamin united them into a church according to the meaning of St. Paul—the Spirit gathered them together out of the world. They pledged themselves to Christian loyalty. Slowly their number grew.

When John returned to Vermont for Christmas, he encountered James Boyle, who was conducting revivals in Brattleboro. James Boyle was a Canadian, born and bred in the Roman Catholic faith. He had escaped from Romanism to preach, in rapid succession, the dogmas of the Methodists and the Presbyterians; and he possessed the arts and graces of the typical red-hot revivalist. On the recommendation of Noyes he was invited to become the pastor of the little group of "perfectionists" in New Haven who had gathered together into the "Free Church." Eventually, after being deposed from the ministry, Boyle became an anti-slavery agitator under William Lloyd Garrison; and some two decades later he was to be rediscovered by his former comrade-in-holiness as the manager of a museum of anatomy in New York.

In August, 1833, with the rest of his class at the Yale Seminary, John Noyes received his license to preach.

During the examinations, he had been drawn into several warm controversies—once with Dr. Leonard Bacon on the subject of faith in prayer, once with the eminent Dr. Nathaniel Taylor on the double sense of the Scripture. These traces of heretical thought were charitably attributed to extreme youth. The final year of Yale's theological course was devoted to "candidating"—actual preaching to scattered congregations too small or remote to have regular pastors. Noyes was appointed to North Salem, a little village eighteen miles east of Peekskill and not far from Ridgefield across the Connecticut line.

On the first Sabbath he waited a long time at the little white meeting-house. Finally, a handful of the faithful appeared. When

he stood before his first flock all the Noyes bashfulness surged over him. He plowed laboriously through a written sermon. Just as the "candidate" was on the point of confessing his ignominious failure, his self-assurance returned.

A week or two later, he delivered three extemporaneous sermons on a single Sabbath. Despite extreme circumspection, a subconscious current of heresy gave an unusual piquancy to his words. This personal flavor did not escape the notice of Mr. Lockwood, an elder of the church, who appeared at John's boarding-place with reproaches and warnings. Mr. Noyes should not have compared the condition of the typical sinner to that of a drunkard—the metaphor was offensive. So, Noyes thought, his very thoughts were to be censored by a set of domineering ministers—and in a land of so-called liberty! But, by the middle of October, when it came time to bid farewell to the little flock, Noyes departed with regret.

He rejoined the little group gathered at Everard Benjamin's in New Haven. They read John Wesley. Exciting talk of *perfection* filled the air. It was no radical doctrine, Noyes realized; in fact, it was nothing but the message of Paul—the great tidings of salvation by grace—promulgated by the mystic of Tarsus and his brethren and rediscovered by that monk of Wittenberg, Martin Luther.

But Wesley had indeed struck the deep truth in asserting that redemption must be intensive as well as extensive, that the *whole* of man, as well as all men, must be saved and kept eternally secure from sin. Perfection must be, not merely a dream of the future, but a guide here and now on earth. Men must become altogether holy—and happy. There could not be two standards of morality, one for the workaday world, the other some spurious religious "perfection" attainable only by monastics and clerics. Perfection must be available for all men and women, and salvation must be a continuous process, not a fixed achievement.

Noyes was out in the open sea now—there could be no turning back into the unthinking conformity of established dogma. Enough of the parchment creeds, of anemic ideals remaining stillborn on the printed page! Of what value was his faith if he could not express it in the length, breadth and thickness of living? "Paul sought a perfect object, by perfect means, with perfect energy," he boldly wrote in an outline for a sermon delivered at the Seminary.

Then a paper which he read before the Society of the Semi-

nary created high excitement. Persecution must be the test of faith, he declared, and adduced the whole testimony of the Bible to support his contention that "those who will live godly in Christ Jesus shall suffer persecution." There were protests and the great Dr. Taylor was called in. That worthy pointed out that the best ministers in Connecticut did not suffer persecution. Though that decree was final and decisive, John Noyes resolutely maintained: "I will never expect or desire to be treated in this world better than Jesus Christ and his gospel are treated."

Meanwhile, James Boyle's Celtic eloquence was producing results. The Free Church was growing. They acquired a meeting place, a roomy hall in the Exchange Building, and Boyle started a series of revivals. He had an able assistant in Chauncey Dutton, who had learned the revivalist craft under the celebrated Horatio Foot. Boyle delegated the services at the Saturday evening meetings to Dutton and Noyes.

Acutely conscious of vague, undefined cravings—"bodily infirmities" he called them—John had sought to conquer them by systematic self-denial, by fasting, by exercise, by a severe regimen of prayer and spiritual exercises. His nervous system had been morbidly excitable; but now, he assured himself, he had checked it with a tight rein. He discovered that he could apply himself to rigorous study for twelve to sixteen hours every day. Preaching was a refreshment and a delight. He was cheerful; his felicity was infectious. But he became thinner and thinner.

Dutton's first convert was a young man named Merwin, the brother of Mrs. Everard Benjamin. Dutton began to apply the tactics of his celebrated teacher, Horatio Foot. He began an open conversation with young Merwin. The rest of the congregation listened with tense excitement. The embarrassed young man hesitated in a long silence; Dutton persisted. By dint of relentless reasoning, alternated with perfervid prayers, he conquered, and Merwin collapsed. In broken gasps, he professed submission without reservation.

Thenceforth crowds thronged those Saturday evening meetings. Every session was crowned with conversions, and Dutton and Noyes took charge of more and more meetings. John Noyes preached the regular sermon; Dutton followed with his exhortations. After these services those interested remained for informal conversation, and sometimes twelve or fifteen would linger on. It was among these that Noyes first became aware of the modest presence of Abigail Merwin, Mrs. Benjamin's unmarried sister.

2

One bleak evening in February Noyes announced from the desk of the Free Church that his text would be: "He that committeth sin is of the devil."

He insisted upon the literal meaning of that text, convinced that he was entering a new field of theology. He knew that such interpretation would be thrust back at him—that he must confess himself saved—eternally saved from sin. Certain that he had committed himself irrevocably, he returned home to the room he shared with his brother Horatio. That night in his bed, he later confessed, he received the baptism he was hoping for. "Three times in quick succession a stream of eternal love gushed through my heart, and rolled back again to its source. Joy unspeakable and full of glory filled my soul. All fear and doubt and condemnation passed away. I knew that my heart was clean, and that the Father and the Son had come and made it their abode." This mystic experience marked the decisive parting of the way for him—the first step in his great venture into the untried and the unknown.

An agitated theological student stood at his threshold the next morning. He had heard the discourse; his head was full of perplexing questions. Did Noyes mean seriously that a sinner could not be a Christian? "If this is your doctrine," he protested, "you unchurch yourself as well as others. Don't you commit sin?"

"No!"

The word came out deliberately and firmly.

The visitor stared as though struck by a thunderbolt. He seemed to doubt his own ears, and repeated the question. Noyes insisted that he actually professed to be eternally free from sin.

Rumors of his heresy instantly flashed through the seminary and the town. "Noyes says he is perfect!" cried the students of the seminary. "Noyes is crazy!" said the orthodox. Students began to crowd to the room of the Noyes brothers, eager for a glimpse of the self-confessed *perfect* man, as unabashed as though they were staring at a tattooed man or a strange monster in a circus. Most of them came to argue with him and to confound him. Every waking hour was taken in answering the questions of students and in disputes with adversaries.

At last, he wearied of being a sideshow. All failed to understand that he did not consider himself perfect in the sense of not expecting discipline and improvement. "I do not pretend to perfection in externals," he cried. "I claim only purity of heart and

the answer of a good conscience toward God.... A book may be true and perfect in sentiment and yet be deficient in graces of style and typographical accuracy."

It was as though he were now living in a new dimension—but the curious hurried away to spread the rumor that "that John Noyes" had lost his reason.

While still a student at Andover, he had written in his diary: "I have been wishing today I could devise some new way of sanctification, some patent, some specific for sin, whereby the curse would be exterminated once for all. In times past I have sometimes thought I had discovered this desirable catholicon; but I have always found that just as I thought my disease was cured it would break out like a cancer in some other spot." The burden of this problem had weighed so heavily upon his spirit that he had determined to give himself no rest until he succeeded in emancipating himself from this heavy burden. After his public confession, he reveled in elation over a desperate battle fought and won. It seemed both a resurrection and a promise of eternal life. It seemed the Kingdom of God into which John Noyes now entered. The solution had come at last!

Only one doubt remained in his mind. He found himself still bound by the formal mechanics of orthodox religion. His conscience, for example, still directed him to get down on his knees three or four times a day and pray by the hour. Gradually, the glory of his new life surged through his spirit, and some new force gave him courage to free himself from these vocal ceremonies. But what would he do when he conducted an evening meeting at the Free Church, as he had promised to do? Old habits inclined him to go through the usual forms—to preach to "sinners," to work up, by tried and tested methods, the usual revival excitement.

When the appointed evening came, and he was on his way to the meeting, he suddenly stood still in the deserted street. His body seemed almost paralyzed with weakness and he felt that he was going to faint. But, as rapidly, as inexplicably as it had sunk, his heart now rose. Again he found himself in the keeping of everlasting love. The old conscience was gone—gone forever, and with it, all doubt. With a light step Noyes went on to the meeting, where a little band of faithful disciples awaited him. He conducted the meeting with new simplicity and disarming directness. As he returned home he was sure that at last he was weaned from the threadbare conventions of orthodoxy.

He was cut loose from the traditions of men, and now, despite ridicule and ostracism, there could be no turning back.

3

The first person to join him in his faith of complete salvation was none other than Miss Abigail Merwin. Already a member of the Free Church, a sister of the young man who had been Dutton's first convert, Miss Merwin had for some time been under conviction. Strangely enough, she had not yet been introduced to fiery young John Noyes. Now she requested an interview.

He hastened over to the house of her brother-in-law in Orange Street, and was there introduced. She was beautiful, she was modest, she was talented. A hidden fire of sympathy and understanding lit up her dark eyes. He felt that there was something of the saint in Miss Merwin's unassuming coiffure. But their attention was not on each other; it was on Christ.

"Will you receive Christ as a whole Saviour and confess him before the world?" Finally, with ill-suppressed excitement, he had ventured to put this ominous question to her.

"I will!" Her answer came without hesitation, without a tremor in the low, steady voice.

Her dark countenance beamed with joy. Abigail was on the verge of swooning; she felt as though she were at the point of death, about to lose her own identity.

The next morning, at the prayer meeting, Abigail Merwin publicly professed holiness. For John Noyes, who was, after all, only twenty-two, that act joined them more closely than any marriage ceremony ever could. Rapidly Miss Merwin advanced in knowledge of the gospel truths; keenly and with sharp intuition she followed his subtlest meaning. It was almost as though they were in flight together; yet there was nothing untoward, nothing sensuous—so he assured himself—in this rhythmic counterpoint of attraction. Their attention was all on the new life—the life of Christ. Even in her absence, Abigail occupied his mind as an angel of light.

She was thirty; he was twenty-two. In those days a woman of thirty was almost relegated to the ranks of hopeless spinsterhood. In spite of her modesty, Abigail must have wondered just when the inevitable proposal of matrimony would come from this burning young prophet, who at times seemed even more than eight years her junior.

However ethereal our aspirations, love has but one language.

To express the relations between God and the individual soul, erotic imagery provides effective symbols. So compactly tenanted is the human mind that the higher and lower emotions often crowd each other like quarrelsome neighbors in narrow corridors. And so, even when the zealous young Perfectionist seemed most detached from earthly ties, his words took on a certain ambiguity, as though his lower nature, like a caged Caliban, thwarted and shackled, were plotting the downfall of his Ariel-like spirit. Sometimes his exalted words awakened in Abigail unmaidenly thoughts; for when John spoke, in Benjamin's house in Orange Street, of his love of Christ, he used terms that were applicable to the carnal affections as well.

For poor, fluttering Abigail, those gleaming gray eyes, those passionate looks, those expansive gestures, those amorous effusions—as John explained the "new life" realized by eternal salvation from sin—were excitement enough. The very tenderness of his words, the passionate vocabulary with which the young man expressed his love for Jesus Christ, spread an invisible net in which Abigail Merwin soon found herself ensnared.

Now, for the first time in his life, John Noyes seemed to himself to be fully awake. He had been living in a lethargy, a sort of stupid sleep, which had seemed impossible to cast off. And through this sleep had run a nightmare of the devil—a nightmare that had darkened his mind and his imagination. Now the future promised a glowing, glorious harvest. Salvation was indeed the voice of God, calling upon him to awake to his rightful heritage, to march forward to the realization of the Kingdom.

Noyes now identified himself with all the goodness of the universe—he felt himself to be the chosen instrument of the Almighty. His spirit leapt for joy. He was impelled to shout out this good news, to communicate the truth of his final emancipation from the net of sin. "Hedges, ditches, limits, narrow bounds," fell away below him as his spirit soared. His first need was to share this joy—and with whom but Abigail Merwin, who understood, and who, so courageously, had joined him?

He began to discover that Abigail possessed a surprising readiness of apprehension, an instinctive facility for communication. Her testimony was bold, yet modest. Her power of argument, and her position as his first convert, placed her at John's side in the front rank of the battle. Together they stood in the full glare of the public gaze; Abigail did not flinch.

Everard Benjamin, his wife, and her own brother, Dutton's first convert, now followed Abigail into the ranks of sinlessness.

Noyes's heretical doctrine gained a complete ascendancy in the Free Church. The "pillars" of that little church were taken by surprise. Until they had time to recover themselves (by appeals to the higher courts of New Haven theology) they were compelled to bow the knee to the new truth. Even Amos Townshend, "father" of the Free Church, was among the anxious inquirers, and Stephen Cook, publisher of the *Christian Spectator*, actually made a partial and temporary profession of holiness.

With a wonderful kind of excitement, Noyes began to broadcast these new views. Letters were sent to an extensive circle of friends. Invitations to preach came from three distant places. To the missionary brethren at Andover he wrote, withdrawing his pledge to go into foreign missionary service. This gesture drew from Champion an expostulatory reply, demanding full explanation. He was already on missionary ground, John promptly replied—"among a people who need to be converted quite as much as the heathen."

Early in April, 1834, Dr. Taylor called at Noyes's room and notified him that he was to be tried by the association which had licensed him to preach. Noyes called attention to Dr. Taylor's own doctrine of man's perfect ability to obey the law of God. Was not this, in essence, the foundation of Perfectionism? God in his benevolence, retorted Dr. Taylor, had adopted a system of gracious indulgence by which absolute obedience was not required. Noyes's view, he pointed out, was nothing more than the old Wesleyan scheme which had been tried and had failed—it could appeal only to the ignorant. "Remember, you are still too young, too inexperienced in these finer points," admonished Dr. Taylor.

Noyes had great reverence and even affection for Dr. Taylor, and this interview left no sting. It renewed his sense of peace and freedom, and it prepared him for the news that the Association of the Western District of New Haven County had, at a special meeting in the theological lecture room, taken away his license to preach . . . "without impeaching the Christian character of Mr. Noyes, this Association do hereby recall his license to preach the gospel." Noyes experienced a certain exultation. "I have taken away their license to sin," he exclaimed, "and they keep on sinning. So, though they have taken away my license to preach, I shall keep on preaching."

He had been holding meetings at five in the morning on the premises of the Free Church for a little group of initiates. The officers of that church told him the premises would no longer be

available. Dr. Taylor called again—and indicated that it was the wish of the faculty that he should retire altogether from the vicinity of the seminary. His departure, John answered, would greatly inconvenience his younger brother Horatio, who was a student in the classical department. Could he not remain there until the end of the term? Dr. Taylor grudgingly consented—and John stayed on.

4

Great importance was always attached by Noyes and his disciples to his "New York experience." This ordeal was his "dark night of the soul"—a sort of *Walpurgisnacht* during which he seemed to be attacked by all the forces of evil. Students of mysticism assure us that the period of ecstasy and illumination is inevitably followed by a precipitate descent into doubt and despair. Often this crisis, among the religious, occurs at the threshold of manhood. With John Noyes, this "dark night" lasted three weeks. He emerged shaken and scarred, to find a new balance and orientation. "By the suffering I endured," he wrote later, "by the mental progress I made, by the revolution of character which was the result, it might deserve to be called three years instead of three weeks."

He went to New York, accompanied by Charles H. Weld, to attend the so-called anniversary meetings of the ministers and theologians from all parts of the country. Many he wanted to meet, especially the celebrated Charles Finney, in whom he expected to find a sympathetic listener. It was to be a splendid opportunity to offer the challenge of Perfectionism. Weld and Noyes left New Haven by sloop, and already the young man began to be exasperated by Weld's wordy preoccupations with official arrangements for the coming dispensation, the physical joys of the resurrection state, and spiritual marriage.

New York was a bitter disappointment. He failed to meet Charles Finney, though Mrs. Finney received him with kindly condescension. He met the fanatic reformer McDowall, too loquacious to listen to any save himself. Weld departed—that was a welcome relief. John rented a room in a Leonard Street boarding-house, and sat down to compose a tract on Perfectionism. Inexperienced, bewildered by the confusion of the city, desperate in his need for spiritual guidance, he found his thoughts wandering. Strange impulses raced through his troubled consciousness. His whole being sought to break loose from the bondage of his Puritan upbringing. He felt himself being bombarded by the nameless,

inchoate powers of evil. The climax came when he was certain that his flesh and blood were about to part. A suffocating pressure tightened about his lungs and heart. He put his little room in order and lay down calmly, to await the coming of death. The distress increased, and his breathing seemed to cease. Suddenly, the pressure was released.

He arose with the joy of victory in his heart. He felt as though he had been released from a dragnet, as though he had been swept down to the very borders of Hades, and then been brought back. After that, all the events of the Crucifixion were etched, line by line, upon his tortured imagination. Not as a mere spectator, but as the tortured victim. He, John Noyes, had been reborn, the Resurrection had occurred in him, and he, John Noyes, had been released from his agony.

All craving for food vanished, and he began to avoid sleep—for then, he discovered, the powers of darkness lurked malevolently, ready to invade his spirit. Night after night he wandered through the dark streets of lower Manhattan. When, after a day of wearisome wandering, young Noyes sought refuge in that little room in Leonard Street, and prayed for a night of calm repose, a sudden horror of those nameless powers would seize him. Then he would creep out of the boarding-house, and take up his wanderings again. Weariness would strike him down, and he would drop on a doorstone, sink down on the steps of the City Hall, stretch at full length along the riverside.

The apparition of that emaciated, bedraggled youth could not have passed without attracting attention, but not even the Watch, as the night police was termed in those days, disturbed the peregrinations of this gaunt, starving pilgrim from Vermont. Like a sleepwalker he staggered into murky alleys from which all virtuous young men had been warned. Vice sprawled ungirt and shameless where once the old Fresh Water Pond had lain stagnant, and escaped slaves had been hanged. There, certain disreputable streets intersected to create the noisome Five Points. Down into dives where abandoned women trafficked with wayfarers who had been blown in from the seven seas young Noyes drifted. Here at last he found ready and willing listeners. The fire in his burning eyes riveted the attention of these whose trade it was to listen to anonymous confessions. He besought them to believe on Christ, to be saved—forever rescued—from sin. These spurious Magdalens were accustomed to the visits of missionaries armed with the Gospel and good words, and "led them on" for the amusement of the unregenerate. Some had even become adept in lurid

recitals of ruin for the edification of godly "workers." So they listened to the distraught young man from Putney without abuse. One of them assumed the rôle of the penitent. Noyes left a Bible with her. To another he gave a Testament.

Like others of his upbringing, he had regarded the use of intoxicating liquors as a sin. Now, for the first time, he learned that no rigid code could guide one through the diabolical zone of experience in which he was tossed.

John Noyes drank ardent spirits, not to defy others, but to defy himself, to eradicate that ingrained habit of legality inherited from generations of Puritan ancestors. His confession of this gesture was to lay him open, decades later, to the charge of drunkenness, just as his confession that he had visited disreputable houses was to be used against him. Such gestures were necessary, Noyes always insisted, to free him from "the grave-clothes." God must protect him from intemperance, as God would protect him from lewdness and all other evils, without the help of pledges.

For a time a sense of impending, catastrophic change filled his tortured mind. All that had been most certain, all that he had accepted as truth, came crashing down. Nothing persisted but doubt. Nevertheless, his mind was preternaturally active.

Like a monument withstanding storm and chaos, still persisted the image of Abigail Merwin. Abigail had courageously joined him in the confession of holiness. Abigail had testified boldly; Abigail had behaved angelically during that crisis in New Haven. To Abigail Merwin he was more attached than to any being on earth. Now, bereft of faith, alone in the ruins of a universe, he seemed to see Abigail standing on the very pinnacle of the universe in all the glory of an angel. But then from the depths a voice, low yet insistent, reiterated endlessly: "Satan transformed into an angel of light!"

Even the character of Jesus Christ, subjected to the spirit of analysis which had taken possession of his mind, now appeared revoltingly hideous—the very prince of devils. Science was a lie, the Bible an imposition for the credulous, Jesus a prince among devils, and God himself could not withstand this storm. For young Noyes, nothing was left but his own experience. And that experience seemed nothing, nothing but a long series of self-deceptions. The darkness of complete atheism enveloped his soul.

At last, the net of Satan seemed to loosen and Noyes emerged into a new dawn of peace. Yet the effect of this mental tornado was to last as long as his life.

Gradually, Noyes began to formulate his own rule of mental economy. "What we positively know is all the mental capital we can count upon as safe and available. What we guess, believe, and hope to be true is paper capital, that may be genuine or may not. It is well enough to have on hand a great heap of guesses, but we must not think of living on them. We should look over the whole mass of our thoughts, select out all that we absolutely know, and keep that by itself, accounting it our specie-basis. If it is but a small store, never mind. A little silver and gold is worth more than a bushel of counterfeit bills. Then we may go on to examine and work our heap of guesses, so as to convert them as far as possible into known truths. This is the only way to keep and get a sound mind."

So, at the age of twenty-two, he emerged from the wreckage of his former beliefs. He was certain of one thing—the malevolent existence of Satan, who could thrust himself into the place of God and imitate the influences of the Holy Ghost. If any spirit tried to crowd him into orthodox belief and obedience, he told himself, that spirit must indeed be the spirit of darkness.

When he looked back on his misadventures in that murky region between reason and madness, he assured himself that no human being ever drank so deeply of the dregs of the cup of trembling. Henceforth, he believed, he was proof against the fire. "Hell has done its worst, and yet I live!"

Meantime his bill at the lodging house in Leonard Street had been steadily mounting. He had given his money away. Three weeks had passed and the bill amounted to twelve dollars. News of his condition had already reached his friends in New Haven and his family in Putney. A young man, an old acquaintance from Vermont, appeared one day at the door of his room, and announced that he ought to write to Horatio in New Haven.

"You are trying to deceive me!" protested Noyes, looking the visitor sharply in the eye. "You think I am crazy, and you have already written to my brother to come and take care of me."

5

The next day Everard Benjamin appeared at the boarding house, settled John's accumulated bill, and hurried the unhappy young man aboard the sloop bound for New Haven. Abigail, it would appear, had inspired this generous gesture on the part of her brother-in-law; but, with the scrupulous circumspection of the

lady of the 1830's, remained so effectively out of sight that John Noyes did not learn of Abigail's presence aboard the little sloop until some time after his arrival in New Haven.

Realization of this tender yet reticent solicitude acted as slender solace, however, for the disgrace in which Noyes now found himself. Wildly improbable stories ran through the little group of New Haven Perfectionists and their intimates. From all that was whispered, Horatio fully expected that his elder brother would be delivered into his hands a raving madman. Reassured at John's arrival he sent off letters to Mary Mead in Chesterfield and to their parents at Putney to allay their fears. Mrs. Noyes responded, urging John to return home immediately for a long and complete rest. He needed, she was certain, her soothing and sympathetic ministrations. So, with no shred of his reputation left, John found himself once more in the sanctuary of Locust Grove by the end of June, 1834.

The coterie of the Free Church in New Haven had received the wanderer with every show of outward kindness, but there was an air of embarrassment at their little gatherings whenever he appeared. When he had departed, his fantastic escapades in New York were openly and thoroughly discussed. At this precise period were planted the legends that persisted for years: that John Noyes had taken to drink in New York City, and had been a regular visitor to houses of ill-fame. On the flimsiest foundations of half-truths towering fabrications were erected.

Pressure, we surmise, was brought to bear on Abigail Merwin, and the danger of linking her future with that of so unstable and unbalanced a character as John Noyes was fully explained. So we learn from an indignant letter written by the loyal Chauncey Dutton, and sent to Noyes in July. It contained the devastating news that not only Miss Merwin, but her sister and Edward Benjamin had deserted the little Free Church and the whole cause of Perfectionism. "If she has gone, as I suppose she has, she has been one of the devil's best counterfeits," commented Noyes with unexpected composure. But the defection of Abigail was a staggering blow, more so than Noyes realized consciously. It may have motivated his somewhat precipitate return to New Haven at the beginning of August, ostensibly to begin the publication of a paper with James Boyle, now also cast out of the Free Church.

However, Noyes refrained from seeking out Abigail Merwin. Living in a rarified realm in which the finer points of Perfectionist doctrine took precedence over all warmly human relations, his whole life grandiloquently consecrated to the promulgation of

new truths, John Noyes felt that marriage should not be permitted to divert him from his charted course. Shyness, too, may have influenced his conduct.

The half-year he spent with James Boyle in launching *The Perfectionist* slipped by with no explanation or communication from Miss Merwin. He found relief in plunging into plans for the new publication. "More or less anarchy always attends revolutions from arbitrary to free governments," he explained, "so it is not to be wondered that our minds in this transition period are not in that orderly, mechanical state that suits a schoolmaster. It is better to move into a new house at the cost of some temporary confusion ... than to live in an old one that is ready to fall on our heads."

They discussed a name for their new paper. "Let us hoist our colors boldly," proclaimed Noyes. "Let the name of this periodical be *The Perfectionist*." He recognized the invidious connotations in the name, but after all, Perfectionism really meant that society could gain nothing while men who had not succeeded in regenerating themselves were attempting to reform others. "Let us," said Noyes, "rescue the name from the disrepute into which it has been thrown." On August 20, 1834, the first number of *The Perfectionist* appeared. After six months, Noyes left and Boyle was in complete control.

At Putney, the elder Noyeses worried about John. They wrote Horatio, proffering the advice that John should return to Putney, or at least go somewhere and begin to earn his living. To his mother John replied: "If you dislike the idea of my dependence upon others, I ask, where will my dependence be more servile, here or at home? Here I am writing for the press and preaching. At home ... I could do comparatively nothing. And am I less in a state of dependence at home than abroad? If you think duty forbids you to succor me here, I pray you be not concerned about my livelihood. Give me up, Mother! For the Lord's sake give me up!"

6

Despite all his activity, he felt an ever-increasing sense of his own isolation. With the exception of the troubling and elusive Abigail Merwin, there was no one to whom he could confide his secret doubts and misgivings. Had not even Luther and Erasmus become frightened, and abandoned the ground of this unexplored realm of spiritual experience? Instead of fighting it out independently, they had reverted to ordinances and dry doctrines.

There the Reformation had failed, and there it had been completely disabled ever since. None of its theologians had dared push through and fight the great battle of emancipation to the bitter end. They had swum out a little way into spiritual experience and found it a jungle stream full of sharks and alligators, it seemed to him: had become terrified and swam back as fast as ever they could! He, too, was finding his own stream full of sharks and alligators; but he was killing them with his bowie-knife as he went along, and would come out victorious on the other side. There was, for instance, that notorious Brimfield episode that aroused so much scandal.

About the first of February, 1835, Simon Lovett and Noyes had set out to visit several groups of Perfectionists in New England. At Southampton they were well received. All hearts seemed warm and open.

John's aim was to divorce the doctrine of holiness from that of Methodist legality. He found that praying and "pumping" for spiritual life still remained the order of the day, even among the adherents of the new sect. At one meeting in a private house it was proposed that they should "pray all around." All present knelt before their chairs and entered upon a series of "new measure" petitions. Young Noyes's place was near the end of the series. When his turn came, John startled the assemblage with these words; "O Lord, we thank thee that thou hast given us all that we need, and we don't want anything more. Amen."

A week later Lovett and Noyes went on to Brimfield. Perfectionists there seemed to harbor a prejudice against important teachings of the New Haven school, and their attitude stimulated the young heretic to preach with extraordinary zeal and contention. The day after Noyes's departure, Chauncey Dutton arrived in Brimfield from Albany. Religious excitement increased, culminating in a frenzy of fanaticism. Mary Lincoln and Maria Brown, leaders among the unattached young women, made their way at midnight to Simon Lovett's room.

The purpose of this visit, it appears, was by no means carnal. Mary and Maria merely intended to demonstrate that the spirit could always triumph over the flesh. "But, as usually happens in such presumptuous experiments," Noyes later explained, "in the end the flesh triumphed over the spirit."

Scandal broke like a storm. Under its pitiless blast, Mary Lincoln imagined that God was about to destroy Brimfield. She warned all true-hearted believers to flee with her to the mountains. Some tried to hold her back; but one young woman, Flavilla Howard,

finally decided to accompany her. They set forth at nightfall, tramped through mud and rain to the top of a neighboring mountain, and scattered their clothing as they ran. Under the stars they prayed that the avenging bolts might be stayed. As a result of this intercession, they afterward claimed, Brimfield *was* saved.

John Noyes was not present at this affair, but in some inexplicable fashion he was held responsible for it. In self-defense he was compelled to explain how and why he left Brimfield. Contact with the Southampton Perfectionists had made him acutely aware of an unguarded freedom between the sexes. Ambiguous expressions like "brother" and "sister," "beloved," and "dearly beloved" were in common use. Had he not blushed when one young woman kissed Simon Lovett the first time she ever saw him? At Brimfield, this group of handsome, brilliant young women, with manners equally free, again embarrassed him. As protagonist of ambiguous doctrines Noyes became the center of special attention and interest. John soon began to realize hidden dangers. One evening, at a social gathering around William Tarbell's fire, Hannah, his daughter, seemed to sink into the depths of despair. Noyes asked her what made her sad. He showed no confidence in her, she replied. He took a seat beside the girl, and finally put his arm around her waist. Hannah kissed him in token of recovery from her distrust. Later that night, while on his bed in prayer, a clear view of the situation suddenly came to him. He received "orders" to withdraw. Next morning before dawn, without making his intention known to any one, he stole out of the house and started on foot through snow and cold—it was zero weather—to Putney, sixty miles distant. He reached Locust Grove within twenty-four hours. The instinct of flight had once again come to his rescue.

When letters detailing the Mary Lincoln scandal began to arrive, Noyes sought to shelter rather than to condemn the young women, who appealed to him against the storm of reproaches. But when sexual irregularities continued and developed into actual licentiousness, and finally into open propaganda, he withdrew all sympathy. The scandal of this Brimfield affair spread so widely and so swiftly that scarcely a day passed during which John Noyes was not called upon to deny participation with the "bundling" activities of those recalcitrant young ladies. The spicy and piquant details were inserted by the enemies of Perfectionism and the story grew into almost legendary proportions; Joshua Longley, a fellow Perfectionist, eventually addressed a communication to Mr. and Mrs. Tarbell of Brimfield, requesting a plain unvarnished

vindication of Noyes. So determined was John Noyes to vindicate his own character and to free himself from the tangled web of sexual slander, that he eventually published Mrs. Tarbell's letter. Besides absolving Noyes, Mrs. Tarbell further explained:

"Mary Lincoln was the daughter of unbelieving parents of high standing and spirits, and in opposition to all her friends, she attended all the meetings, and was very much blest. She seemed to make great proficiency in knowledge. She was very bold in testifying to all, so much so, that she was considered as a head one. . . . She seemed to be happy, and at perfect liberty to say and do as she pleased, and two or three others were not far behind in excitement. One night, she, with some other girls, were where Lovett was, and after he was gone to bed, Mary proposed that they should sleep with him. In the morning they came down and told that two of them went to bed with Lovett. Mary said there was no hurt in it, for they did not commit any sin. The next day her father brought her to our house. He said my husband would have more influence with her than any one else, and he wanted her to stay a few days. Before night there was a number here, and the excitement of four or five was raised to the very highest; they prayed and sung, and kissed, and danced (not in a formal way). Mary would dance around the room. The old gentleman came into the room and began to reprove her, and she stept up and struck him in the face, and said he had got the biggest devil she had seen, and if he would believe, she would cast him out. She stayed until the next morning; we could not keep her any longer, by any persuasion. She went to a neighbor, and then said the center of the town was going to be destroyed that night, and they must flee to the mountain. After it was dark, she and one other set out for the mountain; they traveled through swamps and hedges till they arrived at the mountain, more than a mile west of the meeting house. She said after she got there, that Judgment was laid upon her, and the place was spared. On their return they lost some of their shoes, on the way. They came to a house a mile from where they intended, almost exhausted very late in the evening."

7

John Noyes returned to New Haven and to a summer (1835) of intense suffering and spiritual conflict. Weld proved himself a "wolf in sheep's clothing"; Boyle became cold and critical. The latter still edited *The Perfectionist;* but he notified John that no more of his inflammatory manifestoes could be published, and the

final breach came late in the summer. Boyle pronounced an "everlasting separation" from John Noyes. This rejection, and the hostile influence of James Boyle on the rest of the elect, left Noyes with only a precarious foothold in New Haven.

One afternoon he appeared at the house of his sister Joanna, who had married Samuel Hayes, a New Haven kinsman of Grandfather Hayes. (He was later appointed United States Consul at Trinidad, where Joanna soon died of a tropical fever.) Outspoken, matter-of-fact Joanna Hayes looked anxiously at her haggard brother.

He confessed that his mind had been assailed by a new series of trials and temptations like those of his New York experience. He was fighting back the adversary and had been for the past six months, he confided. The strangeness of his behavior, John admitted, had shaken the confidence of his religious associates. They were turning from him, excluding him from their fellowship. He had no home, no friends "in the wide world." After his abrupt departure Joanna wrote anxiously home to Putney, counseling his return.

His twenty-fourth birthday passed, yet the *Sturm und Drang* period was not ended yet. During the latter half of 1835, Noyes was always searching for sympathetic, understanding ears into which he could pour his eloquence and his hope. There was, for instance, Abram Smith, whom he met in Newark, New Jersey, where there existed the nucleus of a Perfectionist group. A curious man, Abram Smith! An itinerant Methodist parson, always in debt and always preoccupied with new schemes of making money. He alternated between preaching to stray congregations and tentatively farming the land around an old stone house at Rondout, not far from Kingston. Abram was a ready, willing responsive listener, ingratiating in a wily way, and destined to fulfill a curious rôle in the years to come.

Then there was Theophilus Gates, who had for twenty years or more been fighting authority and orthodoxy in the realm of religion.

As early as 1812 Gates proclaimed that sects and parties had been the ruin of all genuine religion in the world. "I have myself been several years without restraint from any society, and under the discipline of no one. I have not lacked anything; nor do I now feel any disposition to turn away from the Lord's service. And hear this, all ye ends of the earth: The true love of God in the heart is the best restraint, and a tender conscience the best discipline." After the first issues of the New Haven *Perfectionist* had

reached Gates, several complimentary exchanges were made between this eccentric Philadelphian and the little group of New England rebels. Gates retained his overwhelming phobia against sects, parties, and churches. "God never made one of the sects now existing!" he exclaimed. "They have been devised, made and fashioned wholly by men. All the present sects in Christendom are the false gods of this day, receiving the attention, homage, and esteem which belong only unto God, and exercising an authority and power solely the prerogative of God."

Gates's writings were infecting the Perfectionists and young Noyes had vigorously warned his colleagues against the insidious, disintegrating influence of such precepts. In October, 1835, he decided to go to Philadelphia to confront Gates. He was cordially received by the eccentric anti-sectarian. Impressed by his earnestness—Noyes was then just twenty-four—Mrs. Gates pressed a five-dollar gold piece into the caller's hand. Meanwhile Gates meandered into a long recital of mysterious acts he felt called upon to perform. Some irresistible impulse had once impelled him to enter the House of Representatives in Washington and denounce the national legislators. Ordered to be silent, he shouted that he must obey God instead of man, and was promptly and unceremoniously ejected.

Noyes listened patiently to Gates's monologue. Finally he cut in abruptly and announced that he considered certain of Gates's published views as so much nonsense. A gleam of anger suffused Gates's watery eye. When Theophilus left the room on some errand, the young man from Vermont observed to Mrs. Gates that battle-clouds seemed to be gathering. He offered to return the gold piece she had given him; but Mrs. Gates graciously refused it. She liked him, and was delighted with this attack upon her husband. Certainly such good straight-from-the-shoulder criticism would do him good.

Gates returned, and resumed the battle.

"You shall leave this house!" Theophilus Gates shouted to his visitor, "or I will!"

"God sent me here to deliver this message to you," John Noyes implacably replied, "I must obey God rather than man. I shall stay until I have finished."

Theophilus Gates was persuaded to submit to his own rule. John Noyes told him without reservation all that was in his mind. "From my first knowledge of your writings, I disliked them for one special reason—they are full of guessing interpretations of Scripture, enforced, not by demonstration, but by an assumption

of prophetic authority." Noyes ended with a sweeping indictment of Theophilus as a false prophet.

Gates commanded his wife to show Noyes to the door. The young man took his leave. Mrs. Gates, possibly satisfied that another dared do something for which she lacked the courage, escorted Noyes out of the house. On the doorstep, the youth tried to persuade her to take back the money she had given him.

"No! Keep it! Keep it!" she exclaimed, and lifted the lamp high to light his way down the steps.

8

Despite these quixotic wanderings, often by foot, and with empty pockets, young Noyes was always, by some invisible power, drawn back to New Haven. Separation only sharpened his interest in the Abigail of his imagination. Miss Merwin remained daily, almost every hour, indeed, tantalizingly present in John's turbulent mind.

Several times every day Noyes crossed an open park and gazed longingly up at the window of the room he knew Miss Merwin occupied. Sometimes, as in the evening a light shone from that window, he lingered and tenderly sought to picture the scene within. Then, one day, turning a corner, he came face to face with Abigail Merwin. A sudden paralysis of action arrested his steps. She gazed with embarrassed fright at the young man. Both found momentary relief in a formal greeting—and then the two of them sought safety in flight.

Even to himself he could not consciously admit that he was in love with Abigail Merwin, that great happiness would ensue if Abigail should consent to become his wife. Months passed by; and instead of a normal solution, their relationship became more and more involved, hedged and harnessed by all the intricacies of their stilted and intricately embellished etiquette. Finally, John Noyes summoned courage enough to request an interview with Miss Merwin. After weeks of self-torture and inner interrogation, he had come to the conclusion that he must break through the walls of silence which they had built up.

When at last he called upon her in New Haven, yearning for reconciliation, hoping for complete understanding, the conventional courtesy with which she received him chilled his ardor. Miss Merwin assured him that she was still in sympathy with Perfectionists—oh, yes, indeed! She expressed great confidence, as well, in Mr. Noyes's religious character. Would he not call again?

Indeed he would—but before he had called again, news came to the Merwins of a bitter, ungentlemanly quarrel that had broken out between Charles H. Weld and Noyes. Those Perfectionists seemed always disgracing themselves with their savage bickering! Mr. Merwin stepped in and summarily informed Noyes that he should not continue his attentions to his daughter. An irresponsible, fanatical zealot, unbalanced and disreputable, was no possible husband for Abigail!

While John walked with a friend one day in September, they passed a young man.

"That," announced Noyes's friend, "is Merit Platt, the young man to whom Miss Abigail Merwin is engaged." But John Noyes refused to credit such news. He thrust it out of his consciousness; he would not receive any such unpleasant fact.

Noyes seemed in love not so much with the real Abigail as with that hieratic image of her he had so deeply graven in his own mind—a creature clothed in white robes, a sort of Byzantine angel chosen by the Lord as his own eternal companion. Even her coming marriage with Merit Platt could not sever that imagined union. The realization that she was really to marry another swept away his inhibitions. From Putney, on December 28, 1835, he wrote to Abigail: "I ask you not to conceal what I write from your lover, your friends, or the world . . . I confess without shame that I loved you as I never loved another, for reasons which I never saw in any other. In these circumstances the thought of marriage was unavoidable. . . . For many months subsequent to our separation I longed after you, but was not permitted to visit you. At length, in the midst of another series of sufferings at Prospect, I saw you again clothed in white robes, and by the word of the Lord you were given to me. My assurance that you would be mine was so strong, that I scrupled not to declare it openly. At the same time I was instructed as to the place which the marriage relation will hold in the coming dispensation. Thenceforward I have been with you in spirit, not doubting that you will ere long return to your first love and dwell with me in the bosom of God. . . . When I heard you were engaged and saw your betrothed, I anxiously scrutinized again the grounds of my faith, lest I should wrong an innocent man. Thrice like Paul I besought the Lord that you might depart from me, and thrice like him I was refused. I know now that my love for you is the gift of God, pure and free, above all jealousy and above all fear. . . . I can tear you from my bosom again at the bidding of God, and again I say, if you are permitted to marry another, herein I rejoice and will rejoice, praying that you and

yours may be blessed of God. Still I have the right and will to love you as the workmanship of God, as my sister, as my neighbor, as myself. I ask no more till God shall make you know that he has joined us in an immortal marriage, and that what God hath joined together man can not put asunder."

John waited impatiently, but to this important pronouncement no answer ever came. Whatever may have been Abigail's true feelings toward John Noyes, there was no dearth of counselors among the Merwins and the Benjamins to admonish the young woman against becoming further involved. A far more sensible, lasting alliance would be that with a steady young man who had been offered a position as schoolmaster at the Ithaca Academy in New York. Though no answer came from the flesh-and-blood Abigail, that twin-soul of his own creation, the angelic white-robed Abigail, continued to live and move and have her being in John's imagination.

At the beginning of 1837, news finally came of Abigail's marriage with Merit Platt. The fact he accepted as inevitable; but he was still convinced, as he had been just a year previous, that the Lord had joined them together. Well, he assured himself, his faith and patience should not waver. Abigail might have expressed a preference for another—but John Noyes was certain of his own leadership in the impending establishment of the Kingdom of God on earth.

Noyes had expressed these convictions to David Harrison the summer before in Connecticut. With this faithful young disciple he had indulged in long, stimulating discussions—monologues in truth, since, as John Noyes expatiated upon intimate aspects of life and love, David usually listened with rapt attention and ardent assent. The interjection of a provocative question now and again was sufficient to launch Noyes into prophetic disquisitions concerning the false standards and the spurious wisdom of the world. David became his trusted confidant: to him he could unreservedly express his convictions.

John Noyes sat transcribing his innermost thoughts in a letter to David. The ever-present image of Abigail's countenance remained before his eyes—an inescapable obsession. In the exalted, prophetic manner which had become almost second nature to Noyes, impulses became articulate, thoughts became formulated and coherent, as they found their way into swift words on the inviting square of paper beneath his eyes. Though he did not suspect that these words were to be thrust back at him, that they

were to be published for all the world to jeer at, some inner urge, imperious and impersonal, guided his pen.

"I will write all that is in my heart on one delicate subject," Noyes confided to David Harrison, "and you may judge for yourself whether it is expedient to show this letter to others." There was a pause. Deeper thoughts emerged, to take shape almost of their own accord; these words set themselves down on the clean white paper: "When the will of God is done on earth, as it is in heaven, *there will be no marriage*. The marriage supper of the Lamb is a feast at which *every dish is free to every guest.* Exclusiveness, jealousy, quarreling, have no place there, for the same reason as that which forbids the guests at a thanksgiving dinner to claim each his separate dish, and quarrel with the rest for his rights. In a holy community, there is no more reason why sexual intercourse should be restrained by law, than why eating and drinking should be—and there is as little occasion for shame in the one case as in the other. God has placed a wall of partition between the male and female during the apostasy, for good reasons, which will be broken down in the resurrection, for equally good reasons. But woe to him who abolishes the law of the apostasy before he stands in the holiness of the resurrection. The guests of the marriage supper may have each his favorite dish, each a dish of his own procuring, and that without the jealousy of exclusiveness. I call a certain woman my wife—she is yours, she is Christ's, and in him she is the bride of all saints. She is dear in the hand of a stranger, and according to my promise to her I rejoice. My claim upon her cuts directly across the marriage covenant of this world, and God knows the end. Write if you wish to hear from me."

Chapter III: HARRIET HOLTON

> I knew a man in Christ above fourteen years ago, whether in the body, I cannot tell; or whether out of the body, I cannot tell; God knoweth; such an one caught up to the third heaven. . . . How that he was caught up into paradise and heard unspeakable words, which it is not lawful for a man to utter. —II Cor. 12:2-4.

I

Miss Harriet A. Holton was an orphan, born in Springfield, Vermont, November 28, 1808, almost three years before Noyes. She was adopted by her maternal grandparents, who lived at Westminster.

Her grandfather, the Hon. Mark Richards, had been a Congressman and Lieutenant-Governor of Vermont, and was greatly respected in his neighborhood. He was also a nephew of the New England theologian, Dr. Samuel Hopkins. William Czar Bradley, Harriet's uncle by marriage, was distinguished in Brattleboro as a scholar, statesman, lawyer. He eventually became the law partner of Larkin G. Mead, Mary Noyes's husband.

The Richards were the aristocrats of Westminster. Heiress of a considerable fortune, and fastidiously brought up, Harriet was looked upon as an ideal match by ambitious young Vermonters.

True, Harriet was neither pretty nor brilliant; but she did possess a good mind—cool and perspicacious, according to the approved Vermont model, and she was the very incarnation of feminine industry. Edmund Burke, a law student in her uncle William Bradley's office in Brattleboro, soon recognized the advantages of an alliance with her.

During the bitter Adams-Jackson campaign, young Burke was drawn into a political discussion with the Hon. Mark Richards and, before he knew it, had been peremptorily shown the door. While Burke stood staring at the house, Mr. Richards announced to Harriet that he would disinherit her if ever she dared marry Edmund Burke. She could never let money or the prospect of money govern her affections, Harriet coolly replied, and refused to break off the betrothal.

But in 1831, Harriet suddenly felt the imperious call of religion, and was converted. "In a protracted meeting I came to the conclusion to devote my life to God," she confided to her diary. Therefore, she promptly announced to Edmund Burke that she had given her heart to God and wished to be released from her promise to him.

"But I am a Unitarian, and you made me one!" exclaimed the astonished young man. He begged Harriet not to abandon him to that outer and disgraceful darkness. Finally, however, they exchanged amicable explanations and parted forever. The Hon. Mark Richards repented, and resolved never to interfere again in the affairs of Harriet's heart.

It was with a great sense of relief, Harriet later confessed, that she was freed from this engagement. Soon, the bonds of orthodox religion were also severed. Gossips began to wonder about Miss Holton's conduct. Members of the church whispered that she no longer attended meetings, did not observe the sacrament, and never contributed to missionary societies. She had even attended a Universalist meeting, had been known to play cards, had been seen dancing. Miss Holton no longer "paid calls," and appeared in calico when the function clearly demanded satin. One distinguished New York cousin sent an eminent clergyman to point out the error of her ways. She received this worthy with characteristic courtesy, and even listened to him preach all one Sunday. Early the following morning the divine returned for a strategic conquest. Harriet was no match for him; and her grandfather, irritated by the endless torrent of words which flowed from the mouth of the visiting clergyman, came to her rescue. Without mincing words, the Hon. Mark Richards proclaimed it ungentlemanly and oppressive to crowd the girl that way. Had she not a right to her own beliefs? Was she not happy in them? Why should she be disturbed? The visitor picked up his hat, and without a word departed from the village.

Then, a friend, Maria Clark, told her of a strangely gifted young man in Putney and of the heresies he was preaching in schoolhouses and taverns. "Many think he is crazy," Miss Clark whispered to her friend. "But what I have heard of his belief has set me thinking!"

"*That* John Noyes," she continued, was promulgating the doctrine of complete and everlasting salvation from sin—a new way to sanctification—and hoped to exterminate the curse of sin once and for all.

To intensify Harriet's interest even more, Maria Clark next appeared with excited, almost incoherent accounts of the Putney prophet. Maria had actually seen some of his writings! She promised to send Harriet her copy of John Noyes's article on the Second Coming. His revelation made everything seem different, the Kingdom of God on earth imminent!

Nine months later Harriet received a hurried note from Maria

Clark. She should come immediately to West Westminster. John Noyes was going to preach in that village—in the schoolhouse. Harriet set out for the Clark house drawn by all the fascination of the forbidden. To herself Miss Holton tried to picture this young man, who so deliberately defied the ways of the world to teach his new covenant, this young man of good family who was reputed mad, who deliberately cast away his reputation to preach to outcasts in taverns and sample rooms.

Her hope was not diminished by his appearance. To Harriet Holton, something almost angelic radiated from the figure of the young heretic. His blue coat seemed to accentuate the disordered halo of the russet hair . . . "his face shone like an angel's." The emaciated figure, the sloping shoulders, the long arms, made him appear taller than he actually was. Deep in her heart, Harriet was happy that he was not handsome. Even his audacity was made doubly attractive by a certain shyness.

Free-thinkers and Universalists made up a large part of the audience that day in the little schoolhouse. Without undue preliminaries, before this handful (who scorned the approval of the orthodox), John Noyes announced as his text the title page of the New Testament—"The New Testament of our Lord and Saviour Jesus Christ."

He said that the word "testament" was identical with that elsewhere translated "covenant," and went on to emphasize the great difference between the old and new covenants. Under the old, the law was written on tablets of stone; under the new, it is written on the heart. Because her spirit had been sensitized by anticipation for the reception of his message, the words so directly and simply spoken by John Noyes seemed incandescent with new meaning, and she felt that at last she was being led out of darkness—on the only right path to life more abundant.

John's horse had been stabled in the Clark barn, and after the meeting, Noyes called at the Clarks, where Harriet was a guest. They were introduced, but both suddenly became tongue-tied. Harriet finally summoned courage enough to ask him if he would be willing to preach at East Westminster. She found him, in intimate conversation, more diffident, more bashful, than she had expected. The Clarks urged the young man to remain overnight—it was a long, dark drive over uncertain mountain roads to Putney. Without apology and without excuse, John Noyes replied that he would rather go home. Harriet admired the directness of his reply. Noyes drove homeward along those twisting Vermont roads, his mind lulled half to sleep by the jog-trot of the

horse and the deepening obscurity; the tantalizing image of Abigail Merwin still remained clearly etched in his imagination.

Without restraint, Harriet plunged into love. With a thrill of anticipation she accepted an invitation from a Putney friend to spend a day or two there. The village lay only a few miles across the hills. But to Harriet the visit took on all the importance of a journey into some remote, romantic kingdom.

Noyes, she learned upon her arrival, was still in Putney. Her friend invited the younger Noyeses—John and his two vivacious sisters, Harriet and Charlotte—to spend the evening. Now Harriet sank into speechless diffidence, though she was three years John's senior.

That evening John was most expansive; a quartette of adoring young women, who hung upon his every word, made an ideal audience for this young prophet of twenty-six. Harriet listened earnestly, and tried to convey her appreciation of the points he made, but somehow she failed to strike any responsive chord. They passed another evening together at Locust Grove; and although on her return to her grandparents, she could not congratulate herself that she had made any personal impression upon John, Harriet nevertheless hoped that she had established the basis of an enduring friendship with Harriet and Charlotte Noyes. That was something gained, at least.

2

Early in March, 1837, John Noyes set out for Boston to carry a message to William Lloyd Garrison. He had prepared, signed and read at a public meeting in Putney, his own "declaration of independence"—against an Administration "drunk with tyrannic power and rampant with cruelty towards Negroes, Indians, and Missionaries."

On March 30, 1837, as William Lloyd Garrison, John Greenleaf Whittier and a few others were discussing abolition politics in the office of *The Liberator* in Boston, this earnest young Vermonter appeared at the conference and waited attentively until the other Abolitionists had left. Then he recited to Garrison the story of his "anti-human government gesture"—his deliberate renunciation of citizenship. He denounced the government as "essentially infidel and reprobate, the seat of slave-power, the instrument of every kind of villainy and oppression, and wholly antagonistic to the spiritual forces which are working for the introduction of holiness, peace and human brotherhood."

The time was ripe, Noyes declared vigorously, for a "revolt of the whole North from the unholy compact, in the interest, not simply of Anti-Slavery, but of the whole regeneration of society." A few days after this personal interview, Noyes expanded in writing to Garrison his conviction concerning slavery: "I am writing that all men should know that I have subscribed my name to an instrument similar to the Declaration of '76, renouncing allegiance to the government of the United States, and asserting the title of Jesus Christ to the throne of the world.

"I will give you my reasons for this 'wild' deed. When I wish to form a conception of the government of the United States (using a personified representation), I picture to myself a bloated, swaggering libertine, trampling on the Bible—its own Constitution—its treaties with the Indians—the petitions of its citizens; with one hand whipping a Negro tied to a liberty-pole, and with the other dashing an emaciated Indian to the ground. On one side stand the despots of Europe, laughing and mocking at the boasted liberty of their neighbor; on the other stands the Devil saying '*Esto perpetua*.'... In view of such a representation, the question urges itself upon me—'what have I, as a Christian, to do with such a villain?' I live on the territory which he claims—under the protection, to some extent, of the laws which he promulgates. Must I therefore profess to be his friend? God forbid! I will rather flee my country. But every other country is under the same reprobate authority. I must, then, either go out of the world, or find some way to live where I am, without being a hypocrite, or a partaker in the sins of the nation. I grant that 'the powers that be are ordained of God,' and this is not less true of individual than national slaveholders. I am hereby justified in remaining a slave—but not in remaining a slaveholder. Every person who is, in the usual sense of the expression, a citizen of the United States, i.e., a voter, politician, etc., is at once a slave and a slaveholder—in other words, a subject and a ruler in a slaveholding government. God will justify me in the one character, but not in the other. I must therefore separate them and renounce the last. Holding simply the station of a subject, as a Christian I may respect the powers that be for the Lord's sake, but I cannot make myself a partaker of their ungodly deeds by mingling in their counsels or assisting their operations.... I have renounced active coöperation with the oppressor on whose territories I live; now I would find a way to put an end to his oppression. But he is manifestly a reprobate; reproof and instruction only aggravate his sins. I cannot attempt to reform him, because I am forbidden to 'cast

pearls before swine.' I must therefore either consent to remain a slave, till God removes the tyrant, or I must commence war upon him, by a declaration of independence and other weapons suitable to the character of a son of God...."

Signs of the times clearly indicated, Noyes continued in this letter to Garrison, that "this country is ripe for a convulsion like that of France; rather, I should say, for the French revolution reversed. Infidelity roused the whirlwind in France. The Bible, by Anti-Slavery and other similar movements, is doing the same work in this country. So, in the end, Jesus Christ, instead of a blood-thirsty Napoleon, will ascend the throne of the world. The convulsion which is coming will be, not the struggle of death, but the travail of childbirth—the birth of a ransomed world."

Garrison read extracts from this letter at a public meeting in Rhode Island in the summer of 1837, and spoke favorably of its sentiment. On October 20th, he published it in *The Liberator*, omitting, however, Noyes's signature. In a communication to *The Liberator*, Whittier denounced this letter as sectarian, and censured Garrison for printing it. Development of the "anti-human government" theory among the radical Abolitionists, and the diversion of the Anti-Slavery Society, followed in the course of a year or two from this time.

Noyes's disciples were always convinced that he had exerted a profound influence upon the great Abolitionist and this influence was freely admitted by Garrison's children who became his biographers. Garrison adopted Noyes's idea of a revolt of the North against the "reprobate" slaveholding Government at Washington, and utilized his concept as the basis of subsequent work against slavery.

The Misses Noyes read a long recital of John's travels with suppressed excitement: "...I went to Lowell, Andover, Boston, Providence and New York, remaining a day or two in each, and returning to my old resting place in Newark.... At Boston I called at the anti-slavery office, found Garrison, Stanton, Whittier and other choice spirits warmly engaged in a dispute about political matters. I heard them quietly, and when the meeting broke up I introduced myself to Garrison. He spoke with great interest of *The Perfectionist*, said his mind was heaving on those subjects and he would devote himself to them as soon as he could get anti-slavery off his hands....

"In my passage from Providence to New York God gave me a view of his wonders in the mighty ocean. We started in a storm, which became so furious that we were forced to lie still

at Newport six hours. Again we put to sea with a strong gale in our teeth. The waves rolled and foamed gloriously. Our boat, one hundred and fifty feet long, jammed full of boxes, with two or three hundred human beings in the crevices, reared and pitched like an unruly horse, till it cracked as though its backbone were breaking. The people staggered about like drunken men. I had a fine opportunity of proving the power of faith in God, although it was a new and appalling scene. I was neither sick nor fearful, not because I trusted in the strength of the vessel or in the skill of its managers, but because I said in my heart, 'The winds and the waves, the steam and the helm are in my Father's hands. I am exposed, not to the fury of the elements, but to the mercy of God.' After two days' contention with the waters we arrived safely in New York. Next day I came to this place (Newark), and directly found myself again exposed to the mercy of God in a new way. A malignant attack of scarlet-fever, which is at work in this place, threatened to prostrate me.... New York is heaving on the subject of holiness and of money. As money goes down holiness goes up. This great people among whom I circulate is full of the elements of heaven and hell. Those elements cannot long remain together. Heaven must begin on earth soon, or hell will."

3

Having overcome the fever by his own highly personal methods of therapy, John Noyes went to visit Abram Smith in the old stone house at Rondout. The disquieting image of Abigail Merwin remained in the background of his consciousness. There was so much he had to say to her—even though she was now Mrs. Merit Pratt, the wife of a schoolmaster.

His face turned toward Abigail, Noyes set out on foot for Ithaca. On his back he carried a knapsack. In his cavernous pockets not one coin jingled against another. At the end of his long day's plodding over the bright spring countryside, Noyes sought refuge in a saw-mill or a barn. The carefree, frontier hospitality made his way easy; and he got a bite to eat wherever he could.

His unflagging resolution to reach Ithaca that spring was based partly on a desire to "confront" Abigail as a deserter. He was impelled, also by what he believed was a call from God, to start a paper for the publication of his new "tidings" in central New York.

By the luckiest chance, at Genoa, he fell in with a group of men who had been in sympathy with the publication of *The*

Perfectionist at New Haven. They made an offering of no less than forty dollars, which made his entry into Ithaca something like a triumph. He took lodgings at a hotel and lost no time in enlisting the sympathy of a local printer. He then discovered the house in which the Merit Platts were domiciled, and once more gazed rapturously at Abigail's bedroom window. Abigail remained in strict seclusion and gave no sign of her knowledge of the embarrassing presence of this persistent suitor.

Notwithstanding this preoccupation, Noyes plunged into his first independent venture in publishing. He decided to call his magazine *The Witness*. It would be modest—an eight-page folio, two columns to the page. He promised his readers twenty-six numbers in all—"sooner or later."

On the last page of the first number he expressed his ideal of a free press. Its terms were *free:* "To such as choose to buy it, *one dollar for twenty-six numbers:* to such as prefer to receive it as a gift, *gratis*.

"I ask you not to become a subscriber to this paper for my sake," he wrote; "I look to God, and not to my subscription list, for support and countenance. 'The laborer is worthy of his hire,' *but he should be paid by his employer, and not by his fellow servants*. I have so fully proved the faithfulness of my employer, that I have not the least anxiety about the future, either in respect to my spiritual or temporal necessities... if you wish for the paper without money and without price, send me simply your name. If you prefer to pay for it, send me your name with one dollar. If you dislike both of these modes of subscription, there is still another, which I prefer myself; to wit, send me your name, with a gift of any amount, more or less. So your money shall be a love-token to me, and my paper shall be, not an article of merchandise, but a present to you. I can buy and sell with an enemy, but I can exchange gifts only with a friend."

The response of this argument could not have been all that Noyes hoped, for in the third number of *The Witness*, he further defended his free press: "If any withhold their names, because they can send no money, let me assure them that in my code of morality, *poverty is not a crime*. I have reason to believe that there are many worthy persons who would be glad to receive the paper, but for some cause or other cannot pay for it. Most heartily I desire such to put away all squeamishness, and send me their names without delay. 'Ask, and ye shall receive.'"

Only three numbers of *The Witness* were published at Ithaca. Between the third and fourth numbers there was an interruption

of more than a year. That interruption was caused by an event that lifted John Noyes out of obscurity and changed the whole course of his life.

4

That letter to David Harrison written by John Noyes in "the nakedness of privacy" sped on its mysterious course. David Harrison read it and reread it. He trembled over its implications. For months he dared not show it to any one. At last he read it to a few intimates, sufficiently initiated into the arcanum of Perfectionist doctrine. They listened breathlessly. "The Lord gave me not liberty to suppress it," Harrison afterwards apologized.

Simon Lovett, the first to whom Harrison showed John Noyes's pronouncement, blushed at the paradise John promised. Recovering his breath, Simon confided his approval of the wisdom and foresight expressed by Mr. Noyes. Could he borrow the letter and peruse it at his leisure? David Harrison reluctantly consented—but exacted a promise from Simon Lovett that it should be returned without delay.

Simon Lovett showed that letter to Elizabeth Hawley, a twenty-three-year-old eccentric, a fanatic in her aversion to worldly conventions. So important a revelation must be sent at once, she insisted, to Theophilus Gates in Philadelphia. Simon protested that he had promised to return the letter to David Harrison without delay—without showing it to another soul. In which case, Elizabeth Hawley retorted, she would leave the house that night, in the thunderstorm, for New Haven. To prevent that folly, Simon Lovett consented.

He confessed all to David Harrison, who, knowing the reputation of Theophilus Ransom Gates, realized that Noyes's ominous words would be shouted from the housetops. He realized that he should write to old Gates at once, forbidding the publication of that document. But, strangely enough—so David afterward explained to John Noyes—he could not get the Lord's consent. "So, you see, the Lord obtained the letter from me, as it were, by stealth."

At the very moment Noyes was preparing to send out the first number of *The Witness* from Ithaca, Theophilus Gates was launching a new paper of his own, entitled *The Battle-Axe and Weapons of War*. It was to be a vehicle for Mr. Gates's own theories concerning the relation of the sexes in the Kingdom of God. With copies under his arm, Theophilus made a special trip to the Philadelphia City Hall, and placed a copy on the mayor's

desk. "We do not use such weapons here!" cried the mayor. Undiscouraged, Theophilus paraded the streets with a placard in his hat advertising *The Battle-Axe,* and spent most of his spare moments distributing *The Battle-Axe* among magistrates, ministers, editors, merchants and lawyers.

Because of its bitter attack upon the sacred institution of marriage, that first number of *The Battle-Axe* attracted much attention. "Men and women had better change their partners twenty times over, under the best regulations they can make with each other, so as at length to have one with whom they can live in harmony and be in the order of God, than to live in any kind of strife and disagreement and live in the order of the devil." Such was the gist of Gates's challenge. Also: "In accordance with this new, more heavenly condition of things, myself and she that was my wife after the fashion of this world have mutually dissolved and forever renounced everything pertaining to such a fashion, and are hereafter to live together only as it is our free and mutual choice so to do."

When the second number of *The Battle-Axe* reached Ithaca, John Noyes read with dismay and mortification all the secret thoughts he had written in strict confidence to David Harrison. How had these words fallen into the hands of that miserable, malicious Gates? He wrote to David demanding an explanation.

Was this the malicious revenge of wily old Theophilus, his retaliation for the young man's implacable indictment? Noyes was certain that it was. However, when the letter was said to have been penned by James Boyle, Noyes courageously refused to hide behind the false attribution. Within a week from the first notice he received that the letter had been published, John Noyes acknowledged his authorship in *The Witness:* "Several persons have written to inquire whether I, or Mr. Boyle, was the author of a letter lately published in *The Battle-Axe.* I answer, I am the author, but not the publisher, of the letter. As an anti-mason, I cannot object to its publication; and as an optimist, I am bound to rejoice. Yet I should never have obtruded upon the public, not for fear of persecution or reproach, but lest my liberty should become a stumbling-block to others. Since it is published, it is proper that I should acknowledge myself as its author, 'that I may bear my own burdens'; and I hereby entirely exculpate Mr. Boyle from any censure which may fall upon it, as I well know that he has long been a decided adversary of some of its sentiments. In due time, if it is demanded, I intend fully to explain the allu-

sions of that letter, as I have the means of manifesting undeniably my innocence in the matter."

Despite Noyes's accusations, it is not altogether evident that Gates was inspired by malice. Noyes's letter expressed views which paralleled his own. Moreover, Elizabeth Hawley had not explicitly forbidden its publication. Gates had made no attempt to use Noyes's name as the author, and prefaced the letter with these remarks of his own: "The open and undisguised manner in which he has expressed himself in the close of the extract on a very important subject, the uprightness and purity of his intentions, and the sacrifices I know he has made, from principle, demand of the reader a candid hearing. . . . God has delivered me from every fear but the fear of offending Him, and therefore, I have no valid excuse to keep back any important truths for the welfare and happiness of mankind when called on by a sense of duty to declare them."

Thus that letter, written in the silence of a winter night in Putney, created a storm of scandal as the "*Battle-Axe* letter." It tossed John Noyes into a spotlight, to face without flinching and without equivocation, the consequences of his own challenge to human institutions. To his eternal credit, he faced them like a man.

Letters from all quarters bombarded the obscure young heretic in Ithaca. Noyes made no effort to escape the storm which broke around his head. "The doctrine of that letter is God's truth, and whosoever contends with it 'rushes upon the thick bosses of His buckler,' " he wrote in the September issue of *The Witness*. "Before the will of God is done on earth as it is in heaven, that doctrine will be preached on the housetops, and its practical tendency, not to confusion and licentiousness, but to 'whatever is pure and lovely and of good report' will be discerned." But he stressed this reservation: "Woe to him who abolishes the law of the apostasy before he stands in the holiness of the resurrection. . . . If the tendency of the doctrine is to be judged by the actions of him who teaches it, truth requires that I should testify as under oath, using an expression of John Bunyan's, that 'I know not whether there is a woman in the world otherwise than by their dress and common report'; and I can say without fear of contradiction to those who have familiarly known my ways, 'Ye are witnesses, and God also, how holily and justly and unblamably I have walked among you.' Liberty never metamorphoses the children of God into swine. If any become swine in consequence of learning the law of liberty, they are only hypocrites made manifest."

Soon the attention of the whole contentious little Puritan civilization scattered along the Atlantic coast was focused upon the "*Battle-Axe* letter." In William Lloyd Garrison's anti-slavery organ, *The Liberator*, James Boyle was severely denounced for his supposed "avowal to the theory of a community of wives." In a letter of explanation to Garrison, Noyes protested against this erroneous statement, but his words were prudishly ignored by the editor of *The Liberator*. "I stand before its readers under the imputation of knavery," he protested, forced to publish this letter to Garrison in his own paper, *The Witness:* "I am charged with the base design of transferring the odium of the '*Battle-Axe* letter' from myself to Mr. Boyle." "As your paper seems to be tossed to and fro with much unprofitable contention about the authorship of the *Battle-Axe* letter," Noyes wrote to Garrison, "and the circulation of *The Witness* is very small, I think you will serve the cause of truth by publishing my acknowledgment of it. . . . I perceive that Boyle and Gates and your New Haven correspondent and even you yourself seem to shrink from exposing my name in connexion with my heresies. I thank you all for the shelter you have given me, but I desire it may be known that my works are not *intentionally* 'works of darkness.'. . .

"The letter was written not for the public, but for the perusal of a familiar friend, with due regard to the delicacy of its subject, and without any intention of obtruding it upon the notice, even of Perfectionists–much less of casting it before dogs and swine. Evidence of this may be found in the letter itself. While I cast from me the fear and shame of guilt, I nevertheless acknowledge myself a follower of Paul in my views of expediency, believing that there are things spoken 'in the third heaven, which are not lawful to be uttered,' and that there is wisdom which ought to be communicated only to 'the perfect.' Though the letter was written in the nakedness of privacy, and therefore may seem uncomely, being thus presented to the public–yet I prefer its nakedness to the filthy garments with which Gates has clothed it."

This public defense cleared the air, and Noyes began to realize that the whole affair was an act of Providence. "God made a glorious move on the checkerboard in that thing," Noyes confided to David. In after years, in reviewing the whole mysterious chain of unexpected events, Noyes confessed that "I felt that I was called, even under the heaviest penalties, to defend and ultimately carry out the doctrine of communism in love. I accepted the commission with a good heart."

But now, the publisher of *The Witness* was confronted by

the blank wall of absolute poverty. The printers in Ithaca were clamoring for payment. The third number of his little folio appeared; but subscriptions came to a dead standstill. A cursory survey of his accounts revealed that he was in debt for his board and debt to the printer—eighty dollars in all. His fertile imagination could not provide the vaguest idea of how to extricate himself from this plight.

Then a miracle happened. As he was opening his mail—it had become thinner and thinner as the reverberations created by the *Battle-Axe* scandal resounded—out dropped an order for exactly eighty dollars. The letter was from Harriet A. Holton of Westminster, Vermont. She was sending the money, she half-apologetically explained, by inspiration. She had obtained it from her dear grandfather in a way that was nothing less than miraculous.

5

Noyes paid his debts, left his affairs in Ithaca in the hands of a friend, A. H. Elston, and hurried off across fields, over split-rail fences, and turnpikes, back to Abram Smith's house in Rondout. Abram Smith listened sympathetically to the recital of Noyes's adventures. Abram agreed that Noyes should bend all efforts toward immediate rehabilitation of his character. So John set out down the river to New York City. Mr. and Mrs. William Green, on whose understanding he relied, greeted the young man with profuse but empty welcomes. At the end of a few days he was made even more painfully aware of the persistent shock occasioned by the *Battle-Axe* letter. The whispering campaign kept growing—it brought blushes to virtuous cheeks. Noyes sought in vain to explain the basic intention of that letter to David Harrison. It was rather, he protested, to commend faith and patience. Its inner doctrine was merely this: when the will of God is done on earth, as it is in heaven, there will be no marriage. He advocated neither a plurality of wives, nor a community of wives, but a *nullity* of wives. Little children, he tried in vain to point out, were of the kingdom of God—and were they not naked and unashamed, as are all God's creatures in heaven and under heaven except man? His letter, he stated, was distinctly not concerned with general practice.

The few who listened turned their heads away, without answering him. But the damage to the Perfectionist cause seemed irreparable.

Noyes once more sought refuge with Abram Smith and re-

mained there until the latter part of March, 1838. Shortly after his arrival at the stone house at Rondout, Noyes received a letter from Ithaca bearing the astounding news that Abigail had left her husband, Merit Platt, and had returned to her father's home in Orange, Connecticut. He sent her a letter, borne by Abram Smith, as official emissary. "My confidence in God concerning you is still complete," he wrote, "and I rejoice in the assurance that the dénouement of our tragi-comedy is at hand. Your reply to this will probably decide the issue." For some unexplained reason Abram Smith did not deliver this letter. Perhaps he failed to locate Abigail, as in March of the following year Noyes implored David Harrison: "Be sure to ascertain where Abigail is," and, a week or two later: "If you can see her, you are authorized to make known to her my mind and circumstances . . . leaving her and the Lord to determine what course is right and expedient for her to pursue. If God does not bring to pass his strange act by her, he will by somebody else soon. The Kingdom of God is swiftly advancing to its predicted collision with the Kingdoms of this world. Like two mighty ships they are coming to a crash, which will shatter and sink one of them."

In April David Harrison finally succeeded in calling on Abigail, and presented two letters to her, as authorized by Noyes. Miss Merwin read them with some degree of interest, but remained noncommittal (all of which, strangely enough, David reported to Harriet Holton!) Within two months Noyes—he was not yet twenty-seven years old—had accepted the inevitable, and composed a farewell poem to Abigail, concluding with this enigmatic touch:

"We'll meet again, be sure of that.
Sometime 'twixt now and never,
An age or two I well may wait,
Since we are one forever."

So the phantom of Abigail Merwin vanished temporarily from the drama of John Noyes's life. Elusive always, it is not so much the real, flesh-and-blood Abigail who comes down to us, as an enigmatic and tantalizing *Belle Dame sans Merci.*

With the intention of resuming publication of *The Witness,* of rehabilitating his reputation and of defending his "thesis" from attack, Noyes went back to Ithaca, arriving late in March. At the postoffice he found letters containing sums of five and ten dollars. These, also, had been sent by Miss Harriet Holton. In thanking

her, he besought Miss Holton to "stop running me in debt, or to make sure that you look at my heart and not at my outward works for evidence that your generosity is not misplaced. . . . I am in the midst of a mighty contest between God's love and Satan's malice. The one heals as often as the other wounds. Woe after woe rolls over me, and alternately joy after joy. . . . If we long for victory, we must long for battle. . . . My daily feeling is that I shall either be killed or crowned soon."

6

Ithaca printers were no longer interested in *The Witness* as a business risk, and Noyes turned again to Putney. New ambitions now filled his head. He dreamed of a great publishing center, as powerful as the great religious book concerns in New York. He was almost twenty-seven—it was time to settle down. He longed for definite, constructive work, and the printing-press seemed the most effective instrument to spread broadcast across the country, nay, the world itself, the message of human regeneration.

He resented the whispering campaign which still sibilated behind his back; and he realized that he could not command respect in the rôle of a penniless, hungry vagabond. His father reprimanded him because he had made no effort to defend his reputation against slander and libel. Mrs. Noyes passed sleepless nights worrying over him. The time had come for decisive action. In this crisis, Harriet Holton emerged as the perfect solution for every problem. Marriage would give the lie to slanders which accused him of lewdness and promiscuity.

His resolution once made, Noyes lost no time in carrying his courtship to a speedy conclusion. On June 11, 1838, he wrote a long letter to Harriet proposing a partnership "which I will not call marriage until I have defined it." A proposal of marriage by the author of the notorious *Battle-Axe* letter might at first glance seem to be a contradiction in terms—for had he not advocated a "nullity of wives"? But Noyes reconciled conviction and gesture. "As believers," he explained to Miss Holton, "we are already one with each other and all saints." But since in heaven there is neither marrying nor giving in marriage, "we can enter into no engagements with each other which shall limit the range of our affections as they are limited in matrimonial engagements by the fashion of this world. I desire and expect my yoke-fellow will love all who love God, whether man or woman, with a warmth and strength of affection which is unknown to earthly lovers, and as freely as if

she stood in no particular connection with me." This generous privilege, of course, was to be reciprocal. He assured Harriet he would neither monopolize nor enslave her heart. Then he enumerated the advantages of this particular union:

"1. In the plain speech of a witness and not a flatterer I respect and love you for many desirable qualities, spiritual, intellectual, moral and personal, especially your faith, kindness, simplicity and modesty.

"2. I am confident that the partnership I propose will greatly promote our mutual happiness and improvement.

"3. It will also set us free, at least myself, from much reproach and many evil surmisings which are occasioned by celibacy in present circumstances.

"4. It will enlarge our sphere and increase our means of usefulness to the people of God.

"5. I am willing, at this particular time to testify by example that I am a follower of Paul in holding that 'Marriage is honorable in all.'

"6. I am also willing to testify practically against that bondage of liberty which utterly sets at naught the ordinances of men and refuses to submit to them even for the Lord's sake. I know that the immortal union of hearts, the everlasting honeymoon which alone is worthy to be called marriage, can never be effected by a ceremony; and I know equally well that such a marriage can never be marred by a ceremony. William Penn first bought Pennsylvania of the British king, then he paid the Indians for it. 'Thus it becomes us to fulfill all righteousness.'

"7. I have the permission and good-will not only of God but of all who are especially concerned in my movements in making this proposal."

This proposal was followed by an assurance that the Abigail Merwin episode was closed; and he frankly assured Harriet that he had recently been released from any connection with Abigail which would interfere with his proposal. "I still believe her to be a child of God and therefore love her. Yet I am as free as if I had never seen her."

As for the irregularity of his career, the seeming instability of his character—questions bound to be brought up by the Hon. Mark Richards—he confidently announced that he knew he possessed "a spirit of firmness, perseverance, and faithfulness in every good work, which had made the vagabond, incoherent service . . . almost intolerable to me, and I shall welcome heaven's order for my

release as an exile, after seven years' pilgrimage, would welcome the sight of his home."

John sent this letter off to Westminster on June 11, 1838. It did not come entirely as a surprise to Harriet, who in her cool, matter-of-fact Vermont manner had evidently been anticipating this alliance. The very next day she inscribed her acceptance. Harriet's joy bubbled through in crisp, light-hearted effervescence. Two or three years ago, Harriet recalled, some one had said of her: "If she will not marry any one who is not of the same faith as herself, perhaps she may marry John Noyes!" And Harriet had retorted: "I should as soon think of marrying the morning star!" "Since that time I have looked at and admired this star, till it does not seem so far off," she wrote. "Yet you will judge how unexpected was the subject of your letter!"

Harriet tripped along in the same vein for a paragraph or two, then she declared: "In gladly accepting this proposal for an external union, I agree with you that it will not 'limit the range of our affections.' The grace of God will exclude jealousy and everything with which the marriage state is defiled as we see it in the world. I only expect by it to be placed in a situation where I can enjoy what Harriet and Charlotte and your mother are now blessed with, your society and instruction as long as the Lord pleases and when he pleases."

However, there remained her grandfather and grandmother. If she went away, who would take care of them? Would the Hon. Mark approve of this penniless vagabondish John Noyes? Problems not to be lightly tossed aside, Harriet soberly realized. Yet she could not let them interfere with the decision of her heart. She put the matter squarely to her grandfather. She realized that Mr. Noyes's ideas on the subject of earning a living must differ from his—but she wished to know without delay if he had any objection to the person. "He said he did not wish to control me; he wished me to suit myself; he had hoped, if ever I married, I should continue in this house; also he had made a comfortable provision for me, and he hoped I would not put it out of my power to enjoy it. He thinks you are old enough to decide for yourself what you intend to do."

The Hon. Mark Richards had heard of the stinging ridicule and slander concerning John Noyes. He put additional questions to Harriet, and these she relayed to her betrothed. "Though I have lived by faith and not by works for four years past," John protested in reply, for the benefit of Mr. Richards, "I owe no man anything; I have defrauded no man; I have never failed."

The illness of Squire Noyes prevented John from going to Westminster to present his defense in person. Instead he wrote a long letter vindicating his past conduct, and detailing prospects for a rosy future: "My profession, though it is a strange one, has satisfactory prospects of being lucrative. My fees during the last year have been numerous and liberal. A lawyer accounts his 'faculty' a fortune. Although I require no stated price for my services as a spiritual counselor, I know that God rewards every man according to his works; and that his people will so value my works, that I shall ere long be abundantly remunerated, even in this world's wealth. I have the intellectual materials for many prospective publications, which will naturally bring an increasing revenue. I am not in the condition of one whose race is run, but of one just commencing business; and the discipline of four years past has only completed my education, not determined my fortune. I have an equal share with seven others in an estate which has borne the liberal expenses of a large family, and the vicissitudes of these failing times without diminution....

"As to a 'certain dwelling place,' I cannot now speak definitely. But negotiations are in progress which will soon determine the matter. My father's infirmities are such that his business already demands the activity of a younger man. Either I, or some one else, will soon take his burden. If God beckons me, and my friends consent, I am ready to engage in the business. In that case, our dwelling place would be my old home. I shall do nothing in this matter without the satisfied consent of a full quorum of those concerned in it, keeping a good conscience toward God, and toward man."

In answering, Harriet assured Noyes of her perfect confidence in him in all things: "Looking below the excitement of present feelings, I am conscious that in my heart God has laid up in store for you a fountain of quiet love, a home, which will be brought forth in due time. I read to my grandfather those statements in your letter which you intended for him. He fled from his first objections, to what has been the only weight in the scale of the world, in my estimation—the care of my grandmother. She requires the care of a mother for a little child, and I have enjoyed giving her that attention."

When he received this heartening reassurance, John answered without delay: "Your letter was sweeter than honey or the honeycomb. That beautiful expression, 'a fountain of quiet love,' is worth more to me than the rhapsodies of Werther, and Juliet, and all such flaming lovers. God grant you may have none other than

quiet love. So we shall 'rest in our love,' I desire (*quietly* to be sure) to hear from you often."

In the end, Grandfather Richards himself went to the minister in Westminster to authorize publishing the marriage expectations. The problem of caring for the aging grandparents was solved by the offer of the housekeeper to act as nurse for the infirm Mrs. Richards, with an additional servant to manage the household.

"You gave me an opportunity of opening my heart in regard to Abigail Merwin," Harriet finally wrote to John. "I do not know much of her, only as one loved by you. In that position I might fear she would be the object of my envy. But I will tell you my feelings, the morning I received your first letter from Putney, and as these came up from my heart I shall depend upon them, whatever may arise to the contrary: I felt that the Lord had directed you to me, and that I was formed in heart to contribute to your happiness and usefulness in this act of your drama, as Abigail Merwin was in the beginning of your testimony. I said, if my fate be that of the Empress Josephine, the Lord will give me a heart to rejoice and say, 'Thy will be done.' I am ready to distrust myself when I look forward, and I say, John, if I *do* betray you with a kiss, the Lord reward me accordingly; a traitor to such gentleness, goodness and truth would deserve the wrath of God. I began, thinking I would write to you particularly about the spirit I have been under which forbids me to marry; but perhaps I shall get my mouth open so that I can talk with you on this subject when we meet."

The allusion to Napoleon and Josephine called forth an immediate reply from the impatient young man in Putney. On June 25 he sent her this outspoken note: "One or two things in your letter today seem to call for an immediate reply. Do you remember that Napoleon always said truly, that his prosperity was identified with his marriage to Josephine? As soon as he parted with her, he parted with fortune; and ere long it might well be said of him, 'How art thou fallen, Lucifer, son of the morning.' If your fate is to be that of Josephine, mine is to be that of Napoleon. I have often thought of Napoleon's case, among others, as a terrible and warning illustration.... 'Take heed to your spirit, and let none deal treacherously against the wife of his youth; for the Lord, the God of Israel saith, that *he hateth putting away*.' Love in the beginning and treachery in the end is the way of the world in all things; a way which I hate, as God hates. In respect to the influence you speak of having been under, I know not how far you

may have imbibed the spirit of Shakerism; but I will say frankly, that there may be no mistake between us, that so far from regarding the act of sexual enjoyment as in itself unholy, I am sure that there is no sacrifice except that of the heart, that is more acceptable to God."

Three days later—less than three weeks after his proposal—they were married in Chesterfield, New Hampshire, where John had first begun his study of the law. That pillar of respectability, Larkin G. Mead, his brother-in-law, performed the ceremony. It was June 28, 1838; the very day when, across the Atlantic in Westminster Abbey, a young girl of twenty was crowned Queen of England.

"Poor Harriet!" exclaimed Edmund Burke, the young man who had once been ushered out of the house by the Hon. Mark Richards. "She has thrown herself away! I would have carried her to Washington." And in truth, this rejected suitor *was* in the course of events elected to the House of Representatives.

"Poor Harriet"—indeed! A strange bridegroom this Westminster heiress had chosen. "By this marriage, besides herself, and a good social position, which she held as belonging to the first families of Vermont," Noyes ingenuously confessed in later years, "I obtained money enough to build me a house and a printing-office, and to buy a press and type."

Their honeymoon consisted of a drive over the hills to Albany, to buy a second-hand printing press at a reasonable bargain; then home again to Putney. There, less than three weeks after their June wedding, John Noyes resumed publication of *The Witness*. In his mind, this took precedence over all else. Hon. Mark Richards provided a handsome allowance—enough for the young couple to live on for the next six years. Upon his death, Harriet was to inherit nine thousand dollars more. In all, the young Noyeses received from this source approximately sixteen thousand dollars.

A few days after the return to Putney, press and type arrived from Albany. The great work of printing—setting type by hand, correcting proof, and all such details—enlisted Harriet and her two sisters-in-law, Harriet and Charlotte, as well as young George Noyes. In order to instruct the rest of them, George, a lad of about sixteen, was to be sent away as an apprentice to a printer in a neighboring town. But they were impatient to operate the press. Skill would come as the fruit of experience, they assured each other.

At last the great day arrived when actual work was to begin.

(Courtesy of Oneida Community, Ltd.)

HARRIET HOLTON NOYES

Above: from a daguerreotype about the time of her marriage.
Below: As the "mother" of the Community.

(Courtesy of George Wallingford Noyes)

JOHN HUMPHREY NOYES, *ætat.* 28
(From an undated daguerreotype made about 1840)

A YANKEE SAINT

Oneida Circular.

A WEEKLY JOURNAL OF HOME, SCIENCE AND GENERAL INTELLIGENCE.

ıblished by the Oneida & 'allingford Communities.

ONEIDA COMMUNITY, DECEMBER 4, 1871.

New Series, Vol. VIII, No. 49 Whole No. 1383.

POST-OFFICE ADDRESS:

ONEIDA CIRCULAR, ONEIDA, N. Y.

TERMS.

The CIRCULAR is sent to all applicants, whether they pay or not. costs and is worth at least two dollars per volume. Those who nt it and ought to have it are divisible into three classes, viz., 1, ose who cannot afford to pay two dollars; 2, those who can afford pay *only* two dollars; and 3, those who can afford to pay *more* ın two dollars. The first ought to have it free; the second ought pay the cost of it; and the third ought to pay enough more than cost to make up the deficiencies of the first. This is the law of mmunism. We have no means of enforcing it, and no wish to do except by stating it and leaving it to the good sense of those conrned. We take the risk of offering the CIRCULAR to all without ıce; but free subscriptions will be received only from persons ıking application for themselves, either directly or by giving express thority to those who apply for them.

Foreign subscribers, excepting those residing in Canada, must nit with their subscriptions money to prepay the postage.

THE UNITED COMMUNITIES.

ONEIDA COMMUNITY

an association living in Lenox, Madison Co., N. Y., four miles ıth of Oneida and a few rods from the Depot of the Midland ailroad. *Number* of members, 205. *Land*, 654 acres. *Business*, anufacture of Hardware and Silk goods, Printing the CIRCULAR, orticulture, &c. *Theology*, Perfectionism. *Sociology*, Bible mmunism.

WILLOW-PLACE COMMUNITY.

Branch of O. C., on a detached portion of the domain, about one d one-fourth miles north of O. C. *Number* of members, 19. *ısiness*, Manufactures.

WALLINGFORD COMMUNITY.

Branch of O. C., at Wallingford, Conn., one mile west of the artford and New Haven Railroad. *Number* of members, 45. *ınd*, 228 acres. *Business*, Publishing, Job Printing, Manufacres, and Horticulture.

SPECIAL NOTICE.

The O. C. and Branches are not "Free Lovers," in the popular ıse of the term. They call their social system BIBLE COMMUNISM COMPLEX MARRIAGE, and hold to freedom of love only within eir own families, subject to Free Criticism and the principles of ale Continence. In respect to permanency, responsibility, and ery essential point of difference between marriage and licentiousss, the Oneida Communists stand with marriage. Free Love with em does *not* mean freedom to love to-day and leave to-morrow; r freedom to take a woman's person and keep their property to themves; nor freedom to freight a woman with offspring and send her wn stream without care or help; nor freedom to beget children and ve them to the street and the poor-house. Their Communities are *milies*, as distinctly bounded and separated from promiscuous soty as ordinary households. The tie that binds them together is as rmanent and sacred, to say the least, as that of marriage, for it is eir religion. They receive no new members (except by deception mistake), who do not give heart and hand to the family interest life and forever. Community of property extends just as far as edom of love. Every man's care and every dollar of the common operty are pledged for the maintenance and protection of the men and children of the Community.

ADMISSIONS.

These Communities are constantly receiving applications for adssion which they have to reject. It is difficult to state in any brief y all their reasons for thus limiting their numbers; but some of m are these: 1. The parent Community at Oneida is full. Its ldings are adapted to a certain number, and it wants no more. The Branch-Communities, though they have not attained the nor l size, have as many members as they can well accommodate, and st grow in numbers only as they grow in capital and buildings. The kind of men and women who are likely to make the Commuies grow, spiritually and financially, are scarce, and have to be ed out slowly and cautiously. It should be distinctly understood t these Communities are not asylums for pleasure seekers or perıs who merely want a home and a living. They will receive only se who are very much in earnest in religion. They have already ıe their full share of labor in criticising and working over raw reits, and intend hereafter to devote themselves to other jobs (a nty of which they have on hand), receiving only such members as m likely to help and not hinder their work. As candidates for mmunism multiply, it is obvious that they cannot all settle at eida and Wallingford. Other Communities must be formed; and best way for earnest disciples generally is to work and wait, till Spirit of Pentecost shall come on their neighbors, and give them mmunities right where they are.

"ALL THINGS CONTINUE AS THEY WERE."

BY J. H. NOYES.

SO said the sleepy souls who jeered at the promise of Christ's coming, eighteen hundred years ago. So say, and always have said the wise fools, who forget the living God, and worship the "natural laws," measuring the future by the poorest experience of the past, and loving the routine of common animal existence, more than the hope of the kingdom of heaven.

But this old argument from experience, which has been used so effectually to batter the watch-towers of faith, may be turned round, and made to play upon the ditch-works of unbelief. We accept the saying, "*All things continue as they were.*" We too believe that what has been will be—that things are to go on "in the good old way." But let us see what the "good old way" has been. The history of the world is not altogether a record of the devil's works and stagnation.

"All things continue as they were *from the foundation of the world.*" Just so. *Before* the foundation of the world there was a God, able to make the world with its "natural laws." He continues mighty as ever. That God, before the world began, had a plan of its whole career and results. He purposed, way back in that old time, to gather together in one, at last, all things which are in heaven and on earth. That plan continues unchanged, and is moving on, as of old, to its accomplishment.

"All things continue as they were." The God of heaven was from the beginning the Judge of all the earth, as was seen in the destruction of Sodom and Gomorrah; in the conquests and exaltation of the Jewish nation; in the humiliation of Nebuchadnezzar, and in the destruction of Jerusalem. Look out for such things in these days.

"All things continue as they were"—God's supremacy in the affairs of men and nations among the rest. There was in old time a covenant with Abraham, that in his seed all nations of the earth should be blessed. That covenant remains as it was. Watch for its fulfillment.

"All things continue as they were." There was "an age of miracles," which they say now is past. But why so? For four thousand years the God of heaven dealt with the world in open manifestations of his power and glory. This is the good old way. Let us have no innovations. What has been will be. The age of miracles is one of the old venerable institutions, which we are bound to cling to, in spite of all the novelties of theologians. "All things continue as they were from the foundation of the world."

The truth is, revolution, progress, and the bursting forth of new things, has been the rule of the world's history; and the routine of which conservatives are so fond has been the exception. The principal things that have been going on since the world began have been subversions of old institutions by new expansions of life: like the subversion of idolatry by Judaism, of Judaism by Christianity, of false Christianity by the Reformation, etc. And such, we might expect, would be the rule of human affairs, if we realize that the living God is at the center of them. None but those who believe that King Log is the center of destiny can reasonably croak for still times.

We vote heartily for the old ways. We trust "all things will continue as they were from the foundation of the world"—speeding onward, from overturn to overturn, till he whose right it is shall reign.

A UNIVERSITY OF DESIGN.

Home-Talk by J. H. N., W. P., Nov. 15, 1871.

LET us look around the room, and see how many specimens of *design* address the eye. Somebody studied a great while in working out the curious plan of that stove and in devising the ornaments upon it. The carpet, also, is a specimen of design. Who knows how much labor was laid out in perfecting the idea of that pattern. Then the paper on the wall has its interesting design, and every dress in the room. In the factories, whence come the material of these fabrics, are men and women devoted to the business of inventing new designs—new figures that will please the eye. Those lamps are specimens of design; and the shade on that largest lamp has a very pretty design; one that pleases the eye wonderfully. Nobody knows how many minds have been employed in perfecting such a design as that. It is not at all likely that it was suddenly invented by one mind. In many instances a thousand minds during a thousand years have been engaged upon a single form, each improving the design of its predecessor, until finally a result is attained which is pronounced very beautiful. In short, we are surrounded by designs that are the accumulated results of the labors of artists, who, in the centuries that are past, have tried to imagine, invent, create beautiful forms to please the eye. Designing has been and is a very great business in the world—thousands and thousands are busy in creating the beautiful forms we see.

Having thus obtained an idea of the meaning and importance of design in things that address the eye, let us extend the idea. There is just as great a field for the multiplication and variation of design in music as in visible art. Every new combination of sounds is a design.

John had picked up some vague notions concerning the rudiments of the composing stick. Surrounded by his adoring Harriet and the two happy sisters, he began to pick up type and construct words. The three women picked out letters and handed them to him. It seemed an interminable task; yet John refused to be hurried. Step by step he felt his way, experimented, studied. At last the "stick" was full. Perseverance and patience had triumphed. His audience applauded. But how to obtain a proof of that "stickful" of type? A hurried hunt for a piece of string ensued. Finally the type was tied fast and firm in the "stick." With infinite precaution the "stick" was laid on the bed of the press. Carefully this miniature form was inked. Then a piece of paper was placed carefully over the type, the press-bed was run under the platen, the arm of the press was pulled around to make the impression. It all came so easily that the amateur printer and his little crew, almost breathless with suspense, could only conclude that no impression had yet been made on that little stickful of type. Eagerness to see a proof could not be restrained. The bed of the press was run out. Type and stick looked as if they had been run over by a locomotive! Had the type been taken out of its iron enclosure and placed on the bed of the press, they saw at once, all would have gone well. A proof, they laughingly admitted, had been obtained —a proof of their own ignorance!

Among this little group, every other interest was subordinated to the press and the publication of *The Witness*. Type-setting and press-work, however, required only a portion of their time. The rest was given to reflection, reading, intellectual studies—and the "home talks" of the leader. Outward ceremonies, long formal prayers, sad, holy-pucker faces were banished. After hours of hard work, study, reflection, and recreation, the evening was devoted to bringing together results for inspection, criticism and edification. All this was done in the free, genial, conversational spirit of a family ever more closely bound together by love.

7

Harriet was promptly to discover that her marriage with John Noyes was no ethereal alliance with the morning star. Not that she suffered any disillusion—for John possessed an uncanny power of evoking unswerving loyalty in the little group that surrounded him, particularly in the women. His very presence thrilled them all. When she discovered that she was going to bear him a child, the adoring females of the little sect shared her joy. But Harriet failed to carry this child to term. It was an agonizing ordeal, and a bitter disappointment to them all.

But such tragedies were common experiences for the women of New England. Putney neighbors offered laconic sympathy; the elder women recounted in elaborate detail their own ordeals in child-bearing. They exhibited a grim stoicism and submission to the inevitable. But, because, most of all, she was animated by the desire to become the mother of John Noyes's son, Harriet uncomplainingly submitted to the renewed hazards of child-bearing. Such was the destiny of womankind. Four of the five infants she carried in the next six years were stillborn. Only one survived. This was a son, who was born in 1841, and given the name Theodore.

John Noyes brooded over Harriet's long martyrdom of child-bearing. He refused to evade his own responsibility in the matter —to accept the current code of respectable silence. His self-righteous fellow-citizens were in the habit of ignoring this torturing problem, dismissing the subject from their Puritan consciences with the remark that "Nature must take its course." John Noyes refused to admit that he, for one, was any mere slave of Nature, the subject of ruthless, impersonal processes. But even more persuasive than this consideration was his rebellion at the recurring physical pain and mutilation inflicted upon his patient, suffering Harriet. He was no feminist—but with malevolent persistence the diabolical injustice of the whole process of procreation stabbed at his conscience. Had they not bowed long and uncomplainingly to the will of God? There was a challenge here, a challenge to his intelligence, a challenge to his pride as an immortal free spirit, born anew in Christ. Why should he—the "perfect"—be caught in this ungodly trap—relentless, mutilating, and frustrating? External Nature seemed to Noyes to be canceling all of man's much-vaunted liberty of action, imposing the shackles of instinct and exacting unspeakable penalties.

Very well, then! John Noyes would accept this challenge. He would pledge his word that he would never again expose Harriet to such fruitless suffering. Rather than break this promise, he made up his mind to live apart from her. Such was the situation in the summer of 1844, six years after their marriage. He kept pondering this problem of marital relations, of the sexual function. Was it not just here that humanity had been brought into slavery, degraded below the level of the brutes? Had God devised this trap—this bait of imperious instinct, this ceaseless, automatic repetition of desire, and with it the destruction of all freedom, the limitation of all progress? Then, in a flash it came to him—the long march of humanity had been *against* Nature, in resolute defiance of her primordial edicts. Cooking, wearing clothes, living in houses, almost everything else accomplished by so-called civilized men—were not these in defiance of Nature, which would keep us slaves of instinct, commanding men to follow the example of the beasts?

Here indeed was a problem for a man who had proclaimed to the world his freedom from sin. In the full plenitude of his power, then in his thirty-third year, John Noyes refused to submit to the general conspiracy of silence concerning such matters or to be driven into the Shaker position of absolute abstinence. From his point of view, there could be no greater cowardice than to "let Nature take its course," to share in the debasement of a function that, properly educated, might elevate, rather than degrade, all humanity. In that widely circulated pamphlet, "Moral Physiology," young Robert Dale Owen had suggested one solution to the physiological problem; but this seemed to Noyes as unsatisfactory as that of the Shakers.

Noyes now began a radical analysis of the whole sexual function, recognizing in it two distinct aspects, the social and the propagative. "I experimented on this idea," Noyes related thirty-three years later, "and found that the self-control which it requires is not difficult; that my enjoyment was increased; that my wife's experience was very satisfactory, as it had never been before; that we had escaped the horrors and the fear of involuntary propagation. This was a great deliverance. It made a happy household."

Such was his "great discovery," which Noyes named Male Continence. To the objection that this practice was a "difficult and injurious interruption of a natural act," Noyes wrote to a correspondent: "But every instance of self-denial is an interruption of some natural act. The man who virtuously contents himself with a look at a beautiful woman is conscious of such an interruption. The lover who stops at a kiss denies himself a natural progression. It is an easy descending grade through all the approaches of sexual love, from the first touch of respectful friendship, to the final complete amalgamation. Must there be no interruption of this natural slide? Brutes, animal or human, tolerate none. Shall their ideas of self-denial prevail? Nay, it is the glory of man to control himself, and the Kingdom of Heaven summons him to self-control in ALL THINGS. If it is noble and beautiful for the betrothed lover to respect the law of marriage in the midst of the glories of courtship, it may be even more noble and beautiful for the wedded lover to respect the laws of health and propagation in the midst of the ecstasies of sexual union. The same moral culture that ennobles the antecedents and approaches of marriage, will some time surely glorify the consummation."

Here, he felt, was a great victory over the tyranny of Nature, and the powers of evil. It meant one more definite step into the Kingdom of God, toward the inauguration of "Bible Communism."

Chapter IV: MARY CRAGIN

I beseech you, therefore, brethren, by the mercies of God, that ye present your bodies a living sacrifice, holy, acceptable unto God, which is your reasonable service.
—ROMANS, xii: 1-2.

I

JOHN ROBERT MCDOWALL early felt the oppression of horrid, abominable, indwelling sin. He was born in Fredericksburg, Upper Canada, in September, 1801, son of a circuit preacher; at an early age he had formed the habit of reproving sinners wherever he found them. He became adept at organizing Sabbath schools, and collecting funds for worthy purposes. At twenty-one he became a law student at York, Upper Canada, but soon answered an inner urge to study theology at Amherst. Later this youth attended Union College in New York. He distributed tracts and developed skill in all the sanctimonious exercises.

McDowall served indifferently as minister in several village churches. Eventually called to New York, a day or two after his arrival he organized the Society for the Moral and Religious Improvement of the Five Points. As the animating spirit of this enterprise, many opportunities came to him to visit forbidden establishments. In the first one he found "the girls were beautiful and elegantly dressed." The next day he visited more of them. His interest in the Magdalens of the Five Points led him to confide to his private journal: "O, the harlots! How numerous! Modesty and purity forbid a minute detail. . . . Some of these women have noble lineage. For strength of intellect, general knowledge, and elegant taste, perhaps few ladies in the city can excel a few at the Five Points."

McDowall soon became a tolerated visitor to most of these resorts. He studied at leisure the inmates and their patrons, including the "City Thieves," a gang of young men, some from the first families of the country. Frequenting the less genteel houses, this gentry shared plunder with their paramours, John Robert was shocked to learn. He gasped as he was told of the prowess of the *blacklegs*, or *knucklers;* of the *sixties*, half-grown lads and apprentices who plundered in gangs; the *forties*, who made up "*gooseberry lags*," plundering excursions to less guarded sections of Manhattan. Mr. McDowall plunged into his self-appointed task of rooting out vice wherever he could find it; he had no respect for the taboo of silence. In 1832, he married Mrs. Carpenter, widow of a Jersey minister, a woman twice his own age, a helpmeet not even his enemies could accuse of inspiring concupiscence. He chose his "dear Phebe," he used to explain, purely on the ground of her fitness for the work in which he was engaged. They occupied a dreary tenement in Thompson Street, consisting of a front room, a back room, a bedroom on the second floor and a small room in the attic. The front room became the editorial office and composition room of *McDowall's Journal.* Into a capacious trunk he thrust obscene pictures and contrivances collected during his indefatigable explorations.

McDowall's sensational exposures aroused the indignation of the virtuous and loosened godly purse-strings. His admirers raised a fund of $1,000, to permit him to visit the larger cities, and obtain other evidence of lewdness. The crusader returned with a rich harvest—quantities of lascivious books, pictures, and licentious devices. One fine May afternoon some three or four hundred respected citizens of New York, fine gentlemen all of them, congregated outside the lecture room of the Chatham Street Chapel. Private tickets had been issued to ministers, Sabbath school superintendents, elders, lawyers, and revivalists. The Rev. John Robert McDowall was to address them that afternoon on the secret sources of enticement and incentives to licentious habits. (He had already created a sensation by the publication of "Magdalen Facts," which produced a vast harvest of sneers, scoffs, reproaches, abuse and caricatures.) Inside the chapel, McDowall and a few willing assistants hurriedly completed their arrangements. Naughty prints and objects, suggestive ditties, curiously designed snuff-boxes, all sorts of unspeakable contrivances were placed on specially prepared tables. Then they were carefully covered by sober draperies. When, finally, everything was in readiness, all those who had been fortunate enough to receive invitations were admitted. Doors were locked then, and a chairman was appointed. Moral earnestness mounted high that afternoon. Mr. McDowall was called upon to present a succinct account of his work. A flutter of impatience began to sweep through the audience. All were on tenterhooks for a peep at those forbidden pictures. Unable to curb the impatience of his audience, Mr. McDowall consented to defer the main points of his address.

Impatiently the coverings were removed. Eagerly the moralists entered upon the business of inspection. Blushes suffused the cheeks of youthful Sabbath-school superintendents. Nervous titters were ineffectively suppressed. One who was present at that eventful meeting was compelled to confess later that a majority of the objects were examples of diabolical skill. All of them were designed to infect the imagination with a perverted passion for sexual pleasures. Some of them were indeed skillfully executed. This fact, in the angry opinion of John Robert McDowall, rendered them far more poisonous to the innocent. Expatiating upon them at length, he pointed out subtle details obvious only to connoisseurs in human depravity. Many of the moralists became so absorbed in examining paintings and prints that they paid no attention to the repeated attempts of the moderator to call the meeting to order again. The bright May afternoon sped away. Paradoxically, angry voices now began to break out, warnings of an approaching storm. Arguments began to flare up; McDowall was the object of their attack; discussions in small groups gradually gathered strength and cohesion: the meeting of moralists ended in a battle of tongues, in bitter denunciation of the reformer's secret motives.

The appearance of *McDowall's Journal* in the winter of 1833 created a sensation. McDowall announced that the principal design of his *Journal* would be to expose public immorality and to devise means of preventing licentiousness. "Your pecuniary aid is essentially necessary. . . ." he announced in his first issue. Subsequent numbers of the *Journal* featured results of Mr. McDowall's investigations as chaplain of the New York Magdalen Society; explained that streams of vice were deluging the land and corrupting youth. Noble men and women were shocked, disgusted, and amazed by his revelations. Money to support his *Journal* began to roll in. Spicy anecdotes of unsuspected depths of depravity were published, but all composed in chaste and "manly" style. Among the ungodly, *McDowall's Journal* was derisively described as "the whore-house directory." For, in the cause of chastity, the Rev. John Robert listed some two hundred and twenty brothels in Manhattan alone. For the edification of visiting clergymen, John Robert specified the streets on which these establishments could be found. Brothel-hunting became, indeed, a sort of sanctimonious duty among his numerous followers.

Spicy bits about the diversions of Yankee mariners on tropic shores also found their place in his columns—as, for instance, how many damsels of Otaheite visited the *Patomas,* "a U. S. ship of war," when she cast anchor two miles off shore of the South Sea paradise; or what happened when the U.S.S. *Franklin* put in to Matanzas; or toothsome bits gathered from such picturesque ports as Gibraltar, Malaga, Messina, Pensacola, or Owahoo in the South Pacific. Such titbits stimulated the Moral Reform societies. Like toadstools, these organizations sprang up almost overnight in every town in the country, declaring a Holy War on Vice. *McDowall's Journal* was literally devoured by a large portion of the religious world.

His call for funds brought liberal and prompt replies. Although he acted as the treasurer of the Female Benevolent Society, most of these remittances were made directly to Mr. McDowall. Unfortunately, Mr. McDowall was not so adept in bookkeeping as he was in exposing depravity. Certain unsympathetic husbands of the lady directors of the Female Benevolent Society began a secret audit of the treasurer's books. Charges were preferred against the good man, investigations called for. McDowall convinced his followers that he was innocent of any intention to misapply the funds sent to the Society. In this predicament, a strong minority in the Female Benevolent Society came out boldly in favor of McDowall, and strongly supported his course. The result of this schism was the organization of the Female Moral Reform Society, headed by Mrs. William Green, and including a number of estimable ladies devoted to Mr. McDowall.

But the ordeal of the martyr of the Seventh Commandment was not to end. Indicted by the Grand Jury as a public nuisance, accused of juggling the funds of the Benevolent Society, John Robert was brought face to face with an even more serious tribulation. Charges were brought against him before the Third Presbytery. Eventually, he was excommunicated from the church, and on March 14, 1834, just a few weeks before John Noyes had met him the Grand Jury presented *McDowall's Journal* as a nuisance: "Under the pretext of cautioning the young of both sexes against the temptations to criminal indulgence, it presents such odious and revolting details as are offensive to taste, injurious to morals, and degrading to the character of our city."

Throughout the trials and the tribulations of John Robert McDowall, Mrs. William Green and the ladies of the Female Moral Reform Society remained staunchly loyal. When it became impossible for him to continue the publication of his *Journal*, these ladies courageously decided to continue the campaign against vice. And so the *Journal* lived on under the new name of *The Advocate of Moral Reform.* Then it became evident to the ladies that they needed a young man to manage the office of the Society and to act as secretary and managing editor of *The Advocate.* After prolonged consideration of various applicants, their choice fell upon young George Cragin.

Handsome, open-faced, his Anglo-Saxon ancestry strikingly marked, George Cragin was well fitted by temperament and education to act as publishing agent for this Female Moral Reform Society. George looked upon John Robert McDowall as the purest, noblest, best-hearted man he had ever met. That the martyr of the Seventh Commandment had been despised by the wicked and aristocratic clergy all the more clearly demonstrated his virtue. Who else, George often asked, in defense of Mr. McDowall, had so successfully disclosed the appalling magnitude of sexual vice?

To Mrs. Cragin, George explained why the ladies of the Female Moral Reform Society needed a man to help them solve their extremely delicate problems. How far was it proper to go in exposing the conduct of vicious men and women? For instance, that sensational murder of Ellen Jewett, beaten to death with a hatchet in her bed in Rosina Townsend's establishment, by her youthful paramour Richard Robinson, brought up a delicate problem. Mrs. Green and her colleagues felt that this great moral lesson demanded the reprinting of the testimony of the trial in *The Advocate of Moral Reform.* Always, George explained, they were confronted with the question of how far details of vice should be published without offending true delicacy and modesty. At every session of the executive board, thorny problems in morals and taste arose. Usually they were decided by the chairman of this board, Mrs. William Green. For this lady George developed unqualified respect and admiration. It seemed to be a constitutional need of George's nature to act as a second-in-command to some dominating personality. This need was amply satisfied by Mrs. Green, who so imperiously wielded her pen in the cause of purity, herself furnishing inspiring column after column of editorial matter and obtaining indignant essays from clergymen, lawyers, and other reformers. So effectively did Mrs. Green cut, trim, and rearrange these contributions that even the clergymen admitted that their productions were improved. At the office of the *Advocate* things were not always pleasant. Almost every day George had to face irate visitors. Many of these threatened to punch in his defenseless head. One rude visitor who had been editorially attacked by Mrs. Green invited George to a fist fight in the street. Such incidents were always fully reported to Mary Cragin upon his return home.

One evening he came home with more astounding news, news that had thrown the ladies of the Female Moral Reform Society into consternation. Mrs. William Green announced her conversion to Perfectionism! The Perfectionists, cried the lady reformers, were as licentious and as dangerous as Fanny Wright or Robert Owen! Had they not all read the *Battle-Axe* letter, written by that young man in Vermont? The Female Moral Reform Society was in an uproar. Mrs. Green was finally expelled. Despite his admiration for Mrs. Green, Cragin diplomatically refrained from resigning. After all, it had been through his efforts that the subscription list of the *Advocate* had increased to twenty thousand names; and branch societies were springing up everywhere.

On December 15, 1837, the *Advocate* published an article denouncing "this dangerous and seductive heresy" of Perfectionism. The intent of this "master-stroke of satanic policy" was "to open a floodgate to every species of licentiousness, and by a refinement of wickedness which puts papacy to the blush, to sanctify the very incarnation of impurity." In April, 1838, a vigorous and detailed reply came from John Noyes. "You will find in my writings no such doctrine on the subject of law as you impute to Perfectionists." Although George agreed with the ladies of the executive board that under no circumstances should the cause of Perfectionism be even indirectly aided by publishing Noyes's defense in *The Advocate of Moral Reform*, he slipped this challenging document out of the files and took it home to read to Mary.

2

Mary Cragin came of unusually fine stock; her father, Daniel Johnson, had been a native of Portland, Maine; her mother a Miss Mary Gorham. At the age of fifteen, Mary Johnson received her certificate as an assistant teacher. In less than three years, she developed a special talent for instructing and governing young children. A number of influential women decided to establish infant schools throughout the city of New York. Dr. Bethune, Dr. Hawks, Thomas Hastings, and other prominent ladies and gentlemen, began at once to look about for suitable teachers. Mary had been promptly engaged and assigned to a squalid section of the city in the immediate vicinity of St. Thomas's and under the patronage of that church. Rooms were secured in the basement of the Union Church in Prince Street. In a short time, the two large improvised school rooms were filled to the utmost capacity—one hundred and fifty little pupils in daily attendance. Mary Johnson's indefatigable labors won the enthusiastic approval of her patrons and visiting committees.

One Sunday morning on the Bowery, Mary, in great perplexity, was seeking the lost mother of a ragamuffin left in her care. A handsome young man stepped up and offered his assistance. He walked home with her and introduced himself as George Cragin.

Friendship developed slowly but surely, and ripened into love and marriage.

Now Mary had two children of her own to bring up in their modest little home just north of Abingdon Square. She was profoundly engrossed in religious matters, and the sensational conversion of both Mr. and Mrs. Green to the doctrines of the Perfectionists interested Mary intensely. She had heard, years earlier, of the New Haven heretics, and had even read certain manifestoes by young Noyes. Some impulse drove Mary to take up these writings again. For weeks she studied, read and reread the Perfectionist pamphlets. The challenge of John Noyes's thought gripped her imagination. On and on, step by step, Mary was led. Face to face she found herself with practical questions of believing, submission and confession; she must find the answers, not at some future time, at a more convenient season, but now—"present tense, imperative mood!" For several weeks she spent most of her days in prayer. She confided nothing of this experience to George Cragin. Her feelings were too intense for expression then.

At last Mary Cragin emerged triumphant from this search. She counted the cost of being thrown out of society, rejected and disowned by relatives, possibly to be turned into the street by her husband—so great was the odium cast upon the Perfectionist heresy.

One day George returned to their little home at 60 Jane Street at his usual hour. They sat down together in the basement dining room. After a silence, Mary solemnly announced: "I confess Christ in me a Saviour from all sin: I shall never sin again."

George sat stupefied. He could not understand. Finally he blurted out: "Do you feel Christ in you?"

"Feelings are not to be trusted or regarded, when they contradict the plain word of God," answered Mary enigmatically.

George had heard and believed all evil of the Perfectionists, and felt strong opposition to what he considered their licentious tendency. But as he heard Mary's words, he must have known that he would be compelled to follow his impulsive wife—for he always had. As *The Witness* came, he read it, and in spite of his prejudices, was convinced that Noyes, whatever else might be said of him, was taught of God. After five years' service in the Female Moral Reform Society, especially as a protégé of the excommunicated Mrs. Green, George felt that his situation had become unbearable. His interest in the *Advocate* gave place to anxiety respecting his own spiritual state; he could no longer respond to the stereotyped preaching of the day. His soul thirsted for a draught of living water. While in this state of mind, Noyes's "Way of Holiness" was put into his hands. He read and believed, and found immediate peace. George Cragin reported to the Society his conversion to Perfectionism and received a summons to meet the board of managers. After a long examination, they put one final question, respecting his belief in John Noyes. They asked his opinion of the *Battle-Axe* letter. To this he replied that he was not a competent judge, but he avowed his confidence in Noyes. Thereupon his dismissal was speedily given.

Less than a month after her conversion, Mary sat down and wrote to John Noyes: "It is now nearly four weeks since I was *translated* from the '*kingdom of darkness*' into the kingdom of God's dear Son.... I need not tell you that my 'peace is as a river.'

"But I have not told you all. No: words cannot express the half. While I am writing to you I am weeping for joy. My dear husband one week since entered the kingdom. When I tell you that he has been the publishing agent of *The Advocate of Moral Reform,* and had been born but three days, when they cast him out, you will rejoice with me. Ah, bro. Noyes, how have 'the mighty fallen.' In him you will find a most rigidly upright character—Grahamism, and Oberlin perfection all in ruins. How he clung to Oberlin, as with a death-grasp! How confident was he that none were saved from sin but mere Grahamites—How disgusted with the conduct of Perfectionists! The Lord has pulled down strong towers. Bless the Lord—on the first of December he will be without money and without business. How this rejoices me! We shall stand still and see the 'Lord provide.'... *We shall be very glad to see you* when you come to the city."

There could be no half-way measures with Mary. "Present tense, imperative mood!" Such was her secret of living. Their conversion wrought immediate changes in their life. After tramping about searching for employment, George came home to find the little basement dining room the habitual gathering place of all stray Perfectionists and religious radicals who passed through the city. These heretics indulged in lush terms of endearment, addressed each other as "brother" and "sister," supplementing these intimate salutations with lingering embraces and sanctimonious caresses. They conversed in an exalted religious lingo. Subconsciously, George found himself scrutinizing their truant hands. There was a certain troubling ambiguity in the symbols that slid so unctuously from their lips.

Frequent among these visitors to the Cragins was Abram

Smith. His discourses upon religious themes were at the same time edifying and puzzling and occasionally discomfiting to George. Mr. Smith clothed his wisdom in a curious vocabulary of mysticism. What most impressed George was to discover the unity of Smith's views with those of their hero—John Noyes. But whatever doubts may have lurked in the background were dispelled by Mary's acceptance of Abram Smith as an ambassador sent by John Noyes himself. They had been intimate friends in Newark. Abram subtly intimated that in some mysterious way he himself had set the Vermonter on the right road.

The ladies of the Female Moral Reform Society now passed George and Mary Cragin with stony, unseeing visages. Both had been expelled in disgrace, just as had their dear friends the Greens. Vague rumors came to them that the Greens might now invite the Cragin family to share their home in Woodbridge, New Jersey. George longed for such an invitation; but it never came. The lease on the little house at 60 Jane Street would soon expire. What would they do then?

Abram Smith pressed upon Mary and George a warm invitation to spend the summer at his home near Rondout on the Hudson, a retreat depicted in the most tempting colors. Finally, for the first time, Abram brought his second wife to meet Mary. His invitation to spend the summer at Rondout was urgently renewed. On previous visits, Mr. Smith had failed to mention this second wife. Mrs. Smith appeared to them prepossessing and dignified, but her good looks, winning smiles, professions of devotion to the cause Mary and George loved, failed, strangely enough, to arouse their sympathy. But, sponsored as she was by Abram, George distrusted his own impressions, and refrained from mentioning to Mary his own secret aversion. So they accepted the invitation for the spring and summer up the Hudson.

Early in March, 1840, Mary and George and their little brood were escorted by Mr. Smith to the Hudson night boat. Mary Cragin was strangely depressed in spirit. With difficulty she repressed feelings, which found release in a flood of tears. With all the tenderness and eloquence of a revivalist saving a sinner, Abram Smith sought to comfort Mary. He won her heart, but his intentions were not clear. Until the last day, Mary had hoped that John Noyes might come to the city and advise them what step to take. Still, she had not dared to implore this personal visit. Lacking that counsel, she had accepted Abram Smith as his representative.

At Rondout, the Cragins found themselves in a family much larger than their own. Besides his second wife, by whom he had one child, there were three more Smith children—a son and two daughters, already quite grown up. Abram's dilapidated stone farmhouse, built before the Revolution, stood in a lonely spot on the south side of a creek directly opposite the village of Rondout.

Innocently rejoicing at finding himself once again in the country, George Cragin promptly began at farm labor. Behind a sad old horse as blind as a bat, with young Joshua Smith acting as a "rider," George followed the plow. Abram Smith took up his work as foreman of a gang of hands engaged in manufacturing lime cement on the opposite side of the river. He placed George Cragin in charge of the farm, while he continued as agent and overseer for the lime company.

Since, under the circumstances, they were to his own advantage, Abram Smith encouraged communistic ideas, and this ill-assorted little group made a half-hearted attempt to carry out a spirit of "holding all things in common." Behind the blind horse, George Cragin tried to delude himself into a belief that he was winning the riches of godliness and contentment.

Inside the gloomy stone house the bickering between Abram Smith and his wife sputtered on to its inevitable climax. The traditional triangle was forming—obvious to all but deluded, gullible George Cragin. Worn out by his long days of plowing, George was the last to sense the storm that was gathering. Long private colloquies between Abram and Mary he dismissed as doctrinal discussion concerning the more intricate problems of Perfectionist ethics. Even after the final pitched battle between Abram Smith and his wife, when the latter was temporarily vanquished and ordered to leave the house for good and all, George Cragin did not suspect that the growing intimacy between Mary and Abram was anything more than theological.

3

Concerning that domestic drama that developed in Abram Smith's house, we may read the naïve account written in after years by George Cragin. John Noyes caught the scent of the drama even in distant Putney. Noyes always read the character of his followers with hypersensitive precision. He knew that Abram Smith, restive as a race-horse, was only awaiting the signal to be off in pursuit of the joys he himself had read into the *Battle-Axe* letter. Eventually, while on a visit in New York, accompanied by the faithful David Harrison and John Skinner, Noyes began to feel that the devil was at work in the Smith house. It was as though he had received a command to intervene in the murky affairs of Mary Cragin. With only cursory explanations, Noyes set out with his two loyal disciples for Rondout.

Without forewarning, three footsore travelers appeared one evening at Smith's door. That very day a warrant had been issued against Smith for a breach of the peace in turning his wife out of doors. The irate Mrs. Smith had denounced her husband in the village. Popular indignation was at the boiling point; an attack upon the stone farmhouse was imminent. What should be done? Should they stand ground and fight it out with the villagers? Abram counseled war. John Noyes took the opposite ground: peace measures with the outside world, criticism and sincerity among themselves—these were the only solution. He sharply rebuked Abram Smith for the course he had taken with his wife. The facts were then told concerning the intimacy between Abram and Mary. The two were admonished plainly but considerately. A claiming, "legal" spirit in poor George was the scapegoat upon which the sins of both parties were laid. Cragin himself joined the rest in denouncing his own spirit of legality, freely forgave the lovers, and confessed himself quite as much in the wrong as Abram and Mary.

Of that first meeting between John Noyes and Mary Cragin, no document remains. From the first, Noyes detected a striking similarity between Mary Cragin and Mary Magdalen—or the woman taken in adultery. Beneath that comparison, we may detect another even more flattering to the Vermont heretic himself. One temptation is to read into the drama an irony which is not borne out by facts. There is no evidence that Mary and John established any hidden entente, nor that anything like "love at first sight" was kindled between these two. Their future intimacy was to be the result of a slow, imperceptible growth.

John's first effort was to extract the poison of bitterness from the whole situation. There was no attempt to place the burden of blame solely upon the shoulders of Abram Smith. Mary, George, and Abram spent that first evening in listening attentively to Noyes. He criticized Perfectionists generally for their intractability, their lack of humility. "All things are lawful for me, but all things are not expedient; all things are lawful for me, but all things edify not." He advised Abram Smith to go next day straight to Kingston, two miles from Rondout, and settle with the magistrate who had issued a warrant for his arrest. Noyes, Smith and Cragin marched up to the judge's office. Abram reluctantly settled bonds to keep the peace and support his wife. But the villagers of Rondout were still indignant and threatening in spirit. Noyes still counseled for peace, and proposed to leave that evening for Putney, taking Abram Smith and his eldest daughter with him. Smith's departure would solve the immediate problem. This plan was carried out. As the Rondout mob looked upon Smith as the chief offender, his absence would pacify their feelings and allow the other members of the family to remain in peace. George took the travelers to Kingston Point, where they embarked upon the steamer for Albany.

On returning, George found everything quiet in the stone house. The talks given them by Noyes during his brief sojourn brought a new hope into George's spirit. He had criticized them sincerely, and yet how forgiving had he been! Until this visit from Noyes, George had been subordinate to Smith and had unguardedly confided in him. But now, as he reflected upon Smith's approaching return, he could think only of Mary, and of his own suffering.

After an absence of two weeks at Putney, Smith came home again. Noyes had cautioned him that there be no further intimacy with Mrs. Cragin. Believing that Smith would keep the faith, George hoped for renewed unity and fellowship between Smith, Mary and himself. In Cragin's presence, the wily divine talked in sanctimonious style. Alone with Mary Cragin, his eloquence was of quite another color. Mary, apparently, was ready and waiting to be deceived anew. Abram loaded George down with hard work, self-condemnation, and evil-thinking. And George wrote, with the pathos of the weaker man, "I very well understood that I could not carry the marriage spirit with me into the heavenly kingdom, if Mr. Smith could; neither could I avoid making the discovery that he was freighting his barge with the same commodity that I was throwing overboard." Toiling alone throughout the hot summer days, George saw but little of Abram or Mary, and knew still less of their movements. George's only recreation was learning to manage a sail-boat. Life seemed hardly worth living, he told himself; he would not mind losing it in a summer squall.

4

During those warm months, Perfectionists from New York descended upon them in crowds. Still the same sing-song pleasure-seekers, they were Perfectionists only in the abstract. George found little satisfaction in this company, and no disposition to open his heart to such brethren. They dissented from his belief in

Mr. Noyes as God's appointed leader of the new church. In discussions concerning the new dispensation, Mary and Abram assumed leadership. In this atmosphere of artificial stimulation, Abram Smith's secret courtship advanced. He was well aware that Mary's confidence in Noyes was greatly strengthened by his providential visit. Accordingly, he made it appear to her that he, Smith, had to the fullest extent the confidence of John Noyes. Skilled in the technique of insinuation and enigmatic hints, Smith renewed his game by suggesting that Noyes approved of their past proceedings; that his late disapproval and public criticism of their acts was chiefly for the benefit of poor, unenlightened George, who was still hovering in the outer darkness. At Putney, Abram confided, he had many long private talks with Noyes on sexual matters. He promised to report these secret doctrines to her, from time to time, if he found her discreet. In effect, said Abram, he and Noyes were one, and whatever course he might pursue in future would receive the endorsement of Noyes. Thus regaining his power over Mary, Smith was even more skillful in keeping her husband in a harmless, helpless condition.

In the latter part of July, in response to a request from Greencastle, Pennsylvania, Noyes commissioned Smith to visit the Perfectionists in that section. John B. Lyvere and several others, who had been spending a few days at Rondout, were about to return to New York, and Smith, on his way to Pennsylvania, proposed to accompany them. Deftly he managed to obtain permission from George for Mary to join the party.

They departed and a week passed. Then Cragin received a few lines from Mary saying that she intended to leave for home the next evening and would be happy if he would meet her at Rondout. This letter melted all the icy feelings toward Mary that had imperceptibly accumulated in his heart. As he entered the ladies' cabin on the boat she met him with subdued yet affectionate greetings. A heavy burden weighed upon her soul, George soon discovered; but he had so disciplined himself that he dared not ask for explanations. By chance he later learned that Smith, instead of going directly to Pennsylvania, had lingered on for a week in New York. A week or two later, Cragin had occasion to go to New York himself, and called upon Mr. and Mrs. Lyvere. From them he learned that Smith and Mrs. Cragin had broken the solemn promise which they had made to John Noyes. Lyvere thought the case should be reported to Noyes, and offered to carry the message in person. Cragin gave him money for the trip. Admonishing Lyvere to report nothing but the truth, George hurried back to

Rondout. All seemed treachery, desolation and darkness. "Do you still believe in the sustaining power of God?" an inner voice taunted him. "Yes!" cried George aloud. "My faith in God and in Mr. Noyes is unshaken."

Next morning, the sun shone resplendently upon the waters of the little bay. In a skiff George rowed himself to the opposite shore. Mary stood on the pier waiting for him.

At the sight of George's woe-begone countenance, "You know all!" she burst out. "The secret is out, and I thank God for revealing it. I will make a clean breast now, for I can carry the works of darkness no longer." Without attempting to screen herself from judgment, Mary unburdened her soul. "George, you can hardly conceive of the terrible dread I have of meeting that man."

"You must put your trust in God," George replied. He took this exhortation to himself also, for he felt keenly his inability to cope unaided with so wily a hypocrite as Abram Smith.

Late the next Saturday night, loud raps on the door woke them. George left his bed to obey the summons. Mary begged him not to allow Smith to enter their room. George finally opened the door. Smith extended his hand.

"No, I cannot take the hand of one who has so cruelly wronged me."

"Where is Mary? I want to see her."

"You cannot. She absolutely declines to see you. She has revealed all."

Next morning the three met in the sitting-room. Smith maintained resolutely that he had pleased God in all that he had done, and regarded Cragin with contempt for presuming to sit in judgment. This curious battle raged with unabated fierceness. In the evening, seeing that he was losing rather than gaining ground, Smith suddenly declared that he would start immediately for Putney. "Very well," Cragin replied. "I will submit to John Noyes's judgment." Abram now became almost affectionate toward George. Would he not write a line to Noyes, confessing that he cherished no unkind personal feelings? Cragin consented. Smith invited Cragin to row him across the creek. On leaving the boat, he asked Cragin to give him a kiss.

Not until Cragin returned to the house did he divine Smith's motive.

"My mind is made up to leave this place at once. We will go first to New York."

Mary seemed overjoyed. They sold most of their furniture for cash, had their few remaining goods taken over the creek, and on the second day of September, 1840, the contrite Cragins embarked for New York. Just an hour before the steamer left, Cragin went to the postoffice, and there found a letter from Noyes. "Mr. Lyvere arrived here today," Noyes wrote, "and has communicated to me facts which compel me to believe that Smith and Mrs. Cragin have violated the solemn engagement which they made when I was at Rondout. They are now adulterers. Before, they might have said and thought sincerely that they did no wrong, because they acted with your consent and not in contravention of any engagement or any law except that of this world, which is of no authority before God. But now they have acted without your consent and in gross violation of their voluntary and solemn promise, and therefore in violation of God's eternal law of truth. ... I see that no real fellowship can exist between me and Smith.

"If you ask what is your duty, I answer, Cut off that offending right hand and follow me. Let not friendship paralyze your honesty and faithfulness to Christ. You are no longer bound to keep the secrets or defend the character of Mrs. Cragin or Smith. Let them eat the fruit of their own doings. Clear yourself of the wreck, if you have to jump into the ocean. ..."

On reaching New York, George wrote to Noyes that his heart was too full for utterance, but that as soon as circumstances would permit he should visit him. After reading the letter, Mary Cragin penned the following postscript: "Since the fatal charm has been dissolved, I see how I have been deceived and taught to believe that I was in an inner circle where it was right and pleasing to God to do what I did. I never in my heart turned aside from the promise I made to you last spring. Again and again I asked Mr. Smith if you would be pleased, for I had terrible misgivings. He assured me that you would, and that he himself would tell you. Guilty as I am, I have been miserably deluded by him. I am reaping the curse of trusting in man, and I deserve it. The instruction I received to lie and deceive began to open my eyes. I do thank God for the judgment that has overtaken me, even if I am to be sent to hell at last, and I wish none to consider me a friend of the gospel until my deeds make it fully manifest."

George and Mary agreed that their personal problems could be solved only by a personal visit to John Noyes. But George set out alone, with new hope in his heart, toward Putney. While waiting for his breakfast in the Dummerston tavern bar-room, George questioned the loquacious keeper of the inn about the Noyes family of Putney. Had he not known Squire Noyes ever since they lived in those parts? "Smart man—the old Squire—made his fortune during the last war [1812] out of the store business. He was a great business man; worked hard for his money, and now, by George! he takes life easy, for he makes his money work hard for him, by lending it to folks who are pushed to the wall; takes mortgages, and gets big interests. Long head that, on the old Squire's shoulders. Nobody can cheat him without feeling the grip of the law, before he knows it."

"Do you know his son, John Noyes?" inquired Cragin.

"Well, haven't seen much of him! He has been off to school. I guess from what I've heard, that his son don't go in for money-making, as much as he does for preaching. He has some new ideas about the Bible and religion. They call him a Perfectionist. Ministers and church-members don't like him; and I don't wonder at it, for he makes them out to be no better than us outside sinners. He used to hold meetings in taverns and schoolhouses about here, and everybody that heard him said he was the smartest preacher that ever opened the Bible." The breakfast bell interrupted this stream of loquacity.

About ten o'clock Cragin found himself at last in the gentle little village of Putney, and inquired for the residence of John Noyes. Their meeting was sympathetic and quiet. George Cragin planned to impart a great deal concerning his own woes, to report in detail the tribulations Mary and he had shared. Now, somehow or other, he was left quite speechless. Those vexations seemed so remote, so evanescent, without significance. He found little to say about himself or any one else. Egoism seemed to vanish. His thoughts did not appear to be his own, but were the thoughts of those about him. His trials seemed nothing. His sufferings, too, what were they? He seemed to forget them. Indeed, his recent ordeals were nothing but the seeds of blessings that were already springing up, where they had been sown.

The little circle George found around John Noyes appeared quite unlike any he had ever met. All of them were kind, quiet, thoughtful, studious—and yet, in spirit, so free. Was it a heaven upon earth he had found at last? Was the change all in himself, or had he found a people totally alien in disposition and purpose from those with whom he had mingled? That sojourn at Rondout had been a hell upon earth; Providence now compensated with a little heaven. By virtue of their liberal education, wealth, and corresponding position in society, the Noyes family naturally belonged to the aristocracy of the land; but all those inherited and acquired advantages had seemingly been cast aside by John Noyes.

An hour or more before George's departure, the two men stood beneath the portico, each silent, with unexpressed thoughts. After a long characteristic pause, Noyes asked simply: "What are you going to do after you return to your family?"

"Find a situation in some counting-room or manufacturing establishment," Cragin replied.

"I have a proposal to make to you," said Noyes; "–return and spend the winter with me in studying the Bible and waiting on the will of God."

"No business in the world would suit me better, but my circumstances would hardly justify me in accepting your kind offer."

"What are those unfavorable circumstances?" Noyes inquired.

"The support of my family."

"You will bring your family with you, of course. My house is large enough for us all."

"You do not really expect that I shall be clownish enough to accept so great a boon at your hands, unmerited, do you?" These words came to his mind, but Cragin refrained from speaking them.

His thoughts were readily divined, for Noyes replied that he used words, not to conceal, but to express his thoughts, and that he expressed sincerely what he thought and what he meant. It was enough. Here at last, George Cragin decided, was a man of solid truth, who recognized no politeness, no human grace of embellishment, however fashionable, except it be the natural outgrowth and fruit of a pure, sincere, truth-loving heart.

"Enough," murmured George Cragin. "I accept the offer as freely as you have extended it to me."

"How soon shall I look for your return?"

"In a week or ten days," Cragin replied, and happily took his leave.

5

Shortly after the Cragins joined the Noyes family in Putney they witnessed John's severity in dealing with his group. John Miller received a kind, but outspoken criticism from Noyes for allowing himself to be carried away by the political storm that was sweeping over New England like a tornado. "No good can come to the Kingdom of God by our aiding either political party now in the field," admonished Noyes. "Both of them are notoriously corrupt, and as a follower of Christ I am bound to avoid them as I would any other evil."

"Let me first go and elect Harrison," John Miller protested, "and then I will come and seek the Kingdom of God."

"Let the dead vote for the dead, if they will: 'follow thou me.' Christ is my candidate, and I will vote for no other if I wait a thousand years," expostulated John Noyes.

During the fall after their arrival in Putney, Mary Cragin passed through the terrible conflicts of unbelief. A probing criticism had been administered to her by Noyes, not particularly for outward offenses and faults, but for a spirit of coquetry evidently engendered by New York City life. Mary's resistance to this criticism took the subtle form of despair. Cast into the depths of self-condemnation, she found herself unable to resist a temptation to suicide. But truth, which Noyes administered to her in love, finally worked to keep a spark of faith alive in her soul, and at length proved victorious. During those darkest hours, Harriet Noyes proved herself a sister and a mother to Mary Cragin, and a great unity of heart grew up between them. To this friendship Mary was indebted for much of the wholehearted acceptance she afterwards enjoyed in the community.

Mary Cragin drank in the wisdom of Noyes with undeviating attention. When he first talked to her, it seemed to him that her intellectual attainments were those of a little girl. Mary, perhaps, felt that this was her most effective rôle. Despite her appealing frailties, Noyes was forced to admit that Mary Cragin was a strong woman—the strongest he had ever met, perhaps. Swiftly her acute, intuitive, penetrating understanding developed. Her judgments revealed an earthy, common-sense quality that could not be ignored. Her wisdom, John Noyes decided, was the wisdom of love. Her virtue was the virtue of love. She resembled Mary Magdalen—this thought had come into his mind when he had first seen her, weeping and repentant, in the house of Abram at Rondout.

Without her strange power over men, women and children, Mary Cragin would have undoubtedly been dismissed as a gushing, sentimental woman. Her power—and it *was* a subtle and irresistible power, as John Noyes was to find out—was hidden in her very infirmities. Never had any woman so strengthened John Noyes's faith in his own divine commission. Although surrounded by adoring females, John received from none of them the exaltation that Mary Cragin gave. Whatever reservations may have lurked in other minds, there was something disarming in the spirit of this effusive, charming woman with her premature outbursts of affection and her occasional bursts of temper. She lived almost exclusively in the present. The *now,* John Noyes observed, was the great all in Mary's behavior.

6

The unfortunate episode of the stone house was not allowed to sink into oblivion. Such experiences are given to us, John Noyes suggested to the group, in order to make us understand ourselves and each other. Before it was forgotten, he utilized the Rondout incident to extract its fullest human significance. To summarize the conclusion in which John Humphrey Noyes acted as a benign yet autocratic *deus ex machina,* we must for a moment skip over intervening years.

In the early part of the winter of 1845, Abram Smith visited Putney—Abram had a way of showing up unexpectedly. It was a period when the revival of Bible-studying and truth-searching was in its zenith of power among the Putney group. All hearts were absorbed in the subject. The search for truth held their undivided attention, creating an atmosphere in the isolated little circle that was decidedly favorable to the rectifying of wrongs and the reconstructing of fellowship on a purer basis. Smith could not have come at a time more propitious for acknowledging the errors of his past behavior, as a ground upon which a new confidence might be developed. In this work Mary Cragin met him half-way. Acting as a mediator between the parties, Noyes drew up a paper, asking the endorsements of Abram Smith and Mary Cragin. Here is the curious document: "The transaction between Mr. Smith and Mrs. Cragin was characterized by two vices—*licentiousness* and *deception.* Both were undoubtedly guilty of both. But I judge from all the evidence I can get, that Mrs. Cragin took the lead and was the principal agent in the licentiousness, and that Mr. Smith took the lead and was the principal agent in the deception. She kindled the fire and he excused and justified and concealed it. This is exactly in accordance with the respective tendencies of the two sexes. Woman is strong in the department of susceptibility; man, in that of intellect. Do the parties heartily accede to this judgment? J. H. NOYES."

"I do subscribe most fully to the above decision and do wish to take on myself the most of the evil. A. C. SMITH."

"I think that Mr. Noyes is correct in his judgment; and that I took the place of Eve in tempting and seducing man, who is made in the image of God. I sincerely ask Mr. Smith's forgiveness for having dragged him down into sensuality. M. E. CRAGIN."

But an ironic twist of this episode came years later, when Smith finally joined the Oneida Community, where he remained for several years. George Cragin could not free himself entirely from his old animadversion toward Smith. Finally, however, in the dormitory arrangements at Oneida, which required the men to accept each other as bedmates, Smith was assigned to occupy a room with George. The two men became bedfellows! "I submitted to the arrangement, believing it to be right," confessed Cragin, "but it was not a dose savory to the self-complacency of the remains of the *old man.* But the new man rejoiced at it, knowing that it was just the medicine the case required. And so it proved. It effectually cured me of the old, unbrotherly feelings with which I had, from time to time, been tormented. Mr. Smith and I got on admirably after being thus disciplined for a while in the same yoke. So there we three were, like brothers and sister in our father's house, having grown better and wiser for the scourgings and sufferings a beneficent and wise providence saw fit to inflict as a means of securing obedience. From that time to the present, I have cherished none but kindly feelings toward Smith, my old comrade in arms against the world, the flesh and the devil."

Chapter V: HEAVENLY ASSOCIATION

> When a superior intellect and a psychopathic temperament coalesce in the same individual, we have the best possible condition for effective genius. Such men do not remain mere critics and understanders with their intellect. Their ideas possess them, they inflict them, for better or for worse, upon their companions or their age.
>
> —William James.

I

Weaving is the basic art. From this primordial craft the rest seem to spring. Could the art of fiction ever have risen had not man first trained hand and mind by generations of weaving? Could music or painting? To intertwine into a single pattern strands fundamentally alien and conflicting, to create a tough, enduring, yet pliant fabric—here is the problem of every creator, whether in art or in life. Between 1838 and 1848, John Noyes toiled to create his own pattern of human lives, content to begin with the humblest elements, and those closest at hand.

He dated the origin of the Putney Community from the year of his marriage, 1838, but the road to communal living was slow and gradual. At first the little group included only his wife, his sisters, Harriet and Charlotte, his younger brother George, then a lad of sixteen, and a few local sympathizers. John and Harriet's home was completed in 1838, and early in 1840 the little coterie of Perfectionists began to hold Sunday meetings there. Out of these meetings grew the Society of Inquiry, designed, as Noyes explained one Sunday in January, "to unite against the contempt of their enemies." John Skinner had come to Putney in 1839, the Cragins in September, 1840; and there were soon funds enough to organize the so-called Putney Corporation of Perfectionists. Formal communal living, however, was of almost imperceptible growth. A number of members were admitted; but most of them, for lack of congeniality, were soon to drop out. In 1843, Noyes was to write: "A spirit of love naturally led us into a sort of community of goods. . . . Our community has no constitution nor written laws. Our object in coming together was not to form a community after the fashion of the Shakers or Fourierites, but simply to publish the gospel and help one another in spiritual things. We found it necessary to investigate many new problems in social economy, but it is difficult as yet to tell what form of social life we shall ultimately take."

The advance into communism of property was made between

the years 1842 and 1846. A "Contract of Partnership" dated February 26, 1844, specified that "all property of every kind, which we are now severally possessed of, or which shall hereafter come into our possession as long as we remain in the Corporation, shall be held as the property of the Corporation." Yet the signers of this agreement were but four, John and George Noyes, and John Skinner and John Miller. The communal investment totaled some $25,940.

On March 9, 1845, this contract of partnership was succeeded by a carefully detailed Constitution, a deliberate leap forward into organized communism, since it recognized the interests of those who merely "invested time" as well as of those who invested both time and property. A president, a secretary and a board of three directors were named—John Miller president, John Skinner secretary, John and George Noyes and George Cragin directors. This constitution provided that unanimous consent was necessary for the admission of new members. But written constitutions were foreign to the genius of the Putney Community, as later they were to be in Oneida. Often, they became out-of-date the day they were written. The path into communism was not deliberate, but rather the outcome, inevitable and involuntary, of Noyes's influence upon his comrades.

Meanwhile, he labored to fulfill the promise he had made to the earliest subscribers of *The Witness.* He continued its publication in Putney until twenty-six numbers were printed. *The Witness* was superseded by *The Perfectionist*, the first number of which appeared on February 15, 1843. Three bi-weekly volumes were published, the last on February 14, 1846. In March, *The Spiritual Magazine* took the place of *The Perfectionist* and was continued until January 17, 1850. Thus John Noyes's dream of a really "free press" became a reality.

Now, let us return to trace the pattern of this human fabric he wove in Putney.

2

On February 5, 1841, Squire Noyes divided his estate among his surviving children. To the four of the Perfectionist faith—Harriet, Charlotte, young George and John, fell something near a total of $19,920, including two farms, dwellings and investments. On October 26, 1841, at the advanced age of seventy-seven, the Squire passed away and John was at liberty to assume, in spite of the anguished and persistent protests of his mother, the leadership of the Noyes family remaining in Putney.

Polly Noyes was terror-stricken at John's ruthless handling of the family funds. Though his earning power was negative, he spent money, it seemed to her, with reckless abandon. Not only that, but he invited a motley collection of disciples to come and live at their expense. Furthermore, he had taken upon himself the arrangement of her own daughters' marriages. She had planned alliances worthy of the patrician status of the Noyeses—marriages like those of Mary, Elizabeth and Joanna. But for Harriet and Charlotte, John refused to consent to any suitors who might lead them away from his influence.

Almost the first person who had severed all family ties to follow Noyes heart and soul was John Skinner of Westmoreland, New Hampshire. His allegiance was unflinching and John Noyes decided he should be rewarded by marriage with his sister Harriet.

As early as 1837, when Noyes preached at Westmoreland, this young Quaker teacher had immediately fallen under his spell. By the spring of 1838 his faith had grown to such proportions that he could think of nothing else. He finally decided to consult Noyes personally and a year later, at Noyes's suggestion, he went to Putney.

His family vigorously objected. Young Skinner could not, they insisted, make his living there; their poor boy had fallen into a bog of delusion. Penniless at Putney, John Skinner appealed to his brother, who owed him the not inconsiderable sum of twenty-five dollars. The latter reluctantly sent him but ten. Disdaining to mention Noyes by name, he added: "I am anxious that you should beware of that *individual* (and his associates) who, to put the most charitable construction on his conduct and principles, is a Monomaniac."

John Skinner waited nearly a month to answer that attack. He finally summoned patience and forbearance, and reserved his defense of Noyes for the last lines of a carefully composed epistle: "Having had a much better opportunity than yourself of becoming acquainted with the individual to whom you undoubtedly allude, I must be permitted to form my own judgment concerning him," he wrote. "As my fellowship with him is a matter which concerns me more deeply than it does my friends, I hope they will do me the justice to believe that I am not acting without examination and reflection."

This defense unleashed the pent-up fury of John's brother, who replied without delay: ". . . That you should spend what will give you future comfort, in following (like the followers of Joe Smith) a scoundrel or a lunatic, I do as your brother object.

. . . With regard to John H. Noyes (if that is the individual you refer to) you say I adduce no proof that his conduct and his principles betoken monomania. I did not at the time, but it was not because I had none. He claims to have arrived at perfection in the Christian character, and to commit no sin. . . . He (Noyes) has been found either *crazy* or *drunk* in the streets of New York. Is that a mark of Christian perfection? He has been seen by a friend of mine, while traveling during the last year, to drink freely of brandy to excess; I think excusing himself by saying, such things would not do in others, but were not sin in him, because of the perfect holiness of his character. Does this seem to you, brother, like the perfection of the Saints? I have numerous testimonials to this state of mind. . . . I do say that the term monomania is the softest horn of the dilemma. To conclude, if his preaching or his doctrine prove false, where will be the advantage in following him? If true, it would be in accordance with Scripture, which makes it the duty of every man to provide for his household and not waste his time and talents in idle speculative theories that the natural laws of creation will be suspended."

John Skinner promptly refuted those calumnies circulated by the malicious and the ignorant: ". . . In proof of the character which you ascribe to Mr. Noyes, you state, that 'he has been seen by a friend of yours, while traveling during the past year, to drink freely of brandy to excess; excusing himself by saying, such things would not do in others, but were not sin in him, because of the perfect holiness of his character.'

"In relation to this charge, he states that he recollects having called for and drank some spirits, while on a journey, in company with a physician from Claremont. But that he drank to excess, or that he excused himself for drinking, in such a manner as was represented, he wholly denies. I apprehend that where he is well known, no person of honesty and intelligence would be likely to accuse him of intemperance. Indeed I am persuaded that his education, his former habits, his moral and intellectual character, and his present *general appearance and daily walk*, would all contradict such an accusation.

"This charge of *insanity*, or *monomania*, which has been made against Br. Noyes, is not a new thing. It is one of the earliest which was brought against him by those who were opposed to his doctrine. And as I could discover no proofs of its being true, either from his writings, or from his public preaching, I was induced, partly with a view to satisfy myself on this point, to seek a personal acquaintance with him, in order that I might not judge hastily, or from the vague reports of others. The results of that acquaintance, and of particular inquiries made of those who have been most intimately acquainted with him, is a full conviction, that the above mentioned accusation is *false;* and that it originated either in the malice of enemies, or in the mistaken judgment of superficial observers."

John Skinner became first assistant in the writing, editing and printing of *The Witness.* He made his home with the Noyeses, and "paid board." The next year he was given larger responsibilities. In February, 1841, he became Harriet Noyes's husband.

3

Mrs. Polly Noyes fought her son every inch of the way, from that moment shortly after his marriage to Harriet Holton, when he had usurped her place as head of the family, declaring that all who attached themselves to him must assume a subordinate place, since a special grace of God qualified him to take full control.

She alone obstinately resisted. He had, she admitted, treated her with a decent civility, but with a cold reserve that made home anything but pleasant. In vain her daughter-in-law assured her that John was a prophet. Mrs. Noyes the elder asked for evidence, but had not listened to the answer. Mrs. Freeman told her John was another David, that he had the discernment of spirits, that he was more like God than any other person she had ever met. Abram Smith compared him to Paul, infallible in all things spiritual, though he might indeed err in judgment. David Harrison called her son leader and commander; and Harriet and Charlotte referred to him as Christ's representative upon earth. Still Mrs. Noyes doubted. "Is there anything more in him than in other great reformers, such as Luther, Calvin and Erasmus?" she wrote ingenuously to a neighbor. "John and all who are associated with him are out of the way and their eyes must and will be opened to see it. . . ."

But they talked her down, mainly by force of numbers. In March, 1839, she capitulated, announcing publicly the "testimony I now give to John H. Noyes as being to me a teacher and father in spiritual things." But when she went to visit her daughter Mary Mead, or talked with Horatio of the strange events that happened in Putney, her loyalty grew strained. It became so unpleasant for her that, once, she left home. Too proud to visit relatives, she sought refuge in a Springfield boarding house. When she returned seven weeks later, Harriet repudiated her mother's authority and

John rebuked her in no uncertain terms. Again and again she might confess renewed faith in the Perfectionist doctrines, but these young people were marching too fast for her simple Vermont mind. The conflict between Noyes and his mother was never satisfactorily settled. Sometimes at night, as she pondered over her miseries, she would resolve that she could not die in peace without plainly telling John that he had faults and infirmities as well as others: but "he soon convinced me that my feelings were under the delusion of Satan; advised me to pray much to be delivered from this accusing spirit and a licentious tongue...."

Mrs. Noyes opposed the invasion by the "foreign" Perfectionists, and objected to all plans for forming an association or community, declaring them impracticable. She fell into the habit of contradicting John, and by so doing brought down upon her head his sternest reproofs. But after each of these conflicts the poor old lady would return, humbled and penitent, to the fold. She would confess, however, that the progress of liberty in the "corporation" remained a mystery to her.

"She thinks herself wiser than all around her in the management of children," John Noyes explained, "and entitled to interfere and dictate in the management of our families.... She is an overseer instead of a scholar. Mother may say that I am what I am in consequence of her administration, and that what I have done for the younger members of the family is ultimately to be credited to her. At my birth she prayed that I might be a 'minister of the Everlasting Gospel.' What did she mean by this? Nothing more than that I should be such a minister as the specimens around her, a minister of the worldly church, which stands foremost in opposition to the everlasting gospel and from which we have come out. What is the real office of such a minister? Simply to keep enough religious influence at work in the community to make men comfortable in the service of Mammon...."

With John stood Harriet, Charlotte and George, just reaching maturity. Leading the opposing family faction were Mary Mead and her husband, representative of the sound, unflinching respectability of Puritan New England. Mary was to become the mother of Larkin G. Mead, the sculptor, of William R. Mead (of the firm of architects, McKim, Mead, and White), and of Elinor Mead, who became the wife of William Dean Howells (he in his turn wrote a "campaign" biography of Polly Noyes's nephew, when the posthumous son of her brother Rutherford became Republican candidate for the Presidency). Horatio joined the Meads in their opposition to John's radical doctrines.

4

There was but a year and eight months between the ages of Harriet and Charlotte. They had grown up side by side, but were quite unlike in appearance and in temperament. Harriet was tall, red-haired, not pretty, impulsive, more or less combative, possessed of an intellect of masculine strength, and of a keen intuition which John said was almost omniscient. More delicate, Charlotte was also more beautiful. She "took after" the Noyeses. She wore her hair, of great length and thickness, in a lustrous crown on a well-balanced head. Her eyes were large, of a grayish blue, with flecks of hazel in the iris; her nose straight, yet feminine; and her mouth was her most beautiful feature. She was gentle and self-possessed and amiable. She was an insatiable and retentive reader, and spent hours absorbed in Sir Walter Scott's heroes and heroines, Milton and Shakespeare, and all the papers and magazines subscribed for by the family. She was very fond of history—particularly English history—and became an excellent teacher of it.

Soon after Harriet's happy, though far from brilliant, marriage to John L. Skinner, Noyes decided upon a young Putney store-keeper, John R. Miller, as the predestined mate for Charlotte.

In 1840, Noyes had proposed to John Miller to dissolve his business partnership, abjure political aspirations, and come to his house to board and to study theology. Miller accepted this advice, put aside personal ambition unhesitatingly, and united his fortunes with those of John Noyes. On the seventh of September, 1841, Charlotte and he were married. There had been nothing romantic about that courtship; it could hardly be termed a courtship at all. Those were earnest days, and the followers of the movement felt like soldiers enlisting for battle, so there was little time for sentiment. Putney, aghast, recalled that Charlotte Noyes had previously received a number of brilliant offers which would have placed her in the most select circles of the land; but these she had declined as temptations of the adversary to draw her away from a sacred cause. Charlotte adapted herself to the position of wife with instinctive grace. She was naturally fitted to be an appreciative and entertaining companion to men of culture and learning. Though affectionate and amiable, Charlotte by no means doted on her husband, nor did she try to wheedle or manage him by feminine arts, yet this union flowered into a deep love.

After Squire Noyes distributed his wealth, and the Putney group came into possession of its capital, a number of persons who had long been in sympathy but owned no property were admitted to membership. Among them were Harvey Bowles, a journeyman printer, who helped on *The Witness;* the carpenter William Sherwood and his wife Lauretta, who belonged to the Newark group. Sherwood arrived in time to superintend the building of their chapel and store. George, David and Alexander Wilder, of Verona, New York, had been brought up in the Dutton school of Perfectionism, and were therefore prejudiced against organization. But in January, 1841, George Wilder, as a sort of delegate of the co-believers in central New York, visited Noyes to observe the Putney Perfectionists. Noyes invited him and his two brothers to come to Putney as Bible students. They were tall, raw-boned young trenchermen and above the average in intelligence. Alexander, the youngest, was preparing for college when he accepted Noyes's offer. Feeling insecure about John B. Lyvere, who had been accused of improper intimacy with women, yet desiring to keep him under observation, Noyes invited him to join the Corporation. In October, 1841, after the death of his wife, Mr. Lyvere came to Putney. A short time previously Almira Edson, a young woman from Halifax, Vermont, whose letters had aroused the sympathy of the Putney Perfectionists, became a member. She and Lyvere were expelled in September, 1842.

At the end of March, 1843, in addition to twenty-eight adults there were nine children: Theodore R. Noyes, son of John H. and Harriet A. Noyes; Joseph J. Skinner, son of John L. and Harriet H. Skinner; George and Charles Cragin, sons of George and Mary Cragin; three children of Clifford and Sally Clark; and two children of Isaac and Polly Palmer. The Community was being supported by the common purse.

5

The Noyeses built a new house and Locust Grove was allotted to the Skinners and the Millers. The Campbell house was occupied by George and Mary Cragin, their children, and other newer members of the association.

The Perfectionist store and chapel were built in 1841 on the east side of the small village square, around which the tavern, churches, stores and village workshops crowded. A more conspicuous place for the chapel could not have been selected; it stood as a challenge to Putney gossip. Interest spread to the borders of the town. The "East Part," a sort of neutral ground, where all religions and no religion held sway by turns, was at that moment the headquarters of Methodism; but that church was not in a very flourishing or harmonious state. Mr. Pierce courageously invited John to preach at the East Part, in the Methodist Church. A revival ensued. Religious and financially substantial families became interested and opened their houses for Perfectionist meetings.

To secure as much time as possible for spiritual culture, the Noyeses adopted a plan of providing but one regular, table-spread meal a day. With the influx of new disciples from all parts, something of the sort became necessary. Curiously, this main meal was breakfast, which was served at about seven or eight o'clock. The morning meal over, Harriet Noyes and other volunteers washed the accumulated dishes, including those that had been used the previous day. They cooked and prepared food of various kinds for the day, and placed it all on the shelves. Upon the pantry-door a printed card was posted, inviting members and guests to help themselves to these refreshments. This notice on the pantry-door read:

HEALTH, COMFORT, ECONOMY AND WOMAN'S RIGHTS

Believing that the practice of serving up in a formal manner three meals of heated food daily is a requirement of custom and not of nature—unnecessary and injurious to health and comfort—subjecting females almost universally to the worst of slavery—we hereby notify our friends that we shall omit, in our ordinary domestic arrangements, two of the usual meals, viz., dinner and supper, and instead of them shall keep in this pantry a supply and variety of eatables, which we invite them to partake of at such times and in such manner as appetite or fancy may suggest.

John H. Noyes
Harriet A. Noyes

Substitution of cold meals at noon and at night became popular in the "family," and this method for saving time and labor was the regular régime between 1840 and 1842. Yet even with this arrangement the women required no small amount of energy and courage to master domestic duties so as to devote three hours of the morning to spiritual pursuits. In two of the families there were infants to be cared for. To give the mothers an equal chance with others, volunteers often took care of the little ones, allowing the mothers to share in the chapel school.

6

Calls came to John Noyes to expound his doctrines through New England. But before setting out, the canny leader took care to strengthen the home organization. About September, 1842, John L. Skinner was elected moderator of the chapel meetings, and John Miller manager of the Perfectionist store and director of the outdoor activities of the little corporation. George Cragin was chosen to accompany Noyes on his missionary tour. The intention was to preach about from place to place according to invitations—not to attempt to establish the truth in any one place, but to introduce their publications and give people a taste of the truth found in their columns.

They went first to Hawley, Massachusetts, the battlefield of a heated controversy. The Congregational minister's attacks on the "immoral" doctrines of the Perfectionists generated intense interest, and even an undercurrent of sympathy for the ostracized sect. A wave of excitement surged through the village when this notice was posted:

> A lecture will be given at Mr. Sandford's Hall, on Thursday next at 2 P.M., by John H. Noyes, on the subject of Sexual Morality. After the meeting there will be opportunity for any one to make inquiries or remarks. The object of the meeting is to go into a free, public examination of the sentiments of those papers which have lately been stigmatized in this place as licentious.

Sexual morality! This frank, unashamed posting of the word *sexual* seemed almost an affront upon public decency. Angry blushes suffused the tight-lipped faces of the Rev. Mr. Thatcher's followers.

Early on Tuesday afternoon, by invitation of two communicants who had been arraigned for heresy, the visitors from Putney attended a church meeting called for the purpose of excommunicating them. About twenty-five members were present. At this meeting Noyes enjoyed the privilege of hearing his name handled very freely by the reverend gentlemen who presided. After prolonged discussion, spiced with unfriendly allusions to the Noyesites, the following resolution was passed:

> Resolved, that Perfectionism, as propagated by John H. Noyes, is a dangerous heresy.

Other resolutions charged the accused members with heresy, disorderly conduct, and breach of church covenant. Sentence of excommunication was passed upon them. Before closing the session, Mr. Thatcher remarked that though he had not before advised the people to attend such meetings, yet under the peculiar circumstances of the case, he felt it his duty to attend the Noyes lecture, and therefore could not say anything against others attending it.

Thursday arrived—blustering, forbidding, rainy. Notwithstanding the threat in the skies, Mr. Sandford's hall was filled and more than one variety of interest excited the gathering.

Noyes opened by vindicating his own character. He offered proofs to show not only that he himself had never been licentious but that his whole influence among Perfectionists had been directed toward putting down this vice. Mr. Thatcher took the floor in support of his charges against Noyes, and held it till nearly dark. Then it was proposed to adjourn till the next day.

The hall proved much too small for the surging crowd eager to attend the next morning. The assembly adjourned, perforce, to the meeting-house. Mr. Thatcher and his friends had packed the meeting. With evident assurance of victory, the reverend gentleman resumed his attack upon Noyes. During his two or three hours in the pulpit, he put upon Noyes's writings constructions so false and so unfair that George Cragin restrained himself with difficulty from rising and denouncing the minister as a liar. When Mr. Thatcher concluded, a noon recess was announced.

At one o'clock Noyes was permitted to take the floor in his own defense. He had taken copious notes during Thatcher's remarks, and was prepared to reply to every specific charge. He presented the fundamental principles of the new covenant. He insisted particularly upon the necessity of being led by the Spirit. For two hours or more, despite his hoarseness, Noyes poured forth a stream of eloquence that seemed to Cragin to wash away the solid wall of antagonism. Replying to each new charge that had been brought against him, Noyes took up his opponent's character as a professed preacher of the gospel of Christ. It was a searching, withering criticism of the typical ministerial functionary. Gradually the sentiment of the audience shifted. When Thatcher rose to reply, the audience signified its verdict of "not guilty," and as their minister attempted a feeble reply the townsfolk stamped noisily out. The discomfited clergyman who had invited his friends to come and witness the contest that they might see how easily and successfully he could annihilate Noyes, the notorious Perfectionist, was placed *hors de combat* with hardly a friend to stand by him in this sudden reverse of fortune. So, at least, George Cragin gleefully reported to Putney.

The village buzzed that evening with unsuppressed excitement. The meeting had been attended by respectable folk of both sexes, shocked because the discussion in the meeting-house had narrowed down to the question of sexual intercourse in Heaven. The Perfectionists boldly answered this question in the affirmative. A shudder passed through the audience, and the sober and religious took that problem to bed with them.

The next day, before their departure, as John Noyes and George Cragin, with their friend Longley, stood in the general store of the village, a woman well past middle age, dressed in prim, homespun garments, and carrying an ear-trumpet, entered. She eyed the little group quizzically and with undisguised curiosity. Then, casting aside discretion, she stepped boldly up to John Noyes.

"Do you really believe, Mr. Noyes, that they have sexual intercourse in Heaven?" The question rang out. The ear-trumpet awaited at a receptive angle for the all-important reply. Trading came to a standstill.

Candidly and without equivocation, Noyes replied promptly, "I do," and looked straight into the eyes of the little old deaf lady.

"So do I!" she said with no diminuendo of pitch. The ear-trumpet descended and the homespun figure, with ram-rod carriage, marched out of the store. The gale of long suppressed laughter broke like a storm.

7

Noyes openly declared war on the clergy. The history of the Puritans seemed to him to prove that this vested interest had always acted as avowed antagonists of any freedom of mind. The clergy, and not the people, were the instigators of many infamous Puritan persecutions. This distinction between the clergy and the people, Noyes felt, reconciled conflicting testimony concerning the character of the Puritans. He agreed with those who condemned the first colonists of New England as cruel bigots; but this condemnation, in his mind, fell first upon the clergy, and upon the people only as the dupes of the clergy. The people could be censured so far as they were identified with the clergy, and no farther. Throughout the world, wherever religious imposture and persecution prevailed, in Popish, Protestant or heathen lands, the clergy perpetuated their monopoly at the expense of spiritual intuition. "But wherever the idea finds place in the people's mind, that any and all may be directly taught of God, there the craft of the learned is endangered. Hence it is perfectly natural that 'educated' ministers should regard every pretension of 'revelation' as a fire which, if not extinguished, must consume the whole fabric which gives them subsistence and reputation. Of course they organize themselves, like fire companies, ready at a moment's warning, with engine and bucket, fire-hook and ladder, to rush forth and extinguish 'the flames of fanaticism' that will occasionally break out in every community....

"Ministers in these days present themselves as witnesses and advocates for the Sabbath, the institution of the ministry, and all the paraphernalia of their own office, as successfully as if they were wholly disinterested in the matter, and were only pleading for the honor of God, and the 'precious' doctrines of the gospel. The credulity and reverence with which their *ex parte* testimony of all such matters is received, is not unlike that manifested by the magistrates.... The time of physical persecution for heresy and witchcraft has passed away. But the same clerical bigotry and jealousy remains, and to a great extent, the same submission of the people to their priests—now as then. The causes of persecution remain, though the form of their effects is changed." Thus Noyes wrote in an early number of *The Witness.*

Even at that early date the word conservative had become odious to reformers of American morals and politics; but Noyes defended "true conservatism." Though the Church, Ministry, Sabbath, and their ceremonies perish, he believed it necessary to preserve the central truth of the Bible. All the better part of human nature, Noyes believed, was essentially conservative: "Whoever in his zeal for reform undertakes an indiscriminate warfare against antiquity, traditions, and existing institutions, dooms himself to a fruitless struggle with human nature.... The true reason why modern reformers fail of their expected triumphs, in their conflict with the representatives of existing institutions, is that they allow themselves to be crowded into an anti-conservative position. The Church and Clergy have got possession of the stronghold of veneration. They stand as the acknowledged conservators of order, government, good breeding, and stability. These things are, in themselves, inestimably precious; and the better and stronger part of human nature cleaves to them. So long as the Church and Clergy occupy this position—however glaring may be their errors and corruptions, and however skillfully these errors and corruptions may be exposed—they cannot be overthrown. The reformers must sit down and count the cost of the war they are engaged in; and not only become, but *prove* themselves more truly conservative than their adversaries, or they will labor in vain."

Such attacks as these automatically sowed seeds of antagonism toward Noyes—antagonisms which were eventually to yield a bumper crop of slander and libel. But evil reports concerning John Noyes and his followers emanated even from the Perfectionists of Oberlin. One of the great heroes of Noyes's youth had been the towering, magnetic Charles Grandison Finney, the very heart of the revival movement of the late twenties and early thirties. But now the great Finney, along with his colleague Asa Mahan, was subsiding into the preaching of a tame, toothless Perfectionism. Mahan, in 1835, had been appointed the first president of the new Oberlin College, in Ohio, and there the two had their headquarters. Noyes suspected that they had helped themselves to some of his most telling ideas, without acknowledging their source, and had utilized them in developing a particularly distasteful school of holiness. Oberlin Perfectionism seemed sentimental and ineffective, and Noyes exposed its inconsistencies. It was no surprise, therefore, that "ludicrous and filthy reports" concerning the Putney group were traced to the central plant of these adversaries.

Writing home from Boston, George Cragin reported to Noyes: "During the anniversary week in this city, I met with a young man from Oberlin. . . . He said, 'The professors of Oberlin institute have reported . . . that Noyes, Cragin and all connected with them at Putney, have abolished the marriage institution and practice promiscuous sexual intercourse.' He informed me further that these professors received this important and interesting information from some of the officers of the Female Moral Reform Society of New York City. I am shocked to think how these professors dared to hazard their reputations, and the ruin of their characters, by conversing with those females on such an indelicate subject. . . ."

Noyes published this communication in *The Perfectionist* (June 15, 1843) with the following sharp comment: "As there is not the slightest foundation in fact, so far as Putney (and we may safely say Belchertown) is concerned, for such reports, it has sometimes been a subject of curious inquiry with us, how even the most malicious persons can put their minds in a state perverse enough to originate them. The philosophy of the matter appears to be this. The tale-teller takes the doctrines of Perfectionism for his basis, and then connecting with them his own consciousness of inward lewdness, *infers* the facts which he conceives correspond to these doctrines. He argues in his own private thoughts thus: 'Perfectionists say they are not under law. Now if I was not under law, I should plunge right into whoredom, might and main. Therefore it is fair to infer that they do so; and I may safely report about them, as facts, any imaginable indecencies. I cannot hit amiss.'

"Evil reports, however base and cruel, have long since ceased to disturb our peace. In fact, so far as our personal feelings are concerned they amuse more than they trouble. Yet, for the gospel's sake, we feel bound to set our heel on the heads of some of the serpents that cross our path."

Rumors concerning Noyes and his band were in general circulation. "If there is any excuse for evil-doing to say it is natural, we allow that the course of the Oberlin professors is in some degree excusable," Noyes commented as early as 1844. "Their circumstances make it very natural that they should slander us. We commenced the testimony of New Covenant holiness. They followed after, and borrowed as much as they dared of our doctrine. Indeed we might say they stole it, for they borrowed it without giving any credit.... They speak evil of us in private circles and from behind the pulpit, where one party only can be heard, and refuse to place their charges on public record. We have invited them to accuse us, in their paper, of those things which we hear of their reporting privately from time to time, but the *Evangelist* is silent. We conclude therefore that they are determined to lynch us, that is, to put us down by *ex parte* force, without due course of trial in open court. Such uncivilized processes may avail for a time. But speedy retribution sometimes overtakes those who practice them, as the editor of the *Evangelist* and others at Oberlin have already had occasion to know. At any rate we shall outlive them and at last God will reward all according to their works."

In spite of his optimism, however, *The Perfectionist*, official organ of the Putney group, showed a loss of seven or eight hundred dollars. It must be made self-supporting. Noyes decided to enlarge it, to publish it regularly twice a month, to concentrate his energies upon the task of presenting his own particular brand of Perfectionism. Cragin should be sent into the field to obtain subscriptions for the venture—not merely to the magazine. With him went Isaac Palmer and the two Wilder boys.

John had even considered inaugurating a campaign in New York City, but his throat trouble was "a thorn in the flesh" warning him against preaching. "I am more and more persuaded," he wrote George Cragin, who was acting as a roving missionary among the scattered groups, "that our strength is to lie in publishing rather than preaching. The invention of printing has changed everything. Our congregations, wherever they are, must do their own preaching, and we must devote ourselves to training a regiment of writers." Though they, as yet, failed even to make expenses, they still dreamed of a grand phalanstery and an enormous business. The phalanstery was to be a great communal dwelling on "the plain"; a sunny plateau on one part of the hilly farm; and the business was to be a printing establishment, (like the New York Bible House or Methodist Book Concern) for the publication of community doctrines and literature.

Chapter VI: THE BEREAN

> And the brethren immediately sent away Paul and Silas unto Berea: who coming thither went into the synagogue of the Jews. These were more noble than those in Thessalonica, in that they received the word with all readiness of mind, and searched the scriptures daily, whether those things were so. —ACTS, 17: 10-11.

I

THE printing press! By this instrument Noyes hoped to educate the world to his new dispensation. Gallant dreams of a Free Press animated all the group—a Press more powerful than Church or State, a Press to revolutionize the souls of men. During the Putney period (1838-1848), Noyes developed his little band into printers, editors, writers, drawing the lesser personalities into his orbit. Their intelligence was a reflected intelligence, deriving light and life from his radiance. The flame of his conviction sent new aspirations pulsating through their veins and brought to fruition inarticulate desires implanted far below the soil of individual consciousness. One question persists: how could one man inspire loyalty so intense that his disciples followed him without hesitation as he led them out of the most deeply entrenched folkways of their time?

That crude, second-hand contrivance transported from Albany, with its primitive daubers and buckskin roller, their first press, exacted endless patience and a vast amount of activity. Yet into the world of actuality this machine distilled the wine of John Noyes's effulgent faith. Lovingly and laboriously Harriet Holton Noyes and her aides copied John's challenging assertions; letter by letter, word by word, sentence by sentence, they set them in type by hand. They minted this new gospel according to John Noyes, not merely upon the clean, handmade white paper; indelibly they engraved it upon their own minds. This labor was no servile task; disciples felt that they were speaking to the world with their leader. They were involved in the whole venture, body and soul, their minds especially sensitized to receive his teaching. Psychologically, the printing press worked miracles in education.

Noyes developed a habit of positive affirmation. In writing, as in speaking, he wasted no breath in negation or denial. From these affirmations, a vitalizing energy seemed to radiate—an energy never dissipated by doubting questions. When, occasionally, timid mouse-like misgivings scampered into the minds of new converts, they were promptly driven back into their hiding places by John's positive yea-saying assurance. Yet Noyes never sought to monopolize the press; he encouraged all of his group to write. But the first requisite was to learn to think. To be steady and effective, thought must be brought into the open. "If you have valuable thoughts, learn to copy them out correctly, just as they exist in your mind, and you will be a good writer." Such was his counsel. If the thinking is sound, he taught them, first drafts are generally better than articles which have been long worked over. Of secondary importance were correctness and elegance of expression, which would be achieved by practice, by examining and reflecting on words and constructions, by habitual reading of the best. Thus Noyes encouraged his beginners, assuring them that "the press is destined to supersede the pulpit in the government of the world; and if we can raise up an army of effective writers, we shall ere long get ahead of the clergy. Their profession was instituted before the art of printing was invented. It belongs to the old world . . . the new world will discard it. . . . Watch and follow your spiritual instinct. Experience has taught me . . . not to force myself into the work. There are times when I feel inspired, and then I write easily and satisfactorily. At other times I have no heart for it, and then I leave it alone."

2

The culminating achievement of this little band of Perfectionist printers was the publication of "The Berean." This compendium of all that Noyes had written, from the days of the New Haven *Perfectionist* ten years earlier, to the very first article he contributed to *The Spiritual Magazine* in 1846, has been characterized as the "Bible" of the Oneida Community. It crystallized into definite expression all the theological convictions Noyes had, for the past twelve years, been formulating. "The Berean" is so closely packed with heresy that orthodox theologians still tear their hair and gnash their teeth over it. Announced as a "manual for the help of those who seek the faith of the Primitive Church," this guide to Noyes's fundamental theological concepts presents a nettling puzzle to the twentieth century mind. The thirty-sixth chapter of "The Berean" is entitled "An Outline of all Experience" and this might well serve as a description of the entire book. Noyes traces the march of the human spirit from primordial savagery through the bondage of externally imposed law, thence through the "spiritual" state and finally to the status of "glorification." Although this book was published less than a century ago, it leads us at times into an almost medieval mentality; but in certain passages its wisdom projects us into a future not yet dreamed of. In a prose vivid, impassioned, occasionally brilliant, he sets forth his convictions concerning first and last things: the purpose of human life on this planet; the reality of rebirth into the universe of the Spirit; the three characteristics of the reborn man; the inadequacy of the Bible as the supreme and literal authority; the only path to the attainment of true and complete liberty; and the significance of the Second Coming of Christ as an accomplished event.

To his followers, these words were accepted as a divine revelation. To us of a later day, with our knowledge of comparative religion, "The Berean" supplies the evidence which admits Noyes to the great tradition of the Christian mystics... Fox, Wesley, or even Blake... driven, as they were, to voice violent opposition to the sterility of the orthodox churches. Genius is always at odds with its own epoch, and spiritual genius most of all. But, like Wesley, Fox, or Luther, Noyes claimed for himself no radical innovations, but only the rediscovery of eternal, unchanging and neglected truths.

The seventy-four chapters of "The Berean" carry the reader back through centuries, beyond the Protestantism of the Reform, beyond formalized and Hellenized Christianity, to the heart of the primitive Pauline church. Noyes revived a faith long neglected in the Occident and sought to recapture the fire, the intensity, the literalness of Paul.

The community of the Perfect, which Noyes hoped to realize in that Vermont village, bears all the earmarks of the mystic community of Islam which extends from here beyond the grave, comprising dead Moslems of earlier generations, even to the righteous of the times before Islam. Noyes's community was comparable to Augustine's City of God, which symbolizes the unity of all believers, the blessed and the angels. And the Albigenses and Waldensian movements of the Middle Ages set up this same symbolical community of the reborn.

As a Perfectionist in the classic historical line, stemming from Wesley, from Puritan and Quaker mysticism, Noyes stood resolutely opposed to the "miserable sinner" ethics derived from Reformation theology. To him, the Augustine "perpetual repentance," which Luther revived because he (Luther) found it impossible to think highly of himself, was unworthy of the sons of God. Noyes reverted to primitive Christianity, to the Pauline church, and came to the conclusion that the noblest destiny of mankind was to grow into ever greater and greater liberty. But that liberty, the heart of Christ's message, must be reached through rebirth into holiness. Avoiding alike the sterile keepers of the letter of the law, and the lawless, licentious Antinomianism in which "everything is permitted," Noyes firmly resolved to clear the way for the superb, outgoing energy of the Spirit as the only power able to create the "life more abundant" promised in the Second Coming.

3

In the pages of "The Berean" we trace the reiteration of those *idées-forces* which serve as guide-lines along his "pathway clearly marked out." The purpose of human life? "Our business is to be co-workers with God in ushering in the last period of man's education—the victory and reign of spiritual wisdom and power." Noyes pleads for nothing less than the complete spiritual regeneration of all mankind. He recognizes the four elements of human nature—physical, moral, intellectual and spiritual. But he warns against the danger of making this division a permanent one. Soul and body are one. Soul is eternal spirit; it is energy free and self-directing, indestructible in its essence. Spirit is the dynamo of the body. The life of the body must be directed as an integral part, but only a part, of the life of the spirit. The life of the soul and the body are essentially one—yet the body may die and the soul still live and renew its strength. To think of physical life as independent of the soul is a basic fallacy. Christ never divided life into two parts; but viewing the life of the body and the soul as one, he affirmed that life would never relinquish its consciousness and its growth. All artificial distinctions between the life of the soul and the life of the body Noyes dismissed as perplexing and false. Thus represented, Spirit is seen as one creative mind, one energy, which animates all humanity. Muscle, nerves, bones, thinking, feeling, are but differentiated and integrated instruments of that dynamic spirit. "Know no man after the flesh." We must see human beings as they are—immortal spirits, sharers of a common life and a common hope, and never as mutually conflicting and destructive, atomistic "egos."

Once we grasp his conception of the Spirit as pure Energy—dynamic, life-giving, autonomous, and therefore perfect in its freedom—we understand Noyes's antagonism to "external" law. For him, legality was synonymous with restraint, compulsion, prohibition, while the Spirit rules by grace and truth. He insists upon the importance of this distinction, and discovers in it the yawning chasm between the old and the new dispensation. Under the old, the law was written on tables of stone. Under the new, it is written in the heart. "I will put my laws into their mind, and write them in their hearts." External law presupposes internal depravity. "The law was not made for righteous man, but for the lawless and disobedient." "Who ever heard of a law requiring that men shall eat or sleep?" Noyes asks with scorn. Because all men are sufficiently disposed to eat and sleep, such a law would be ridiculous. Likewise, were men sufficiently disposed to love God with the whole heart, a law requiring them to do so would be equally ridiculous. External law attempts to check the leprosy of sin by external medication: the new covenant purges the blood and by this purging removes the necessity of external medication.

Incomparably easier to receive deliverance from all sins than to conquer one! So he proclaimed. Pride, envy, anger, sensuality were but limbs of the tree of sin; its trunk was that unbelief which rejected the Spirit. The man who commenced the work of exterminating sin at the top of the tree, or among any of its branches, would soon discover that the branches which he had once lopped off grow again, or send their juice into other limbs. Easier to lay the ax at the root and fell the whole tree at once, than to extirpate effectively a single limb! Under the old covenant, God said: "Do according to all I command you, and ye shall live." Under the new covenant, when its powers are fully developed, He may safely say: "Do as you please; for I promise that your pleasure shall be mine. I will write my law upon your hearts." Thus perfect liberty is the one implied promise of the new covenant. This is the prize for which man must strive. But, admonishes Noyes, there is but one path to its attainment: it is fulfilled in believers by the energy of the blood of Christ, the spirit of the living God.

Noyes defended this wholesale, sweeping defiance of "law," saying: "We do not mean that we are not under government. ... But government may be administered in various ways. Law is not the only means by which a king may seek and secure obedience to his will. Even earthly governments, in many cases, rely on education more than on law. ... In the Christian dispensation, God reigns not by law, but by grace and truth." Fundamentally, this was not a moral but a prudential question. Even God could not drive men into love by threatening law, but only by exhibiting to them His own love.

Noyes envisaged the universe as a theater of action—a battlefield, whereon the Son of God and the Devil arrayed themselves and clashed in decisive conflict. Satan's spirit is the external atmosphere that envelops mankind, pressing (we may say figuratively) with a weight of fifteen pounds on every square inch of human life. Wherever there is a vacuum in men's hearts, that evil atmosphere enters, manifests itself in selfishness, covetousness, and all evil works. Wherever the laws of life are violated, physically or spiritually, evil may infuse its poison, aggravating and perpetuating the injury.

This theory of "spiritual pressure," forced as it may appear, serves at least to dramatize effectively the eternal conflict of external versus internal; the battle between the outer world of Nature, with its incessant counterplay of forces inimical to Man, and that inner world of the Spirit which, for survival, must actively deploy its energies, must press onward to ultimate victory. This contrast and its tragic implications brings to mind the famous passage in which Marcel Proust describes the *agonie* of his grandmother. "When the abyss of sickness and death opens within us, and we have no longer any resistance to offer to the tumult with which the world and our own body rush upon us, then to endure even the tension of our own muscles... even to keep ourselves motionless in what we ordinarily regard as nothing but the simple negative position of a lifeless thing, requires, if we wish our head to remain erect and our eyes calm, an expense of vital energy that becomes the object of an exhausting struggle."

In similar vein, John Noyes writes of the endless battle between the outer world, seeking to invade the soul, and of the resistance of the outgoing energies of the Spirit. The external world, with its inhuman, natural power, may claim us as mere biochemical organisms subject to relentless laws and tropisms; but the universe of the Spirit gives us the strength to assert our inviolable freedom, our immortal destiny. Only as we pledge allegiance to the Spirit can Man wrest victory from the outer universe.

4

Regeneration, rebirth into the spiritual world, is the peculiar attainment of the Christian dispensation; and John Noyes set down for his disciples three marks of the reborn man.

His first discovery was that the spiritual man exhibited a renewed mind. "He that is spiritual," says Paul, "judgeth (i.e., discerneth) all things." His intellect was not only under the influence of that Spirit which "searcheth the deep things of God," but was assimilated by it, and acted in unison with it. This renewed mind is strong and penetrating, Noyes asserted; "quick and powerful, sharper than any two-edged sword"; and "all things are naked and open to it." The reborn mind receives without staggering and really apprehends divine mysteries which mere human intellects are unable to see or bear. "We speak wisdom," says Paul, "among them that are *perfect*,–even the hidden word of God in a mystery. Eye hath not seen, nor ear heard, neither have entered into the heart of man, the things which God hath prepared for them that love Him."

The second characteristic of the reborn soul is a loving heart. In proof of this point, Noyes adduces almost all of John's first epistle, exclusively devoted to the definition of the characteristics of the regenerate. No truly reborn man can be envious or contentious. Among spiritual believers, quarreling cannot persist. The spiritual man "dwells in love." He has gained the crown of all attainments, that bond of perfectness which is charity.

As we explore these pages, we cannot fail to admire Noyes's power to infuse piercing significance into those old ideas which have now, to follow Paul Valéry's striking figure, gone to "join, in the cases of the numismatists of language, so many other verbal coins which are no longer in circulation." Thus Noyes insists that charity is far from meaning that outward-bound, bustling quality of character which usually passes for religious benevolence. Its elements, on the contrary, are mostly negative. The idea of doing good in conspicuous and ostentatious fashion is never prominent in charity: but, as Paul says "it worketh no ill." It is just that quality which fits a man to live in social contact with his fellows without giving offense and without taking offense. Thorough extinction of selfishness, a perfect appreciation of the interests of others, of the value of peace, quiet reliance on the faithfulness of eternal love,–such are its prime implications. The man who has it will live in peace, in spite of all the sons of discord. He cannot be drawn into any envious, grudging, murmuring, evil-eyed spirit.

This unobtrusive spiritual quality was far more needed to cure the world's miseries, John Noyes was certain, than the "doing good" sort of institutional philanthropy, empty-voiced Peace Societies, or the visionary programs of Fourier or Robert Owen. Was not egocentrism, in the final analysis, the universal and inveterate malady of human society? Charity, as defined by Paul, was the one infallible cure for this malady. With charity of this type the world might become a comfortable Paradise, even though external institutions were to remain unchanged. Without it, he realized, the most perfect organizaiton could become no more than a disciplined Bedlam. Charity, then, was the very fruit of the re-oriented psyche. Except as they were used as designations of charity, the very terms *holiness, perfection, salvation from sin,* would remain mere shibboleths.

The third characteristic of the reborn, Noyes specified, was an unquenchable desire for unimpeded growth. "I count not myself to have apprehended: but this one thing I do; forgetting those things which are behind, and reaching forth into those things which are before, I press toward the mark for the prize of the high calling of God in Christ Jesus." Was there ever more stimulating expression than this affirmation of Paul? Such thirst for ever greater conquest in the field of spiritual attainment belonged to the very nature of the renewed mind and the loving heart. No priggish imagination of the attainment of unimprovable perfection; no idea of being a passive subject of grace, could ever prevent the truly regenerate from pressing onward in knowledge and service. Such was the only valid meaning of progressive conduct.

In recapitulation, Noyes sums up the leading characteristics of the spiritual man, as a discriminating and stable mind; a quiet, loving heart; and energetic ambition for improvement. Without these characteristics he could not name any man "perfect" or "spiritual" in the primitive sense. "He belongs among the *nepioi,* not among the *teleioi.*" Such were the main outlines of "human experience" and the goal of human endeavor as John Noyes traced them to his little band in Putney.

5

The thorny problem of the Parousia—the Second Coming of Christ—occupies a crucial point in Noyes's theology. It was first brought to his attention while he was a student at Andover. Noyes placed himself firmly in the so-called preterist position: Christ predicted, and the Primitive Church expected, the Second Coming to take place within one generation from his First Coming. All signs of its approach actually came to pass before the close of the apostolic age. Consequently, simple faith was compelled to affirm that He did come again at the time appointed, and that the confusion about His coming had not been in His predictions or in the expectations of His disciples, but in the imagination of the world as to the physical nature of the event. It was an event, Noyes insists, of the spiritual world. To affirm that the Apostles were mistaken, or that time has proved the fallacy of their anticipations, seemed to Noyes to undermine the very foundations of the Christian faith. Either the predictions—including the destruction of Jerusalem, the coming of the Lord, the resurrection of the dead, and the rewarding of the faithful—did take place before the passing away of that generation, as predicted by Christ, taught by the Apostles, and expected by the whole church; or else, the hope of the Church was a delusion, the teachings of the Apostles an error, the predictions of Jesus a dream.

For Noyes, believing that the Second Coming was a *fait accompli*, one conclusion was necessary and inevitable. He reiterated his faith in the existence of the spiritual world, independent of the temporal and spatial order—"the original organization instituted by Christ and the Apostles is accessible to us, and . . . our main business as reformers is to open communication with that body." The tenacity of this belief is, perhaps, difficult for the twentieth-century mind to grasp, but it is essential for a comprehension of the religious foundations of the Putney and Oneida Communities.

6

Noyes liked to refer to himself as a true conservative; but in the minds of his Puritan contemporaries, he was a devastating iconoclast, condemned, as we have seen, as an aberrant monomaniac. Indeed, even to his own well-disciplined New England intellect, the dissociation of the inward substance of virtue from external conformity was a difficult operation. "We tell them that a pure heart, and its counterpart, a good conscience (which is all we mean by perfection) are inward spiritual matters, which may be produced instantaneously by the infusion of the purity and good conscience of Jesus Christ, and are independent of external conduct—though necessarily productive, more or less, of outward righteousness." The love of right must be the whole substance of virtue; for outward actions are only completed manifestations, having no merit or demerit in themselves. In order to be free from sin, man need only to have a perfect love of the right. External actions are to be estimated by their relation to such love—that action being the best which most effectively expresses confidence in God, and that action the worst which most decisively exposes isolation of heart.

This principle, Noyes asserted, was destined to work tremendous revolutions in the moral codes of this world. Pursuing this theme, he concludes that in the service of God, freedom is the primary ethical necessity. But, since liberty to serve the devil is the worst of bondage, Noyes proclaims that there is but one road to true spiritual freedom. That is through holiness–to be born anew in Christ, to become dynamic instruments in transforming and transmitting the energy of that Spirit.

By perfect holiness (using the expression in its most elementary sense) Noyes meant that purity of heart which gives a good conscience. While it equips the spiritual soldier with a pure heart and good conscience at the outset, this theory of the life of the Spirit nevertheless does not exempt him from service. To win the glory of God was not the accomplishment of one brief moment. The battle between flesh and spirit would go on. Nevertheless, the rule which allows men to *hope* for heaven without presumption allows them to *receive* heaven here without self-righteousness. "While, therefore, we shrink not from the odium connected with the name *Perfectionist*, we cannot despair of disabusing all honest men, ere long, of a portion of their prejudices against it, by convincing them that we join in the testimony of our living head, that 'there is none good but one, that is God,' and believe that by the energy of his goodness alone we are delivered from sin."

To Noyes, the Bible was not, in itself, a revelation to men. Without outside help, it could not reach the human mind. The scale of human intelligence ranged, he said, from mere ability to read to the perfect clairvoyance of inspiration. The intelligence of the *literati* stood, as he estimated it, only midway between these extremes. Had the Bible no mysteries to disclose to those who had attained that higher intelligence which comes by inspiration? Assuredly God provides in His revelation seasonable food for all: milk for babes, strong meats for men; simple truths for the ignorant, deeper truths for the learned; and still deeper mysteries for the inspired. Noyes found the Gospels a revelation of the deeper things of God, to those who could read with the help of the Spirit of Truth. This, he said, was the only means by which the Bible could be a "revelation to men." Without rebirth into the realm of the Spirit, man is utterly incompetent to interpret the "deep things of God." The Paraclete must be the ultimate arbiter of Biblical interpretation. "How irrational it is to suppose that the same agent which once gave to man gifts of supernatural wisdom and power, is still present, but only as a latent auxiliary of the clergy! What a blasphemous descent is this, from the sublime to the ridiculous! As well might a purblind dotard say that the sun still shines, but the age of daylight is past, and only one of the seven colors which were the elements of ancient sunlight—and that the dimmest—is now given to the world!"

Insight into "first and last things" was the primary requisite for spiritual wisdom; then the squaring-up of such direct revelation with the hidden meanings of the Gospels. In this fashion John Noyes sought to reconcile his iconoclasm with ancient truth. His disciples drank in his challenging affirmations, set them in type—and, willing but unsuspecting helped him plant these ethical explosives among the folkways of New England.

7

No sooner had John Noyes begun to publish this "Berean"—anathema to respectable churchgoers—than he found himself the center of a fierce struggle for leadership of the amorphous sect of Perfectionists. Between the ethical sterility of the Oberlin school and the willful and irresponsible anti-legality of the "left wing," which threatened to lead the whole movement into a bog of promiscuity, a clear course had to be charted. James Boyle, John's colleague of New Haven days, was still active. Boyle was a traitor to the gospel; and, rather than put his neck into the yoke with Boyle and company, John Noyes vowed he would break brotherhood with every friend he had. In Belchertown, Massachusetts, Alexander Wilder had assailed Noyes's theories, and had plunged that little group into doubt concerning Noyes's qualifications as a leader. David A. Warren also attacked the Putney prophet as an autocrat, accusing him of usurping credit for every new truth, of "behaving as pugnaciously as a pugilist."

These men were ill-equipped to hold aloft the banner of the new life. Equally unfitted was Dr. Josiah A. Gridley, a "brassy, smart, witty and licentious pill-vender," whose lecherous visage could deceive no one. Gridley lived in Southampton, Massachusetts, and had shared in the scandalous proceedings in Brimfield in 1835. Noyes had long corresponded with him. "On the subject of sexual morality," he wrote Gridley as early as July 8, 1840, "the church and the world have swung men far beyond the center, to the right. Perfectionism took away the restraining force, and some swung far beyond the center to the left. In this case, the church and the world are the cause, for they placed men in a position of unnatural restraint; Perfectionism was the occasion, though the innocent occasion; for the abolishment of law is an essential feature of the gospel, and must not be kept back let the consequences be what they may. . . ."

"I have no desire to conceal the fact that in 1834-35 . . ." Gridley had written to John Noyes, "the Devil pressed hard upon our souls, and thus drove some of us beyond the sea of discretion. . . . Several that were direct from New Haven have declared most emphatically that they received their first lessons, in theory at least, directly from yourself; and that it was not superior grace but your natural timidity of woman that saved you."

With men like Gridley setting themselves up as teachers of the new covenant, Noyes saw that irreparable harm would be done to the cause. Acknowledged adulterers and fornicators must not be permitted to act as spokesmen. "A man who has once been guilty of adultery," he protested in a letter to Joshua Longley, "ought to be watched, especially if he asserts his innocence in that adultery, though he may confess its folly and inexpediency. . . ." In order that there should be no confusion concerning his own standard of sexual conduct, Noyes published in *The Perfectionist* (July 12, 1845) this warning: "No shame or fear of consequences shall ever make us retract the sentiment of the *Battle-Axe* letter. The unwise have converted those sentiments to purposes of licentiousness against our strenuous resistance. . . . The present is not the time of realization but of preparation; . . . the resurrection of the body must precede the everlasting marriage. Our own example has been blameless, and we have faithfully exposed all offenders that have come within the range of our influence and responsibility. By these means Perfectionism has been to a large extent cleared of the corruption which once threatened to overwhelm it. But within a few months we have seen indications that the old spirit of confusion and uncleanness is still alive, and we therefore address all pure-minded believers the following suggestions:

"1. The worst enemies of the cause are those who disgrace it.

"2. Beware of allowing a leading influence to those who have been formerly involved in licentious disorders.

"3. Brotherly love stands ahead of sexual love.

"4. Be on your guard when you see religious teachers fond of indulging in bodily contacts.

"5. Believe no one who professes to have attained the resurrection of the body.

"6. Believe no one who boasts that he is free from sexual desire.

"7. Bear in mind that the Shaker and the libertine are alike in their fundamental error, an over-estimate of the importance of the outward act of sexual union.

"8. Beware of engaging in or conniving at deeds which it is necessary to conceal."

This manifesto indicates that Noyes's challenge cannot be dismissed as "rationalization" of unconscious sexual impulse. His sexual philosophy was elaborated while he himself lived in the strictest monogamy. By the publication of this manifesto, the author of the *Battle-Axe* letter hoped to demonstrate the purity of his motives to the world. It might have been an easy matter to gloss over the challenge of this famous letter, to let it sink into oblivion. This he refused to do; and his courageous refusal served to excite much curiosity concerning his handling of "such tremendous machinery as that of Bible Communism."

8

Swedenborgianism, rising to full tide across America in the early forties, inevitably drew Noyes's fire. Swedenborg's writings promised still another new Heaven and a new earth; and the intellectuals acclaimed him a Messianic son of science. Emerson and the members of Brook Farm were bowled over completely. Even Oberlin Perfectionists took up the study of Swedenborg. Professor George Bush, who championed Swedenborg in a course of lectures at the College of the City of New York, urged Noyes to lose no time in examining the Heavenly Doctine. This led to a long study and controversy, published during 1845. Noyes printed his criticism on newspaper galley proofs, and, strategically, sent them to all religious papers in the country. In the words of Dr. Bush, he thus "riveted the prejudices of thousands of minds." Noyes declined to pay tribute to Swedenborg. "I cannot fully account for the astonishing attributes of Mahomet, of Jacob Boehme, of Shakespeare, of Napoleon, without looking toward superhuman sources, but I do not therefore receive those men as plenipotentiaries of God." The Swede, insists Noyes, attempts to "cashier" St. Paul and supersede him. "Paul is in possession of the field, and Swedenborg is the ejector. I insist then that the question to be settled at the outset is whether Paul was a true man or an imposter. Now I have long ago settled it in my mind that Christ revealed himself in Paul, and committed to him the dispensation of the everlasting gospel. I can truly say of Paul that I have found in his writings all the essential truths of Swedenborg and a great deal more; and I do not find in Paul the gross errors which I find in Swedenborg. Therefore in my view the balance is altogether in favor of Paul."

Noyes's primary objection to Swedenborg's ethics was that his morality was essentially that of a bachelor. Even his God was a bachelor! "Swedenborg seems not to have thought of providing for any interests but those of men." After his reading of the celebrated "Conjugial Love," Noyes noted that though Swedenborg permitted paramours for husbands, no such privilege was permitted to mere wives. "His plan necessarily involves the immolation of a large class of women to the lusts of the other sex." On this subject Swedenborg's mind had been warped by the worldly eighteenth-century atmosphere in which he had lived. Too sophisticated, too courtly, too urbane, the whole thought of this well-advertised mystic was conditioned by his background—that of the petty nobility of a minor European kingdom. Noyes condemned his outline of sexual morality as "a soft raiment fit for those in kings' houses." Swedenborg, who proffered his modest claim that he had lived for twenty-six years in free and easy intercourse with all the heavens and hells, who had indeed formed a habit of daily conversation with angels, devils and ghosts, made himself the apologist of worldly concubinage and divorce. Did he not specify at least fifty good reasons for both? Yet even in his heaven, safe, middle-class marriage remained the foundation of society. Swedenborg's saints and angels remained devoted husbands and wives. John Noyes thought that domestic picture a bit tame and unconvincing, just as were Swedenborg's pedestrian accounts of courtship among the heavenly lovers. Yet this edifying picture of bourgeois respectability was in contradiction to Swedenborg's free and easy morals for the unmarried on the mundane plane. It was the bachelor psychology once more.

Here, then, was another new saviour of intellectual young America! Brook Farm's *Harbinger* became the organ of the new vision. The popular rush to Swedenborgianism became as palpable, as portentous, as the old revivals. From his detached vantage point of view of Putney, John Noyes looked at these various movements which stimulated the will-to-believe among his fellow countrymen. And as he looked, he was more convinced than ever that all were wandering, lost, far from the fountain-head of the great central truths.

Chapter VII: ATTACK

The Vision of Christ that thou dost see
Is my Vision's Greatest Enemy;
Thine has a great hook nose like thine,
Mine has a snub nose like to mine:
Thine is a friend of All Mankind,
Mine speaks in parables to the Blind.
Thine loves the same world that mine hates,
Thy Heaven doors are my Hell Gates . . .
Both read the Bible day and night,
But thou read'st black where I read white.

—WILLIAM BLAKE.

I

WHILE reaffirming Noyes's unchanged allegiance to the thought expressed in the *Battle-Axe* letter, as well as the unsmirched purity of his motives, the manifesto published in *The Perfectionist* in July, 1845, specifically declared that the "resurrection of the body" had not yet occurred. The resurrection state, when relations would exist on earth as in heaven, was still a promise of the future.

Still the rumors of sexual irregularities persisted, magnified and exaggerated by his enemies. Noyes always protested that he had never "known" a woman in the Biblical sense until his marriage to Harriet Holton; and that he had never ventured outside the bounds of strict monogamy until the formal acceptance of complex marriage by the Putney family. This man who was always so startlingly frank in publishing the details of his inner life cannot, in all fairness, be discredited in these statements.

His discovery of "male continence," in 1844, was another factor which brought the theory of complex marriage into the realm of practicality for the spiritually eligible. Coupled with an ever-intensified religious fervor, and the increase of community solidarity in confronting the attacks of the outside world, the success of this practice hastened the time for the plucking of the communal fruit.

The Putney group looked upon themselves as a little army, formed into a hollow square, a maneuver necessary for their infantry to meet the cavalry of Vermont respectability. Each of them was helped and protected by the whole. A firm face was presented to the enemy on all sides. Hell might rage outside, but within those closed ranks they found an inner retreat, the abode of peace and love. Thus cut off, they felt, every day, the coming approach of the Kingdom.

They stood now at a crucial point in the establishment of the Kingdom of Heaven on earth. Soon they were to change their testimony from future to present tense, to announce fearlessly and decisively: The Kingdom of God has come! "Sooner or later, we shall have to stand forth," John announced to his thrilled listeners on the first day of June, 1846, "and face the principalities and powers of the world with this declaration."

Then he put this momentous question to them: "Is not *now* the time for us to commence the testimony that *The Kingdom of God has come?* To proclaim boldly that God, in his character of deliverer, lawgiver and judge, has come in this town and in this association?" Public confession, he warned them, must sometimes be made in the face of surrounding unbelief. Inevitably it would unleash a storm of persecution. Yet such a confession must mean the first great step toward the splendid goal. "I believe we are now called upon to take our stand on this great truth as a corporation: and our confession of it to ourselves and to the world will be the beginning of a new development of its power in us.... The full results which pertain to the kingdom of God will never come, so long as we fearfully wait for them as a basis of confession.... The thing now to be done is for each one to look around, and see... whether we are prepared to let the truth of our confession have full sweep in the world around us, whatever the collisions arising from it may be.

"With a mighty hand, and marvelous wisdom, God has gathered us together here.... We have been able to cut our way through the isolation and selfishness in which the mass of men exist, and have attained a position in which, before heaven and earth, we trample under foot the domestic and pecuniary fashions of the world. Separate household interests, property and exclusiveness, have come to an end with us. Our association is established on principles opposed at every point to the institutions of the world.

"Our association... is the mustard seed of something that was not developed in the Primitive Church until the Second Advent, when they raised the banner of the kingdom of God in the spiritual world."

A current of excitement surged through the gathering. The great moment, all felt, had come at last. Out of the diversity of their characters Noyes had woven his web, and tied them into invisible, yet indivisible, unity. One after another, each professed unfeigned love for one another, and avowed the certainty, every day more compelling, that they were members of the invisible

Kingdom of God. Finally, with full realization that all were involved, all irrevocably committed, the little body unanimously adopted the declaration: "*The Kingdom of Heaven Has Come.*" It seemed more momentous than the Declaration of Independence, that declaration of the first of June, 1846. It was to unleash a storm, they well realized, as soon as it was published to the world. As the vote was being taken, a clap of thunder, like a salvo from some heavenly cannon, crashed over the meeting-house. It seemed the response of Heaven to their act; and it was the only sound of thunder they heard that evening.

2

Mary Cragin began a journal to record the extraordinary developments. The pattern of their personal relationships became complex and puzzling. During an absence in Belchertown and Southampton, Massachusetts, George Cragin wrote a confidential letter to Harriet Noyes, expressing his love for her as a sister in Christ. Mrs. Noyes was brought in tribulation by chance remarks of other members concerning George's letter; but to John she freely admitted her love for George Cragin. John Noyes heartily approved these feelings, and upon George's return, he arranged for a meeting of the two couples. "We met one Saturday evening about the middle of the month," Mary wrote. "Mr. Noyes requested Mr. Cragin to read the letter of counsel referred to, and added words of caution, which Mr. Cragin confessed were needed. Mr. Noyes said this was the negative side of the subject; we would now turn to the positive side. He then called upon Mrs. Noyes to speak. She said that she was pleased by Mr. Cragin's letter, and that her heart was drawn out toward him by it. Mr. Cragin confessed a similar feeling toward her, which prompted the letter. Mr. Noyes then asked Mr. Cragin's leave to tell me that he loved me. Mr. Cragin heartily consented. I said that I have loved Mr. Noyes so much that I feared he would find it out; for I was not certain, my awe of him was such, that he wanted me to love him so much. After these avowals we considered ourselves engaged to each other, expecting to live in all conformity to the laws of this world until the time arrives for the consummation of our union. The effect was most refreshing to our spirits. We have formed a circle which it is not easy for the Devil to break. We find this evidence that our love is of God: it is destitute of exclusiveness, each one rejoicing in the happiness of the others."

Such, then, was the prelude to "complex" marriage. A few

days after this meeting, Noyes announced that he wished to extend the blessing to all as fast as they were able to receive it. He found Harriet Skinner far more prepared for a community of hearts than he had supposed. Mr. Miller also gave satisfactory testimony. But, until John Noyes gave the signal, no actual steps were to be taken. With this end in view, Noyes gave a lecture upon the proper bounds of demonstrations of love between the sexes. He warned his disciples against kissing, and everything which might be considered licentious. This "tendency to unity" increased. To find out if confidence was sufficient to prevent jealousies and evil surmises, he called the Millers, the Skinners, the Cragins, and the Noyeses together. They expressed a unanimous agreement that as head and pilot John Noyes could go ahead as he saw fit.

However, Charlotte confessed that she did not think John Miller loved her as formerly. Mary Cragin had, she admitted, perhaps unconsciously, attracted him the year before. Embarrassed by Abram Smith's unexpected arrival at Putney, Mary confessed that she had turned for consolation to Charlotte's husband. "Finally, Mr. Miller," Mary wrote in her little journal, "acknowledged that he might have been imprudent, and Charlotte said she thought her mind would become calm. So we parted. The next day Mr. Cragin tendered his sympathies to Mr. Miller, and begged him not to be so sensitive, assuring him that we all loved him, and that what had taken place was an external affair.... Charlotte remains distressed. Alas! That I should be an apple of discord in a family to whom I am under such untold obligations! But this seems to be my fate."

Under the influence of an interview with Noyes, Mary admitted that she did love John Miller more than she had been aware. "I still love Mr. Miller as well as ever, but with a firm determination to infringe on no one's rights. 'Love worketh no ill to his neighbor.' I will just add that I think Charlotte has not been jealous of me without cause." Beneath the placid surface, the atmosphere in which this little band was living was surcharged with excitement. The air crackled with the suppressed conflict of sacred and profane love. The little army awaited its orders to advance.

John Noyes and Mary Cragin fell into the habit of strolling off by themselves under the cathedral-like arches of towering trees. One evening, deep in the discussion of some point concerning heavenly association, upon which Mary was seeking special instruction, they wandered far from the village. Before either realized the distance they had covered, fatigue overcame them, and

(Courtesy of Mrs. Albert Kinsley)

MARY CRAGIN

(The only portrait extant)

(*Courtesy of Mrs. Albert Kinsley*)

GEORGE CRAGIN

(From an early portrait)

a common impulse led both to sink down upon the inviting surface of a flat rock. Under the magic of the stars and the pulsating breath of the night, their stilted theological vocabulary was transformed into one of almost inarticulate murmurs. Words could no longer express what they had to say to each other. The painful ecstasy of this effort to remain apart—the temptation to merge bodies into a complete unity produced a sort of exquisite torture. On this we have John Noyes's testimony.

Noyes resisted that imperious impulse with all the strength of his will. "I said to myself, *I will not steal!* I resolved in my mind, as before God, what to do, and when I thought of going home for confession and consultation with those who had rights in the case, I got a signal that that was the true thing to do. After a moment we arose and went toward home. On the way we stopped once and took some liberty of embracing, and Mrs. Cragin distinctly gave me to understand that she was ready for the full consummation. I said, 'No, I am going home to report what we have done.' On reaching Mr. Cragin's house, I called a meeting of the four, related our doings, and offered the transaction for criticism. A searching talk ensued; Mr. Cragin at first was tempted to think I was following in the footsteps of the man who had given him so much trouble years before; but he soon recognized the difference between my course and that of his old enemy, and finally gave judgment of approval. My wife promptly and entirely sanctioned our proceeding. The upshot of the conference was, that we gave each other full liberty all round, and so entered into complex marriage in the quartette form. The last part of the interview was as amicable and happy as a wedding, and a full consummation soon followed." Thus Noyes arrived at the position toward which his path had led since the writing of the *Battle-Axe* letter. John and Mary entered upon a second honeymoon, and George Cragin and Harriet followed in their footsteps with the docility of true believers.

Their secret became an open one among the inner group, and gradually the nucleus grew. Still, all were not ready for the advance in Bible communism as a letter, written about August 1, 1846, indicates. John Miller had not yet succeeded in throwing off the shackles of mundane morality. In a letter, slightly unusual from brother to sister, we find John Noyes addressing Harriet concerning the husband of her sister Charlotte: "'He that doubteth is damned if he eat.' Mr. Miller doubteth. His last position in conversation with me was that he would not do again what he did on the road from Clarendon. He stands opposing my theory and withholding submission. Yet he is availing himself of the privileges of my theory. He embraced Mrs. Cragin last evening. What advances he is making to you I know not. But I wish you to be on your guard. You must tell him you will not allow him to do anything which he thinks is wrong and will be ashamed of afterwards, for to him such things are licentious. I cannot go along with him until he has decisively adopted our principles and has put himself wholly into my hands. He will need much discipline, and he has never yet shown that he knew the value of discipline. He will need to be instructed in regard to secretiveness and the law in relation to propagation before he can safely be trusted with liberty. But in his present spirit and position I cannot instruct him. I wish you therefore to hold yourself aloof from him, or at most to coquette with him, and not allow him to feel free with you until he openly avows our principles and submits to my instructions."

By August 18, John Miller expressed his faith in John Noyes as a guide through these uncharted regions of experience. "I believe that God is able and willing to show me the whole truth on this subject in due time, and I will wait patiently. Your whole past life has been such as to inspire me with confidence. I can point to no one act which I do not think was right and directed by the spirit of God. In all my past difficulties I can plainly see the hand of God directing them for my good."

3

The case of Lucinda Lamb added fuel to the spreading conflagration of village protest. Miss Lucinda Lamb was drawn into the Community circle through her friendship with Helen Campbell. During the winter of 1846-1847 these two Putney girls were pupils at a seminary for young ladies in Charlestown, Massachusetts. Helen was twenty; Lucinda was only fifteen. Helen received letters from Mr. John R. Miller; and, because her parents had been among the earliest converts to John Noyes's Perfectionism, was thoroughly familiar with the doctrines of the Putney group. Dr. Alexander Campbell and his wife, Achsah Richardson Campbell, had become followers of Noyes as early as 1835. Helen's father had passed away in 1839; and his position as a leading physician in Putney had been taken over by his son John, Helen's stepbrother.

In May, 1847, John Miller seems to have undertaken the conversion of Helen and her elder sister Emma, who was then twenty-four years old. Mr. Miller engaged Mrs. Campbell in a plain talk concerning the spiritual welfare of her daughters. Helen resisted his efforts. She was not yet ready to confess Christ. Miller urged her to talk with John Noyes, who was so much better qualified to lead the young woman out of the dark wood of confusion in which she was wandering. Helen was in great distress of mind; yet John Miller was certain she would come to him. Such a conversion, it was hoped, would exert a tremendous influence upon all the younger set in Putney. Yet in the letters that passed, there is a hint that Mrs. Achsah Campbell entertained certain misgivings concerning John Miller's preoccupation with the spiritual welfare of her daughters. We find Miller writing to Mrs. Campbell (May 11, 1847) that "in all my association with Emma and Helen my only motive has been to bring them to the knowledge and confession of the truth. If you or they supposed that I had any other motive, you have altogether undervalued my friendship."

The conversion of Lucinda set off the fuse of Putney's pent-up rage. Already townsfolks were whispering concerning the "goings on" in the families of the "Noyesites." Despite the policy of "Bible secretiveness," which permitted withholding facts from those who were babes in their comprehension of the higher wisdom, the group could not live in air-tight seclusion. Tradespeople, servants, and village gossips could, and did, distort facts and fabricate rumors on the basis of slight truth. Foes of the new doctrine were horrified to discover that Noyes and his group were attempting to draw in innocent young girls—the very "flowers" of their village. Still, conversions were soon made. Almost before May was half over, the Campbell girls were drawn in. On the evening of May 20, John Miller coolly called upon Lucinda to explain that, before entering a serious conversation with her concerning the deeper things of the Spirit, he would first seek to obtain her father's consent. The following morning he called Mr. Lamb into the Perfectionist store, and with George Noyes, they went upstairs. There John Miller told Mr. Lamb that he wished to invite Lucinda to attend their meetings at the Chapel. The father gave his consent reluctantly.

Exulting over his success with Mr. Lamb, John Miller hurried over to impart this news to Lucinda herself. She was delighted that her father had given his consent, and promised to join Miss Emma Campbell that very evening in a soul-searching talk with John Noyes. "Is not this first-rate?" Mr. Miller asked Helen Campbell. "I feel as though I were in a powerful revival, and that it will not stop here."

Less than a week later, the little group jubilantly celebrated the winning of these three novices. Harriet Skinner broke the good news to George Cragin, away on one of his missions. "The old Château is a bower of foliage and blossoms. But our spiritual bloom is more remarkable. Emma, Helen and Lucinda, the flowers of the village, were all at our meeting last evening, regular participants at our Lord's supper. What new-born feelings! John was delighted. To finish we danced, and George and Mr. Woolworth saw the damsels home."

Antagonists of the Community hurried to Lucinda's father. Perhaps it was the indignant Dr. John Campbell, Helen Campbell's step-brother, who whispered his suspicions into the ears of Lucinda's amazed parent.

Therefore to postpone the initiation of Lucinda was the better part of discretion and delicacy. John selected the youthful George as mediator to visit Mr. Lamb. John Miller went with him, and persuaded Mr. Lamb of their innocence. "But the next day her father changed his mind," Harriet wrote to George Cragin, "and without knowing that the covenant had been made, desired Lucinda not to join any church, but to have a conversation with the Rev. Mr. Foster! . . . Something is going (on) every day. You must not expect this prize is carried off and nothing said. The church and the village are astir, people are taking sides, gossips are lively, men collect in the corners of the streets, suspicious conjunctions are observed. . . ."

The Perfectionists gathered in the parlor for their evening meeting. The case of Lucinda was exhaustively discussed. The village seemed to be in arms against them—and angry whispers circulated concerning this "seduction" of one of the fairest of village maidens. Their foes had opened the eyes of Mr. Lamb. What should they do? The rebellious young lady was, next day, to be shown the error of her ways, by Rev. Mr. Foster. After the meeting a solution seemed to come to John, and he went up to Harriet Skinner's room to discuss it. She wrote Cragin: "John has just been up here with a fancy. What if George should go tomorrow morning and ask Lucinda if she will marry him, and then ask Mr. Lamb's consent? (One of Mr. Lamb's great troubles is that John dictates our marriages, but he has signified his acceptance of George for his daughter.) This would be a perfect counter-check to the plans of the enemy, and place Lucinda independent of her parents under John's instruction. George makes no reply, but the morning will decide. So good night. . . .

"Thursday morning, bright and beautiful: Mr. Lamb has just gone by with a horse and wagon. George has seen Lucinda and invited her to ride this afternoon; is considering John's fancy with favor."

With all the obstinacy of youth, and through the very opposition of her father and the village gossips, Lucinda remained firm in her new convictions. Although she was prevented from attending their meetings, and every movement she made was watched, she managed to convey secret messages indicating that her father, with his clerical counselors, planned to send her away, out of the State, far beyond the influence of her newfound friends. When this news came to Noyes he decided to write a formal protest to Mr. Lamb.

The haughty tenor of Noyes's epistle seems to have driven Mr. Lamb to a violent and immediate decision. Weeping and rebellious, the girl was bundled off to relatives in Massachusetts, and nothing could now come of John's plan to make her the wife of George. It may have been a belated realization of the serious nature of Putney's indignation that hastened a double wedding the following month (July 12, 1847). Young George Noyes was married to Helen Campbell and William H. Woolworth to Emma Campbell. There was no orthodox religious ceremony. Once more Larkin G. Mead was called upon to effect this compromise with "external law."

Adversaries congratulated Mr. Lamb upon the "narrow escape" of his daughter. So, like the elusive Abigail Merwin, Lucinda fades out of the Perfectionist drama. Today the privileged may gaze upon Lucinda's portrait, hanging in an old Putney house. The primitive *naïveté* of this painting only faintly suggests the mutinous spirit of this damsel of fifteen. In it Lucinda is all innocence and obedience. She stares out at the intruding visitor a veritable lamb of God.

In the spring of the same year, 1847, Lydia, wife of Dr. John Campbell, obtained knowledge of certain astounding facts by cross-examining Harriet Skinner. A family tempest followed this disclosure. Achsah Campbell entreated Lydia to request an examination in person from Noyes. "I do not believe that men or even devils can deceive you," she said to Lydia. Accompanied by Helen Campbell, Lydia called on Noyes. He gave them the explanation they asked. After conversing with several others of the Noyes household, Lydia was finally convinced that Noyes was right, and without pressure from him, she persuaded Mrs. Achsah Campbell. Mrs. Achsah Campbell tried to persuade Dr. John Campbell, her step-son, to talk with Noyes, but Dr. Campbell refused. He too was thenceforth definitely allied with the "enemies."

4

Disease was to be banished, and Death abolished in the good time coming. The last result of Christ's victory over sin and the Devil would be the abolition of Death. Bodily ailments, Noyes proclaimed, grew out of the central "lust of the flesh." Anxiety about the body, encouraged by physicians—the celebrated Dr. Graham was one of the worst offenders—grew out of this besetting sin. "Body tenders," Noyes named all who placed physical well-being above the life of the spirit.

This was the period in our national history when faith healing was gaining a foot-hold in all classes and states of society. New theories—mesmerism, magnetism, mental healing—were being read, talked about, practiced even in the stronghold of the orthodox and the Puritan. Though without success, magnetism had earlier been practiced in the community group. The fact that it was the dissenting Alexander Wilder who introduced it did not diminish the influence of its theories.

In a series of lectures delivered in Putney, Noyes declared his absolute independence of all the medical systems in the world. Christ was declared to be the only physician of the Community. Dr. John Campbell remained skeptical, and the orthodox of Putney jeered at Noyes's claims. This spurred him on to undertake the cure of Mrs. Harriet Hall. For eight years this Putney woman had been a hopeless invalid. She had been forbidden by the doctors even to walk or stand on her feet. Then, after three years, total blindness came over her. Some time in 1843, after she was converted to Noyes's doctrine of perfect holiness, the invalid was transported to the home of the Noyeses. Under his ministrations she regained ability to walk and to see. But upon her return home, his patient fell back into her state of prostration and darkness, and lost all faith in John Noyes. Yet, incredibly enough, on November 2, 1845, this invalid was married to Mr. Daniel J. Hall. Daniel, it seems, was an infidel. "I was barely able to sit up long enough to go through the marriage ceremony," the bride later confessed. "After this I was separated still farther from Mr. Noyes and at last became as nearly a skeptic as my husband." But her two sisters and a brother renewed fellowship with John Noyes, and they persuaded Mrs. Hall to permit him to undertake a second cure.

"On the twenty-second of June Mr. Noyes in company with Mrs. Cragin visited me. I was at that time in a very low condition, lower than ever before. I was unable to move or be moved without excruciating pain. A mere crack of the window below the curtain was all that I could endure. Yet I expected to be healed, and even to go home with Mr. Noyes at his first visit, and had told my husband so that very morning.

"Mr. Noyes at one time spoke of going home, but I could not believe that he would go till I could go with him. At length I told him that I would do anything that he would bid me. He told me to sit up in the bed. I did so with ease. He then commanded me with great energy to 'get up,' and taking me by the hand, led me to a chair. Without pain and with great delight I sat before the window. Mrs. Cragin raised the curtain and let in the blaze of day. My eyes were perfectly well, and drank in the beauty of a world all new to me with wonderful pleasure. I was constrained to declare again and again that I was perfectly well. I called for work, and found myself able to knit with facility. It was soon determined that I should go home with Mr. Noyes and Mrs. Cragin. I was immediately stripped by my sisters and Mrs. Cragin of my extra flannels and caps and my grave clothes in general, and in an ordinary dress without spectacles or veil I took my seat in the carriage and rode two miles in the light of a midday summer's sun without the least fatigue. That was indeed a joyful ride. I was conscious of perfect health. All pain had vanished."

She was restored to health again—so Mrs. Hall was convinced. Her appetite returned. She began to attend the evening home meetings, the Sunday meetings at the Perfectionist chapel. Gradually she learned to recover the use of her limbs; she taught herself, like a little child, to walk. The jubilant Perfectionists advertised this victory over disease. It was, they claimed, an authentic miracle. But the Rev. Hubbard Eastman, the Rev. Mr. Foster, Dr. David Allen, Dr. John Campbell and the rest of the village cynics jeered at this new example of the overwhelming impudence of "that John Noyes!" Noyes, writing on July 3, 1847, declared that he had been challenged to a public contest with death. "I made up my mind not to go to her until I could go in the fullness of faith, and I had an assurance that my dealings with her at this time would not be like those of the former trial but swift and decisive." He described the "cure" in dramatic terms. Subsequently, under the influence of the storm of "Putney unbelief," Harriet Hall suffered a relapse. Yet eventually she was taken to Oneida on a cot, and recovered sufficiently to live to the age of seventy-four.

For months Mary Cragin sought to save the life of a young girl, Mary Knight, doomed by tuberculosis, but her ministrations failed. Mary died on September 2, 1847, during the absence of John and Harriet Noyes. The bitterest enemies of the heresy now met and plotted the downfall of the absent leader; they took secret oaths that the little sect should be smashed to pieces, and its adherents driven out of Vermont.

5

John and Harriet Noyes went to central New York, representing the Putney group at the two important Perfectionist conventions held in September, 1847. The first meeting was called by John B. Foot, and assembled on the third of September at the Baptist Meeting-house in Lairdsville, Oneida County, New York. Foot's object in calling the convention was to increase friendship and to further the spirit of coöperation among Perfectionists. Specifically, he mentioned his invitation to Noyes and the Community at Putney, and expressed a desire that this meeting might result in unity of the east and west branches of the sect. Jonathan Burt was chosen moderator, and William H. Cook secretary. In a long speech against "fussing and fixing things for God to do," Charles Jones of Deruyter seemingly directed his fire against Noyes. The address precipitated a discussion of John's character and position, and the majority expressed satisfaction with the claims of the Putney leader.

That afternoon Noyes preached. While Noyes was speaking, Alexander Wilder and Dr. Lee stalked in, and later in the day Jones launched into a terrific tirade against the pretended cure of Harriet Hall. The next morning when the meeting opened Foot spoke of Jones's accusations. Despite the opposition of Noyes's adversaries, the Lairdsville convention expressed its faith in Noyes by unanimously passing these resolutions:

"*Resolved*, That we heartily approve of the general course of the press at Putney, and believe it to be an appointed and useful agency of God.

"*Resolved*, That we will coöperate with the brethren at Putney by circulating their publications, procuring subscriptions, and furnishing means and matter for the paper."

The second Perfectionist convention was called also by John B. Foot. This meeting was at Genoa, Cayuga County, New York, opening on September 17, 1847, and continuing three days. A committee consisting of Noyes, Edward Palmer 2nd, John B. Foot, John Corwin and William H. Cook reported two series of resolutions, among them the following:

"*Resolved,* That we will devote ourselves exclusively to the establishment of the Kingdom of God; and as that kingdom includes and provides for all interests, religious, political, social and physical, we will not join or coöperate with any other organization.

"*Resolved,* That, as the Kingdom of God is to have an external manifestation, and as that manifestation must be in some form of association, we will acquaint ourselves with the principles of heavenly association, and train ourselves to conformity with them as fast as possible.

"*Resolved,* That one of the leading principles of heavenly association is renunciation of exclusive claim to private property.

"*Resolved,* That it is expedient immediately to take measures for forming a heavenly association in Central New York.

At the end of the day these resolutions were passed without a dissenting voice.

Sunday afternoon Noyes urged believers to enlist in the army of heaven, to substitute Christ for death, to make no excuses on account of worldly engagements. His discourse was followed by a full surrender of many hearts to the call of Christ. With great fervor the strongest men of the convention came forward and pledged "their lives, their fortunes, and their sacred honor" for the enterprise of "establishing the Kingdom of God in this world."

6

While the Noyeses were thus occupied, the conflict in Putney was increasing in intensity. Four days after the death of Mary Knight, Mary Cragin brought twins into the world. They were named Victor and Victoria. Mrs. Achsah Campbell acted as midwife. "I thought... I should have an easy time," Mary wrote to Harriet Noyes. "Instead I had a hard time and now sit up very little. But I am perfectly satisfied. Nobody has heard me say, I shall die, for my faith has never wavered, not even when Death was staring me in the face.... My heart is with you both, and my thoughts sleeping and waking wander off and bring you before me hourly. How glad I shall be to see you!" Victoria survived only a few days. The son was named Victor Cragin Noyes.

In the face of all ordeals, in the face of the gathering storm, Mary Cragin wrote a poem expressing the new joy that welled up from the depths of her being. It was published in *The Spiritual Magazine:*

The earth, ice-bound by winter's chilling sway,
Lies lifeless as in funereal array;
No genial warmth her frozen bosom thaws;
Her pulse stands still 'neath Nature's sterner laws.
But when to Spring the desolator yields,
And life's glad warmth broods o'er the grateful fields,
Then, bubbling up from myriad secret stores,
And rushing out through countless unseen pores,
Those juices flow which yield earth's fruits and flowers
And clothe the hills with glorious forest bowers.
'Tis thus with hearts; unblest by love's warm rays,
In death's drear barrenness men pass their days—
Blind to the boundless treasures heaven holds.
But when love's sunshine dawns upon the heart
New hopes, new joys, new powers, its beams impart;
Its quickening fire invigorates the mind;
'Tis health and hope and joy and zeal combined.
Ye weary moralists, who vainly toil
To plow and fertilize a frozen soil,
Behold your only hope—the fount of bliss—
God's perfect love—the sun of righteousness;
'Tis rising, and shall renovate the earth;
Destroy all evil; to all good give birth.

The birth of Mary Cragin's twins was looked upon as of no concern to the townspeople of Putney, and there is no evidence of any birth record. But with curiosity sharpened to the utmost, the enemy, without doubt, suspected much that went on within the hollow square.

Rumors of the "complex marriage" system among the Putney Perfectionists proved to be too much for the slow-witted Clifford Clark. Was his own precious wife involved? If not already, she soon would be, decided Mr. Clark. To Brattleboro Clifford rushed, poured out his troubles to a lawyer, came back in hot haste, and removed his two children from danger of infection, placing them in the home of the equally indignant Hubbard Eastman, the Methodist minister. To that scandalized pastor, Clifford Clark confessed everything. Impelled by some inexplicable automatism of his subnormal mind, Clifford Clark immediately repented and was received back in the camp of the Perfectionists; but the secret was out.

Ever since the "miracle" wrought on his wife, Daniel Hall had been a trusted friend of the Association. He was making rapid advances into the faith—he had progressed far enough to hear from the lips of the leader himself the attractions of community life.

Such revelations were given with the idea of furthering the enlistment of Daniel Hall, but they failed dismally. Within a week Mr. Hall drove deliberately down the country road toward Brattleboro, and there reported the Putney scandal to the State's Attorney. The latter presented this evidence to the Grand Jury.

Without a dissenting voice the eighteen shocked Grand Jurors of Windham County had found a bill against the Putney heretic, charging that on June 10, 1847, he "with force and arms did carnally know one Fanny N. Leonard, she the said Fanny N. Leonard then and there being a married woman, the wife of one Stephen R. Leonard, and with her did commit adultery—contrary to the form, force and effect of the statute in such case made and provided, and against the peace and dignity of the State." Furthermore: that on the twentieth day of August . . . "at Putney aforesaid," Noyes "with her the said Achsah Campbell did have that intercourse and connection which in case the said Achsah Campbell had been a married woman would have constituted the crime of adultery."

On October 26, Noyes was arrested, and charged with adultery.

He was led before a Justice of the Peace at the local tavern. That dignitary turned out to be none other than Royall Tyler, an old schoolmate of Brattleboro.* Upon the advice of his attorney, W. C. Bradley, Noyes waived examination, and his old playmate held him for trial, under bond, for the next County Court. There was something ominous in the archaic document:

> Whereupon, the said Royall Tyler, Justice of the Peace as aforesaid, doth order and direct that the said John H. Noyes be held for trial before the County Court next to be holden at Newfane, within and for said County of Windham, on the fourth Tuesday of April next, by giving bonds, by way of recognizance, with sufficient security, in the sum of Two Thousand Dollars, to the Treasurer of the State of Vermont, conditional on his the said John H. Noyes's personal appearance before said Court, in answer to the things which shall then and there be objected to him on this behalf, and abide the judgment of said Court thereon.

The arrest had been conducted with the most punctilious courtesy. The sheriff apologized for his "unpleasant errand." John Miller furnished the necessary bond. Without a single word of insult, Noyes left the tavern court-room. But his own unrepentant

* The son of the famous chief justice of Vermont, who had achieved something like national fame as the author of "The Contrast," reputed to be the first American comedy, which the elder Tyler had published in 1790.

manner, as he strolled homeward through Putney, was more than enough to send the rage of his enemies to the boiling-point. He might have indeed been a visitor from Mars.

His countenance radiant and half-amused, his step elastic, buoyant, unashamed, his cane flourishing almost impudently, John Noyes suppressed his laughter until he reached the intimacy of the community home. There he recounted the whole adventure of his arrest. He had been in duress less than four hours that Indian summer day. As John recounted how he had parried wit with the lawyers, the Community all laughed and shouted with glee. The attorneys might have the first picking of this affair, Noyes told them; but the last word could not be determined by his arrest—nay, nor by his imprisonment either.

Larkin Mead, Noyes's brother-in-law, was horrified. He wrote at once to Mrs. Polly Noyes, visiting in Hamden, Connecticut, and the latter, never suspecting the facts, wrote to Charlotte. "Mr. Mead of course is dreadfully horrified, shudders, begs and warns, has wept and prayed. He is really to be pitied on some accounts, but in others he is only reaping what he has sown. He has never acted a manly part towards a confession of Christ, and now I don't know how he will come out unless he is an infidel. Poor Mary! I hope her tears are worthy of a bottle for future use."

Larkin Mead also wrote to John Miller, considering him without doubt as the most level-headed among the Putney group: "I was glad to hear from so good authority that you Perfectionists are not going to the devil. To all I hear of Putney affairs I have only to say, I am not able yet to associate in my mind the names of my dear family friends there with—adultery. When I become convinced that John's theological speculations end in a community of persons, I shall think the sooner he is shut up in some kind of a prison the better for all concerned. . . ."

Mary Noyes Mead hurried home to remonstrate with her brother John. But he soon recaptured her respect. "There are two or three particular days in my life that project into peculiar prominence," he wrote later. "The day I found Christ and gained victory over sin at New Haven was one. And there was one day in our terrible campaign at Putney that was as soul-stirring as any I ever saw. It was when Mary Mead came down from Montpelier to Putney. There was no time in the whole course of our trials when the storm beat so heavily as it did that morning. I went to my bedroom and lay down to think. My mind was in chaos—no light in any direction. All that I could say was, that God knew how things were going and would see that all went right. But it seemed as if the vindication of the truth was impossible, as if the Devil in the shape of law and brutality had won the entire advantage. While in that state of mind I had an inspiration as distinct as a voice from heaven, that victory had come, and that God would give me a sign of it immediately. In half an hour Mary came.

"The circumstances of her visit were these: Mr. Mead was in the Senate, and she was with him at Montpelier. When they heard about my arrest, she decided to come. She held her mind calm, and entreated Mr. Mead not to commit himself until he heard from her. The importance of her visit was greatly increased by the fact that she had the respect and confidence of the surrounding community. As Colonel Keyes said, she was 'not a woman to be humbugged,' and the people stood watching. They all expected her to fall upon us and sink us. And truly, her coming did not look like a sign of victory. To take a mind like hers fresh from the world and bring it up square to such tremendous doctrines as we professed and practiced seemed hopeless.... God took charge of the conversation. I had great freedom in setting before her our position. To my astonishment she yielded point after point, and took all quietly. When I had finished, she was satisfied that we were true and good people."

The village buzzed with excitement. Men congregated at the postoffice, discussed the "immorality" of the Perfectionists, threatened to drive "foreign" members out of town. If Noyes were innocent, demanded the Rev. Hubbard Eastman, why did he waive an examination before the Justice of the Peace? He could not have feared false witnesses, for were not the witnesses from his own group? If he were innocent, an examination should have resulted in honorable acquittal.

The next day John Noyes hastened off to Brattleboro. He called upon his brother Horatio, who was cashier of the Brattleboro bank. Scarcely able to believe his own ears, as John openly avowed his principles, Horatio, furious and blushing, resolved to go home to rescue his two younger sisters, Harriet and Charlotte, and his brother George, from this web of immorality.

Thursday evening the embarrassed and mortified Horatio appeared in Putney. Young George announced to his elder brother that they were all involved, and that they were willing to go to prison for their principles. Harriet and Charlotte appeared nettlingly cheerful and courteous. Their disgrace need not affect him, they assured Horatio. If he wished to help them, they insisted, he should take a calm, rational view of the situation—"to regard the matter not in the light of statute law but of common law, which says that if no one has been injured, no wrong has been done, and then to persuade such men as Chandler and Israel Keyes to let us alone till we hurt somebody." Charlotte and Harriet remained adamant. Even more helplessly furious than when he had come home, Horatio drove off. A disgrace to the whole family—he would wash his hands of the whole affair!

To her mother, temporarily boarding with the Dickermans in Hamden, Connecticut, Harriet wrote a long letter explaining everything. Poor Mother Noyes! Had she read that they were all dead, the shock could not have been greater. Her cup of bitterness was overflowing—she could only thank God that she was not in Putney, where she had been respected for twenty-five years. Thoughts and feeling rushed upon her so swiftly that Mrs. Noyes sat down on her bed to keep from reeling. Something of the sort had been hinted during the summer, she recollected, but she had never credited such rumors. "They will do no wrong!" she managed to reassure herself; "they cannot; God will not suffer it." It was indeed providential that Mrs. Dickerman and Caroline were away from home. Mrs. Noyes managed to regain her composure by the time the two ladies returned, and said nothing about Harriet's letter.

In Putney, the disgraced Perfectionists calmly went on preparing the next issue of *The Spiritual Magazine*, to be published the first of November. On November 26, Larkin Mead and William Bradley sent word to John Noyes and Miller, requesting them to come at once to Brattleboro. There they learned that warrants for the arrest of George and Mary Cragin were in the hands of the sheriff. A long discussion ensued. Seeking the best and easiest way out of the whole business, which was intensely distasteful to him, Larkin Mead recommended that all Perfectionists who were not actual residents of Putney should disperse without delay. John Noyes should not return to Putney at all, it was decided, but should leave that very evening for Boston.

"We shall beat the devil at this game!" With a burst of laughter John Noyes danced across the law office and snapped his fingers in high spirits. Larkin Mead glanced disapprovingly at his brother-in-law. A stiff jail sentence, he was convinced, would put a stop to such untimely capers.

It was arranged that the Goulds should leave the Community next morning for central New York; that Louisa Tuttle should go home to Connecticut; and that the Burnhams should return to northern Vermont. Other "foreigners" were directed to leave without unnecessary delay. John Miller was appointed leader of the strategy of this retreat.

Returning to Putney, George Cragin broke the news to Mary. They commenced hurried preparations for departure. At midnight they fortified themselves with supper, and then waited nervously for the sound of the carriage at the door. It was two in the morning when William Hinds, the fourteen-year-old store boy, drove up with faithful old Bob. Mary stepped into the carriage, and George followed with the sleeping Victor. As William Hinds drove them through the dark road of the hillside village, they knew that, at any moment, they might be hailed and arrested by officers of the law. Just a mile outside Brattleboro, their hearts seemed to stop. A man was approaching them. He stopped the carriage—and inquired the way to Dummerston. Mary's fright subsided after that; they passed through Brattleboro at dawn, and offered thanks to God that their progress into Connecticut had not been hindered.

At about one o'clock after noon of the next day they crossed Mill River. Old Bob had already been watered, but George Cragin insisted that Willie Hinds stop again. On an eminence overlooking the river stood a little inn. As they glanced up at it, they saw a man standing at the door. It was none other than John Noyes. Scheduled to take the early stage to Boston, Noyes had left Brattleboro the previous evening. He had decided to go instead to Leverett, Massachusetts. It was a miraculous reunion, they all agreed. "If we had gone by without stopping to water old Bob," William Hinds liked to explain, "we should not have seen him."

They were with the Silas Morgans in Leverett that evening. Three months old, Victor endured like a little soldier this flight of forty miles over rough roads. The older Cragin boys had been left under the care of Mrs. Harriet Noyes. On Monday Noyes went on to Boston, and thence back again to Hamden, where his mother was staying with the Dickermans. The Cragins remained with the Morgans at Leverett until Wednesday morning. They proceeded to Amherst, thence by stage and railway to Wallingford. From Wallingford, after dark, a private carriage took them to the Dickerman home at Hamden.

Mary Cragin and little "Vic" met with a chilling reception by the Dickermans, even though little Victor behaved like a gentleman. Mrs. Polly Noyes, however, received the outcasts with cheering warmth. To Mary the atmosphere became so cold that she embraced the opportunity, as soon as she conveniently could, to move over to the Tuttles', where the exiles received a hearty welcome. Mrs. Dickerman, with whom the elder Mrs. Noyes was boarding, was in a state of great tribulation, not so much with regard to the new doctrines of sexual morality as on the ground of confidence in John's divine mission.

Noyes and Cragin planned to establish themselves in New York. Noyes compared this expulsion from Putney to the driving of Paul to Rome. The Kingdom of God assaulted the religious dynasties at New Haven, was driven out, took refuge in Putney, and there assaulted the civil powers. Again it had been apparently driven out. Its final resting place might soon be at the center of both religious and civil power–New York. Putney was not up with the times in religion and revolutionary progress. New York, after hearing Fanny Wright, Fourier, Bush and Davis, might listen to John Noyes with more moderation. So he mused. In New York he had been crucified. Perhaps he would now be called to deliver his great final testimony there. At all events, New York should be his temporary headquarters.

7

The exodus of John Noyes, the Cragins, and other disciples added new fuel to the fury of the hillside village. On the evening of December 2, indignant citizens met at the vestry of the Congregational meeting-house "for the purpose of taking into consideration the outrageous proceedings of the Perfectionists, so-called." They organized by appointing Preston W. Taft chairman and William Houghton secretary. On motion of Dr. John Campbell, a committee of five was appointed to draft and report some appropriate resolutions at a future meeting. "Israel Keyes, Esq., Rev. A. Foster, Rev. H. Eastman, Hon. John Kimball and James Keyes, Esq., were appointed said committee."

On the following Monday, resolutions demanding the immediate dissolution of the Perfectionist association were unanimously adopted. "Perfectionists ought to renounce those principles which tend to or do violate the statute laws of the state; that those persons in this town who receive serious injuries from said Association ought to be suitably remunerated by said Association; that the editors of the *Vermont Phœnix*, *Windham County Democrat*, *Semi-Weekly Eagle*, and *Bellows Falls Gazette*, be respectfully requested to publish the proceedings of this meeting and that the Secretary furnish each of them with a copy of the same."

How respectable Brattleboro estimated the Putney Perfectionists is indicated by an editorial published in the *Vermont Phœnix:*

"When such monstrous doctrines as these are promulgated and practiced, and when there is such indubitable evidence as the history of this sect has furnished us, to prove that the young, the innocent and the unsuspicious, are enticed to disgrace and ruin by them, and that systematic seduction and licentiousness are practiced under the specious garb of religion—or rather made impiously a part of religion itself—it is time for the public press to expose the true character of its principles, and warn the young and credulous, at least, of the snares that are spread for them."

Indeed, newspapers of the whole Vermont countryside unanimously condemned Noyes and his Perfectionist disciples. Putney respectability boiled over in renewed fury. Public indignation meetings were held almost nightly; committees of visitation were appointed; resolutions were passed affirming that the community must be dissolved. Arrests were made, suits commenced, writs of attachment issued, mob violence threatened, vows taken that "Perfectionism" should be killed in the seed. Members of the community were left without a shepherd! Yet not wholly—still gallant and unflinching stood John R. Miller, John L. Skinner, George W. Noyes, Harriet A. Noyes, Harriet H. Skinner, and Charlotte A. Miller.

Gradually, however, after days of anxiety the storm seemed to be dying down; then on the morning of December 13, Gates Perry, deputy sheriff, called with two writs against John Noyes. The writs were for $3,000, and Perry attached the real estate, even wished to attach the Perfectionist store, but was persuaded to give that up. Then came the rumor that Mr. Lamb would prosecute George for his offer to Lucinda.

They gleaned some consolation from the discord that broke out among their opponents at the town meeting held at the Congregational meeting-house. When Dr. John Campbell wrathfully spoke against Noyes, he was heckled by certain young fellows in one corner. Nevertheless, a Vigilance Committee, consisting of five, was appointed—John Campbell, Israel Keyes, Timothy Underwood, and two others. John Miller and young George almost collapsed under this new threat. Emma and Helen made matters worse by their complete discouragement and plaints against their new isolation.

Enemies of the Perfectionists continued in their wrath. Now they talked of prosecuting the Corporation for gross lewdness and similar offenses against "chastity, morality and decency," named in the ninety-ninth chapter of the Revised Statutes of Vermont. Noyes and his followers should not, the enemy protested to Larkin

G. Mead, be permitted to inculcate principles subversive to moral and statute laws. Even a promise of external conformity would not be enough—as long as they continued to publish Noyes's principles, such behavior would be an insult and a mockery to Putney virtue.

Although he continued loyally as their legal defender, the sputtering, outraged Larkin harshly berated John to his relatives. If he continued carrying out such principles in New York, Mr. Mead assured John Miller, Noyes would soon be transferred to the city prison.

After a long silence Noyes wrote to Miller from New York City that he would not abandon the testimony that the Kingdom of God had commenced, nor acknowledge that they had done wrong. That was out of the question. He would suffer, cheerfully, the spoiling of goods, or imprisonment, or death rather than bend in that way. He refused to concede either to friends or enemies the right to stop his mouth or muzzle his press. The threat of losing two thousand or ten thousand dollars would not deter him from speaking what justice to God and man demanded. Yet he would not brave public opinion unnecessarily.

George Cragin and Noyes found lodging in a parlor on the first floor of sympathetic Catherine Wadsworth's house, genteel with carpet, glass ornaments, eight mahogany chairs, and sideboard. A bed had been placed in the room; and there was a cozy coal fire. Catherine was delighted to wait on them, and willingly constituted herself the factotum of the Putney exiles. Perfectionist company flowed in upon them. Noyes communicated his views to all who called, and was heard with interest and respect by his new disciples.

During this New York interlude, Noyes and Cragin held several sympathetic conferences with Thomas Cogswell Upham, the "Quietest," a distinguished mystic, and professor at Bowdoin. Upham shocked some of his associates by his fraternizing with the heretic from Putney

In New York, Noyes's only worry had been the thought of perils and pressures of the Putney family. It seemed unfair that he should go free and comfortable while they were left to face the storms of the irate villagers. But he reminded himself that his presence would only increase the fury of the storm, and that it would do his followers no good to see him imprisoned or assassinated. Throughout Windham County a report was now circulated widely that the Perfectionist heretic had "absconded"—had deserted his followers by a cowardly flight from justice. That he had evaded the consequences of his criminal conduct, abandoning his disciples, John Miller and John Skinner, to defend the little group against the fury of the Putney mob, was the unpleasant charge against Noyes circulated by the Rev. Hubbard Eastman, who was to publish a book entitled "Noyesism Unveiled" shortly after the excitement died down.

By dint of repetition, this charge grew into ugly legend; decades later it was revived by the dissentients of the Oneida Community. Noyes always denied it vigorously. He had not left Putney on account of the arrest and bonds, Noyes claimed in self-defense, since he remained there a month after the law had taken possession of his case; he went to Brattleboro because Mead had advised him that mob violence was impending; nor had he any thought of leaving Vermont when he had gone to Brattleboro, but had carried on his person a written proposal to surrender himself to the custody of the law without bail, on condition of the assurance of peace to the rest of his followers. Mead and Bradley disapproved of this proposal, he recalled, and advised his withdrawal. The same action was advised in the case of the Cragins. "The main point is that we left, not to escape the law, but to prevent an outbreak of lynch law among the barbarians of Putney." Noyes recalled the menace in the reported remark of Dr. John Campbell: "If there is no law that will break them up, the people of Putney will make law for the occasion." Previously Dr. Campbell had made a physical attack upon John Miller. "Who then were the law abiders, and who the law breakers?" Noyes demanded indignantly. "I was content to abide the issue and settle with the law as best I could. But Dr. John Campbell could not wait on the law, and he may thank his own turbulence that I escaped its clutches and saved him and his confederates from committing acts of disgraceful violence and perhaps murder."

The Millers and the Skinners found little consolation in facing the music in Putney. At Christmas time, John Miller was still receiving anonymous threats, one letter assuring him he would be tarred and feathered and ridden on a rail, if he did not leave town. The Meads, too, came to exert pressure. If John thought he was raised up to introduce this doctrine, Mary Mead assured them, she herself was raised up to put a stop to it.

But by January, Miller reported to the absent leader, even the bitterest opponents, ladies and gentlemen, began to drop in the Perfectionist store again. "It has been amusing. Ladies would come into the store with faces as long as a yardstick, and leave with their prettiest smiles.... Those who used to trade with us are anxious to get back.... People begin to say: 'Well, I shall trade with you, let folks say what they will.' Last Saturday, the store being open in the evening, so that the ladies could come under cover of night, we had our store full all evening. . . . Our most bitter enemies grow more and more mad as they see symptoms of our prosperity."

From New York, John Noyes sent words of encouragement, urging the little band at Putney to see things as God saw them, to hate the fire-eye of fanaticism and the fish-eye of unbelief: "Our warfare is an assertion of human rights; first, the right of man to be governed by God and to live in the social state of heaven; second, the right of woman to dispose of her sexual nature by attraction instead of by law and routine and to bear children only when she chooses; third, the right of all to diminish the labors and increase the advantages of life by association. These are certainly the dearest of all human rights, and we cannot spend or be spent better than in their defense.

"The governments of this world positively forbid the social state of heaven. . . . We have drawn the issue deliberately, and as humanely as possible. No one has been injured; no one directly concerned makes any complaint. All within our own circle are conscious of benefit. We have moved out of the fashion of this world soberly, cautiously, conscientiously, and after a long, severe course of preparatory education.

"Our position is defended on the spiritual side by open manifestations of the power and wisdom of God attending us; on the intellectual side by a complete and splendid theory of sexual rights and relations; on the moral side by great improvement in our characters; and on the physical side by many cases of healing and a general advance of health among us, promising ultimate victory over death.

"The head and front and whole of our offense is communism of love. No other charge is brought against us by our enemies. If this is the unpardonable sin in the world, we are sure it is the beauty and glory of heaven."

PART TWO

ONEIDA

Chapter I: COLONIES AND COMMUNITIES

. . . Not a scheme in agitation
For the world's amelioration
Has a grain of common sense in it
—Except my own.
—THOMAS LOVE PEACOCK.

I

THE era was one of disintegration. Portents of disaster, even of destruction for the nation, abounded. Many believed that the Union could not endure. Kabylism—the impulse to split up and to disperse into tribes—was a prevalent symptom of the early decades of the nineteenth century. The Mormons, under the leadership of Brigham Young, had just successfully completed their epic migration into the western desert, following in the footsteps of the Donner Party, which encountered so shocking a tragedy in the snows of the Sierras. Only a few years had elapsed since the Millerites had awaited in vain for the end of the world—had indeed set the very day in 1843, and had won such a following that all worldly affairs were settled by tremulous thousands. This day came, in 1843; came and passed, and yet survival by no means destroyed the faith of Miller's followers. Scattered like weeds over the continent, all sorts of theories proclaimed the immediate regeneration of society, the advent of a New Jerusalem. Josiah Warren's much-discussed doctrine of individual sovereignty, a sort of thorny anarchism, exercised a strong appeal to "rugged individualists." Fourierism was putting forth its ephemeral blossoms, known by the grandiose name of "phalanxes."

Catastrophism was in the air. The Abolitionist movement, headed by William Lloyd Garrison, was looked upon as a menace to the Union—as indeed it was. Every Utopian obsession somehow found a soil in which to strike root and flourish. No theory of social organization seemed so fantastic that it could not attract a little band of fanatical adherents. The very expanse of the North American continent, across which, even at the middle of the nineteenth century, the white race had as yet but faintly penciled in a vague outline of its civilization, invited social experimentation. When not to be had for the asking, land was almost dirt cheap. Natural resources seemed inexhaustible. To the dissatisfied, the gullible, the maladjusted and the adventurous, excursion rates to Utopia were offered by reformers, fanatics, or mere madmen gifted with the power of persuasion.

As early as 1824, Robert Owen had stirred the life of the

nation with his appeals to kings and congresses, and soon afterward inaugurated his vast experiments at New Harmony, Indiana.* At the age of fifty-four this prophet of a new social order succeeded in gathering, on a farm of no less than thirty thousand acres, a family of nine hundred members. The world thrilled at his grandiloquent promise. Owen's influence assumed the proportions of a religious revival. No less than ten smaller communities of the Owenite type were organized in various states. New Harmony lasted about three years; the others dispersed at the end of three months. Through lectures, newspaper publicity, and the organization of local societies, Owen, his son Robert Dale Owen, and that indefatigable prophetess, Frances Wright, disseminated this new Utopian seed, until some elements of the plan were even injected into the platform of the Democratic party.

In studying these unprecedented manifestations of social reform, young John Noyes had been sharply struck with the similarity between the unquenched craving for social reconstruction and the revival wildfire that had swept over the country nearly twenty years before. Each had two great leaders, each two eruptions of enthusiasm. Nettleton and Finney led the religious revivals; Owen and Fourier (by proxy) injected the virus of Utopianism into the imagination of all who hungered for escape from harsh realities. Between 1831 and 1833 Charles Finney swept the nation like a tempest. The religious movement and the social movement, as Noyes surveyed them, seemed to alternate. Neither seemed able to rivet the attention of the public at one and the same time. Between 1831 and 1834, the American people seemed on the point of surrendering all earthly ties for the Kingdom of Heaven. A decade later (1842-43), Fourier, with his enticing picture of an earthly paradise, awakened new hopes. Hypnotized by the siren song of Fourier's apostle, Albert Brisbane, the credulous felt that they stood at the threshold of a new Age of Harmony.

John Noyes was early convinced that salvation of soul and body could not be separately attained. Revolution must begin within. A man's deepest experiences, he insisted, were those of religion and love. These must be brought into the open—and were these not precisely the experiences about which men habitually remained silent? Noyes claimed that the great revivals and these laboratory experiments in socialism were among the most significant phases in American history. But both religion and social

* "The shrewd, gullible, high-minded, illustrious and preposterous father of Socialism and Coöperation"—so Lytton Strachey characterized Robert Owen. "Queen Victoria," p. 11.

experiment had failed to bring heaven to earth, because they despised each other; because they could not coördinate their two great animating energies. Noyes saw that the salvation of the soul, for which the revivalists had cried in the wilderness, could never be attained under the *status quo* of social chaos. Equally impossible was social revolution—"for want of regeneration of the heart."

Delving into various experiments in communal life on the North American continent, Noyes discovered that Robert Owen was not the pioneer in this field of social reconstruction. At the beginning of the nineteenth century, George Rapp had led away from persecution in Europe a little band of German burghers and peasants who thrilled with the anticipation of the imminent advent of Christ and the coming of the millennium. In 1803 Rapp sought refuge in America. He bought five thousand acres of land in Butler County, Pennsylvania. Six hundred disciples followed in 1804. In 1805 they organized their community on the model of the Pentecostal Church. Though their fare was hard, they lived down calumny and suspicion, and under their patient toil, the acres yielded rich harvests. In 1807, the community adopted celibacy; but in other respects they were not ascetics. They indulged in music, painting, even sculpture. To the envy of surrounding neighbors, they cultivated their gardens. Yet, homesick perhaps, for a gentler climate which might remind them of their native Württemberg, they sold all, and migrated to Indiana. On the banks of the Wabash they built up a new village—which once again they named Harmony. Their numbers increased to nearly a thousand; but soon these Rappites were on the march again, driven perhaps, by some strange herdlike or atavistic instinct. They found themselves back in Pennsylvania, in Beaver County, near Pittsburgh. There, at last, in a village which they named Economy, they settled permanently, boring oil-wells, accumulating wealth. Close union protected this sect from persecution, from pestilence, from false brethren. But in the end they succumbed to the virus of accumulated wealth.

These Rappites taught Robert Owen his first practical lesson in communism. From them he purchased the cultivated tract in Indiana. This Montgomeryshire "infidel" found, ready-made, the village those chidlren of faith had spent ten years in building up. When the migratory impulse had come upon them, the Rappites had sent as envoy Richard Flower, an Englishman, to interview Owen at New Lanark, and try to kindle his interest. Owen came, saw, and was conquered by this Utopia waiting only for the new social order to move in! Of the thirty thousand acres of land, three thousand were already under cultivation. There were nineteen detached farms; six hundred acres of improved land occupied by tenants; and a substantially planned and built village. He bought it all. Adherents flocked to this "New Harmony." The "industrious and well disposed of all nations" were invited—how soon was Owen to regret this promiscuous invitation! Within six weeks eight hundred men and women had accepted and that motley company was soon to grow to nine hundred. Inevitably, rapidly, black sheep crept into the fold. To the sputtering candle of Owen's idealism the needy, the defective, the discontented fluttered as moths to the flame. Indiscriminately, Robert Owen welcomed them all. Disconcerting incidents were excused on the ground that the change from an irrational to a rational society could not be accomplished overnight. Leaving all vexatious details of "transition" to his second-in-command, Robert Owen departed for Europe. When he sped back in January, 1826, Mr. Owen found all sorts of amusements flourishing. In the old Rappite Church a brass band blared; balls and concerts took up most of the evenings; five military companies did duty from time to time on the public square, and all at the expense of the founder. Differences of opinion soon led to the establishment of a second community, now also settled on the New Harmony estate.

In this lush, Utopian soil, the ignoble traits of human nature flourished like weeds. Though Robert Owen deluded himself into the belief that the community idea was making marked progress, it soon became imperative to abolish all offices and officers, and finally to appoint three worthies as a triumvirate. Dissatisfied adherents began to drift away. By December, 1826, an order decreeing the abolition of ardent spirits was prominently posted. With its nine hundred passengers, but with no captain or organized crew, Owen's ship was floundering helplessly to disaster. In consternation, Owen began to sell property to individuals. New Harmony was cut up into separate lots. Painted signboards began to appear on deserted buildings. On June 18, 1827, Robert Owen met his disillusioned followers to bid them a bitter farewell.

Owen had based this venture upon an ingenuous assumption of common honesty among his adherents; he was repaid with dishonesty. He had hoped for temperance, and was rewarded with drunkenness. Instead of industry, habits of idleness were all too evident. Dirt instead of cleanliness; waste instead of thrift; apathy instead of an appetite for knowledge—these were the successive steps to his complete disillusion. If the thousand persons who gathered at New Harmony had possessed all those sterling qualities of character which Owen naïvely assumed, there would have been small possibilities of attracting them to the community. Owen had never thought of that. Certain die-hards remained after the catastrophe. Among these survivors Socialism became an almost forbidden name. They were nauseated by their protracted diet of idealistic theories, appetizing to the inexperienced palate, but wormwood and gall to those who witnessed and lived through the recession of the new harmony into ancient discord.

Poor Robert Owen! This metaphysician of the old school, his idealism suckled, without doubt, on Jean Jacques Rousseau, endowed with an innate talent for fault-finding and intellectual negation—this cautious, thrifty son of a saddler, long habituated to the servility of cotton-mill hands, or to his New Lanark disciples, possessed no technique to defend himself against the "rugged American individualism" of that migratory era, against rogues who unerringly sniffed out his weaknesses. While he professed his conversion to socialism, Owen still held title to those thirty thousand acres he had bought from the equally canny Rappites; but his armor of idealism proved to be no protection against scoundrels who insinuated themselves into his confidence, exploited his vanity, swindled him, and deceived him in a manner worthy of the mad extravagance of a Ben Jonson comedy. Taylor and Fauntleroy, for instance, became Owen's associates and counselors. When Taylor's rascality became evident even to Owen's deluded eyes, Owen managed to rid himself of this rascal only by granting him a large tract of land. Taylor promptly announced that he would form a community of his own. An agreement was signed that he should have the land and all upon it. But previous to the signing of this document, this precursor of the modern racketeer made sure that a large quantity of farming implements, as well as livestock, had been transferred to his section of the land. And then, instead of founding the community he had planned, he began to operate a distillery. To add to the troubles of New Harmony, Taylor was soon dispensing whiskey. To his dismay, Owen discovered that he was not dealing here with any starved, servile peasantry. These Yankees retailed whiskey under his very nose. Taylor's distillery only hastened the castrophe—and it twisted the knife in the wounded spirit. A few years later this disillusioned Socialist sought refuge in the spectral comforts of nineteenth-century spiritualism. This mild opiate helped him to forget Taylor and his rascality and all the rest of the Utopian saturnalia at New Harmony. The fault, Owen reassured himself, was never in his own theories, but in the ineradicable depravity of human nature.

2

In 1842 young Albert Brisbane returned to his native land, bearing aloft the banner of the incomparable Fourier, celebrated inventor of a panacea for all social disorder. In Paris, this wealthy young American had studied the ideas of all the great French reformers and reconstructors—the Saint-Simons, the Comtes, the Considérants, the Cousins. Theories of socialism were boiling merrily in the French *pot-au-feu* of the late thirties. Young Brisbane traveled far—to Greece, to Turkey. He had left his Buffalo home, a typical young American of the upper class, carrying with him all the conventional, dogmatic assumptions of his caste. Lacking nothing himself, he believed the world as it was could hardly be bettered. Greece awakened in young Mr. Brisbane the certainty that a woeful deterioration of man's estate had occurred since Pericles ruled Athens. By the time he had retraced his increasingly indignant steps to Paris, Brisbane's mind was awake and receptive for the message of social reconstruction. With burning interest he listened to the belligerent Saint-Simoneans, to the whole army of grandiloquent theorists and Utopians. Most impressive of all, to this susceptible young man from Buffalo, was the rosy vision of Charles Fourier.

When at last Albert Brisbane was ready to return to his native land, he had made the gospel of Fourier his very own. He was bent upon the establishment of "phalanxes" in all the states. To propagate this idea, Albert Brisbane made an arrangement with Horace Greeley for the outright purchase of a column in the New York *Tribune*. Albert Brisbane may be described as the original "columnist" of the American press. The widely-syndicated column of Arthur Brisbane, son of Albert, may be considered a direct heritage of this early venture in personal journalism. He put all conventional ideas of the typical American of the forties out of his head. He postponed marriage and the duty of raising a family. More important work confronted him. Albert Brisbane had already published "The Social Destiny of Man"—a little book which excited the Transcendentalists and laid foundations for an epidemic of social experiments.

Brisbane's articles at first appeared only twice a week; but in a few months they were appearing thrice a week, and then, due to growing interest, every day. A powerful rival, the New York *Herald*, twitted Horace Greeley as "our Fourierite contemporary." Albert Brisbane's agreement with Greeley gave him unrestrained freedom in publishing the ideas of his master. Before the growing

toward extreme individualism—toward an ideal of civil rebellion. Just as in the troubled realm of religion the Antinomians swung to a pole opposite the legalists, so in the realm of social theory, Josiah Warren promulgated the doctrine of "individual sovereignty." Warren had been a member of the Owen Community at New Harmony; and out of disillusion at that celebrated fiasco, developed his gospel of the unqualified supremacy of the individual—thus winning himself a place as one of the pioneer philosophers of anarchism. Elaborated to the smallest detail, his theories included detailed plans for "equitable commerce" and "labor exchange." After the failure of New Harmony, Josiah Warren appeared in Cincinnati. There he opened a "Time Store," and operated it long enough to demonstrate, so he claimed, the truth of his basic principles. He divided off a portion of this shop by a lattice-work containing many racks and shelves, upon which was a variety of small articles. In the center of this lattice an opening was left, through which the store-keeper handed out goods and took pay. On the wall, back of the store-keeper and facing the customer, like a presiding deity, hung a great open-faced clock, and underneath it a dial. Molasses, corn, buckets, dry-goods and other commodities cluttered up the store. On the wall, conspicuous enough for all to see, hung a board on which were placed bills that had been paid to wholesale merchants for all the articles in the store; also orders of individuals for various things. Walking up to the wicket, the customer might request the store-keeper to serve him with some glue. He was immediately asked if he had a "Labor note." If he replied in the negative, he was told that he must get some one's note. His object in going there might have been to find out if Mr. Warren would exchange labor with him; but the abrupt reception had a disconcerting quality and many departed hastily. Those who were not thus discouraged procured a written labor note, promising so many hours labor at so much per hour. Entering the Time Store with note and cash, such customers informed the keeper of their needs—a jug of molasses, a few yards of Kentucky jean, or a bag of corn. As soon as the clerk began conversation or business, he set the dial under the clock, and marked the *time*. He then attended to his client, handed out the articles asked for, and in return took cash to equal the wholesale price of the article, and time out of the customer's "Labor note" to equal the time spent in making the sale. Five per cent was added to the cash cost, to pay rent and to cover incidental expenses. The apostle of individual sovereignity characterized himself as a "peaceful revolutionist" and published a paper of that name at a village he endowed with the modest name of Utopia. Apparently, if we may trust his editorial entitled "A Peep into Utopia," Warren was an adept in negation. "No organization, no delegated power, no laws or by-laws, rules or regulations, but such as each individual makes for himself and his own business; no officers, no priests nor prophets have been resorted to; nothing of this kind has been in demand. . . . We build on individuality; any difference between us confirms our position. Differences, therefore, like the admissible discords in music, are a valuable part of our harmony." Noyes characterized this type of revolt as *Porcupinism.*

In this discordant, inchoate social scene, Noyes saw no dearth of malcontents. Our country seems perpetually to replenish its caste of dissenters—of those, colloquially, "ag'in" the *status quo.* Compared to some of them, Mr. Thoreau seemed a timid conformist. There was, for example, John Collins of Boston. An agent of the Massachusetts Anti-Slavery Society, Mr. Collins had become more and more radical in his dislike of the government. In a series of "articles of belief and disbelief," to advertise the community he proposed to start on his farm near Skaneateles, Collins proclaimed his disbelief in the rightful existence of all governments based upon physical force, declaring them all organized *banditti* whose authority was to be challenged. "We will not vote under such governments, or petition to them, but demand them to disband; do no military duty; pay no personal or property taxes; sit upon no juries; refuse to testify in courts of so-called justice; and never appeal to the law for a redress of grievances, but use all peaceful and moral means to secure their complete destruction."

With these no-government and non-resistance principles, John Collins set out sanguinely to found "the most radical and reformatory" colony yet attempted in North America. But by May, 1846, he was forced to confess that his venture had been premature, owing chiefly to the moral defects of those who had with alacrity accepted his invitation to become members. Like the disillusioned Robert Owen, John Collins abandoned his cherished schemes of philanthropy and social improvement, and soon was seeking refuge in "the decencies and respectabilities of orthodox Whiggery."

Brook Farm, too, crashed to an ignominious finale. On March 3, 1846, a great fire swept through that well-publicized phalanstery and extinguished its energies and hopes. Thus closed dramatically the final phase in the six years of Brook Farm's existence. Through *The Dial*, and later *The Harbinger*, the little band in Putney had watched with the closest attention every step of its progress—its inauguration under the banner of Fourier, its conversion to Swedenborgianism. Yet John Noyes had an instinctive distrust of Ralph Waldo Emerson and Margaret Fuller.

4

There was, however, one group of colonies, those of the Shakers, which possessed the power of survival. These were like monasteries for both sexes, and had been founded by the followers of Mother Ann Lee. Their earliest communal home had been established in 1776, at Neskeyuna, New York. Toward the close of the eighteenth century, these monastic farms were established in other townships in New York, thence throughout New England and even as far west as Kentucky, Indiana and Ohio.

Mrs. Ann Lee, founder of the sect had, in her early years, passed through an inferno of sexual experience, during her marriage to an incurable drunkard. She had suffered the agonies of torture and martyrdom in several child-births, and all her babies had died in infancy. After the birth of the last infant, extracted by forceps, Ann Lee lay for several hours at the very edge of death. As she fought her way back to life, step by painful step, she then and there decided that she would never again indulge in carnal intercourse. By revelation, she avowed, she had received knowledge that this indulgence was the root of all evil. Soon thereafter, she began her impassioned testimony against sexual intercourse and against marriage.

Of great physical strength and endurance, Ann Lee set an example of hard work and rigid discipline. Her celibate followers developed into extraordinary designers and builders. An unimpaired, undiverted intensity of spirit animates the furniture they built for their community homes, as well as the building themselves—enduring records of the sublimation of their impulses.

Noyes had long admired the achievements of the Shakers, though their ideas concerning sexual love were diametrically opposed to his own. Not long after his marriage to Harriet Holton, finding himself near Harvard, Massachusetts, where a Shaker colony existed, he paid it a visit. He was courteously received by an elderly Shaker sister and engaged her in a sort of Socratic dialogue on the problems of earthly and Heavenly intercourse.

"The Lord commands husbands to love their wives," proclaimed Noyes. "We must be obedient to this; we must have the armor of righteousness on the right hand and on the left."

"Yea, that is all right," answered the Shaker sister. "But the world is not now as it was when Paul wrote: he had to deal with heathen that were in the worst state, and they had more than one woman; and Paul told them to love their wives so as to keep them from going to other women. This ceremony of marriage—the being 'published' and going before a minister—is nothing!"

"I agree with you that the ceremonies and ordinances of men are of little or no value," admitted Noyes. "But the connection of the sexes is altogether another thing. This is in accordance with the desires and organization of our nature as it was created, and is therefore an ordinance of God. If I understand your books, you yourselves allow that sexual intercourse was originally appointed by the Creator, under certain restrictions as to times and seasons."

The Shaker sister shook her head gravely and finally, without embarrassment, replied: "I guess not. We don't know what God did appoint: man did not wait to see. You will see; you are in the right way, but you have not traveled through. I have been where you are, and I have gone on. I have been looking at this matter a long time."

"I have been looking at it, too, a long time. I have been where you are, that is, I have taken the common and literal view of the text 'They that are accounted worthy,' but I have gone on and taken another lesson."

"You have backslidden, and will have to go over the ground again," the old woman retorted gravely. "If you are traveling any place and stop and go back, you will never get there. You turned back because you were thinking of getting married."

This outspoken reference to his own life brought a quick reply. "Not so!" exclaimed the young man from Putney. "I made up my mind about the matter before I had any idea of being married, and when I never intended or expected to be married according to the custom of this world."

"Well, be that as it may, I know that you are in an error. I have been where you are." Perhaps the good sister wished to bring this futile interview to a close. But she did not know John Noyes.

"And I say again, I have been where you are! As you say of me, so I say of you, you have traveled part way toward the truth, and have stopped. Now if you travel on you will find, as I have, that the Shaker doctrine is a great error."

The Shaker sister was not offended—not even shocked. "Do you think that we have not any light?"

A disarming innocence seemed to lie behind this question.

"No, I don't judge you, because I am not sufficiently acquainted with you," Noyes replied courteously. "I came here to reason with you. If you have had so much more experience than I and think me in error, you must convince me by argument. . . . In Christ all are one, and each owns all and all own each, and all are married to all. Of course, the supposed difficulty of determining whose wife the woman should be could not exist there (in heaven). We must remember that the exclusive and artificial marriage of this world is one thing, and natural sexual intercourse another; and Christ's answer only determines that such marriage as would make the difficulty proposed does not exist in heaven, while he leaves entirely untouched the question whether sexual intercourse exists there."

The Shaker sister gazed at the young heretic in silence. Finally she answered: "I should really think that one who has so much understanding of Scripture as you have would see the true meaning of that text. It says they are like angels; we must be like angels in this world."

"Well, how are the angels?" he demanded quickly. "Christ says, 'Except ye be converted and become as little children, ye shall not enter into the kingdom of heaven.' If we would be like angels then we must be like little children."

"We Shakers are like little children; we are all brothers and sisters," she answered, hoping for an escape from this argumentative visitor.

"Little children do not think evil of any part of their bodies or separate the sexes on account of it," he retorted. "Are you in this respect like little children?"

She became confused; she had no training in the finer points. But he could not leave without delivering his message: "You are not and never expect to be like little children. The truth is, little children are no more like Shakers than they are like the world. Little children represent the purity and innocence which belong to the kingdom of heaven; and so long as Shakers regard any passion or department of human nature as necessarily impure and carnal they cannot be in the child state, and so are not in the kingdom-of-heaven state."

"I wish some of the brethren who know how to handle these things were here. I am but a poor old woman!" the Shaker sister exclaimed.

Young Noyes found the Shaker brethren well able to defend their point of view in argument, unexpectedly penetrating in their analysis of the sexual customs of worldly society, yet with an intuitive comprehension of his point of view. Some mysterious attraction of opposites drew him to them.

Despite their limitations and apparent eccentricities, they demonstrated, for the shepherd of the Putney flock, that a communal life could be successfully lived within the framework of the nation.

Now, facing a new problem, and surveying all the various ventures in colonization that had been undertaken for almost a century, Noyes realized the almost insurmountable obstacles that might defeat the successful development of a Perfectionist Community. Yet, for reassurance, there stood the long record of success that had rewarded the patient efforts of the Shakers. Their colonies had, by some miracle, perpetuated themselves—though their members had not! Modestly yet eloquently their example testified to what might be accomplished.

Noyes was convinced that the success of the Shaker communities had encouraged the successive emigrations and experiments of the Rappites, the Zoarites, and the Ebenezers. These subsequent experiments in communal living were mere echoes of Shaker initiative—echoes which grew fainter and fainter, as the initial impulse toward a new form lost its *élan*.

When in England, Robert Owen had undertaken to convert his world to communism, consciously or unconsciously he was following the paths hewn out by the American Shakers. Was not Owen a distant follower of the Rappites? Noyes even went so far as to claim that Frenchmen like St. Simon and Fourier had been influenced by the Shakers. Tracing the genealogy of the movement for communal living, (at a later date) he declared: "it is no more than bare justice to say that we are indebted to the Shakers more than to any or all other social architects of modern times. Their success has been the 'specie basis' that has upheld all the paper theories, and counteracted the failures, of the French and English schools. It is very doubtful whether Owenism or Fourierism would have ever existed, or if they had, whether they would have ever moved the practical American nation, if the facts of Shakerism had not existed before them and gone along with them. But to do complete justice we must go a step further. While we say that the Rappites, the Zoarites, the Ebenezers, the Owenites and even the Fourierists are all echoes of the Shakers, we must also say that the Shakers are the far-off echoes of the Primitive Christian Church."

So Noyes sought to find inspiration in the example set by the followers of Mother Ann Lee.

Surely the territory of the United States was vast enough, extensive enough, free enough in tolerance of spirit to permit the fulfillment of another experiment. The country at large was far more open-minded than Putney.

But, confronted on all sides by the collapse of other colonies and communities, the outlook was far from encouraging to one who now found himself a fugitive from Vermont justice, accused of adultery and fornication; whose community had been dispersed, and who was reduced to the ignominy of sitting in exile, in the front parlor of a modest New York house—wondering how he could reassemble his scattered flock, how move forward in establishing the Kingdom of God.

Chapter II: RESURRECTION

But now we are delivered from the law, that being dead wherein we were held; that we should serve in newness of spirit, and not in the oldness of the letter.

—ROMANS 7:6.

I

DURING the autumn of 1834 Chauncey Dutton had carried the message of the New Haven Perfectionists to Chittenango, in central New York. In that little settlement Dutton preached Christ a whole Saviour, with faith the only condition of full salvation. After one meeting, a young man named Jonathan Burt followed Dutton to the home in which he was stopping. Burt engaged Dutton in argument; but the young evangelist from New Haven swept away all objections. Next day, Jonathan Burt had made a public confession of his everlasting salvation from sin. Dutton gave him a copy of *The Perfectionist* containing John Noyes's theory of the Second Coming of Christ. As young Burt sat at his workbench a day or two later, eating his midday meal and musing upon this new revelation, he related that something like an electric current struck the top of his head and spread a tingling glow through every part of his body. "My mind was illuminated to understand the Bible as I had never understood it before. I wanted to share my all with God's people." From that day Jonathan Burt was a Perfectionist, subscribed to all of Noyes's subsequent publications, and became a loyal disciple of the Putney prophet.

Eleven years later, in the autumn of 1845, at the suggestion of a fellow Perfectionist, an opportunity came to Jonathan Burt to go into partnership in the purchase of the so-called Indian sawmill on Oneida Creek. Although he had expended something like $1,800 for his property in Chittenango, Burt disposed of it for about $900, and bought a share of the Oneida sawmill and a forty-acre timber lot. By January, 1846, he had erected a house, and moved to this new wilderness. But felling trees and hauling logs to the mill put a heavy tax on Burt's strength, and he broke down under this strain. During his illness a spring freshet carried away the dam. Everything seemed to go against poor Jonathan. He had not bettered his lot by this radical change; he was in debt; to buy out his partner would increase his burden to an amount he could not carry. Nor was his uncongenial partner able to buy him out. To make matters even more unendurable, his brother Horace was now discharged from the Worcester hospital for the insane. Horace proposed to sell his own property and to buy the partner's share in the mill. He did so; but, since his madness promptly shortly returned, he proved an additional burden.

The Genoa Convention of Perfectionists (September 17, 18, 19, 1847) selected a committee of twelve to draw up plans for the formation of a "heavenly association" in central New York. Two possible sites were discussed. One was John B. Foot's farm at Lairdsville, the other Jonathan Burt's Indian sawmill. Noyes favored the latter location. However, Mrs. Burt had not been converted to the new ideas. The committee of twelve was divided in its opinion. William H. Cook, its special executive agent, briskly proposed an association in Syracuse, where he happened to be a salesman in a store. The commercially-minded Cook envisaged a great mercantile business as a basis of support for the new community of saints. To a majority of the committee his scheme was not appealing; and after a meeting at Manlius, when Cook outlined his rose-colored vision, the committee ceased to function. One of its members, William G. Gould, however, was delegated to visit Putney and study Noyes's community. Gould happened to be in Putney when the storm of disapproval broke, and the leaders were scattered.

Meantime, early in October, 1847, Joseph C. Ackley, William S. Hatch, and Daniel P. Nash were organizing a little community of their own. Two other families—twenty-three men, women and children in all—were gathered into a semi-communistic group at Beaver Meadow, near East Hamilton. On the first of November, Joseph Ackley appeared at Burt's place with the proposal that they should join him at the sawmill. Arrangements were quickly concluded. Burt dismissed his sawyer and other hired help—it was decided that Ackley's band should replace these hirelings. Mrs. Lucinda Burt obstinately demurred—the business should, she insisted, be carried on in the name of her husband. However, all hoped for her speedy conversion. So, on the very day of the dissolution in Putney, November 26, 1847, the Ackleys moved into Jonathan Burt's home. The next day, digging was started for the foundation of a community house to shelter the rest of the Beaver Meadow group. It was little more than a shanty, but by the middle of December it was already sheltering three families. The newcomers brought not a penny with them—nothing but one horse and a troop of ravenous children. To make matters worse, no snow fell. The mud became so deep that the two teams could not be moved out of the barn. No logs to saw at the mill, no money coming in from the sale of lumber, though the railroad would have bought all the mill could turn out. Payment on the bank-note was drawing near. Never in his life had Jonathan Burt placed his trust in God to such a test. News of the Putney scandal and debacle came as the climax.

As soon as he discovered the whereabouts of Noyes, Burt wrote him a letter describing the new activities at the Indian sawmill, and invited Noyes to visit him. Without hesitation, Noyes decided that here was a most promising haven for the Vermont Perfectionists.

Arriving at the Burts', Noyes found the men all wheeling dirt to stop a leak in the dam caused by high water. In the evening they all assembled at the new house to listen to his story. "He explained to us the principle of male continence," Burt later recounted, "rehearsed the circumstances that led to its discovery, and finally frankly opened to us the fact that they had at Putney stepped over the marriage bounds and introduced a new relation between the sexes. He spoke in a spirit and manner that evinced great purity of thought and feeling, and though the subject was new to me I had data in my spiritual experience which enabled me to accept what he presented as God's truth.... The women were somewhat disconcerted, but on the whole there was a good deal of candor."

The next day, Saturday, Noyes called on Dr. Gould at Oneida Depot. Gould had been at Putney as the representative of the committee of twelve, and had there, evidently, evinced some impatience to share in the privileges of "complex marriage." Noyes had forbidden that step. Dr. Gould vigorously protested against any such "arbitrary" restraint upon his personal freedom, censuring Noyes as aristocratic, snobbish, dictatorial. Subsequently, however, for reasons of his own, Gould renewed his allegiance, and wrote in glowing terms: "Your dispersion and apparent overthrow has only increased my interest and determination to sustain you, and ... your orders shall be as promptly executed when issued from the Tombs of New York as from the White House at the Capital."

No sooner had Noyes appeared in Oneida, however, than the old conflict broke out anew. On Sunday morning, Jonathan Burt, Daniel Nash and young Hial Waters arrived at Dr. Gould's house, only to discover the ravages of a storm. Noyes was on the point of departing, planning to return to New York City. At the conclusion of a private conference between Burt and Noyes, Jonathan pledged his allegiance to the Vermonter as an inspired leader. Noyes pulled from his pocket a heavy bag, and with a whirl tossed it upon the bed. Out of the bag, on to the bedspread, rolled a stream of ten-dollar gold pieces—five hundred dollars in all.

"There, Mr. Burt! If that will help you in any way, it is at your service. I offer it as my first contribution to a New York community!" Jonathan Burt accepted it thankfully, as from the Lord. He invited Noyes home with him. Henceforth he would cleave to Noyes, Jonathan informed Dr. Gould.

For the comfort of John Noyes, Burt bought a sturdy parlor stove the next day, and set it up in the best room. Even the recalcitrant Mrs. Burt was persuaded to do her utmost to make things pleasant and comfortable for the exile. Without delay, Noyes plunged into a task that was crowding everything else out of his mind, the writing down of his "Bible Argument, Defining the Relations of the Sexes in the Kingdom of Heaven."

By February 4, Noyes reached a final decision: his scattered flock should be reassembled at Oneida. Tacitly he had been accepted as leader of the little group of New York Perfectionists. "They see for themselves . . . that I am as hostile as ever to licentious spirits, and that my 'tyranny' instead of being an annoyance is highly useful in protecting them from the wolves." Thus he wrote to the Cragins, waiting in New York. Now at last he had found a place for them all. His letter glowed with the fire of his hope for the new community to emerge out of the ashes of the old. This letter reveals Noyes on the threshold of his great adventure. "Do you recollect a small timber house across the road from Brother Burt's? There is one comfortable room with buttery, a back-kitchen for summer, a bedroom upstairs, a good barn, a small shoemaker's shop, and twenty-three acres of land included, mostly in the long bend of the creek, good-looking meadow with a small wood lot. Crane, the present occupant, offers to sell his interest in it for five hundred dollars, and to give possession within one week from the time of the bargain. This land, like most of the lands in this region, is held by articles from the State, pledging to give deeds when the purchase money is paid. About four hundred dollars remain to be paid, but the State does not call for this so long as the interest is kept up; also there is a probability that the present Legislature will throw off one-quarter of its claim. I think you can live at least as comfortably there with your children as the Beaver Meadow folks live in their shanty (and I assure you they are happy), until we can build a Château. There is some romance in beginning our community in the log huts of the Indians. But your house, though built of hewed logs and by the Indians, is well plastered and papered, warm and pleasant. . . . And the money which we should have to pay for one year's rent of a decent house in New York City will make you the owner to all intents of quite a little farm. Brother Burt's plans for water-power will be furthered by this purchase, and he will make common interest with you in managing your land. As to occupation, he wants just such a man as you are to take charge of his accounts and superintend scattered business so that he can devote himself to his mills; and the community will need Mrs. Cragin's help as teacher of children, for which purpose the little shoe shop seems to have been constructed. We can send to Putney for furniture, and Brother Burt will provision you. All here will receive you with acclamations. Shall I close the bargain?

"If you decide to come, I shall probably send for my wife and the children. Harriet will go into the yoke with Mrs. Burt, who needs her help and is quite sure to prove a fine woman under right influence.

"By these movements the original four-square nucleus of the Putney Community will be re-united, and will give tone to the Oneida Community."

Noyes, on the same day, hastened to break the news to Harriet of the coming migration: "I opened my whole heart to them. Some of my disclosures of course caused temporary suffering, but God found means to convince all that I am not walking after the flesh. I lectured and talked abundantly, and the result is a joyful quickening of all, full confidence in one another, increasing hope. Mrs. Burt, hitherto not a believer, is yielding. She gives me liberty to invite you and Theodore as soon as I please. . . . On the whole I think you had better come. You will be needed with me in laying the foundations of the new Association."

By the fifteenth of the same month all was settled. The Noyes and Cragin families would arrive at Oneida Depot at three o'clock on the afternoon of March 1, there to be met by teams from the sawmill. "I cannot stop to tell you all that is going forward here," John Noyes wrote exultantly to Harriet. Purchases of land and buildings adjoining Jonathan Burt's property were under negotiation. The appearance of no less than twenty-eight hundred dollars in gold in that frontier settlement gave rise to fantastic tales. A domain of some one hundred and sixty acres, with two houses and two log cabins, was being assembled.

George Cragin was appointed to take charge of the exodus. Harriet Noyes, with her son Theodore and the Cragin boys, was to meet the Cragins in Springfield, proceed thence to Troy (where they were to spend the night), and finally to be met by John and a team at Oneida Depot.

2

Like the passage of the Jews from Egypt to the land of Canaan, they used to tell each other, was that venturesome migration to Oneida. Rather more like falling out of a balloon from a height of a thousand feet, John Noyes used to retort, and "not only landing safely but in the very garden of Eden!" But no garden of Eden welcomed them, that stinging March afternoon when George and Mary Cragin and Harriet Noyes arrived at Oneida. George and Mary had left New York on Saturday, spent Sunday in New Haven, and arrived in Springfield Monday at noon. The Putney delegation, in charge of John Miller and John and Harriet Skinner, had departed from the village Monday morning and arrived in Springfield that evening. After the vexing events of the past three months, it was a joyous reunion. Mary and Harriet seemed more closely bound together than ever, and made glowing plans for the future. Next day the Millers and the Skinners returned to Putney; the Cragins and the Noyeses began their venture into the unknown —"the West." George counted twenty-two persons and pieces in all—boys, babies, boxes, bags and bundles!

Precisely at three the next afternoon this first installment of pilgrims arrived at Oneida Depot. Completing their schedule to the second, they found themselves peering out into a forbidding wilderness. Anxiously their eyes searched for the team, across the plain of hard-packed snow, but John was nowhere to be seen. At last two double teams drove up, and young Abram Burt and Hial Waters introduced themselves. Into their two sleighs the travelers piled, bundled up like Eskimos against a wind that lashed across a black-and-white landscape. Stripped of all foliage, stark trees swayed like drunken genii. The unending horizon of the white plain was punctuated by squat, black boxes. Over the icy surface of hard-packed snow, with cracking whips, Hial and Abram guided the newcomers into the heart of the Old Indian Reserve, —territory formerly set aside as a residence for the Oneida tribe. Those log huts had formerly been occupied by the Indians. The State bought back the territory, and had, six or eight years previously, opened it upon easy terms to white settlers. It was located almost precisely at the geographic center of the State. Later, George Cragin used to stick a pin in the very center of a map of New York, and with a piece of string describe a geometric circle.

Starting at Niagara Falls, on the western boundary, that circle passed through Rouse's Point, the State's most northern extremity, and, at its southernmost point, through New York City. The pin to which the string was tied, he explained to the children, marked the geographic center of the Empire State. The pin-point was Oneida, the very domain of the new Community.

Oneida Creek entered the sawmill territory at its southeastern corner, made a great sweeping curve, half encircled the plateau upon which the community buildings were eventually to be erected, and a good two miles to the northwest continued its way through a valley. To the south, the valley gradually widened till it seemed to become a boundless expanse. In that direction, some nine miles away, from the higher points, Oneida Lake could be seen on a clear day. Five miles north lay the long unbroken line of the Erie Canal, which was then in its heyday as a waterway.

Cold and hungry, the bewildered newcomers reached the Burts' at last. Jonathan Burt's hearty welcome rang out reassuringly; but its warmth was tempered by the reserve of Mrs. Burt. Her house was already crowded to overflowing–and the poor woman had not yet fully recovered from the initial shock of the revolutionary doctrines enunciated by John Noyes. The slight reserve of this welcome may have contributed to the decision of the newcomers to move without delay over to the log hut. The gold payment had been made; the cabin stood ready for the Putney family. There was only one room on the ground floor; but its huge fireplace suggested intimacy. Despite the chill which crept, razor-like, under the sills of the little square windows, Mary Cragin and Harriet Noyes chattered gayly of the hut's manifold attractions. Climbing up a narrow ladder, euphemistically named "stairs," they discovered under the low roof a single "bedroom." Except under the ridge-pole, they could not stand erect. But even that detail produced exclamations of delight.

It was a lark to cook for the next few days over the broad smoky fireplace. The boys were sent out for wood to keep the fire alive and the pots boiling. However, as soon as finances permitted, the pioneers bought and installed a cook stove. They resolved to keep the number of their "external wants" as low as possible, to contrive with their own hands rather than to purchase every essential household article. They borrowed a table and chairs. Their crying need, however, was for beds. They decided to build their own. Basswood boards were cheap and close at hand. Without hesitation, they made bedsteads entirely of these. They even talked of taking out a patent upon this invention: bedposts were constructed so that each stood alone on its own individual base, preventing any general collapse of the whole structure.

To organize communal life in the log hut required only a few days. Nearby stood the little "shoe shop." It caught the eye of Mary Cragin—the very place for a schoolroom, she decided at once. Education of the young was Mary's ruling interest. She proposed to Mr. and Mrs. Burt that she open a school. The little "shop" measured no more than twelve feet by twelve. In a few days, twelve boys and girls were captivated by Mary Cragin's musical voice as she read to them—almost entirely from the Bible.

Mrs. Cragin's school had the additional advantage of taking youngsters away from the hut, where Noyes was composing the conclusion of his "Bible Argument." Unfaltering Harriet spent long afternoons copying in her firm handwriting this challenging declaration. The manuscript was to be sent to Putney, to be rushed through the presses by Charlotte and Harriet and the others who had been left in charge of the printing press.

Outside, the men were busy preparing for the arrival of other followers. They were building a rough board shanty, similar to that already occupied by the Beaver Meadow contingent, to be used as a dormitory for the younger men. On March 22, Lemuel and Sarah Bradley arrived; on April 1, James L. Baker, Catherine Baker, and their daughter Mary; and on May 6, from northern Vermont, Henry Burnham with his family.

Originally the Community was composed of three general groups. First, and centrally important, came the Putney "family" —a sort of cabinet surrounding and supporting Noyes with unquestioning loyalty. Secondly, there was the original New York group, headed by Jonathan Burt, with the Ackleys and the Nashes, already settled, though precariously enough, at the Indian sawmill. The third group was recruited from staunch disciples of northern and southern Vermont. When the call came, they sacrificed the farms and homesteads they had so patiently and painstakingly wrested from the wilderness, to follow Noyes to a new frontier of human experience. Henceforth these Vermonters would date everything before or after the year 1848—the year of the "great change."

Among the chief Vermont families to follow the leader to Oneida were the Kinsleys, the Barrons, the Joslyns, the Bakers, the Burnhams. Typical were the Kinsleys—Albert and his wife, Maria Ellsworth. A man of importance in his own remote little community, Fletcher, Vermont, Kinsley had filled the offices of Justice of the Peace, sheriff, and deacon of the church. His somber dark eyes peered steadily out with a courageous certainty of vision. A progressive, forward-looking man, Albert Kinsley had introduced the first cooking stove into his section of Vermont, and the first matches as well. The Kinsleys also might have boasted of the best pump in the countryside, but they were not given to boasting. As sheriff, Albert used to bring his prisoners home for a good dinner and night's lodging—even though that gesture might mean that Maria and he would be forced to pass a long night in wakeful vigil.

Strangely enough, the message of John Noyes awakened an immediate response in Kinsley's soul. To him, it seemed irrefutable, logical, clear as crystal. Nor did the good Maria ever falter—she became Albert's equal in earnestness and conviction. Unfaltering and unexcited, without a moment's hesitation or misgiving, the Kinsleys severed all their cherished home ties, and sold all, to follow John Noyes. They packed a few home treasures, along with the cash the farm brought, into a "mover's" or covered wagon, and set out for the new life they were to undertake. Their team and wagon were ferried across Lake Champlain; and they completed the long journey on a canal boat, which set them down at Durhamville, the port of landing nearest to Oneida. There they took up the long haul through roads deep in mud to the new settlement of the Perfectionists.

Sarah, the eldest daughter of Albert and Maria Kinsley was nineteen years old, and Jane was just seventeen. Their two boys were younger—Martin fourteen and Myron twelve. Looking into the travel-wearied visages of these youngsters clad in Vermont homespun, Noyes welcomed them as heartily as if he could foresee the lifetime of loyalty they were to give him.

3

Presently George Cragin was sent forth again, to collect funds to build the Mansion House. George was rigorously cautioned not to beg—even if he did not receive a farthing. His task was to present the simple facts of the situation to loyal Perfectionists, to convince them, whenever possible, that this new undertaking was the "cause of God and of humanity." His aim was to raise, if possible, the sum of fifteen hundred dollars. Labor, material, and skill were to be supplied by members already assembled at the sawmill. Double that amount was cheerfully subscribed by disciples, many of whom afterwards became members of the Community.

Meanwhile, in Jonathan Burt's mill, lumber was being put in condition for seasoning. This group of amateurs faced the task of the construction of a cellar wall for the new Mansion House. Not one of them had ever had any practical experience in masonry. All were firmly resolved, however, not to call in outside help. They would tackle this job alone. Providentially, in this crisis, there arrived from Baldwinville a first-class stone-mason, a Mr. Ruggles, who took charge of the construction of the foundation. Then Erastus Hamilton appeared, and he was an experienced carpenter and joiner, a boss-builder, an architect.

Youthful enthusiasm radiated. The spirit of youth enabled them to turn disappointments into jokes, to face hardships with laughter. Erastus Hamilton and his wife were twenty-seven and twenty-four years old, respectively. Henry Burnham was only twenty-eight and his wife Abby twenty-seven. Only seven of them had yet attained the age of forty. Jonathan Burt had indeed turned forty; and Harriet Noyes and George Cragin were just at that turning point. John Noyes and Mary Cragin were not yet thirty-seven.

4

In the log hut, Harriet Noyes industriously copied Chapter Seven of her husband's "Bible Argument." John had appended two notes: she paused over each word as she wrote: "The present dress of women, besides being peculiarly inappropriate to the sex, is immodest. It makes the distinction between the sexes vastly more prominent and obtrusive than nature makes it. In a state of nature, the difference between a man and a woman could hardly be distinguished at a distance of five hundred yards; but as men and women dress, their sex is telegraphed as far as they can be seen. Woman's dress is a standing lie. It proclaims that she is not a two-legged animal, but something like a churn, standing on castors! Such are the absurdities into which the false principle of shame and sexual isolation betray the world.

"When the distinction of the sexes is reduced to the bounds of nature and decency, by the removal of the shame partition, and woman becomes what she ought to be, a *female man* (like the Son in the Godhead), a dress will be adopted that will be at the same time the most simple and the most beautiful; and it will be the same, or nearly the same, for both sexes. The dress of children—frock and pantalets—is in good taste . . . taste not perverted by the dictates of shame, and it is well adapted to the free motion of both sexes. This, or something like it, will be the uniform of vital society."

Harriet and John Skinner, with their son Joseph, arrived from Putney on June 16. Almost immediately, in the garret of the log hut, the three women sat down to devise a costume suitable for everyday life in the Community. First of all, they agreed, it should be simple, modest, attractive. They experimented and contrived, cut and snipped, discussed various possibilities, and finally decided upon a radical innovation. They cut down their long skirts to knee-length. With the materials clipped off they tailored pantalets, as a compromise with convention. When they tried them on they were almost afraid to look at themselves. It required all their courage to appear thus clad before the rest of the Community. Compared with this, complex marriage seemed an easy step. But, encouraged by John's daring ideas, they decided to face the consequences. They created a sensation; there could be no doubt about that. Their appearance was greeted with uncouth laughter from the younger men. A number of the women were shocked—a few actually distressed. The new costume was denounced as absurd and ridiculous; but a majority of the little Community commended its trim appearance; and after the first surprise most of the family were converted.

When George Cragin returned from his unexpectedly successful financial tour, two fantastic looking figures came skipping out from the "white" house to the road. As the short skirts and pantalets worn by Harriet and Mary burst upon his astonished sight, George burst into a peal of uncontrolled laughter. Never had he seen anything quite so odd in the way of women's fashions. But the two women vigorously defended their new uniforms, and George was forced to admit that they were right.

Several months later another innovation was made. The women decided that short dresses and long hair were incongruous. The fashion of letting the hair grow indefinitely, which necessitated an hour's time in properly combing and arranging, was decreed incompatible with true simplicity in feminine attire. Several women declared it distasteful and burdensome. The idea of wearing their hair short occurred to them; but Paul's theory of the natural propriety of long hair for women seemed to stand in the way. After a careful examination of the subject, they found that Paul's language expressly pointed out the object for which women should wear long hair; and that was not for ornament, but "for a covering." The popular fashion of combing and coiling the hair upward on the top of the head made it anything but a covering.

The style of little girls, with short hair falling round the neck, conformed more closely to Paul's advice. The argument was conclusive. Without hesitation, they began to clip their hair. Short hair altered the looks of the women even more than the short skirts. But no one could deny that short hair made the women appear younger; and all rejoiced in this new freedom. In those days of chignon and "folly," of bustle and crinoline, abbreviated skirts and short tresses gave them all a sense of rejuvenation.

5

The colony now numbered fifty-one: thirteen men, thirteen women, twenty-five children and youths seventeen years or younger. An informal census revealed many assets in the way of craftsmen, and artisans. They discovered one shoemaker; one lead-pipe maker; one millwright, pail-maker and general jobber; one carpenter and joiner, architect and builder; one merchant, reformer and publisher; two sawyers; one-half blacksmith and one-half farmer, good at all work; one printer; one cabinet-maker and miller; one stone-mason; and one teamster, landscape gardener, and executive agent. Few useless professions were represented. Literary and academic culture was mostly stored in the brain of John Noyes.

One moonlight night Noyes and Erastus Hamilton selected the site for the Mansion House. With the north star as a guide-point, they staked out the ground for the foundation walls of the Community's new home. Standing on an elevated part of the domain, it would command an extensive view of the surrounding country. The basement was to be divided by partitions across the whole width into three apartments of equal size, thirty-five feet by twenty. The first was to run back into a rise of ground on which the house would abut, and serve as a cellar. The second would be the dining room. The parlor over the dining room would be of the same size; on the second floor, also, would be the reception room, the school room, the omnipresent printing-office. The third story was to be devoted to sleeping apartments for married pairs and for females. A garret, extending over the whole house, and without partitions, was to serve as the dormitory for the unmarried men and boys.

This building of their home was the first enterprise that mobilized the full strength of the Community; all were equally interested. It was their main summer work. The force of men was not large: therefore little attention could be given to any other work. Under the direction of Mr. Ruggles, the job of stone work on the cellar walls was undertaken enthusiastically. As chief assistants, Mr. Ruggles had Daniel P. Nash and Noyes himself. Soon they became expert masons.

Dressed in their new uniforms, the ladies themselves became daily helpers. Harriet Noyes and Mary Cragin toiled from two to four hours every day, handling trowels, small stone and mortar, with a dexterity equal to that of most men. This work was not drudgery, but a thrilling pastime—a real pleasure, they were to recall always with satisfaction. Fresh air, manual exercise, free and easy mingling of the sexes, and the consciousness of rendering public service, all contributed to a novel sense of freedom. Among the women Mrs. Cragin and Mrs. Noyes set a pace in zeal and enthusiasm, with Harriet Skinner and Charlotte Miller close seconds. When the structure was far enough advanced to allow of it, and even before the sideboards were on, planks were placed across the joists, and the women commenced lathing. The greater portion of that task was accomplished by the women.

The business of collecting materials had been promptly attended to, even as the work of excavating the cellar was going forward. With the sawmill in operation and a wealth of timber cut on the domain itself, with a goodly number of carpenters and joiners already members of the Community, this undertaking progressed pleasantly and successfully. With the exception of the plastering, the whole of the task was done by Community members. Noyes himself worked at the sawmill in getting out siding for the house, and when everything was ready acted as one of the principal masons in the job of laying the walls.

Inhabitants of the sparsely settled countryside looked on with astonishment. Strange stories concerning the ideas of these "foreigners" were bruited about. Here, in a few weeks they were completing the cellar-wall of their house—a mansion indeed in that frontier where only log cabins dotted the landscape. Even more rapidly the frame of the structure had arisen—it was at least sixty feet long and thirty-five deep, and it rose almost four stories into the air! More like a factory it looked than a dwelling place.

"Why didn't you people locate that big building on the creek, so that it can be used for factory purposes when you break up and scatter?" one storekeeper asked.

"We may not break up and scatter."

"What is going to keep you from quarreling and scattering?"

"Our religion unites us—it will hold us together."

"I thought you were all Sabbath-breakers. Have you people got any religion?"

"No, we haven't got religion, religion has got us. It will make us honest, do honest work, pay honest debts, and it will make us do so from choice, and not from compulsion...."

"I guess you folks are honest in your business dealings," admitted the storekeeper, "but some say that you hold queer notions about marriage...."

6

The August sun beat down relentlessly upon this band of amateur builders. With little protection from the excessive heat, they toiled on the foundation, stark on its little hill. Despite their ambition to finish the new house as soon as possible, a suppressed lassitude became painfully evident. A mysterious weakness seemed to overcome many who had been most ardent. This malaise spread insidiously. Henry Burnham seemed most downcast. Days passed before any dared to mention this secret affliction. They were victims of dysentery.

But these battle-scarred veterans valiantly assured each other that in the endless warfare against the devil's strategies they had served too long to succumb now. Their enemy was no longer a mystery; they struck back with the weapons of good nature and buoyancy of spirit. The epidemic was spoken of only as "this." Mainly by determination, rather than by any knowledge of medicine, they managed finally to rout the invader. Had Burnham been carried off, they admitted later, panic might have ensued and the whole enterprise abandoned.

The precariousness of their situation was most keenly appreciated by George Cragin. It was George's special task to go out and raise funds. As appointed financier, Cragin pledged himself to see the obligations met. To this end he worked day and night. Under his management, the domain had been paid for, so far as the claims of previous occupants were concerned, subsistence provided, building expenses met, and debts to the amount of about two thousand dollars canceled. A letter from Cragin to John R. Miller indicates the state of the Community exchequer at this critical moment.

"Oneida Castle, Aug. 16, 1848

"Dear Bro. M.:—I am very happy to comply with your request to send you a statement of our financial affairs. Probably I was reflecting with some interest on the subject just at the time you were penning your letter; quite an interesting coincidence to me. Our liabilities are about $4,820. Our assets may be thus stated:

Burt's Mill	$2,500.00
Wood Lot	950.00
Crane Farm	1,000.00
Francis Farm	3,600.00
Personal Property	1,350.00
Total	$9,400.00

"We are at present nearly out of funds. I expect to collect, for lumber sold and a note held by Mr. B., about seventy-five dollars, to be applied toward taking up a note that falls due the 20th inst. We shall require for the purchase of sash, glass, paint, brick, etc., five hundred dollars, besides five hundred more for current expenses this fall, and the payment of interest due the State. We are expecting about $1,600 from Northern Vermont, with which the notes on the Francis place can be met."

No money on hand—a house to build, a printing-office to maintain—and a hundred persons to feed and clothe! But when a sharpening chill made fires imperative in the log huts, the Mansion House remained unfinished and unready for occupancy. Unless some new method of constructing dormitories could be devised, the whole project would have to be abandoned.

At length, for temporary convenience, a plan was devised. One-half of the third story, a space of thirty-five feet by thirty, was finished as a single room. There were windows on three sides of the room, ten in all. Twelve sleeping apartments, called tents, were devised. Partitions of curtains of cotton cloth, hung on wires, were supported on upright wooden frames, seven feet high, about two feet below the ceiling, allowing full circulation of air and light from the windows. The large interior space, forming a hollow square, became a comfortable common sitting-room for the occupants of the "tents."

One large stove, placed in the center of this sitting-room warmed the twelve rooms around it. Two reflectors (those were the days of candles) were suspended conveniently in the central part of the room and furnished light. A space designed only for six bedrooms, each of which would have required separate stove and light, was converted into twelve bedrooms, with a sitting-room in the midst. Cloth for the tents cost ten dollars; the labor of constructing them was slight. Suspended upon wires, the curtains could be drawn, or the whole space thrown into one large room. As quickly it could be restored to separate inclosures, private enough, they were convinced, for persons of sound morality.

Harriet Skinner, Mrs. Noyes, Mary Cragin and the rest of the women were determined that the "tent-room" should be as attractive as they could make it. Soon drab moreen curtains were substituted for cotton and surmounted by a neat little valance of blue woolen delaine. This gave the effect of a cornice, with a finished, and even elegant appearance.

The dedication of the new "tent-room" took place on Christmas Eve, 1848. The families had moved in the day previously; each assigned a "tent." Nothing could exceed the delight with which they entered these new apartments. They praised the novelty and simplicity of this new room. No one could wish for larger quarters! The tents were trimmed with evergreens. At candle-light the whole family, including the children, gathered in the "tent-room," and in the midst of green festoons, the occasion was celebrated.

This "tent-room" soon gave rise to a squall of slander concerning the sleeping arrangements of the Oneida Community. The little sect had prematurely congratulated itself that here it had found a haven safe from intrusion, remote from village gossip and calumny—"clear of the clashings of village interests," as John expressed it, and in a neighboring population less bigoted than that of Putney.

Because of the rapid increase of members, an addition to the Mansion House became necessary during the spring and summer of 1849. A wing running west—two stories high, with an attic lighted at its end and sides, was erected. The basement was utilized as a wash- and bake-room, with large boilers for heating water, and with a large brick oven (eight feet by ten on the inside). The second floor was designed as sitting- and sleeping-rooms; the attic was for boys' sleeping apartments, commonly known as the "boys' garret." Projecting south from this, another wing, eighteen by twenty-five feet, was soon added. This was also two stories high—the basement designed for a wood-shed, the second story for sitting- and sleeping-rooms.

The frequency with which the Community made alterations in its buildings, and moved them from place to place, gave rise to many local jokes. "The Community folks should hang their partitions on hinges, and set their buildings on castors, they change so often!" exclaimed a visiting workman. In defense of this readiness to change, the Community boasted of its flexibility in meeting the necessities of circumstance.

Other wooden structures were eventually constructed. Standing within thirty-six feet of the Manson House, and connected with it by an underground passageway, was the first "Children's House," which, like the tent-room, was to provoke no little gossip. Previous to its erection, the children had continued to occupy the old "White House" until it became overcrowded.

The erection of a large frame house, twenty-five by forty-three feet, two stories high, with an attic, was undertaken in the months of June and July, 1849. Into it the whole family of children moved before the first of September of that year.

All their resources seemed to be expended upon an almost endless effort of "getting started." Scattered groups of Perfectionists, chiefly in Putney, northern Vermont, Massachusetts, Connecticut and New York, hastened to join. Membership totaled only eighty-seven at the end of the first year, but increased to one hundred and seventy-two at the end of the second, and was to increase to two hundred and five at the end of the third year. More lands were purchased and cleared, dwellings erected, communal housekeeping inaugurated. Children and those few adults who joined in an irreligious state were converted. The fundamental principles of the new social order were taught.

Eventually it was essential that they should develop some basic industry. For the present they could depend upon farming, the saw- and grist-mill, a store, a shoe-shop, a blacksmith-shop. Branch communities were soon maintained at Manlius in New York, and at Cambridge in northern Vermont. A few of the faithful still held the fort at Putney. Members constitutionally unfitted for communism were sent away or allowed to withdraw after a period of probation. Congratulating himself that he was transmuting this motley crew into true communists—homogeneous, compactly organized, equipped with religious and social ordinances, even respected by their neighbors, John Noyes now looked forward to larger conquests.

Chapter III: SACRAMENT OF SEX

> *Shall I not then*
> *Delight in these most Sacred Treasures*
> *Which my Great Father gave,*
> *Far more than other Men*
> *Delight in Gold?*
>
> —TRAHERNE.

I

NOYES's "Bible Communism," an argument "defining the Relations of the Sexes in the Kingdom of Heaven," was written and published in 1848. This document became the Magna Charta of the régime of sexual communism inaugurated in the Community; we must now pause in our narrative to summarize its basic ideas and the manner in which they were adapted to the life at Oneida.

Despite his attempt to marshal the wisdom of the New Testament in support of his philosophy of sex, and to find its vindication in the Bible, it is possible that Noyes was influenced by the current of neo-Malthusian thought which was then rising throughout the Anglo-Saxon world. As early as 1833 Charles Knowlton, a Boston physician, had published a booklet entitled "Fruits of Philosophy" advocating certain elementary methods of birth control. In 1836, Robert Dale Owen, the Americanized son of the founder of New Harmony, published his "Moral Physiology," in which he advocated, as the surest check upon overpopulation, the method of withdrawal. Despite the shrieks of orthodox moralists, a large section of the American people were discussing Owen's proposal with unvarnished plainness and sobriety of speech. Ladies of the Female Moral Reform Societies were shocked by Mr. Owen's offensive frankness in discussing the technique of sexual intercourse. Their denunciations naturally whipped up interest in the Owen book, which attained, so it is said, its greatest popularity among the clergy. Moralists denounced it because it suggested a safe and certain method by which the "consequences of sin" might be habitually evaded.

Years later William Hepworth Dixon, an English journalist, stated that Owen had given the first hint of his system to Noyes. Noyes denied this, and called attention to a review he published in an early number of *The Witness*, printed in Ithaca (1837): "The *last* part of the book I cannot commend, because it shamefully advocates the most atrocious robbery of which man can be guilty; a robbery for which God slew Onan, and for which I doubt not He will in due time destroy all who practice and commend it. Yet the pure in heart, those who are clad with the armor of light, need not fear to read the book, for it contains its own antidote, inasmuch as it most beautifully portrays and inculcates that fearless simplicity which is the very essence of genuine modesty, and a most perfect preventive of the crime which the book was designed to propagate. I may say this is one of the best and the worst books I ever read; *best,* because it teaches the liberty of innocence; *worst,* because it forges and gilds the chains of guilt. It is a dish of foul poison, garnished with the most wholesome and delicious viands. I advise the reader to take the garnishing as lawful spoil, and leave the poison for those who distilled it. . . ."

Noyes always vigorously denied that the Oneida "system" was derived from that advocated by Robert Dale Owen: "Ours is Male Continence; his is Male Incontinence, plus Evasion. If I got my 'first hint' from his book, the 'system' that resulted shows that the hinting must have been 'by contraries.' . . . Owen's book probably helped to turn my attention to the study of the sexual question: and this is all there is in the language I used. I was reading Shaker books also in 1837, and they had quite as much influence on my studies afterwards as 'Moral Physiology.' In fact, the 'system' of Male Continence has more real affinity with Shakerism than with Owenism. It is based on self-control, as Shakerism is based on self-denial; while Owenism is the usual self-indulgence evading its natural consequences." His theory of male continence, Noyes insisted, had been filched from no book: it was in fact the fruit of bitter experience. His sensitiveness to the long, heart-breaking, though always stoically uncomplaining suffering of his wife had opened Noyes's eyes to a fact accepted or ignored by a majority of men of his time: that ordinary sexual behavior as practiced within the bonds of matrimony involved a tragic waste for both participants, and was responsible for a life-long reign of terror for many women. All about him, Noyes witnessed the spectacle of women of every level of society debilitated by excessive childbearing and, as he bluntly expressed it, husbands becoming blandly unconscious murderers of those they loved and had pledged themselves to protect.

2

If the more restrained members of the new community harbored any secret hopes that Noyes would give up his theory and practice of sexual communism, their hopes were speedily dashed. Even more important for Noyes than the building of the Mansion House, or the laying of a sound fiscal basis, was the publication of his "Bible Communism." To the world at large he must herald his marvelous discovery—the "only certain highway" to the recreation of "vital society." Male continence could not fail to effect a complete revolution in love and marriage. Of this John Noyes was firmly convinced. Yet, he was careful to qualify, any attempt to revolutionize sexual morality, before personal settlement with God, would be out of order. "Holiness must go before free love." Moreover, he was careful to explain, these ideas had already been put into practice and successfully vindicated by an association composed of members "of the most respectable families in Vermont . . . educated in the best school of New England morality and refinement, men and women who by ordinary standards had been above reproach in their sexual behavior." Deliberately they had inaugurated this experiment of a new state of society "on principles which they had long been maturing and were prepared to defend before the world." Sober, substantial men and women, of good character and social position, all of them were. Moreover, their innovations would be restricted to the family circle at Oneida. Society at large, therefore, could have no just complaint that its taboos were violated or its customs indecently invaded.

"The first thing to be done in an attempt to redeem man and reorganize society is to bring about reconciliation with God; and the second thing is to bring about a true union of the sexes." Thus the keynote of Noyes's argument: ". . . Religion is the first subject of interest, and sexual morality the second, in the great enterprise of establishing the Kingdom of God on earth."

Just how the sexual function was to be redeemed and true relations between the sexes to be restored was the primary question Noyes sought to answer. His solution, written generations before the advent of modern psychology and the flood of "literature" concerning the sexual problem, remains a landmark of courageous thinking. Noyes foresaw many problems that bewildered humanity is attempting—though with only fragmentary success—to solve in the present century.

It would be impossible to enumerate the number of times this simply stated point of view has been paraphrased—without acknowledgment or thanks—by the counselors of sex-technique in the twentieth century. Noyes's outspoken directness in dealing with such intimate problems should be enough to acquit him of the charge of fanaticism or of any obsessive compulsion. Rather this evidence strengthens our contention that his primary aim was to elevate a bodily instinct into the service of religious ecstasy.

At a later date Noyes admitted that the ideas expressed in 1848 had not then been put to any wide practical test. But they definitely and eloquently expressed the ideal toward which the Oneida Community, for the following thirty years, was to strive.

Noyes declares that the amative and propagative functions are distinct from each other and must be separated in practical expression. Both in the theories of physiologists and amongst the unenlightened, these functions were then confounded. The amative function was regarded merely as a bait to the propagative, and merged in it. But communion which consists in a simple union of persons, making "of twain one flesh," and forming a medium of magnetic and spiritual interchange—is distinct and independent, as superior to the reproductive function as love is to propagative ejaculation.

He proceeds with his proof that this method of controlling propagation is natural, healthy and effectual. Natural, first of all, because useless expenditure of seed cannot be defended. "God cannot have designed that men should sow seed by the wayside, where they do not expect it to grow, nor in the same field where seed has already been sown and is growing; and yet such is the practice of men in ordinary sexual intercourse. They sow seed habitually where they do not *wish* it to grow. This is wasteful of life, and cannot be natural. . . ."

With a courage extraordinary in one whose whole outlook was conditioned by a starkly Puritan background, Noyes refused to evade the evidence that an imperative instinct of human nature demands frequent congress of sexes, not for propagative, but for erotic ends. Simple congress of the sexes, *without the propagative crisis*, he insists, is the order of nature for the gratification of ordinary amative instincts; and the act of propagation should be reserved for its legitimate occasions, when conception is intended. "The idea that sexual intercourse, limited to the social part of it, is impossible or difficult, and therefore not natural, is contradicted by the experience of many."

No less emphatic is Noyes's claim that his method is a sane and healthy one, inasmuch as it renders woman secure from the curse of involuntary and undesirable procreation. The habit of restricting the action of the organs so as to avoid the spasmodic crisis could easily be established, it was his contention, "and then there is no risk of conception without intention." Ordinary sexual intercourse, the egotistic physiological release of organic impulses, the performance of the act without the intention of procreation, Noyes frankly classes with masturbation.

To initiates, this doctrine of male continence stressed moderation and appreciation of the first stages of enjoyment—counseled delay, instead of hurrying over into the abyss of sensuality. The young men were assured that, if they *would*, they *could* stop at any stage. Lust for filling the belly with food in a greedy spirit, hurrying over the preliminaries, corresponded to the lust for the propagative crisis. To Noyes, ordinary custom in sexual intercourse seemed to be on a par with the drinking habits of the English country gentleman of earlier times; for at that period it was esteemed decent for a man to end his dinner under the table.

In actual practice, many delicate problems and complexities arose. Yet the Community experiment confirmed his conviction of the essential importance of his "great discovery." Undoubtedly there were failures, abuses, even abnormalities. But even his scientific and conservative son Theodore, who was educated as a physician, wrote some twenty years later (1870) in defense of male continence: "It must be borne in mind, that, when speaking of sexual abuses, we do not mean our system of male continence, but the perversions to which it is undoubtedly liable. We hold that sexual intercourse, carried on with moderation which does not approach the orgasm, is not injurious to either male or female.... Errors have undoubtedly occurred in the application of our system, through a lack of exact definition in the minds of many; but not more, we believe, than occur in the application of the ordinary method."

3

"I would spear the tallest arch-angel if he should undertake to meddle with my wife!" With this indignant protestation, William Hatch had once set a meeting of Perfectionists into an uproar. Fortunately, perhaps, William Hatch never became a member of the Oneida Community.

Even amongst more docile disciples, Noyes realized that it would be no light task to eradicate the exclusive marriage spirit from the dominating males. Yet he was resolved that the ideal of "idolatrous, exclusive love," so long perpetuated by novelists, poets and sentimentalists, should not take root in the Community. He spurned the notion that romantic love was an inevitable fatality, an epidemic which must be allowed to run its course. Therefore at the daily meetings of the members, he set about to uproot the fallacy of selfish, monogamous love, to demonstrtae how "the law of marriage worketh wrath." He labored hard to dissipate all misgivings, to dispel the timidity of the women, to visualize the inspiring ties of the compact, vital, loving society they might create.

Selfish desire must be subordinated to the greatest good. The law of marriage, he reiterated, inevitably provoked to secret adultery. Adultery of the heart was far more sinful than that of the body. By affording the sexual appetite only a "scanty or monotonous allowance," monogamy bore as its fruit the vices of "poverty, contraction of taste, and stinginess." Love must flow from within outward—only by the fullest and unimpeded expression could it grow. "We must *love*, or the spirit withers and dies." But Noyes was careful to point out that emancipation from these cast-iron rules by which selfishness regulated the relations of the sexes in the world must never be allowed to descend into license, unregulated speech or conduct, or any unseemly familiarity between the sexes. The whole matter of love should be placed under the guidance of the wiser and more experienced. For these reasons, it soon became the main subject for discussion at the evening meetings of the Community, and subject to mutual criticism.

At these meetings Noyes broke down that inherited respect for the holy bonds of matrimony that had been ingrained in these Yankees for generations—that petty business, as Noyes expressed it, of "chaining individuals in pairs for life,"—a pattern, he insisted, completely in conflict with the demonstrated laws of human nature. No matter how the prejudices of the worldly might attempt to conceal the fact, "men and women find universally that their susceptibility to love is not burnt out by one honeymoon, or satisfied by one lover. On the contrary, the secret history of the human heart will bear out the assertion that it is capable of loving any number of times and any number of persons, and that the more it loves the more it can love. This is the law of nature, thrust out of sight, and condemned by common consent, and yet secretly known to all. There is no occasion to find fault with it. Variety is, in the nature of things, as beautiful and as useful in love as in eating and drinking. The one-love theory is the exponent, not of simple experience in love, but of the 'green-eyed monster' jealousy. It is not the loving heart, but the *greedy claimant* of the loving heart, that sets up the popular doctrine that one only can be truly loved...."

"Love is something to give, not to claim," he answered the timid. Love that torments is not true love. "There is peace and rest in true love. Do not think that you have to work and scratch and worry for love—it is the gift of God. . . . We should pray, Give us this day our daily love, for what is love but the bread of the heart? We need love as much as we need food and clothing, and God knows it; and if we trust him for those things, why not for love? And if he gives us love, he will give us rest with it. Love without rest is misery."

But this complex problem could not be solved merely by eloquent words of wisdom. There were long secret consultations among the "central members." Mary Cragin and Harriet Skinner voiced the point of view of the women. However, the final decision concerning intimate relations was always left to Noyes himself. In this realm he remained the supreme and final arbiter. He believed that it would be better for the young of both sexes to associate in communion with persons older than themselves, preferably with those initiated into the practice of self-control. It would be deplorable, he concluded, for two inexperienced and untutored persons to rush into intimate fellowship. Initial steps into the principle of male continence, to which Noyes attached basic importance, must be taken under skilled guidance. The custom was that young men, who had not as yet attained self-control, were initiated by women who had passed the menopause.

After prolonged deliberations, the "central members" decided that they must devise some system of supervision. Exclusive, idolatrous bonds between two members, attachments "unhealthy and pernicious to the whole system of complex marriage," must never gain a foothold in the Community. Hearts must be kept free to love all of the true and worthy. This precaution suggested the intervention of a third party—so that all attachments might be brought under the inspection of the Community; so, also, that women members might, without embarrassment or restraint, decline proposals that did not appeal to them. No member should be obliged to receive—to this they pledged themselves—at any time, under any circumstances, the attention of those they had not learned to love. The Community promised to protect its members from social approaches that might, for one reason or another, either temporarily or permanently, be deemed unattractive. Every woman was to be free to refuse any, or every, man's attention.

John Noyes always resented the application of the terms "free love" or "promiscuity" to the régime of the Community. On the contrary, "complex" marriage signified that each was married to all. So sacred was this pledge during the thirty years of the existence of the society, one of the members claimed in retrospect, that not a single instance of infidelity occurred. When two members aspired to closer relations, an intimation to that effect was given by the man, but always through the medium of an older woman, who represented the Community and was authorized to control such negotiations. This was for the double purpose of overseeing and advising the young people, and of allowing the woman so approached to be perfectly free to decline without embarrassment.

This entire freedom of the women to accept or reject the advances of their lovers kept men as alert as during more conventional courtships. Men sought, as always, to prove themselves worthy of the favor of their sweethearts; and that made their life, they confessed, one continuous courtship.

4

Fundamentally, Noyes's aim was to integrate sexual love with the life of the spirit, to make a sacrament of physical love, the outward and active sign of inward, spiritual grace. Love should be a science as well as an art—the deepest and most engrossing of all sciences. Only through this function, so long abused and misunderstood, could men ever truly experience unity with God and Humanity. Its value was not merely in a rite sacredly fulfilled, but in its power to awaken complete realization of divine unity—the knowledge that all love is one and indivisible. Sexual love, transcending individual consciousness, Noyes explained, provided the experience through which we, as members of the human race, are enabled to experience the ecstasy of true communion, to break through the dark isolation of egotism and self-hood. He might have insisted that there is no more meaning in sex for sex's sake than there can be in "art for art's sake"; for this portal to the mystic experience is defiled when it is used merely as the means of sensual pleasure. Egotism here defeats its own end and closes the door to more profound and exalting experience. Noyes would have agreed with Miguel de Unamuno that sexual love is the generative type of every other love, that we are constitutionally unable to dissociate the concept of love from the idea of sexual love, which creates an ineradicable symbol of its true character. The Spanish mystic has written: "In its essence, the delight of sexual love . . . is a sensation of resurrection, or renewing our life in another, for only in others can we renew our life and so perpetuate ourselves."

The new covenant, as Noyes interpreted it, must reverse and revolutionize not only religion, but also the love experience. There was in humanity an inertia, a racial tendency to drop back into the ordinary habits of the world—a law of spiritual gravity that must be incessantly counterbalanced. He insisted that, on the contrary, all experience, all living, whether religious or emotional, must be infused with novelty, must battle endlessly against habit and repetition. Only thus could life become a continuous unfolding. Most deeply in error were those who claimed to have solved the great enigma of sexual love, those men who fatuously assumed that they "knew all about women"—or *vice versa.* The mystery, he insisted, could not be so promptly nor so simply fathomed. Those who feel that they have solved the mystery and that it is, after all, no great affair, are indeed lost to the deeper significance of living. Such an attitude—the philosophy of the *homme moyen sensuel*—he denounced as an insult to human nature, and to the God who created male and female.

"In such a simple instrument as the violin, you may find men who devote their lifetime and all the powers of their musical nature to understand it and they still say they are just beginning to fathom it, and every few years some one comes out with a new understanding of its capabilities and powers. I must be a poor, wooden character," Noyes expostulated one evening, "a more worthless thing as an instrument of pleasure, than a violin, if the mystery of our companionship is fathomed, and we know all about each other. I say such a conclusion shows a very poor view of human nature; it shows that people have no respect for God. I should have more self-respect than to believe this; and back of that, more respect for God; for we are fearfully and wonderfully made. We are wonderful musical instruments; made to give and receive great pleasure in love. What a poor compliment to him to say, after merely tasting of each other, that the enigma is solved, that we have mastered all there is on that instrument. So to a true heart, one that appreciates God, the same woman is an endless mystery. And this necessarily flows from the first admission that God is unfathomable in depths of knowledge and wisdom."

There was, Noyes insisted, a way to use every form of external enjoyment as a method of worship and interchange between man and the divine; and contrariwise, that there was a way to use the world and its pleasures as a medium of exchange between men and the devil. "The right use of the things of this world depends on our digestive power. . . . There is a digestive power that can spiritualize and sanctify everything." Wisdom, he said, consists in the discernment of what we can bear. When men pray "Lead us not into temptation," they pray to know how to proportion their use of this world to their digestive power—to be kept from using any more of this world than they can thoroughly assimilate. "We cannot regulate ourselves by reference to others; for one can digest more than another. Neither can we make any general rule for specific conduct. We must have instinctive discernment for ourselves."

When a natural attraction among younger members, youths and maidens standing at the threshold of maturity, seemed to be toward those of their own age, great care was taken to make them understand the law of the ascending fellowship, the state in which a person's companionship was with those above him in spiritual life. The descending fellowship was a state in which a person loved those below him in spiritual life, so that the drawing of the fellowship was downward. The ascending fellowship was preferable; of course, all should associate with those who drew them upward. But ascending fellowship also implied descending fellowship. The only principle on which the descending fellowship could be justified was that it was sanctioned by the superior, identified with and authorized by it. True, legitimate, descending fellowship carried with it the inspiration of the superior. "I would not set up a distinction of right and wrong between general and special love, except that special love, when false, makes more mischief," explained Noyes to his family. "I insist that all love, whether general or special, must have its authority in the sanction and the inspiration of the ascending fellowship. All love which is at work in a private corner, away from the general circulation, where there are no series of links connecting it with God, is false love; it rends and devours, instead of making unity, peace and harmony. There is a great deal of that kind of fellowship which is tolerated; for God is merciful. He waits on prodigals, reaches after them, follows them and brings them back from unfathomable depths of idolatry. . . ."

Earnestly and innocently the Community listened to the counsel of the leader as in the family meetings he guided them out of the darkness of the world surrounding them: "The soul must go down into the body and have fellowship with its pleasures just as far as God and the heavens send it and no farther; and the body must go down into the businesses and pleasures of the material world just so far as the soul sends it and no farther. The superior sending and limiting the inferior is the principle that starts from the example of the Father and the Son, and runs through all the descending links of celestial and terrestrial love."

Scandalized whispers were gathering momentum throughout Oneida and Madison Counties. Children were sent away as elders discussed the amazing practices at the Community—"They say . . . they say . . . they say!" To his critics Noyes retorted: "A just scrutiny would disclose less familiarity of the sexes—less approach to anything like 'Bacchanalian revelry'—vastly less unregulated speech and conduct than is found in an equal circle of what is called good society in the world. That we have disclaimed the cast-iron rules and modes by which selfishness regulates the relations of the sexes, is true. . . . Amativeness, the lion of the tribe of human passions, is conquered and civilized among us."

5

Noyes, the inveterate and indefatigable propagandist, decided to dispatch his "Bible Communism" to the Governor of the State, to prominent men in public life, and to many advanced thinkers. Just as assiduously, he circulated the first Annual Report of the Oneida Association. The sexual practices of the Community became an open secret. Wild tales concerning Noyes and his followers aroused increasing scandal and gossip. In defense, the Community claimed to be a private family, unashamed of its open secrets—no matter how piquant these might seem to the prurient. "We are not ashamed of them, yet we have always preferred that they remain veiled. We have given credit to the public for that delicacy which respects the proper veil of private life, and have found the better part of mankind . . . respectful toward our internal affairs. . . ."

The more sensitive, however, always felt vague premonitions of the coming storm. They remembered Putney—the betrayal, the persecution, the threats of mob violence, the final expulsion from Vermont. Was this ordeal to be repeated in New York?

In 1850, enemies complained to magistrates of both Oneida and Madison Counties concerning the "unmoralities" practiced within the Community. The question was referred to the Grand Jury of Madison County. To that august body information was given and complaint made by certain persons residing in the town of Lenox, that there was in their midst a collection of individuals of both sexes, living in a mixed manner; that they did not hold to marriage; that their numbers were steadily on the increase; that their example was corrupting and demoralizing to the community in which they lived, and that, in fact, they were a public nuisance. The Grand Jury was asked to find a bill of indictment against them. A number of witnesses backed this complaint. Many questions were asked of the complainants and witnesses, from which it appeared that such a collection of people did live in the county. But it also became evident that they were industrious, peaceable and law-abiding, apparently minding their own business, and harming no one, not differing from other people essentially except as to their views of marriage. A number of the jurors were for finding against Noyes and his followers. Finally the Grand Jury tactfully decided not to notice the complaint, but to keep an eye on the behavior and the influence of the Communists.

In 1850 the Community had not been long enough in Oneida to make many influential friends. While it remained in ignorance of the complaints and proceedings in Madison County, a real storm broke on another battle front. Though the Community was not located within their proper jurisdiction, the authorities of Oneida County carried proceedings against Noyes even further. Community men and women were summoned to Utica and put through a merciless examination by an exasperated District Attorney before a very chilly Grand Jury. It was not fair nor lawful that they should be called on to incriminate themselves, but they were; and they told the truth and the whole truth.

Sensitive and high-minded women were asked obscene questions about the most private experiences; but without evasion or complaint they told all. The women were never to forget the ignominy of this ordeal. Their nostrils were assailed by that odor which seemed to pervade all courthouses in the olden days—an odor emitted by some strong, crude disinfectant that suggested a nearby jail and motley criminals. They ran a gauntlet of the curious gaze of idlers, the leers, the suppressed obscenities, the quips of the lesser functionaries, the malicious probing of lecherous lawyers and dignitaries. But their dignity, their perfect manners, and their honesty carried them through. They saved the day for John Noyes. They were fully conscious that they were in the lion's mouth. How they ever got out, they never quite discovered. All they could ever recall was that they told the furious District Attorney and the excited newspaper world that they were willing to go back into marriage or Shakerism if that were demanded of them. Their inquisitors answered with scorn and wrath; they had no confidence in John Noyes. They advised his followers to break up and "clear out." The women answered meekly that they had no idea of resisting the will of the magistracy and people around them; that if it was really the will of neighbors that they should clear out, they would do so. Calculations and measures for dispersing were actually commenced—some to Vermont, some to Massachusetts, all to various former homes. But fairly to test the question whether neighbors really wished them to "clear out," the Community circulated the following document:

TO THE DISTRICT ATTORNEY OF THE COUNTY OF ONEIDA AND ALL WHOM IT MAY CONCERN:

This is to certify that we, the undersigned, citizens of the towns of Vernon and Lenox, are well acquainted with the general character of the Oneida Community, and are willing to testify, that we regard them as honorable business men, as good neighbors, and quiet, peaceable citizens. We believe them to be lovers of justice and good order—that they are men who mind their own business, and in no way interfere with the rights of their neighbors. We regard them, so far as we know, as persons of good moral character; and we have no sympathy with the recent attempts to disturb their peace.

Nearly every one to whom they appealed willingly signed this document. The Hon. Timothy Jenkins, largest land-owner and most influential citizen of the Oneida Reserve voluntarily declared that he considered the Community members not only good, peaceable citizens, but the best class in that region; and that he regarded it as a blessing to the other citizens to have these in their midst. Other influential men spoke a friendly word in the right quarter. And so they found themselves saved from the lions!

Chapter IV: WILLOW PLACE

> . . . nor life, nor angels, nor principalities, nor powers, nor things present, nor things to come, nor height, nor depth, nor any creature shall be able to separate us from the love of God. . . .
>
> —ROMANS: 8.

I

THE "Brooklyn period" in the life of John Humphrey Noyes extends from 1849 to December, 1854. This period marks the culmination of his Messianic ambitions, and ends with his willing, though chastened return to the Oneida Community to resume the task of shepherding his flock through the years of famine confronting it. Noyes's motive in leaving Oneida for Brooklyn is not altogether clear. Persecution was gathering like thunder clouds following the publication of his "Bible Communism," and was, a year or two later, to gather into the storm recorded in the last chapter. But we discover evidence indicating that Noyes also felt called upon to convert the world at large to his astounding beliefs. This ambition was fostered by Abram Smith, who seemed to have exercised a shrewd power in persuading the "central members" to accept policies advantageous to his personal ambitions. The third annual report of the Oneida Association, published in 1851, states that "Mr. Abram C. Smith, an old associate in the cause of holiness, upon joining the Community in the spring of 1849, bought for its use the house at 41 Willow Place, Brooklyn, N. Y., at a cost of $3,300. This has been the residence for most of the time since, of Mr. and Mrs. Noyes, and Mr. and Mrs. Cragin. Mr. Noyes chose to live here, as affording a more quiet place for reflection, and a better place to act upon the Association than a residence directly in it. Friends from Newark are generally present Sundays, and some of the evenings of the week." The house adjoining (No. 43) was also bought by the Oneidans for $3,300, and eventually the two Willow Place houses were converted into one.

Among the little group of Newark Perfectionists who came on Sundays to listen to Noyes's counsel, the leading figure was William R. Inslee. He was an expert machinist and the proprietor of a modest little machine shop in Newark. Several of the younger men from Oneida were sent there as apprentices, and acquired a solid training as machinists. This education was characterized by Noyes as the cornerstone of the later prosperity of the Community. The Brooklyn family was soon convinced that it could maintain itself through the manufacture of gold-chain, and the house at 43 Willow Place was purchased to provide room for a communal workshop.

With its cultural advantages and its proximity to New York, Brooklyn in 1851 appealed to the communists as a stimulating change from the incessant toil at Oneida. Fire had destroyed the press at Oneida, and Noyes resolved to set up a new one in Willow Place. "The fire which destroyed the printing-office and press at Oneida, and thus abruptly terminated the *Free Church Circular*, spared the greater part of our type—sufficient for the use of this paper—and made occasion for the transfer of the printing department to Brooklyn. We have since built a printing-office in the rear of our dwelling, procured a power-press, and made all arrangements necessary for efficient and permanent service in the work before us.... We commence a weekly paper at the center of communication (for Brooklyn is a part of New York), surrounded by radiating lines of railroads, steamers, telegraphs and expresses. Our working company of writers, reporters and printers, is stronger than ever before, and ready as one man for any amount of service that the times may demand. Thus our enterprise is in good condition at the outset, and may grow."

But the heavy burden of these plans for the conversion of American civilization fell upon the struggling little community at Oneida. It required all of John R. Miller's "financial genius" to make both ends meet. The financial pinch became sharper and sharper. Often money was not on hand at night for the necessary expenses of the next day. Once the last dollar in the dwindling treasury was given to a visitor to pay his way home. Oneida paid the bills for Willow Place and until the end of the Brooklyn venture, economy, industry, and dexterity in converting property into cash were all that staved off disaster.

It was proposed at one evening meeting in Oneida that all who could spare their watches should place them in the hands of a committee to be sold. Twenty-five watches were given up, and the next evening fifteen more. In September, 1851, a letter was read to the Community proposing that the Oneida family should furnish Willow Place with butter. This appeal was greeted with merriment; no butter had been served on the Community table for days.

Despite all these hardships at Oneida the leader in Willow Place insisted upon continuing the paper, believing that they owed everything to the publicity they obtained through *The Circular*. "I do not think we ever began to make our living at Putney, by the farming or housekeeping, or anything else that we did; but we kept the paper going," he explained. The paper had prepared the way for these conventions which led to the establishment of the Community. The paper had brought in the Burts, and the Hamiltons, and the Wordens and the Abbots; from northern Vermont came another thirty thousand dollars or more from the Kinsleys, the Barrons, the Halls. The Connecticut brethren brought in eight or ten thousand more. The paper had turned their hearts; the paper had burned out egotism and selfishness; the paper had gathered a capital of one hundred thousand dollars, more or less. Noyes admitted that the Brooklyn family was a heavy expense, that a great deal of money was spent publishing the paper and carrying on the educational enterprise, for which no immediate return was in sight. But they were keeping communications open with the men and property of the world. It would be a confession of failure to close this communication, to retreat, to become an isolated little family, grubbing and scratching, making all the money they could and hoarding all they made! No: it would be, he insisted, much better to sustain the paper, to adhere to the principle that truth would ultimately find its way into the hearts of men and make them generous and self-sacrificing. "Let the private fortune of the Oneida Community be what it may, its first business is to see that God has a Press. If it does that, it will have God's blessing as I have had it."

So the house in Willow Place provided a refuge from the storm of persecution that had led to the ordeal in Utica. Even the epidemic of cholera in the metropolitan region seemed preferable to the dismaying protests that swept over Madison County. Despite John Noyes's ambitions, his hopes for the expansion of his free press, and his indomitable leadership of his scattered forces, Destiny loaded the dice against him. As in Putney, as in Utica, the moralists took up arms against him. Now planted squarely under the nose of the rulers of public opinion in the metropolis, the little band of Perfectionists drew new fire.

A self-righteous and pontifical religious weekly, the New York *Observer*, discovered the obscure little community in Brooklyn, and promptly trained its long-range guns of moral indignation upon the "family" in Willow Place. The most significant fruit of that crusade of pompous verbiage is a letter it drew from the elder Henry James. With all the characteristic gallantry of that disarming eccentric, that letter indicates that Mr. James himself—accompanied (we like to think) by his sons William, aged ten, and Henry, eight—crossed the ferry in person to investigate this new variety of religious experience, budding in so extraordinary a fashion in Brooklyn and Oneida. Mr. James made clear to the editor of the *Observer* that he was no champion of the doctrines and practices of Noyes, but love of justice and fair play compelled him to write in defense of the Perfectionists. The elder James denounced "the cowardice which . . . hints and insinuates the calumny it dares not boldly mouth." He went on: "From a conversation or two which I have had with some of their leading men, I judged them to be persons of great sincerity, but of deplorable fanaticism, who were driven to the lengths you so sternly reprobate strictly because they exemplify what you are not,—a logical abandonment to their own religious convictions. I told them candidly that any man of common sense must give short shrift in his regard to a deity who elected men to the privilege of leading disorderly lives; but at the same time I saw that they were no way amenable to the tribunal of common sense. An unhappy religious fanaticism, the flowering of your fundamental principles, has lifted them out of that wholesome judicature, and they must henceforth drift whithersoever the benignant powers—who after all are paramount in this world, spite of many *Observers*—will let them. But at the same time I must avow that these strenuous and unhandsome sectarians appeared to me far worthier of tender compassion than of brutal public vituperation. Honest, upright souls they seemed at bottom, though sadly misguided by an insane sense of duty, and delicate women were among them, too, full no doubt of women's indestructible truth. They were fathers, and husbands, and brothers, like myself, disfigured, to be sure, by a morbid religious conscience, but no less capable of suffering on that account whatever I suffered. And so I could not help saying to myself how surely must errors like these involve this poor unprotected people in permanent popular disgrace, or what is worse, perhaps, provoke the fatal violence of a disgusting pharisaic mob; and how gladly, therefore, must good men of every name rather lessen than deepen the inevitable odium in which they stand! Accordingly it appears to me about as unmanly a sight as the sun now shines upon to see a great prosperous newspaper like the New York *Observer* gather together the two wings of its hebdomadal flatulence, 'secular' and 'religious,' for a doughty descent upon this starveling and harmless fieldmouse!"

But Henry James, the elder, charmingly eccentric and seemingly irreverent—from the Puritan point of view—must have shocked the Brooklyn Perfectionists, as much as he had shocked the admirers of Bronson Alcott in Concord. Perhaps, like Mr. Alcott's, Mr. Noyes's authority was not to be questioned, especially by an outsider. Despite the service Mr. James rendered them in springing to their defense, the Brooklyn disciples tactfully hinted that his lack of reverence to the Deity made him an unwelcome visitor.

2

The Willow Place family insisted that John should go to the World's Fair in London as a reward for his arduous labors. Robert Sparrow de Latre, an English disciple who came from Canada, planned to go with him. They obtained passage on *The Baltic*, and not without apprehensions and ill-disguised fears the women in Willow Place packed the belongings of their hero. John Noyes was going to "look the world in the eye." They were sure that he would be under the protection of Providence—but it was a long, perilous voyage across the Atlantic in the spring of the year—it would take at least twelve days to reach London. John's departure left them leaderless, and Harriet Noyes, Mary Cragin and Harriet Skinner sought to buoy up their drooping spirits. But outwardly, their bravado was splendid. Perhaps in their dreams they pictured the wreck of the good ship—shipwrecks were frequent calamities; but during the day as they set type or "held" proof, they remained conspicuously cheerful—though each of them counted the days till he would return.

Meanwhile, *The Baltic* was soon running into heavy seas. Mr. Horace Greeley, who was aboard, remained appallingly seasick in his cabin on an upper deck. When Robert de Latre and John Noyes ventured on deck, they were enveloped in clouds of soot and cinders. They found it more comfortable to remain in a little semi-private saloon which opened off Noyes's berth. This room was heated, and gradually certain passengers discovered its seclusion—and even the great editor of the New York *Tribune* accepted Noyes's invitation to join the group of intelligentsia. The little saloon became the scene of a series of lively debates. Greeley upheld Noyes in a discussion with a Swedenborgian on the Second Coming of Christ, but disagreed with the Oneida heretic on the benefits of transatlantic travel. Literally green with seasickness, Horace advanced the position that Americans should remain on their own continent. Christ's place, retorted Noyes, was on the sea. There citizens of all nations and races might meet in peace.

In London, after the long, turbulent passage, Noyes was taken to see the famous sights. Robert de Latre led him off to the visitors' gallery in the Commons, to Westminster Abbey, St. Paul's, and the British Museum. But their main interest was concentrated upon the celebrated Crystal Palace. Early one Monday morning, De Latre and Noyes were among the first to arrive at the hall. Noyes went to the central transept, bought a synopsis of the exhibition, and sat down to read. After a few minutes he rose and without any purpose of his own, wandered down the west aisle. Suddenly his way was stopped by a little gathering of people, who seemed specially interested in some sight. Noyes stepped among them, and took his place at a railing. A few steps within the railing there was a group of ordinary-looking folk, examining exhibits of the show; and among them a plain sort of matron leaning on a gentleman's arm. Noyes asked a bystander who that lady might be.

"My dear sir!" replied the Briton, "it is the Queen!"

"There I was with my republican hat on, face to face with her majesty, not ten yards distant," wrote John in a letter to Willow Place. "The latent loyalty of the old Norfolk blood awoke, and I respectfully uncovered. 'And who is that tall gentleman with the Queen?' said I to him of the distinguished air.

" 'That,' said he, 'is the Prince of Prussia.'

"I had an opportunity to inspect the royal countenance at my leisure for some minutes without crowding or bustle. The Queen is not beautiful—the portraits flatter her. She appears simple and sensible. Her stature is short, and her features rather coarse. But there is something good and even majestic in her eye. Her dress was quite ordinary. After some minutes, she with her suite came directly toward the railing at the point where I was, passing me within reach of my hand, with her face toward me, and bowing two or three times as she swept along to another stall. Soon there was 'racing and chasing' up and down the aisle, and in and out the stalls, when it became known that she was in the building; but few had the quiet opportunity that I had of seeing her. In fact, I find that old Londoners and British subjects fairly envy me the lucky view."

This seemed to have been the most memorable incident of those brief three weeks in London and Paris. In seven weeks, almost to the hour, De Latre and Noyes were back in Willow Place. The women rejoiced upon their safe return. Secretly they assured themselves that this homecoming was nothing less than miraculous.

3

Not long after the hegira to Brooklyn, Abram Smith stepped forward with an arresting idea. Shortly thereafter the Association came into possession of a sloop, the *Rebecca Ford*. The ex-

Methodist minister sold it to them. During the season the *Rebecca Ford* was regularly employed in freighting limestone from Kingston to Brooklyn and New York. No less than sixty passages were made, and the financial experts of the Community rejoiced in the *Rebecca's* earnings of $1,250. So elated were they that they could not refrain, in all seriousness, from announcing in their annual report: "With these two arms, a competent and organized Press, and a suitable Marine, truth is furnished for the conquest of the world. In sailing the sloop as in all other business, it was found necessary at the outset to get free from the trammels of the world, to follow inspiration, and keep the spiritual foremost.... The sloop men make their home with the Brooklyn family when in this port, and at Kingston with friends there."

But the "conquest of the world" was not to be effected by that "suitable Marine," the *Rebecca Ford*. And "inspiration" was to prove a poor guide for Hudson River navigation.

Aboard the *Rebecca Ford* a gallant little crew left Brooklyn one Tuesday afternoon (July 22, 1851) at about four o'clock. Abram Smith acted as captain of the sloop. His crew consisted of Henry Burnham, Henry Seymour and Francis Long. Radiant with enthusiasm Mary Cragin also joined this summer cruise up the Hudson, and Eliza Allen echoed Mary's delight. She had come from Wallingford, Connecticut–she was less than a year older than Mary, and she was as inexperienced in sailing as she had been in the complex codes of the Community.

Through the waters of the bay, before a stiff south wind, plowed the *Rebecca Ford*. With full-bellied mainsail the sloop made its way through the North River into the Hudson. Each new aspect of changing shores found expression in appropriate quotations from the Scriptures. For forty miles they went on through the pageant of the late afternoon sun, until they reached Stony Point. There they anchored the *Rebecca Ford* for the night. In the morning they floated up to the Highland ice-houses; they visited Montgomery Lake, and late in the day returned to the "yacht"–as they delighted in calling that workaday sloop. Then slowly in the late afternoon, as innocently pleased as children with a new toy, the little crew moved on up the Hudson, studying the river-map they had brought with them. With little cries of delight Mary identified the summits and highlands, more famous in those days than today. They discovered decayed landmarks of Revolutionary activities, and commented upon them all with lively interest. From West Point, across the gleaming oily surface of the river, came distant strains of martial music, echoes of marching feet. On Thursday, the gallant *Rebecca Ford* reached her destination. Then, for the three men began the drudgery of loading the sloop with limestone. Mary Cragin and Eliza Allen served the meals in the cabin of the boat. During the day, the two women found time for excursions—even to the neighborhood of Abram's old stone house. "We rambled through the woods and picked several quarts of berries," Mary wrote to George Cragin on the night before their departure. "I like a 'sea-faring' life very much. It breaks up effeminate notions and takes the starch out of folks wonderfully, and is, I think, very conducive to health; certainly it quickens my appetite and digestion. Miss Allen stands it well. Tonight, after we had finished our day's work, we visited the *cave*, and had a fine time. Tell Mr. Noyes that things go well, *interiorly* and *exteriorly*, and we feel satisfied that the angels are watching over us and are full of 'good will' to us. We shall have one or two adventures to relate to you which will prove it. I had some emotions of wonder, and admiration of God's power and wisdom in bringing us through safely in 'the days of old' which these scenes revive. Surely, after what has passed, we can trust him to pilot us through anything, confident that he has the machinery sufficient; only give him time."

On Saturday, Mary, Eliza Allen and Henry Burnham left in the yawl to visit the old stone house at Rondout. Two hours of loading remained to be finished. The "crew" planned to pick up Mary, Eliza, and Henry as the *Rebecca Ford* passed downstream.

As the three of them were sculling in the direction of the stone house, Mary read to them from her Testament. She chose the eighth chapter of Romans. She read slowly, emphasizing passages that most impressed her:

" 'For the law of the spirit of life in Christ Jesus hath made me free from the law of sin and death.' " Each reading, it struck Mary Cragin, revealed fresher meaning, deeper truth. Eliza and Henry listened attentively as Mary's voice lifted across the surface of the sparkling, sunlit water:

" 'Nay, in all these things we are more than conquerors through him that loved us. For I am persuaded, that neither death . . .' " her voice rose exultantly, " '. . . nor life . . . nor angels . . . nor principalities . . . nor powers, . . . nor things present . . . nor things to come . . . nor height, nor depth,' "—Mary paused to peer downward into the depths of the river, "nor any other creature . . . shall be able to separate us from the love of God, which is in Christ Jesus our Lord.' "

Silence. "What more do we need than this?" cried Mary at last.

The three of them clambered aboard the *Rebecca Ford* again at about eleven o'clock. It was a glorious, breezy morning. Henry Burnham took his post at the helm. The wind blew mainly from the west—to Henry it seemed a bit contrary, as though it were playing tricks with their cumbersome craft. He paid strict attention to his task. Abram Smith and Long were attending to the mainsheet. Soon they were shouting congratulations to one another upon the speed they were making. The heavily laden *Rebecca Ford* seemed to be flying—plowing deep furrows through the swift current.

Below, Mary and Eliza busied themselves with the preparation of the midday meal. Dinner would be ready for the "crew" promptly at one o'clock. The wind subsided into a steady, quiet breeze. The three men on deck could hear the gay chatter of the two women below. Finally Mary Cragin cheerfully shouted that dinner was ready. Her course laid, the *Rebecca Ford* was cutting steadily downstream. Already they were little more than a mile north of Hyde Park. While Henry Burnham went below for his dinner, Francis Long offered to stand at the helm.

They sat down to dinner but had scarcely begun to eat when the *Rebecca Ford* lurched suddenly. Without any particular apprehension of danger, Henry Burnham looked out the porthole. Was it the beginning of a squall, this sudden gust of wind?

"Captain" Smith and Henry hurried back up on deck in an instant. Smith saw that the inexperienced Long was maneuvering badly—he seized the helm from the frightened young man. But his gesture was too late. The *Rebecca Ford* had gone over too far ever again to right herself. Water was rushing through the open hatches—there was no getting back into the cabin. Henry Burnham clung to the guards of the starboard quarter. The *Rebecca Ford* careened over. Burnham and the men clutched hopelessly on the side that remained longest out of the water.

From that point, with a sort of stunned detachment, Henry Burnham could see everything—the cargo of limestone on the deck dislodged and crashing, the waters rushing down into the cabin. Did he hear the voices of the two women trapped there? Seymour caught a terrifying glimpse of Eliza Allen, but could give her no help. The sloop filled almost instantly. There was a deafening roar of air escaping through the stern windows. Through the spray Henry Burnham suddenly saw a brilliant rainbow. Never afterwards could he forget that curious detail of the most helpless, agonizing moment of his life. He could not swim; so he clutched first at an oar, then at a plank, buoying himself up, waiting and waiting, until at last even the mast of the *Rebecca Ford* disappeared beneath the surface of the water.

A yawl from the schooner *Shaw Abbilena* picked up the four survivors. They were hauled aboard by Captain Hotaling. Henry Burnham pulled his watch out of his pocket. It had stopped, water-soaked, at just six minutes after one. He remembered having glanced at it at the table—and it had been then but five minutes after one. He asked himself, unbelieving, how so much could have been compressed into sixty seconds.

At twilight a messenger delivered a telegram to Noyes. It read: "Serious news to communicate. At six minutes past one o'clock this afternoon in a squall of about two minutes' duration, the sloop capsized and sunk. The women went down with her; the men were saved. She was homeward bound, one mile above Hyde Park. I shall take the seven o'clock train this evening for Brooklyn. Your stricken brother H. W. Burnham."

Later that night at Willow Place, Henry Burnham appeared, repeating over and over again the details of the swift tragedy. Noyes set out early next day. He found Smith and Seymour at Rondout; they left at once for Kingston Point. The two men told Noyes that at low tide the mast of the *Rebecca Ford* extended some feet above the surface of the water, and that Francis Long had been there to guard the lantern which hung from the tip of the mast. Smith had tried to secure at Rondout means of raising the vessel, but without success. They were advised to try further at Poughkeepsie. Burnham was sent on to Oneida; and Smith, Seymour and Noyes set out on foot for Hyde Park, a distance of some twelve miles. They met Long, and spent the evening on an inquest into the "causes of the judgment we have suffered." They arrived at a "unanimous decision that Long's mismanagement and cowardice was the direct cause; that a perverse spirit in him which had resisted criticism and kindness so long, was the previous chronic cause; and that the loose habits of fellowship which have admitted him among us and employed him in responsible business, have involved the Association in his culpability; so that this chastisement is deserved, and necessary for us all."

This jury did not spare poor Francis Long! They pointed out that for months he had been in a gloomy, unbelieving and non-consulting spirit. One of the main objects of Mary Cragin's excursion had been to make an effort to conquer him by kindness and spiritual advice. Abram Smith reiterated the accusation that as he had ascended the companion-way just before the disaster he had seen that Francis was holding the helm the wrong way, and had ordered him to put it "hard down." But a moment later, averred Abram Smith, the helm was wrong again. Smith had sprung to the tiller—but it was too late!

Noyes ordered Long to prepare a confession of his rôle in the disaster. He promised to do so. He must prove his penitence. Yet there was no light on the mast of the *Rebecca Ford* on Monday night. Poor Long confessed that he had seen the light in the lantern flicker and go out during the long hours of the night, but that he had felt so miserable, the river was so dreary that he was afraid to go out and relight it. So Smith and Noyes went out to replace the light over the resting place of Mary Cragin.

"At eleven o'clock in a dark night, to go out in a small boat half a mile to hang a beacon over the bodies of our loved ones was as solemn a thing as ever I did; and yet it was pleasant. We spoke not a word of sorrow, but cheerfully hailed the spirits of the dead, and left the scene with reluctance."

Smith and Noyes trudged to Poughkeepsie, seeking help to raise the sloop. Then they returned to Kingston Point, traveling about the docks in quest of boats. Many discouragements confronted them, but Noyes refused to abandon the task.

Not until the nineteenth of August were the two bodies rescued from the cabin, laid side by side in one coffin, clad as they were at the time of the disaster in the short dresses of the Oneida uniform, and carried up to the cemetery of the Episcopal Church of Esopus. The spire of the church, which stood out on the west bank of the Hudson, nearly opposite Hyde Park, became for Noyes the monument to Mary Cragin and Eliza Allen. Eli Hitchcock of Hudson presented a white marble monument, erected over the grave of the two women in the hilltop churchyard.

4

Death now stalked into the house in Willow Place. Miss Sophronia Tuttle, only twenty-one years old, was prostrated by dysentery, and died on September 12. "A few days before she departed, we requested her to bear our love to Mrs. Cragin, and tell her we were waiting for a re-union." Later the family discovered this "unusual liberty with the dying and the dead" had been sanctioned as early as 1840 by the great Dr. Bushnell, who had suggested the propriety of sending messages by the dying to departed friends. Indeed, Dr. Bushnell expressed surprise that this custom was not oftener observed.

The communal family in Willow Place could not be discouraged by these blows, nor by the reports John Miller sent from Oneida, although month followed month and still there was no change for the better in their fortunes. They were sure they could rely upon the energy, financial skill and tact of John Miller, the second-in-command at Oneida. Had he not always turned aside the shafts of persecution, averted the Community bankruptcy more than once?

Then, in 1853, came the ominous news that John Miller must rest. His health had broken under the strain.

Poor John Miller, as some one remarked, had "ticked too fast." Years of unrelieved effort in behalf of the struggling communities had cost Charlotte's husband his health. A level-headed business man, John had also proved himself a skillful tactician in meeting all threats of mob violence. It had been Mr. Miller who had diverted the angry currents of opposition in Putney. At Oneida, during these years of the Brooklyn epoch, the outlook for tolerance had become more and more hopeless. Late one night, he had been aroused by a straggling crowd of countryside roughs standing outside the Mansion howling threats. John Miller dressed and went down to meet them under the butternut tree. So peaceful, so neighborly, so frank was his talk, addressed to them in their own terms, that this leaderless gang was soon satisfied that the "free lovers" were after all decent, law-abiding, and only concerned with their own livelihood. Temporarily appeased, the mob dispersed.

But such attacks were the least of John Miller's worries. For as business manager, there were six "families" or communities that depended upon him. Not only Putney, Willow Place and Wallingford, but the smaller flocks at Newark, Newkirk and at Putney were almost incessantly crying for help. If any of them were to survive, John Miller realized, they must be organized on a self-sustaining commercial basis. They must have some industry that would yield an income. Some one had suggested the possibilities of the silk peddling business. John Miller sent the community men out, two by two, peddling sewing silk throughout the region of central New York. The first traveling bag business, initiated in Willow Place, demanded his close attention, as did the grist mill at Putney, the peddling of fruits and vegetables at Wallingford and at Oneida. In addition to all this, to John Miller fell the Herculean task of finding money to continue the publication of *The Circular* in Willow Place.

Despite all Miller's efforts to establish peaceful relations with the surrounding inhabitants, the outlook at Oneida became more and more threatening. In 1852, it seemed certain that they must scatter once more. John Miller made a special trip to northern Vermont to investigate the possibility of establishing a refuge on the foothills of Mount Mansfield. But fortunately, due to his level-headed tactics and unfaltering courage, that crisis was later averted. The dark clouds of persecution lifted. But at last Miller had collapsed under the strain of those years.

Despite his mental and physical exhaustion, John Miller was temperamentally unable to relinquish his duties. Unflinching in loyalty to the absent leader, he made a desperate effort to regain his strength, to devise new ways of raising money so that the publication of the tri-weekly might be continued. In May, 1854, he undertook the long, fatiguing journey from Oneida to Willow Place, in order to outline his plans for the future. Cheered up by this contact with Noyes, John Miller returned to the Community a few days later. A month later this martyr was laid to rest on the hillside behind the Mansion House, and Charlotte was left a widow with three children—Tirzah, George and Helen.

5

The death of John Miller seemed to be the final blow to Noyes's grandiose ambition for converting the world by the instrument of a daily press. Confronted by disaster compounded and multiplied, Noyes passed through that zone of despair that many men must traverse in their early forties—to the rocky barrenness of the road ahead when the excess trappings of youthful ambition and Messianic ideals must be cast away. Now he could go forward warily, but one step at a time. Noyes did find some consolation in his study of geology. It taught him, he confessed, the necessity of faith long-continued—a willingness to wait patiently for far-distant results. He became more realistic, less visionary, more practical. "I took in an element of patience; and since then I have not been in so much of a *hurry* for a daily paper, for the Millennium, and for the manifestation of victory over death. But if I am more ready to wait, I have a faith surer than ever in regard to the coming of these things. Geology had been supposed to favor a state of unbelief, but to me it has been a source of faith. It has disclosed the *time* in which the music of the universe is written. I hear in it the movement of the grand anthem of creation; and it enabled me to correct my step so as to keep time with it. . . . I learned not to be desirous of dancing a jig, when everything around is moving to the time of a grand march."

In December, 1854, Noyes and the rest of the Willow Place disciples returned to Oneida. They resolved upon a policy of retrenchment and concentration. Branches at Brooklyn, Newark, Putney and Cambridge, in northern Vermont, were closed. Henceforth Oneida would be the chief community, while Wallingford, in Connecticut, was to be developed as a printing center. *The Circular* was to be published weekly as a sort of news-letter going to scattered groups of Perfectionists, as well as to residents.

The Community was seeking tentatively to discover an industry that would assure its security and permanence. Noyes issued a call for manual labor, and insisted that no work could be considered humble or degrading if it would help the Community to its feet.

The majority of the members responded with enthusiasm. They worked long hours at the humblest tasks; they volunteered for all sorts of industrial experiments; they joined in the innumerable "bees" organized to overcome unpleasant drudgery. But the shadow of the approaching national crisis, in those final years of the fifties, darkened the outlook of the Community, isolated though it stood from the passions of the world. The famine years continued. Something like $40,000 had been sunk without trace in the publication of the paper in Brooklyn. By 1857, the net earnings of the whole Community sank to $5,478.00, and the year following, the financial situation became even more alarming. The Community earned less than two thousand dollars. Finally, by Spartan methods they succeeded in reducing the cost of board and lodging for each adult member to less than eighty-four cents per week. A typical breakfast might consist of boiled potatoes, tomatoes, gravy and bread; a midday dinner of baked potatoes, bread, pickles, butter and cocoa; and supper the same day of wheatbread, molasses cake and apples. There is a record of one supper which consisted solely of blackberry shortcake—but "plenty of it—" and cold water. Bread and cheese and melted sugar for supper afforded little variety in this monotonous diet. But the little army of Heaven remained cheerful and uncomplaining, so thoroughly disciplined was it by defeat and adversity.

Two of the members had been peddlers before joining. Noyes suggested that a peddling department be organized, in order to insure the distribution of Community products. His suggestion "cut across the pride of some, especially the women," but, inspired by the enthusiasm of the leader, all were soon begging, men and women alike, for the privilege of going out. One man cried that he would shoulder a razor grinder "and joyfully too" if it would serve the Community. Few women were sent out, because in the entire feminine wardrobe of the Community, there remained but one dress and hat made according to the fashions of the day; one woman at a time wore this costume on their sallies into the world.

So the Community peddlers ventured forth, two by two, on foot like disciples of Christ. Usually they were not absent for more than a week. On their return these men were cleansed of the worldly spirit by a thorough scrubbing and the criticism of their comrades. They carried pins and needles, silk thread, combs, lace, edging, ink, collars, palm-leaf hats and all the other products manufactured at one time or another by the Community. They acquired a thorough training in the Yankee art of salesmanship: and soon they no longer trudged dusty roads on foot, but rode in "the cars"—and conducted a sideline by preaching John Noyes's gospel of salvation and by taking orders for the publications of the Community.

So it was that the Community entered the field of business. But it was not these worthy endeavors that established the foundation of its conspicuous prosperity. That was to come upon it from another, and quite unexpected, source.

Chapter V: TRAPS

Qui veut faire l'ange fait la bête.
—Pascal.

I

Before the erection of the Mansion House, that first summer at Oneida, there had been no room large enough for a full gathering of the faithful. Noyes sometimes held levees in the little log hut. Listeners sat on window-sills, door-steps and floor, until every inch of space was crowded. At last, so great was the eagerness to hear the leader that a barn was furnished with benches, hand-hewn from logs at the sawmill. "Outsiders" from the neighboring country-side sometimes attended; and one Sunday afternoon a genial, neighborly couple in Sunday attire descended from a carriage and appeared at the door of this improvised chapel. To the Noyeses, Jonathan Burt proudly introduced Mr. and Mrs. Sewell Newhouse, from Oneida Castle.

Sewell Newhouse appeared as indigenous to the old Indian Reserve as its woods and streams, its birds and game. There was something of the stag in his majestic walk, something of the hawk in his far-seeing eye, something of the Indian in his taciturn dignity. Like John Noyes, Newhouse was a native of Brattleboro. His family had migrated to this western country in 1820, when Sewell was fourteen years old, and he had spent his youth exploring the woods and streams of the vast territory. He became a hunter and trapper of almost legendary skill.

Dissatisfied with the traps of that epoch, which he condemned as crude and faulty, Sewell Newhouse had set himself the task of forging more efficient instruments. He succeeded; huntsmen around Oneida Lake clamored for the new contrivance and soon he found himself master of a special craft. He bought a blacksmith's forge and anvil, a hand-punch, a swaging mold, a hammer and file. In a short time, Newhouse was turning out approximately two thousand traps every year. Their fame and the demand for them spread rapidly; and the more these spread, the more carefully he hid his special secret of tempering springs. Hunters relied unreservedly upon these Newhouse traps. They could catch, and what they caught they held. After a season's service they were sometimes resold to the Indians at sixty-two cents apiece.

For twenty years Sewell Newhouse toiled at this craft—sometimes with partners, sometimes with hired help. But with clock-like regularity, between seasons of trap-making, he disappeared into the Northern Woods, or explored and reëxplored the wilderness around Oneida Lake. He knew every foot of its wooded swamps, every one of the thirty-six creeks that flowed into it, its bays and woods, its birds and wild life. As if he were one of its own people, migratory instincts periodically took command, and set him in the direction of the forest. His cronies never tired of repeating stories of his feats in running and wrestling; in and about the Indian Reserve, his fame came to rival that of Davy Crockett, Robin Hood, and other woodsmen of legendary powers.

Sewell's almost fabulous muscular strength was never misused nor brutalized. On the contrary, Newhouse was gentle and shy; he refused to discuss or to hear discussed his feats of strength. A strange character, individual to the point of eccentricity, and the last man in the world, his boon companions thought, to be induced to join the Community at the Indian sawmill.

When he was young, this demi-god of the forest fell violently in love with Miss Eveliza Hyde of Oneida Castle. They were married and set up their home there, and both became faithful members of the Presbyterian Church. However, even as early as 1835, Sewell had been attracted to the advanced views of the Perfectionists. It may have been because, like himself, this sect mingled caustic humor with profound sincerity. As evidence of Newhouse's dry wit, the story was told of a minister, setting forth the unhappy condition of the wicked in the realm of Satan, who proceeded in a clerical sing-song: "There'll be no-o-o Sabbaths there; there'll be no-o-o churches there; and there'll be no-o-o ministers there!"

"Yes there *will-l-l!*" Sewell Newhouse broke forth, from his place in the congregation.

Shortly after their first call upon Noyes, and almost fifteen years after Newhouse's initial interest in Perfectionism, he and his family were received as members of the Community. Habit occasionally drove Newhouse back to his old craft; occasionally, too, the brawnier young men laboriously hammered out at the forge a few dozen traps, all of a single size. But until the return of Noyes from Brooklyn, in 1854, no thought was given to trap-making as a possible Community industry.

Suddenly orders for traps began to trickle in from New York and Chicago. Confronted with the problem of lifting the Community out of the starvation zone into which it had sunk, Noyes began to investigate trap-making as a business.

Even to John Noyes, Sewell Newhouse held the door of his little shop hard shut, almost locked. He finally but reluctantly consented to initiate two or three of his young admirers into the mysteries of trap-making, but he still concealed the inner secret of his craft. But Noyes appointed himself the representative of what he termed the "communizing, democratic power of inspiration"; at last he wore down Newhouse's resistance, and gained admission into the little trap-shop. Unaided and unwelcome, the leader fumblingly tried to pick up the elements of this craft. Newhouse grudgingly permitted him to undertake bits of the simpler work. Curiosity led Noyes on; he soon began to push further, and persuaded one of the young men to teach him how to split bows, another how to weld them. Finally, young Homer Barron took him in hand and led the leader, step by step, through the whole process.

Homer and Noyes became inseparable. The Community band was just being organized; both were enthusiastic members. They drilled away at music every noon and discussed music over their work in the trap-shop. "We became very much attached, and this play of affection had something to do with the revolution in the trap department." Their mutual enthusiasm brought others in, and before a great while the whole Community was making traps.

2

From a little shop which had utilized at the beginning no more than three hands, the business was now transported into a building equipped with water-power. New mechanical appliances were introduced. Noyes, Newhouse and their crew of young machinists exercised all their inventive powers in devising machinery which should supplant hand-work in fashioning the different elements of the traps. The first machine to be introduced was a power-punch. Next followed a rolling apparatus; then it was discovered that in parts of the traps, malleable cast-iron could be substituted for wrought iron. The steel-spring presented a most vexatious problem; its fabrication demanded long, arduous labor. Only by hand, with hammer and anvil, apparently, could the spring be made. It required two stalwarts, a two-hand sledge, heavy hammer, and no less than one hundred and twenty blows, to reduce the steel to its elementary shape. This task once accomplished, the spring was completed by a long series of lighter manipulations. Yet, one by one, the ingenuity of that little band of amateur machinists conquered all these difficulites. At length, without a single hammer-blow, they performed the whole process of shaping the trap-spring, from its initial state as a long steel bar, into a bent, bowed, finely tempered and elastic instrument ready for its relentless use.

In the years that followed, the Community manufactured steel traps by the thousand dozens and shipped them to all the frontiers of the continent. Even in October, 1855, orders were beginning to exceed the possible output, and they kept on increasing. In March, 1856, six hundred orders came in, and in April of the same year, a single order for one thousand traps came from Milwaukee. The Hudson Bay Company sent in an order so large that the whole labor force of the Community was temporarily mobilized. What should they do about the other Community industries? —the printing plant, the manufacture of traveling bags, the preserving of fruits under the direction of Henry Thacker?

Community farmers were afraid that the voracious trap-shop would require all hands through the harvest season. But, in comparison, profits from the traps were enormous. Before they realized it, the Community was definitely committed to an industrial régime. In December, 1863, business increased to such a degree that the school was closed and the youngsters were marched into the trap-shop with the promise of an extra week of study after production caught up. The leaders converted this task into a "bee," just as they were accustomed to do in other communistic duties.

3

By 1864, they were making six sizes of traps, for different types of fur-bearing animals, from muskrat to bear. The Community was capturing the American and Canadian business in this field, and driving foreign competitors out of the trap market. The number of hands directly employed had increased to sixty, with an additional twenty-five or thirty finding employment in the machine-shop. Forty skilled laborers from outside the Community were also given employment; the pay-roll for these was more than $1,100 per month.

The old mill throbbed and buzzed with industry. Men, women, boys and girls all toiled happily together. In a neighboring room, young Hial Waters supervised the grist-mill, grinding out that "superfine extra" in which the Community took special pride. In the machine-shop above, Mr. Reid and Mr. Inslee directed the labors. Abram Smith and William Hatch toiled at the carpenter's bench. In the inevitable printing-shop nearby, George Noyes, Harriet Skinner, and Theodore Pitt kept compositors busy with endless relays of copy. Precisely at the clang of the great bell, at ten o'clock every morning, labor ceased. Trap-makers, machinists, millers and printers dropped their work. Into the printing-office they trooped, appetites whetted by the aroma of warm gingerbread and steaming coffee, sent over from the kitchen of the Mansion House. After this mid-morning repast, ten minutes of recreation followed—usually dancing in the garret, where the spacious floor inspired them. "Money Musk" was the favorite dance; but they were passionately devoted to almost all of the old "contra" dances—"Chorus Jig," "Cheat the Lady," and "Chain Figure." They dashed into the figures with vim, though this ten-minute recess was not nearly long enough to do "Money Musk" justice; fully twenty minutes were required for each head couple to go through the figures of that favorite. However, they all swept into it with a zest that had no savor of steel traps or Perfectionist theology. The fiddler scraped his bow! Excitement was in the very toes of the dancers; they became carefree children again for that fleeting recess. The dance swung on to an exhilarating crescendo. Suddenly, the fiddle stopped; just as promptly the trap-makers returned to their forges and their steel springs. "Ah! Money Musk! how we liked to dance it—and as years roll on, how we like to think of how we danced it!"

Noyes was no advocate of any mere return to the soil, of innocent reversion to simple rural life. "The business that afterwards built our houses and improved our surroundings, and placed us before the world as a successful business Community, everybody knows was the manufacture of traps. And this business, it should be remembered, was the offspring of another. The foundation of our material prosperity goes back one step further than trap-making, to Mr. Inslee's Newark machine-shop, with which we came into connection while printing *The Circular* in Brooklyn, and in which several of our young men were educated in a knowledge of machinery and mechanics. Mr. Inslee, as a machinist, and the educator of machinists, was in an important sense, the father of our success in trap-making. We thus trace the lineage of the industrial character of the Community to Newark, and find it to be a birth out of that manufacturing city, drawing from thence its developing skill and invention of machinery."

Noyes gave Sewell Newhouse full credit for the precision and faithfulness with which the traps were manufactured, and which enabled them to conquer the market. Newhouse kept the standard as near perfection as possible. "He has been placed in a trying position," Noyes explained to the Community. "It is the fashion of the world that a man should hold his trade as a kind of mystery. Mr. Newhouse had the aristocrats of the machine-shop coming down on him from above, and me with the whole Community at my heels coming up from below, all like the Goths and Vandals, invading the territory of his mystery."

4

One more paradox in an adventure marked by the unexpected at every turn was this prosperity suddenly thrust upon the little colony of Heaven at the very moment when the nation was plunged into internecine strife. South Carolina declared its secession from the Union. On May 11, 1861, the Second Massachusetts regiment marched southward chanting "John Brown's Body...." The fever for war was spreading like a virulent contagion throughout the North. Noyes sought to render immune his own "soldiers." They were all, he assured his army, on the battle-front of another war. "There is many a reckless soldier who would turn a cowardly back to the batteries we face," he reminded them, assuring his flock that a policy of discretion need not imply that they were cowards in this national crisis. In the first days of the secession the Community withheld its sympathies almost entirely. When the first conscription took place, Noyes fully expected to find several of his men drafted. Chances were a thousand to one that some of the Community men would be drawn; the estimated proportion would have been ten or twelve. There was but one draft in Madison County; and when the chosen names were posted, not a single Community man was among them. At Wallingford, only one member was drawn, for whom the commutation fee of $300 was paid by the town.

"He has bribed the enrolling officer," whispered Noyes's enemies throughout Oneida and Madison Counties. But the Community had never seen the officer. Through his own stupidity, or under the confusion of circumstances, he had overlooked it. Oneida Creek was the boundary line between Oneida and Madison Counties. Although the Community was located in Madison County, its nearest neighbors on the public road which passed directly in front of the domain were residents of Oneida County, and its water-power and mill were in that county. The enrolling officer of Oneida County came to the north bridge and noted that the Oneidans were residents of Madison County. "All right," he said, "I have nothing to do with them." The enrolling officer of Madison County passed along the road half a mile west, and, looking over, supposed the Community to be in the same county as their nearest neighbors on each side, that is, in Oneida County. "All right; I have nothing to do with them," he thought. There was no bribing, as everybody saw when the matter was explained. "Community luck," was the word that went round. The Community remained unconscious of any evasion of duty.

In subsequent drafts, both at Oneida and Wallingford, the towns were fortunate enough to secure volunteers to fill their quotas. At the final draft in Madison County, however, by a mistake of the provost marshal in not giving the town of Oneida its proper credit of volunteers, a draft took place, by which two of the Community's men were drawn. The credits were afterwards allowed, the drafted men discharged; again the Community escaped conscription. And the same Providence which saved the Community from the repeated drafts, saved it also from "war fever." During the periods of greatest excitement several young men were affected by the surrounding fever and talked of volunteering; but finally they chose to remain on their own battle-front. This objection to personal service in the war was not "on the ground of disbelief in the rightfulness of war, in itself considered, nor in the use of carnal weapons (though they considered war a very poor way to overcome evil or settle difficulties), but mainly on the ground of want of orders from the supreme Government of God."

The great uprising of the North as one man, in response to the call of President Lincoln for volunteers, immediately after the attack on Fort Sumter, convinced Noyes that deep below the surface, in the popular heart, a love of right and justice still burned. The North would emancipate itself entirely from Southern influence, he felt; from all complicity in the great crime of slavery. Thenceforth the Community followed the drama of the war with deep interest. As it progressed, their sympathies were drawn out in proportion as they saw the war tending to develop in the people and government a recognition of the rights of man, and a realization of the providence of God in the affairs of the nation.

The Community bore its full share of the financial burdens and losses incident to the War, responded to repeated calls for aid to soldiers, lent the town of Oneida money to help in raising volunteers. In consequence of heavy bounties paid by the State and counties for volunteers, the Community's direct federal war taxes were more than quadrupled.

• 5

Outside criticism of the Community's conduct was most effectively silenced by its expanding business. As early as 1863, it had become necessary to employ outside labor for the emerging industry and in the years following the number of outside employees increased steadily until hundreds were on the Community pay-roll. Transportation was provided to carry the workers to the factories, and working conditions were far superior to those in ordinary capitalistic industries. In the industrial sphere at least, Noyes's communism was vindicated.

Thus Noyes and the central members were brought face to face with the complex labor problem. From a self-sufficient communism, mainly devoted to home industries, they found themselves "capitalistic" employers of labor, on a constantly increasing scale. Noyes met this problem with tact, foresight, and more than justice. With prophetic intuition, he foreshadowed by more than half-a-century some of the tenets of the so-called "modern" school, asserting that *every* man is entitled to a *great deal more* than the product of his labor.

As an employer of labor, Noyes cemented the respectability and popularity of the Oneida Community with its neighboring townsfolk and business men. By generous policies he built a well-nigh impregnable wall against the yapping attacks of moralizing critics. Community traps were becoming the wellspring of material prosperity for the surrounding county.

By the beginning of 1866, a regiment of workmen and workwomen was steadily employed at the Community. A new power-site in Turkey Street had been added; it was a half-mile nearer the Oneida freight depot, it was built of red brick, and it was named "Willow Place" in memory of the Brooklyn epoch. In addition to the thriving trap industry, most ordinary employments were still continued at the Community—farming, gardening, blacksmithing, milling, carpentry, wagon-repairing, dentistry, printing. Traveling bags, involving considerable labor and capital, were manufactured. Previous to 1862, the annual sales of this department did not exceed $3,000; by 1865, they were more than $50,000 and the bag department had twenty-four men and twenty-six women at work for wages.

Under the direction of Henry Thacker, the business of preserving fruit remained popular with the Community, and promised to grow to large proportions. It gave pleasant employment, during the summer months, to all the women of the Community, and to many neighbors. Most of the fruits and vegetables used were grown by the Community itself. These preserves gained a wide reputation; during the season of 1865, the department used twenty-three laborers and brought in more than $20,000.

Much of the manual labor in the trap factory came to be performed by other than Community men. For some of these outside workers, the Community erected comfortable houses and planned to furnish pleasant homes for others. These first houses were the nucleus of an idea that has developed so far that a town today stands on the old Community farmlands, erected by the descendants of these industrial pioneers.

But out of all these growing industries, it was Sewell Newhouse's steel trap which was to become the cornerstone of prosperity. The Community—like the nation at large—closed its eyes to the fact that the beasts caught in these traps suffered prolonged and excruciating pain.

To absolve the Community completely of its share of the guilt in this crime in which all civilization has shared, would be to miss a significant aspect of the venture. No phase of the experiment more sharply illustrates how closely interwoven in all spiritual life are the web and woof of nobility and ignobility, the heroic and the all-too-practical. Even "Perfection," even "Holiness," to survive in this alien and hostile world, must be alloyed with baser motives.

6

In the autumn of 1864, Noyes went to New York and established the Community's agency in the Moffat Building at 335 Broadway. For the next few years he made only occasional visits to Oneida; but despite this fact, newspapers continued to jibe that he had established a paradise of Mahomet at the center of the Empire State. One day in the New York office, appeared Richard Realf, who had just been mustered out of the Army. This fantastic Anglo-American adventurer sought, he said, final refuge from the bitter cruelties of the world. He had been a member of John Brown's "cabinet," and possessed an insatiable appetite for every variety of religious experience, from Shakerism to Catholicism. He applied for membership in the Community and Noyes invited him to make a temporary visit. But Realf never put in an appearance; fifteen years later they learned of his suicide in Oakland, California. Richard Realf atoned in part, at least, for the faults of his split personality by his mystical poem "Introspection," which has won its place in the anthologies.

During this New York period, in the late sixties Noyes spent his week-ends at the Wallingford Community. Sunday was not observed here, or at Oneida, except in so far as to avoid annoyance to orthodox neighbors, but a religious meeting every evening was as constant as the stars.

The Connecticut Community stood at the foot of Mount Tom, pleasantly remote from the village, on the old turnpike between Hartford and New Haven. Toward the east flowed the Quinnipiac, a respectable river running from north to south. The country on the east side of this river rose by a succession of easy slopes and terraces to a height of perhaps a hundred feet. The elevation was a long, smooth, nearly level ridge crowned by the old village of Wallingford. In 1851, a farmer named Henry Allen became convinced that the doctrine taught by Noyes was a sound one, and resolved to adopt it for himself, his wife and four children. Acting on this conviction, Mr. Allen invited members of the Oneida institution to come and join them in the formation of a branch community upon his land. The invitation was accepted, and the immigrants and a number of Wallingford people began a communistic mode of life which resulted in a well-to-do company of hard-working people. From the small farm which Henry Allen donated to the cause, their lands were to increase until their acres on the hillside numbered two hundred and forty or more.

Wallingford was comparatively rustic. Its small wooden buildings, without ornament, inside or out, were also without "modern conveniences"—even without a door-bell. Here, "our Hall is a plain, unshapely room, and for music we have only a parlor organ and some singing girls."

This Wallingford Community was, by train, only a half-hour distant from New Haven and Yale, and was to be used in the sixties and seventies as headquarters for the young men from the Community who were sent to the University. Three hundred miles away from Oneida, the Connecticut Community was eventually to develop a distinct character of its own. It was in this secluded refuge that Noyes was to seek sanctuary when the Community at Oneida had developed into a "show place," and the hue and cry against him reached its highest pitch.

Chapter VI: MUTUAL CRITICISM

...excessive sensitiveness is a great fault.
—J.H.N.

I

THE DEPARTMENT OF JUSTICE in the Community was embodied in a system called Mutual Criticism. Self-government was impossible without discipline; and discipline, which implied subordination of the "I-spirit" to the "we-spirit," was found to be most effectively yet mercifully enforced through Mutual Criticism. Much importance was attached to the system inaugurated by Noyes. Even as early as the pioneer days in Putney, every member of the group was encouraged at regular periods to submit silently while associates analyzed his habits, his virtues, and his vices, and pointed the way to character development.

Painful, humiliating, more than mortifying at times this ordeal was to novices who had not lived long enough in the Community to get rid of self-consciousness and egotism. But eventually they welcomed these cleansings of the spirit. The bitter pills they swallowed were usually coated with praise. As we read the records of these "criticisms" today, they seem innocuous and innocent enough. But in the beginning they were undoubtedly humbling ordeals.

Noyes of course acted as Chief Justice of this Community court. He developed the technique of Mutual Criticism out of the exercises practiced among the members of the secret society at Andover, called "The Brethren." This type of criticism Noyes introduced and expanded into every-day use in the Putney Association, during the crucial stage of its rapid advancement into the spiritual life. Any person wishing to be criticized submitted his name. His character became the subject of special scrutiny by all members during the interval preceding the next meeting, when his "trial" took place. On the presentation of the case, each member in turn was called on to specify, as frankly as possible, everything objectionable in the character and conduct of the person criticized. Thus he had the advantage of a many-sided mirror. He found himself placed at the focus of a spiritual lens composed of all the judgments of his associates. Rarely was any complaint of injustice registered by the subject of such scrutiny. Chastening was accepted with fortitude, submission, and gratitude. As a rule the subject felt relieved and purified by the process. Among various objectionable features of the character under criticism, one or two of the most serious faults would usually elicit censure from the whole circle; and the judgment of these points would thus have the force of a unanimous verdict. Any soreness resulting from the operation was removed at the succeeding meeting by administering a round of commendation. This system of open and kindly criticism became so attractive, by its manifest good results, that every member of the Putney Association submitted to it in the course of the winter of 1846-1847. To it Noyes attributed the accelerated character improvement which marked that period. Instead of hurt feelings, abounding love and good works followed.

Often, under the verbal scalpel of Noyes, members discovered that their most prized virtues—virtues at least from the worldly point of view—were dismissed as faults. What must have been the feelings of prim, Quakerish John Skinner, as his brother-in-law announced that while Skinner was honest, he was deficient in those qualities which made honesty attractive! "The compound of a perfect lover is goodness and a musical external nature.... A compound of innocence and skill is the perfection of character. Mr. Skinner is an honest, serious, conscientious man; but these elements of his character are not sufficiently embodied in cunning, romance, and emotion. Love, perfected, is very cunning. Mr. Skinner is unpracticed, green, deficient in skill to make himself attractive—*deficient* and yet *promising*. He has improved very much since he came here. One person has confessed that she loves him very much now, though she could hardly endure him when she first saw him, he was so pedantic and awkward.

"I will mention some of the hindrances in his case," Noyes continued: "His strong tendency to intellectual development is one. It is a proverb in the world, that a book-worm is awkward in love—slow to be smitten, and likely to behave foolish when he is. In other circumstances, I think, Mr. Skinner would have been predominantly intellectual, and had but little development of his social nature. His cast of mind is very unfavorable to poetical thought; he might make rhymes, but they would lack the sparkle of poetry; and it is the poetic element which makes us lively and attractive in social intercourse. He has a warm heart, and a geniality of feeling which counteracts somewhat the pedantic and sober element of his character; but in the world, the pedantic would probably have prevailed.... A second hindrance is this: I have observed an interference between one affection and another.... The tendency to high enjoyment of food, wherever it exists, is a hindrance to the development of life in the form of amativeness. Epicures and drunkards extinguish at last the sexual attraction. In order to attain the highest development of our social nature, it is desirable to be abstemious. As in religion, sensuality of appetite is a hindrance to spirituality, so it is equally an enemy to love, and the development of the highest power of fellowship between the sexes." At the end of this criticism, Noyes inquired what had been the effect of his criticism upon the subject. Mr. Skinner replied that it had not produced much mortification.

At Oneida, the system of criticism was continued with various modifications and adapted to increased numbers. At one time in the early days of the organization, the Community appointed four of its most spiritual and discerning judges to criticize in turn all members. Their method was first to ascertain as much as possible concerning the character of the individual, by inquiring among his associates, and then, after discussing his character among themselves, to invite him to an interview, tell him his faults plainly, converse with him freely about his whole character, and give him their best advice. At another time, members formed classes of ten or fifteen persons, and each separate group carried through a course of mutual criticism of all its members. Various other modes were also tested, though the general tendency was to public criticism of individuals by the whole family, at their evening meetings.

Instead of having its day and dying out in favor, as legal ordinances generally do, Mutual Criticism grew more and more popular, more firmly fixed as a vital agent of organization and improvement. With the passing of the years, it became an instrument highly valued and sought after by old and young alike. The Oneidans claimed that such criticism probed deeply, penetrated more and more effectively into the inner recesses of character, and thus operated beneficently on the springs of conduct.

Thus developed, criticism took its place as the regulator of society in the Community, superseding legal rules, developing character, producing harmony, and conserving all that was true and beautiful in mutual relations. All claimed for it high efficacy as an agent of health, a powerful means for the influx of new life. Heart-searching criticism brought about an almost immediate and rapid improvement in bodily health. During the Community's epidemic of diphtheria, in 1863, "criticism" was even practiced for its therapeutic value. It became a common custom for every one who was attacked with some disorder to submit to this unique remedy, by sending for a "criticizing committee" of six to eight persons in whose faith and spiritual judgment he had confidence. An element of Butlerian fantasy enters the scheme. The result, when administered sincerely, was usually to throw the patient into a sweat, often to bring on a reaction against disease, and to restore him soon to usual health. "We have seen this result produced, without any other agency except the use of ice, in perhaps twenty cases of sore throat within a few weeks. We have seen it take effect at an advanced stage of chronic disease, and raise a person up apparently from death's door. It seems a somewhat heroic method of treatment when a person is suffering in body, to apply a castigation to the character through the spiritual or moral part; but this is precisely the thing needed to cleanse and purify the system from disease." Had they not tried it and found it to be invaluable? They commended this prescription as a medium for conveying healing and life. "If you are sick, seek for some one to tell you your faults, to find out your weakest spot in character and conduct; let them put their finger on the very sore that you would best like to keep hid. Depend upon it, there is the avenue through which disease gets access to you. And if the sincerity which points this out and opens it to the light, hurts, and is mortifying for the time being, it is only a sign that the remedy is applied at the right place and is taking effect."

2

Loyal members looked forward to and welcomed drastic criticism from John Noyes; outsiders spread rumors to the effect that the shepherd of the flock himself had never submitted to the ordeal of Mutual Criticism. At last these whispers reached the ears of the Community. In April or May, 1870, some one wrote in to inquire: "Is it true that Mr. Noyes, Sr., Cragin, Sr., and a few others are practically excepted in your criticisms?" *The Circular* (May 16, 1870) replied that Mr. Cragin had been the recipient of severe and repeated criticisms; that leading members of the highest grade next to Mr. Noyes were still under criticism, and none had ever been long exempt, and that Mr. Noyes himself had been among the first volunteers for group criticism always holding himself amenable to it, and frequently offering himself for criticism, private and public. Mr. Noyes, however, had failed so many times to "draw fire" that he had latterly left matters to take their course. "If he is practically exempt from formal criticism nowadays, it is to be considered that all the informal grumbling in the Community falls on him, and that he takes the principal share of the criticism that comes from the world outside; which is whipping enough to keep one man sober."

Vigorously and repeatedly Noyes disclaimed any secret desire to utilize the instrument of criticism to bend the members of the Community into servility to his will. At Willow Place in Brooklyn he had renounced an intention to act as a "chart-maker to men."

Free, unimpeded behavior was forever impossible while a person remained burdened with the heavy armor of sensitiveness. Fundamentally, Noyes was aiming for the development of free, outgoing personality, but not the development of the pathological ego. Noyes was an enemy of the *culte du moi.* Always, in his spiritual syntax, he translated the *I* into the *we.* Excessive sensitiveness, he insisted at the meetings for criticism, was a great fault. Every one should strive to reach the point where he could judge himself, could look at himself truthfully by the grace of God and cultivate what he called the superior consciousness, should look at his own faults as he would at another's, and feel no more pain in dissecting his own character than in dissecting that of any one else. This superior consciousness led, Noyes explained, into fellowship with God and His judgment; and in that condition it was possible to rejoice in pulling to pieces our own works.

Upon this method of catharsis was conferred the name of "krinopathy." Its curative properties were held in such high esteem that it was applied even to the youngsters in the Children's House. A severe epidemic of colds broke out among the children and there were various complaints of head-aches, sore throats, coughs, ear-aches. Temperatures danced up and down, with accompanying crossness and lethargy. The house mother attributed all this to the presence of an evil spirit. Acting on the conviction that disease comes and goes out through the spirit, a course of exhortation and criticism with the children was promptly inaugurated. Ailing children were counseled to confess Christ as their physician, and invite criticism as their medicine. One feverish lad did not seem to mind what was said at the time; but before night he manifested symptoms of returning activity. Another whining boy was criticized for hardness of spirit, which had come by being petted. He was in his place the next day among the children. One little girl, suffering seriously from croup, was plied with simple remedies for a day or two without much improvement. A dose of truth-telling to the spirit that oppressed her produced prompt results. She appeared refreshed, and grew steadily better. One morning, when the children were called together for a talk, one girl remained lying on the bed crying. Invited to submit to criticism as the only possible help, she consented after some little delay, got up, and courageously took her seat within the circle.

With accuracy and directness, the rest of the children told the little patient what was in their minds, showing very ready discernment. A few of the first shots appeared to add to her pain; she was tempted to criticize criticism. But finally she listened quietly and the pain stopped. A good-natured, loving spirit immediately took possession of her; she became her own bright-eyed and happy self again; she smiled with thankfulness, and seemed conscious of a new experience. Other children were likewise affected, and after a week or so of "krinopathy," the youngsters were all well.

All this was reported in full detail by the guardians of the Children's House, probably as an inducement to the elders to submit to criticism. Recalling the penalties inflicted in Samuel Butler's "Erewohn" upon those guilty of common colds, "krinopathy" proved to be a sharp weapon in deflating that cherishing tenderness most humans exhibit toward their own ailments.

3

To those outsiders who were eager to ridicule and condemn departures from current conventions, mutual criticism, as practiced at Oneida, was only one more eccentricity instituted by John Noyes. Between the lines of some contemporary newspapers we may detect a rudimentary respect, even admiration, for the "queer people of Oneida," but most dailies of that period did not encourage social innovations. The New York *Times* took up the editorial cudgels against Mutual Criticism, in a malicious, acidly amusing comment: "Hitherto the believers in Communism, as . . . understood before the Paris Commune gave it a new meaning, have had but one solitary theory to which they could point with pride," the *Times* tartly declared. "Every experiment in practical Communism has been a ridiculous failure, with the solitary exception of the Oneida Community. . . . How it was possible for Noyes to induce hundreds of men to enter his sty and to live there year after year, is a problem which the public has been totally unable to solve. The real secret of the prolonged life of the Oneida Community is obvious to the thoughtful student of human nature, although it has, to a great extent, escaped notice. When Noyes devised his plan of 'social criticism' he proved himself a man of unusual cunning. . . .

". . . Here was scandal reduced to a system and made infinitely more effective and delightful than it is elsewhere. The brethren enjoyed the pleasure of publicly abusing Brother Smith to their hearts' content, knowing that if he showed any resentment he would be at once cast out of the Community. Brother Smith, on the other hand, felt that he could sacrifice everything else in order to have the opportunity to criticize his assailants. As but one person could be criticized at any one meeting, it would take Brother Smith eight or ten weeks to revenge himself on all his enemies, and at the end of that time he was liable to undergo another course of criticism. What was true of Brother Smith was true of every one of his fellow-Communists. No matter how much any one of them might wish to leave the Community, he was always determined to stay till he could give each one of his critics as heavy blows as he himself had received. This was the real tie that held the Community together. They lived on in order to 'get square' with their fellows at some future meeting for 'social criticism.' Of course, their criticisms were never ended, and, of course, the Community was never ready to dissolve. This was the secret of its long success, and that Noyes should have recognized the fact that he could bind his followers together by the bond of mutual hate stamps him as a man of real, if perverted genius."

4

But Mutual Criticism was no panacea. The devil invaded the colony of Heaven in subtle disguises. Often Noyes called the "central members" into confidential consultation; and more than one crisis arose which demanded prompt decision and drastic action.

Misfits and malcontents who soon became dissatisfied with the rigors of community life passed in and out during the first years. Grumblingly they confessed that this attempt at heavenly association was not at all as they expected it to be. Weeding out uncongenial and undesirable candidates became an inevitable and necessary process. Aglow with enthusiasm they entered; grimly and silently they departed into the outer night. Reasons for leaving were as varied and fantastic as their motives for joining. After the Community took possession of its new house there were twenty or thirty withdrawals.

The catalogue of departures suggests a recurrent clash of temperament. The Community sought to devise tactics to ease this friction, often of emotional origin. Supplicating and humble, however, converts still begged to be admitted to the Community. Eager to enter, most were unwilling to take no for an answer. After long correspondence, followed perhaps by a short personal acquaintance, they were received at last. Labors of love were bestowed upon them, confidences extended, privileges enjoyed. Disillusion, alienation, discontent ensued. Connections made in apparent candor and sincerity could not be severed without painfully affecting the whole Community. Not, however, until the Community was unwittingly drawn into the so-called "Mills war" was it compelled to devise a rigorous policy to defend its existence against rogues and rascals. William Mills was the first member ever to be expelled by physical force.

In the early Sixties, William Mills, with his elderly and unattractive wife, a son Charles, and his two daughters, Ellen and Grace, were received into the Community. Mills's advances toward the women of the Community, although begun in the prescribed fashion, failed utterly. This unexpected rebuff nettled Mills and even led him to advocate new methods of consummating the desired intimacies, such as drawing lots out of a hat. He quarreled violently with the leaders because they would not compel a certain woman to respond to his advances. Their principles left all women free, they explained, and protected from compulsory association.

Spurned by the older women, William Mills seized every opportunity that came his way to undertake the initiation of the young girls. He had invented and constructed a dish-washing machine for use in the Community kitchen—an invention, it appears, that he alone could successfully operate. Presiding over his dish-washing machine, a high functionary in the kitchen, he worked in turn with all the younger girls as their kitchen service came in rotation; he decided to make the most of this intimacy. Mills made advances to nearly every girl who served in the kitchen. Grace, his youngest daughter, belonged to the class just becoming young women (about the age of sixteen), and was a leader among them. She never dared go to her father's room alone, and avoided intimacies by bringing with her the whole of her class of girls. For several months in the summer of 1863 Mills held daily meetings with ten or twelve girls, varying in age from eleven to fourteen. They went there first because Grace Mills asked them to go with her. They continued to go because it was a place where they could "carry on," and meet each other, without being criticized. They despised Mills but they found the fascination of the forbidden about his room. He kept apples and pears and "goodies." He gave them *eau de Cologne* and beads. He tempted them with candies and sugar-plums which he kept hidden in his trunk; offered them wine of his own making and urged them to drink. He teased them to kiss him; he promised them candy if they would, and he joined them in a game they played—a mock "confession of Christ."

Mills never tired of enumerating all the women he had loved, and teased these young girls to tell what men they loved, guessing this one or that. He himself had no secrets, he said; they ought to confide in him, as he did in them. He flattered the girls, telling them how pretty they were, then steered the conversation into dangerously intimate fields.

The breaking up of his embryonic *seraglio* severed the last tie that bound Mills to the Community. He set his face toward secession, and began plotting war and blackmail. Early one morning, with the firm resolve to exterminate Noyes and his Community, Mills set out for Syracuse to present his grievance to the Grand Jury. This angry excursion placed him in the attitude of an open enemy of the Community, and threw him out of even the semblance of membership. Yet, true to the stick-and-hang instincts of all parasites, he remained where he had become a nuisance and a horror. The *impasse* became an intolerable one for the central members of the Community. Once again they were confronted by a problem that seemed to require a diplomatic solution, if a new storm of public protest was to be avoided. Finally however, diplomacy was cast aside and they decided to put him out bag and baggage.

Mills found himself, one winter night, suddenly, inexplicably, unceremoniously, horizontally propelled through an open window and shot, harmlessly but ignominiously, into the depths of a snowdrift. It was the first and only compulsory expulsion in the history of the Community. Mills first sought refuge with a neighbor, and finally put his case in the hands of Messrs. Sedgwick and Andrews, attorneys of Syracuse.

The Mills war lasted four months; not until February 18, 1865, was peace concluded between the belligerents. Terms were substantially the same as those Noyes had originally offered in a letter to Mills. The agreement signed by both parties gave Mills $2,250, in satisfaction of all demands, complaints, and suits, against the Community or any members thereof. One-third of this was to be paid with interest at the expiration of one year, on condition of Mills's peaceable behavior. A note for this $750 was placed in the hands of Mills's attorneys, and they were to be the judges of his fulfillment of the condition. The Community agreed to cease hostilities. Mills went West. And Noyes wrote:

"If we are ever indicted for keeping a disorderly house, the principal specification against us ought to be that we have received and harbored for years such a licentious scoundrel as Mills. In that case we shall beg the authorities to consider, in mitigation of our offense, first, that this man, with all his salacity and impudence, has had very little success among the women and girls of the Community; and, secondly, that as the United States has had grace at last to shake off the foul spell of Slavery, so we are proving ourselves strong enough in courage and righteousness to expel and defy Mills and his demons."

5

But William Mills was not the only trouble-maker. From Illinois, in the early sixties, there came a somewhat erratic youth, Charles Guiteau, who had not yet attained his majority. At the urgent solicitation of his father, one of the outside adherents of Noyes, and evidently a loyal subscriber to *The Circular*, he was accepted on probation. The youth brought with him a sum of nine hundred dollars. The leaders explained to him that each new member or probationer must agree to accept board and education in the Community as an equivalent for services rendered. In the autumn of 1864, when he had attained his majority, the probationer voluntarily signed this agreement, thereby ratifying all he had done under it before coming of age.

During the whole period of his membership, this youth taxed their patience. Moody, self-conceited, exhibitionistic, unmanageable, he was never amenable to criticism, and as a worker he was inefficient and unreliable. The communists were relieved when at last the young man announced his decision to depart. Voluntarily they reimbursed the $900 he had brought with him. Yet, strangely enough, he was soon humbly begging for re-admission.

Even more inexplicable, in the light of subsequent events, was the Community's second acceptance of the young man. In 1867 he departed forever, this time firmly resolved to make trouble for Noyes and the Community. At the Young Men's Christian Association in New York, this malcontent found eager ears into which to pour his tale of injustice and immorality. To his prurient and scandalized listeners, the youth's "exposures" had the effect of certifying his own inherent virtue. He was introduced to John H. Dean, a Pine Street lawyer, who naïvely considered Guiteau's presence at the Y.M.C.A. a guarantee of his honesty. The attorney sent a demand to Oneida for $9,000 and interest, in payment, at the rate of $1,500 per annum, for Charles Guiteau's services at Oneida, and $150 interest on the money he had originally brought in.

Noyes himself answered the lawyer's communication in a letter temperate but unyielding. Before the matter was dropped—the unreliability and insane delusions of Guiteau soon became apparent to the New York attorney—the ex-member's exposure of the "social principles" of the Oneida Community had come to the scandalized ears of the Y.M.C.A. president. And that worthy promptly brought pressure to bear upon the Phelps Dodge Company, one of the country's largest manufacturers of metals. Young Mr. Dodge refused to sell anything more to the representatives of the Community.

On July 2, 1881, Charles Guiteau fired the shot that caused the death of President Garfield, and subsequently died on the gallows as an assassin. Theodore L. Pitt was sent to Washington to absolve the Community of any responsibility, direct and indirect, for Guiteau's act.

Charles Guiteau's abortive attempt to "break up the Community" was indirectly responsible for the emergence of a new counselor of the Community. From Cleveland, Ohio, on December 12, 1867, James William Towner wrote to Noyes, advising him to let the courts settle the extortion case. "You will be annoyed every now and then by demands of this sort from those who may for one reason or another withdraw themselves from membership as this young man has done. I take the liberty now of saying that there are decisions of the courts of the country which have been made in similar cases, and in every case recovery has been refused."

Sound counsel this was indeed, coming from a lawyer who had made a special study of Community contracts. To Noyes, it seemed providential that new friends always sprang to the defense of the Community when trouble-makers threatened its existence.

Noyes and his "cabinet" began to realize the weakness of the Community's constitution, and the need for iron-clad legal protection against recalcitrant members. The problem was submitted to Ward Hunt, an attorney of Utica. The original constitution was changed to a so-called "constitution of the four." Following the suggestion of Mr. Hunt, all community property was transferred to four "property owners"—a committee which consisted of Noyes, Erastus H. Hamilton, William H. Woolworth, and Charles Otis Kellogg. It was understood at all times, and specifically stated, that this arrangement was merely one of convenience, and that every member had equal ownership of the Community's assets. This arrangement was devised to render the Community itself impregnable to blackmail or extortion.

Automatically almost, following the publicity which was provoked by the Mills war and the Guiteau threat, came a flood of applications for membership into the Community. These applications were courteously declined, for Noyes and his cabinet were now fully awake to the dangers of opening their fellowship to the mentally unbalanced and those who were seeking merely for an escape from their own difficulties. Regularly, on the front page of *The Circular*, appeared a plain statement that the Community was not seeking new members, and was not interested in opening correspondence with individuals on the subject. For the few who were from time to time admitted, a prolonged period of probation was deemed absolutely essential, a period during which the behavior and character of the initiate were placed under minute scrutiny.

Chapter VII: HOME TALKS

> What, then, is the new mission of Don Quixote, today, in this world? To cry aloud in the wilderness. But though men hear not, the wilderness hears, and one day it will be transformed into a resounding forest.
>
> —UNAMUNO.

I

CERTAIN men seem selected by destiny to transmute the souls of those who fall under their influence. Some implied or spoken promise of emancipation, of redemption from the bondage of the world, some unspoken invitation into a new garden of Eden, seem to lie at the root of the fascination such men exercise, seem to vivify the simplest words they utter. The late D. H. Lawrence exercised this spell, mainly upon women: J. H. Noyes evoked the unquestioning allegiance of men as well. His alchemy transmuted the souls of Harriet Holton, of Mary Cragin, and of most of the women of the Community. But, also, it completely swept level-headed men away from the traditions of their solid New England Puritanism. Lawrence could only translate his vision into words: Noyes translated his into action. He disdained literary expression, abandoned it, almost, before his flight from Putney. Yet every word he uttered—and he could seldom speak above a whisper—was accepted by his followers as divine. To share his presence was to experience an exhilarating influx of new life and energy. An innocent joy, a felicity of spirit, of renewed vigor seemed to suffuse his listeners, as they echoed his Jovian, though almost silent, merriment. Since 1842, a chronic affliction of the throat had rendered public speaking almost impossible for Noyes. This condition recurred at frequent intervals throughout his life; and he accepted it—not without humor—as a warning against the indulgence of too many words.

In 1849, after the Brooklyn family was established in Willow Place, Mary Cragin began to take notes in her effort to catch the spirit of Noyes's carelessly tossed off wisdom. She had taught herself the rudiments of phonography and devised a system of abbreviation, and after the meetings, Harriet Noyes and Mary Cragin would sit down together and patiently decipher these notes. They were often imperfectly reported; but these talks, read often, long remained favorites with the Oneidans. They were printed and reprinted long after Mary Cragin's death, and something of her incandescent enthusiasm seemed to glow in the talks she reported. After Mary's passing, William A. Hinds mastered the art of phonography, and presently was setting down verbatim reports. Soon there were several competent shorthand reporters among the young men and women of the Community. A little group of trained journalists prepared the "home talks" for publication in the Oneida *Circular*, and Noyes was given the opportunity to correct and revise his spoken thoughts. As pencils scurried across their notebooks, seeking to pin down every elusive word, Noyes warned his attentive listeners that he could not and would not offer, pontifically, any panacea for personal problems. He rebelled against all conventional teacher-pupil, master-disciple relationships. They should not come to him for ready-made cut-and-dried answers to personal problems. After all, there could be no categorical answer to any problem.

After Noyes's flight from Putney, the Rev. Hubbard Eastman published an exposé of the Perfectionists, under the title of "Noyesism Unveiled." Noyesism! To the delight of the family Noyes had translated "Noyesism" into No-yes-ism—that was the very essence of his philosophy! One day in Willow Place, Noyes warned them against thrusting upon him the task of thinking for them: "My theory and my experience is continually no and yes—it is No-yes-ism! The definition of all righteousness is contained in this idea. There is no such thing as understanding me, or the Bible, or God, unless a man is able to understand the righteous combination of no and yes. You cannot propose a question in morals but that I cannot answer it both ways. Is it right to do thus and so? No—yes; and both shall be true. If you say this is puzzling, this confounds me, there is no straightforward chart in these instructions to go by such as we want: I say, very good—I am glad of it. . . . And here I protest against being used as your chart. I don't stand up as a teacher with any intention to save you the trouble of being wise for yourselves. I have no chart to offer, to save you the necessity of being inspired, or to save you the trouble of rightly interpreting the word of God, and of becoming skillful in handling it. And I renounce the office of chart-maker to men, in any such sense as will enable them to dispense with being wise and inspired themselves. My instructions are to be received as hints and helps in the action of your own minds to things to which I shall call your attention, but not as substitutes for the actions of your minds."

Convinced that words as words were useless currency unless measured by deeds and conduct, Noyes confessed that he spoke simply "as the spirit gave him utterance." With his final emergence into the full plenitude of his power, Noyes's talks probed more directly into those persistent problems that timelessly and immediately concern all human welfare.

To trace the movement of this extraordinary mind, to capture the wisdom of John Humphrey Noyes in its essence, we can do no better than to examine these home talks. Their accumulated volume is immense. They contain much that we can no longer accept. But inevitably the reader is brought up with a shock as he stumbles upon some passage that flashes like a long-range gun across creeds and temporalities, pierces the limitations of time and space and aims at eternal truths.

The self-centered, he said, live in terms of the first person singular, and the servant class always in the third person—"He said this—she did that—they are doing this!" Real advance is to escape both the egocentrism of the first person singular, and the starved vicariousness of living in the third person, singular or plural, into living in terms of "We." Newman wrote "The Grammar of Assent": Noyes sought to instill in the minds of the Oneidans what may be described as the grammar of communal living. "The possessive feeling which expresses itself by the possessive pronoun mine," he explained, "is the same in essence when it relates to persons as when it relates to money or any other property. Amativeness and acquisitiveness are only different channels of one stream. They converge as we trace them to their source. Grammar will help us to ascertain their common center; for the possessive pronoun *mine* is derived from the personal pronoun *I;* and so the possessive feeling, whether amative or acquisitive, flows from the personal feeling; that is, it is a branch of egotism. Now egotism is abolished by the gospel relation to Christ. The grand mystery of the gospel is vital union with Christ; the merging of self in his life; the extinguishment of the pronoun *I* at the spiritual center. Thus Paul says, 'I live, yet not I, but Christ liveth in me.' The grand distinction between the Christian and the unbeliever, between heaven and the world, is, that in one reigns the We-spirit, and in the other the I-spirit. From the *I* comes *mine*, and from the *I*-spirit comes exclusive appropriation, of money, women, etc. From *we* comes *ours*, and from the We-spirit comes universality of interests."

2

To act is of greater significance than to talk—of this John Noyes was certain. Until it was put into practice, no virtue was to be trusted. Before the invention of the word, he was a pragmatist in a typical Yankee sense. Doing teaches us, he insisted. We must walk, as the Apostle expresses it, in "the light of life." A person whose whole life consists of thought and speculation is incapable of forming any true theory. Noyes prided himself upon being an active man and a realist. Vision, he said, develops by action; experience corrects mistakes. Action establishes balance in behavior and corrects our course across uncharted seas of life. Only the doing man sees clearly. "Dr. Lardner demonstrated some years ago, from philosophical principles, that no steamship could cross the Atlantic—that it could not carry sufficient coal; and one of the English lords said he would eat the boiler of the first steamer that crossed the ocean! Now probably the men who actually *did* the thing were indifferent talkers, and could not have explained the matter very well; but they saw the essential facts better than the lords and doctors. They could see far enough ahead to know how to work, but not far enough to explain, philosophize and talk. Light sufficient to work by is the best possible amount. If a man has more, it will be a curse to him."

Christ moved in no plodding, theorizing manner. Christ and Paul *hugged realities.* Noyes reiterated his faith in the realism of the Spirit, the power of its inner vision. Eternal life is one of the things which are unseen, but it is as real a thing as money or blood, added Noyes. To him, Heaven was "a present, existing state, one that ought to be admitted into this world."

As for progress, despite all the heady boasting of the mid-nineteenth century, Noyes told his family, the age of Christ and Paul was the most wonderful epoch of all. Although he was untrained in the rigor of scientific thought, Noyes's vigorous insight informed him that the very spirit of modern science—catalytic, destructive, revolutionary—was at one with the Spirit of Christ. "The personal influence of Jesus Christ is the cause of all this great development of civilization that is going on around us; he is, silently and secretly, the great Master who is unfolding the sciences, who is the inventor of railroads and telegraphs and all the improvements in which the modern world glories. Let it be shown, as it will be shown, that he is the originator of this great march of progress, and then the prophets of the time may turn upon mankind and say, See what you have been doing in your unbelief! See what neglect and contempt you have thrown upon your instructor and leader! See how you have gloried in the attainments he gives, as if they were your own; and how your petty schools of sciences have distinguished themselves as much for their infidelity as for their discoveries!" *

* Cf. H. Bergson: *Les Deux Sources de la Morale et de la Religion,* pp. 242 *et seq.*

3

In the subtle art of dissociating ideas, John Noyes reveals himself a precursor of Remy de Gourmont. Gentle and patient in leading his disciples out of the morass of preconceived ideas, Noyes soon realized that the majority of them had been "conditioned" by generations of Puritan repression. Afraid of their bodies, afraid of their appetites, afraid most of all to acknowledge sensuality, they followed him timidly. To such repressed minds, enjoyment, carefree, happy indulgence, seemed evil in itself. Therefore, Noyes sought to dissociate the concept of sensuality from evil connotations with which the Puritans had chained it. Sensuality had been an innocent enough word originally, signifying the enjoyment of the senses and the pleasures of the body. But the word had been degraded by those who had imposed upon the world a monkish system of abstinence. Pleasures of the body are not necessarily evil, and "it must be part of our religion to bring the senses in as helpers of devotion.... The body will assert its rights. It is fearfully and wonderfully made. It is a part of God's creation that is full of power," pursued Noyes. "If you do not make it serve you in a godly way it will rule you in a destructive way. Abstinence will not subdue it.... You must find a better way to treat it."

Noyes continued: "Mohammed said that he took special delight in women and perfumes, and that they helped his devotions. His sensuality, if it was not spiritual, was of a higher order than some people think. If I were to choose the two senses in nature most elevated and refined I would choose these. The sense of smell is comparatively neglected by the common taste. But you will see it exalted in the Bible....

"People must work out their own salvation with fear and trembling. In general I should say to all: 'You must not serve the lusts of the flesh; if you do you will be damned. You must not make monks of yourself; if you do you will be damned. You must find a way to make your senses promote your spirituality, or you will be damned.'"

Inspired always by the pressing problems of community life, these Home Talks, simple, direct, and colloquial, became with the passing years the staple spiritual bread of the little band. No phase of their lives was overlooked, from table manners to the clothes they wore. The homeliest and most trivial questions often produced the most stimulating comment.

In the first years of the Community's existence, economy was "a virtue of necessity." Means were almost desperately limited, and the struggle for existence grimly sharp. Members lived much like soldiers—content with the shelter of log houses and rough shanties, with plain diet and spare wardrobes. Noyes's talks infused a certain element of romance into a life not unlike that of the pioneer and backwoodsman. He succeeded in turning their eyes to the future, to the possibility of an ideal community home. As they approached the realization of it, step by step they surrounded themselves with increasing comforts, even with luxuries. In the transition experience, they learned how to "suffer need." With the advent of prosperity, Noyes sought to teach his followers "how to abound."

This second lesson was more difficult than the first. Thriving businesses brought in greater rewards, and it was almost inevitable that personal wants should expand, that the Community should fall into habits of luxury, even of extravagance. Noyes's instinctive antagonism to the hoarding precepts of Ben Franklin found characteristic expression. Dr. Franklin taught men how to hoard, Noyes asserted; Jesus Christ taught them how to spend. Better to expand, to give out, than to develop niggardly habits of acquisitiveness.

Always, Noyes integrated practical counsel with his central aim. With the passing of the years, his theological terminology falls away and his expression becomes more direct. Yet the passion for freedom remains as stirring as when, a youth in New Haven, Noyes first entered the battle. Much that he spoke concerning the ethics of liberty may strike our ears today as threadbare truisms, but such ideas were mad heresies in nineteenth century America. "Common sense teaches us that we must ultimately find our way to a liberty greater in degree than is at present allowable in the world. A person who is sick cannot safely take the liberties that a healthy man can in eating and drinking. It would be cruel and presumptuous to put a sick man on the diet of the healthy; on the other hand, it would be no less cruel and oppressive to put the healthy man on the diet of the sick. Because an invalid can bear nothing but water-gruel, must that be the regimen of the healthy?

"If people are still determined to quarrel, and say, 'You think that what is sin in others is not sin in you,' we beg leave to introduce the apostle Paul as an expounder. . . . He distinctly avows our very principle repeatedly. . . . 'All things indeed are pure, but it is evil to him that eateth *with offense*.' . . . According to Paul's definition of the true working of conscience, persons in a certain state of feeling in regard to the propriety of freedom may do things which others under the law and with a different conscience may not do. If we are ashamed before this taunt, then we shall have to be ashamed of Paul and his moral philosophy."

Noyes was happiest when grappling with conventional moralists on the subject of universal right and wrong. The seventh commandment he characterized as "good penitentiary morality," destined to pass away with the fashion of this world, as a law adapted to a state of selfishness. One of the most foolish ideas in the world, he insisted, is that morality is a fixed thing. Men find out what is right for a given time and in certain circumstances, fix a mold, promptly cast a whole system of rules—solid, cast-iron morality, for the world. The real spirit and meaning of lockstep morality, Noyes believed, resided in laziness. "How much easier to put every one under cast-iron regimentation than to discriminate between persons and give attention to particular cases. How much easier to practice on Dr. Sangrado's plan of bleeding and blistering every one *secundem artem* than to study the human system and get an accurate knowledge of every specific case, and adapt the medicine accordingly!"

Liberty, however, Noyes is convinced, must come as the reward of virtue—as a bounty on good behavior. If an insane person can hope for no enlargement of his liberty by rational conduct, what encouragement has he? Under the cast-iron system of the world, the most disobedient enjoy the most liberty; hand-cuffs and strait-jackets are put on the intelligent. The wicked are free, the virtuous cramped. But they will never get their liberty by complaining. "Those only who set their heart toward God and attain salvation from sin and inspiration will have perfect freedom. Encouragement to the good is quite as important an element of government as threatening to the bad. It is just as wrong to discourage the righteous as it is to countenance the wicked; just as mischievous to say that men shall not have liberty as the reward of virtue, as it is to say that they may have liberty without virtue. The governments of this world have little but threatening for the bad: there is no premium offered to the good, and cannot be while the same liberty is given to both."

These two types of freedom—the liberty of egotism and the liberty of unity—Noyes took great care to dissociate. The so-called natural liberty vindicated by such anarchs as Max Stirner in "The Ego and His Own," Noyes would have condemned as pathological—a mad reaction from the prison of social coercion. Noyes could indeed understand such gestures, but, from the ethical point of view, egotists and anarchists are recidivists—retreating, as Noyes aptly names their attitude, into infantile *porcupinism.* The sole legitimate freedom must be full-grown, autonomous responsibility. "There are two kinds of liberty, and they look in exactly opposite directions. One is the liberty of *independence.* 'Hands off, leave me alone!' is its language: 'I want to do as I please without interference.' The other is the liberty of *unity*—the liberty of fellowship—liberty to approach one another and love one another—the liberty of communism. There is but little conception, generally, of this second kind of liberty; and yet it is greatly superior to the first. If I were called upon to say what is the greatest conceivable blessing, I should have to reply that it is a genuine love-feast—a flowing together of hearts. This is possible; we may enjoy perfect communism of life, and so realize that 'we sit together in heavenly places in Christ Jesus.'

"Now which liberty will you choose—the liberty of independence, or the liberty of union?—the liberty of an insect to fly off into darkness and isolation, or the liberty of children of God to come into communism with him and with one another—the liberty to be alone, or the liberty that makes a happy home? I have chosen the liberty that makes a happy home, and the liberty to enjoy that home with all who love God. There is but one way to make such a home, and but one way to obtain the liberty of its highest enjoyment, namely, by all receiving Christ into our hearts, and each becoming, as he was, 'meek and lowly' enough to live with others in peace and harmony.

"There is a great deal of talk about the right to freedom. What is that right?—and to whom does it belong? It is evidently not a right that attaches to mere animal life or personality. No one will affirm that animals have a right to unrestrained liberty; for they would abuse it, and make it a curse to themselves as well as to others. If our cattle were all let loose and allowed to go wherever they please, they would ruin our interests, and finally ruin themselves. Then there are certain classes of men—thieves, murderers, lunatics—who also have no right to unrestrained liberty, because they would abuse it. Then, as we rise in the scale of beings, where shall we stop and say, 'Here is a class that may have perfect liberty—here are men and women who can be trusted with liberty, because they will use it without abusing it'? Perhaps some would answer, 'American citizens are in general entitled to the highest liberty.' I doubt it. Different classes of American citizens are entitled to different degrees of liberty, but it cannot be said that they are in general entitled to perfect liberty, for the simple reason that they are not prepared to make good use of it. 'Who then is entitled to perfect liberty?' I answer, Only those who have the meek and lowly heart of Jesus Christ, and who have been saved from selfishness; for they only know how to rightly use that liberty. I am certain that sooner or later, in the ages to come, it will be regarded as the very climax of absurdity to imagine that a sinner–a man governed by selfish passions –deserves liberty.... When our hearts are purified, so that we can live in harmony, without envy or jealousy or grabbing, then we are prepared for true liberty, and not till then.... That is what I mean by perfect liberty; and no one can gain it, except as he gains the meek and lowly spirit, and has his heart purged of all selfishness by Christ. He is the door, and the only door, leading to perfect liberty.

"A person may ask, 'Don't you desire other liberty than that you have described? Don't you crave centrifugal liberty– the liberty of independence and isolation?' I answer, No, I don't think I ever appreciated that kind of liberty as some do; but if I did, that appreciation is now gone from me. I have no taste for it. My prayer now is that God will restrain any tendency of that kind that may exist in me–that he will clip my wings, if I undertake to fly in that way, and put me through any experience necessary to purge out of me any remaining desire for that kind of liberty. The liberty of isolation and war I would hate; it is the liberty of death and destruction....

"The liberty of isolation and independence is false and deceiving. It promises what it cannot perform. It promises to make men free by sending them away from God into the darkness of unbelief. That kind of liberty proves in the end to be horrible bondage. In praying for liberty we ought first of all to pray for deliverance from the false liberty of infidelity–from the temptation to doubt our immortality and the integrity of Christ. Our cry should be, 'O Lord, bind us, bind us to thyself; shut us up to faith; force us, if need be, into the liberty of heaven–the liberty of unity.' " *

4

No æsthete, no believer in "art for art's sake," Noyes scorned literature created for the sake of mere expression or as an exhibition of vainglorious virtuosity. He suspected even the brilliant

* It is profitable to compare Noyes's interpretation of Liberty with that of Nicholas Berdiaeff, who attacks this religious problem in "*Esprit et Liberté*." (See Bibliography.)

eloquence of Ralph Waldo Emerson. Noyes was convinced that "the tendency to literature, as represented by Emerson, is the farthest opposite of communism, finding its *summum bonum* in individualism and incoherent, instead of organic, inspiration." "It seems to me that the great condemnation of mere literary art, and indeed of art of any kind insubordinate to religion and science," he declared in September, 1869, "is that it is an enemy to earnestness. It is very absorbing, but with superficial things. It cultivates the sense of beauty to the keenest point; but it is sensual beauty, irrespective of righteousness. With this keen appreciation of artistic beauty, one could live all his days in a dream. The real issues of life, the knowledge of God and his kingdom, would go unheeded unless some sharp affliction, old age and death had the power to break the illusion. Better to be like John the Baptist, a dweller in the wilderness, clothed in sackcloth and leathern girdle, and feeding on locusts and wild honey, with his deep, clear-sighted earnestness, than to float through life wrapped in the most delightful and artistic dreams."

Noyes diagnosed Hawthorne as an apostate from the faith of his Pilgrim ancestors, a faithless reactionary. Hawthorne's "inveterate languor of principle, his doubting sneer at all religion, the lurking virus of remorse that appear in all his writings" were revolting to Noyes. Hawthorne, he asserted, was an apostate Socialist. His "Blithesdale Romance," based on the Brook Farm experience, revealed only a talent for sneering contempt. "We have no faith in the permanence of Hawthorne's reputation. In the long run, no skill in the music of words can make evil-worship popular. That which is vitally pernicious will sooner or later be disgusting to good taste."

Noyes distrusted eloquence, and rhetoric, all pretentious façades of literary art. If poetry is to be alive, he said, the energy of the Spirit must vitalize it. For: "The best part of truth is unspeakable. I can see or feel at a flash, instantaneously, a sum of truth that is perfectly intelligible to me, and yet that cannot be expressed in words. And if these spirit-openings could be translated into words, a mountain of books would not contain them. We want . . . a deeper language; and as we launch out beyond the range of mere intellect into the domain of heart and feeling, and get free to see things by intuition, without requiring them to be put into logical shape in words, we shall find that there *is* another utterance—a language of the heart and spirit, that will condense volumes into one instantaneous glance. That is the real meaning of poetry, as far as it has any valuable meaning. It is an approach to this language of the heart.

"The ambition of words that labor for expression . . . characteristic of some poets, appears to me as despicable incontinence, such as would spoil the real poetry of life. It is not to be believed that the poets who make books have therefore the most real poetry in them. On the contrary, the amount of poetry in persons is probably, in many cases, inverse to their amount of talk. The deeper persons are in love, the less, generally, they have to say; and so God may see more poetry in those who can neither write nor talk, than in those who fill books."

In 1864, William Blake was discovered to the cultivated American world by an essay published in *The Atlantic Monthly*, entitled "Pictor Ignotus." The genius of Blake was immediately recognized by the Community, and more than eight columns of *The Circular* (May 9, 1864) were devoted to him. While Noyes himself was not, apparently, responsible for the essays on Blake which appeared in *The Circular*, his influence and counsel were unquestionably responsible for the enthusiasm which spread contagiously among the group whose minds he had cultivated.

5

Men, women, and children were encouraged to "confess Christ." Puzzling to the young, especially, was this mysterious duty. Often they appealed to Father Noyes as a confessor. In simple, elementary terms—yet with penetrating psychological intuition—he explained the benefits of this spirtual exercise. With the precision of a mechanic explaining the working of some complex machine, Father Noyes traced the steps out of egotism into the larger life—out of the "first person singular" into "we-ness." To one young man, he explained: "We must first conceive of ourselves as members of Christ; recognize whatever there is in us of faith and goodness as the working of his life. We can say that we *are Christ;* not that we are Christs in the plural—that would be an assumption that we are independent, individually, both of Jesus Christ and of one another—but we *are Christ as members of him and one another*. Christ is a unit, and his life fills his whole body. We humans are Christ as the hand or the foot is part of the person to which it belongs. Such is the first great overruling conception of Paul's gospel. From this concept, we are able to work out our character. We assume a position in some respects like that of an actor or dramatic artist. After conceiving of a character which he is to delineate, he goes on to perfect details. Under the conception that we are Christ, our life purpose naturally is to act as Christ would act in all circumstances, 'to do all things in the name of Christ.' This fundamental confession, impressed upon us from the beginning by the Holy Spirit, and growing stronger and stronger by every confession of it, and reflection upon it, comes to be an ever-present, all-controlling element of character-building.

"We know how powerful self-respect is in helping people to do right. A man who habitually regards himself as mean will inevitably behave meanly; a man who conceives of himself as honest and respectable leads an honest and repectable life, or at least is protected by his self-respect from many temptations." With immensely greater power, this principle works when we sincerely confess Christ in us, Noyes told the young man. "The standard of self-respect which we assume as embodiments of Christ lifts us toward superhuman goodness. Our character is formed by the action and reaction between our conception of Christ and our efforts to realize or personate that conception in our daily life. By confession and reflection we renew our self-respect as members of Christ. That helps us to behave well. Then our behaving well goes beyond our expectations, and proves itself to be really the working of Christ. That helps us to confess and renew our conception of Christ in us. This is the working of Paul's gospel, as I understand it. This is the way we 'work out our salvation, knowing that God worketh in us.'"

6

When he turned his attention to education, Noyes found himself in complete disagreement with contemporary ideals. This new idol could become the most pernicious instrument to sow seeds of selfishness and competition. As he grew older, Noyes became aware that the younger generation was worshiping at the altar of this new god, that the principal motives which impelled young men to study were a love of gain and a love of fame. He felt compelled to warn the younger generation against such motives. Unless harnessed to communal development, he believed, education might become an evil. He protested against the utilization of education as an instrument, a weapon, no matter how disguised or concealed, for the cultivation of acquisitive traits. Did not the entire rank and file of professional men pursue their careers as lawyers, doctors, and writers solely for the purpose of making money? In the one case, education was followed as a means of living; in the other, it was made the stepping-stone to personal distinction; but in both, the motive was false. The Community itself, Noyes admitted, had entered the field of education, sending its young people off to college with the promise of all that modern science could teach them. All the more important, therefore, that each should rightly determine his motives. The young students might be discharged from the lower motive—the love of money; the Community guaranteed their support. But the other motive, the love of personal distinction, was a subtler one, one to be specially guarded against. "Unless we take great pains to prevent it, a tendency will rise among us to seek learning from the same motive of ambition that works in the world."

Thus Noyes warned his "family" against worldly love of personal distinction. "We shall need to watch and pray and set our faces as a flint against it. We must keep it from getting among us as we would the cholera. I believe we can handle all the tools the world handles, and master all its sciences, and yet keep clear of this vice. We can do for the love of God and the truth more than others can do for the love of money and personal distinction."

In 1872, when some of the younger members of the Community were studying the catalogues of the various universities, a copy of the Cornell University Register fell by chance into the hands of Noyes. He gazed at its frontispiece—a portrait of the Honorable Ezra Cornell, with these words surrounding the picture: "I would found an institution where any person can find instruction in any study." Commenting on these words, Noyes is reported to have said: "I would like to find an institution where a person can get systematic instruction

on *the way to find God;*
in *the art of walking in the Spirit;*
in *the art of love, general and special;*
in *the theory and practice of social life;*
in *the art of conversation;*
in *the art of sexual intercourse;*
in *scientific propagation as applied to human beings;*
in *the art of managing infants;*
in *the art of rearing boys and girls;*

and to sum up all,

in *the art of making a happy home.*

"Where is the institution that gives systematic instruction on any of these subjects?"

Noyes advocated a periodic return to manual labor as "the only condition of healthy life." Looking back over his career, at the age of sixty-four, he confessed that "education, so far as it sets up an interest that is separated from and independent of productive industry, has gone off in a wrong direction." Again we feel that in the back of his mind, he was beginning to suspect that the prosperity that had come to the Oneida Community might corrupt the third generation.

"The system that tempts young men to despise manual labor and look down on mechanics and their works, and to live a monkish kind of life, devoting themselves to brain labor, is a wrong system. We have got to discriminate and not consent to lose any advantages the world has gained by the colleges and that kind of education; but look well into it and see what the deepest truth is about the whole matter. We do not want to educate ourselves or our children for specialties. We want an integral education that will fit us for eternal uses."

Unpredictable, sometimes shocking, yet invariably stimulating were Noyes's home talks—destructive always of presumption in favor of things as they were and had been; against all old-established sentiments, old-established institutions, which were habitually assumed to be correct, and which demanded the right of way, putting all burden of proof on the innovator. "I believe in my soul that the presumption is all the other way—that it is *against* established sentiments and institutions. . . . The institutions that have come down to us by tradition from our fathers originated with men who were not qualified to lay eternal foundations."

"But will there not come a time when revolution will no longer be necessary?" some timid listener might ask. "Is it necessary always to have new things breaking out? Will not the spirit of Christ come at last into coöperation with a settled state of things?"

"In the sense in which you want it, there will never be rest," Noyes answered. "The infinite life in Christ cannot abide the rest you want; it will be entirely impossible ever to attain a settled state of things such as will suit the lover of cidermill routine."

Chapter VIII: MUSIC

> So it is with music; the written notes are not the main thing, nor is even the heard performance; these are only evidences of an internal invisible emotion that can be felt but never fully expressed.
>
> —SAMUEL BUTLER.

I

ON the elevated land just north of the old Mansion House, an imposing new Community House of red brick was erected. The old wooden buildings were removed, and the new home was surrounded by spacious stretches of lawn and trees. Wings were added to this dignified building in the seventies, so that a cloistered inner quadrangle was eventually formed. Behind the new home, to the west was erected the "Tontine," named after a new hotel in Boston. The Tontine housed the kitchens and dining-hall, and was connected with the basement of the main house by an underground passage, for use in bad weather. This new house was equipped with all the conveniences that the period offered. On the second floor, the commodious assembly hall was fitted with a balcony running around three walls; and a stage, equipped with a footlight trough, was used for the Community entertainments—dancing by the children, tableaux, dramatic performances, concerts, and even recitals by celebrated, traveling virtuosi.

Downstairs, in an office off the main entrance, two members received callers, for the Community was attracting an ever-increasing number of visitors. In 1870, the Midland Railroad built a line which extended for more than a mile through the seven hundred acres comprising the Community domain, and a station named "Community" was established within a stone's throw of the dwellings. This convenience made it possible for dwellers in neighboring towns and cities to organize excursions to the Community. All visitors were encouraged to picnic on the lawns, to inspect gardens and factories, and free concerts were given in the Community Hall. Trainloads of men, women and children, often from considerable distances, visited this little Utopia. They roamed through the new Community House, completed in 1871, enjoying its comforts and luxuries. Hundreds of the curious wandered over the six hundred and sixty-four acres of "the best farm and grazing lands in the State." They were guided in parties through the vast trap-shops and canning factories. Under courteous supervision, they trooped through the substantial farm buildings, paraded through stables well stocked with thoroughbred Ayrshire and Holstein cattle, Cotswold sheep, Berkshire swine. As at a county fair, they inspected the Imperial Pekin and Aylesburg ducks with their snowy plumage and fantastic crests, the white Holland turkeys, or Langshan fowls, the Light Brahmas, the Houdans, Leghorns, and pigeons. Magnificent, thoroughbred cattle dotted the green pastures—cattle which won many livestock prizes at Lenox Fair.

These visitors undertook lengthy cross-examinations, imperious interrogations into the mysteries of the Community's existence. In the public rooms, at the table, at the barn, under the butternut tree, wherever indeed they managed to buttonhole stray members, the visitors implored: "Tell us now what you are about!—tell us everything! Tell us what holds you together. You are getting rich and are happy, we don't understand it. Out with the secret! You can't explain to persons on our plane? Yes, you can,—come, let us have it. How do you manage about the women? I would knock any man down who should think of loving my wife. I would shoot him. You do not have such feelings? Well, tell us how you stand it. You don't believe in marriage; how are you going to multiply and replenish the earth? And whose are these children round here? What is your object in getting rich? What good do you do? Did you do anything for the war—for the Sanitary Commission? You publish a free paper, you say—well, your object is to proselyte, you expect to make money by that. If you are right, why don't you go abroad and preach the gospel to every creature? What do you shut yourselves up here for?" Even more embarrassing questions were sometimes put, and the youth and innocence of Community members was not always a safeguard. But such visitors usually departed with voluble disclaimers of any intention to be impolite, and with positive expressions of respect.

Most prying, most impertinent of all were the visiting ladies —padded, upholstered, overstuffed, harnessed and bustled paragons of virtue who seemingly cast discretion to the wind, and went on a moral spree. Was it not true, these ladies confidentially inquired, that at the Community all men and women slept in one large room? Their insatiable curiosity could not be appeased by cool assurances that in the Community, with few exceptions, each individual member enjoyed his own private room, where, without disturbance of any kind, he might be free to meditate and pursue plans of spiritual improvement. "The simple truth is that we do not live nearly so closely together in the external way

(Courtesy of Mrs. Dorothy B. Leonard)

THE "NEW" COMMUNITY HOUSE ABOUT 1871

(*Courtesy of Oneida Community, Ltd.*)

A BAG "BEE" ON THE LAWN

Traveling bags were manufactured by the women.

as the majority of married people," the guide might explain, but usually in vain.

But the Community women? Alas! Alas! Such strange, slender creatures, with sun-tanned visages and short hair, were not in the taste of the overstuffed Seventies. Such figures then seemed positively "unhealthy," but actually they were a great deal healthier than any average lot of the same number in the outside world. Nearly all newspaper correspondents wrote in scornful derogation of the appearance of the Community women. Outdoor life had brightened the eyes and tanned their complexions– "A discoloration which they take no pains to conceal with powder." They were fresh, bright, active, intelligent, poised and well-formed; if they had been dressed in the excess of feminine harness and upholstery, approved by the Seventies–corsets, paint, whitewash, false hair, long trains and bustles, they would have held their own with the belles of any fashionable assemblage. These were facts obvious to unprejudiced eyes, but most visiting journalists came not to dispel, but to re-inforce, current prejudices.

Intelligent visitors, who came expecting to be shocked by lewdness and license, left with praise only. The gentility and good-breeding of the Oneidans were disarming. Thomas Wentworth Higginson published a testimonial to this effect. "As a matter of fact, I am bound to say as an honest reporter," Mr. Higginson confessed in the *Woman's Journal*, "that I looked in vain for the visible signs of either the suffering or the sin. The Community makes an impression utterly unlike that left by the pallid joylessness of the Shakers, or the stupid sensualism which impressed me in the few Mormon households I have seen. The fact that the children of the Community hardly ever wish to leave it; that the young men whom they send to Yale College, and the young women whom they send for musical instruction to New York, always return eagerly and devote their lives to the Community,–this proves a good deal. There is no coercion to keep them, as in Mormonism, and there are no monastic vows, as in the Roman Catholic Church. This invariable return, therefore, shows that there is happiness to be found in the Community, and that it is of a kind which wins the respect of the young and generous. A body must have great confidence in itself when it thus voluntarily sends its sheep into the midst of the world's wolves, and fearlessly expects their return."

The army of little sleds outside the main entrance of the Community house had seemed to the Bostonian, as he alighted from his carriage one winter day, a very good omen. He had been cordially received in a sort of "palace of plain comfort, admirably warm and ventilated." The manner of all was cordial and inoffensive, and he sat down to a well-cooked dinner, well-served on a snowy tablecloth. But most of all, Mr. Higginson was impressed by the musical education of the members. For after dinner he was escorted to the assembly hall for a concert. The orchestra that day was small, but excellent—under the leadership of a thoroughly trained director. And to the delight of Thomas Wentworth Higginson, they performed "good German music."

The Community's experiences in music are so characteristic of its attack upon all education, and so vivid a part of the whole picture, that no account of Community life can be complete without a record of its musical history.

2

From an early date, music was encouraged in the Community. The story has come down by word of mouth that Noyes himself could never carry a tune; but he had theories of his own concerning musical appreciation and musical composition. He recognized it as another path to communal sharing—a hint of the great superconsciousness ruling the universe. The Community was not primarily interested in passive musical appreciation—although the great musicians of the time, men like Ole Bull and Remenyi, turned aside from tours to give recitals in the Community hall (without remuneration) and were received by intelligent and appreciative listeners. For the followers of Noyes, however, music was essentially an activity, a beauty one must re-create. Here again, they were precursors of modern ideals of musical education.

This history of Community music seems to recapitulate the progress of music in nearly all civilizations. Starting with youthful, fecund amateurism, it almost ended in the sterility of professionalism. One difference was that the Oneidans discovered this corrosive disease and sought to arrest its advance. On the return, in 1854, of the Brooklyn leaders, scattered freshets of musical interest soon began to converge. The nucleus of what was to become a Community orchestra soon germinated. At half-past twelve, on alternate days, some half-dozen embryonic musicians used to gather together in the parlor of the old Mansion House. For fifteen minutes the tuning of fiddles and bass viols, the endeavor to harmonize a pair of recalcitrant flutes created what they termed a "mellifluous" confusion. An equal period in the performance of pieces selected from two or three well-worn collections of music followed. To accommodate the increasing number of instrumentalists who joined this circle, a four-sided stand was constructed. On this were placed the well-thumbed music books. One row of performers was seated; the others, from behind, looked over their heads. Huddled around this square blue box, the company of anxious, would-be musicians earnestly endeavored to glimpse the music from the one or two books on the stand. All were untutored beginners in instrumental music, possessing neither system nor musical experience. Some of the music was arranged in one, some in two, some in three parts. At first they were content merely to read it through with tolerable accuracy. As some one expressed it, "we had no leader; every man did what seemed good in his own eyes." Sometimes they acted in turn as leaders. This office consisted in selecting tunes and giving word to the rest in a commanding tone, "*All ready, play!*" But as "all" were seldom ready at the same time, ear-splitting discord often came forth. Still, no sophisticated critics hovered over them to discourage those rude but sincere attempts. So they pressed on; and the enthusiasm and ambition of each member elicited the praise and encouragement of the Community at large.

From the first, this impassioned interest in music was coincident with an equal progress in manual labor, the flute and violin forming an accompaniment to the clang of the anvil. In the spring of 1856, the orchestra consisted of one piccolo, two flutes, six violins, one violin-cello and an "orphicleide." To supply instruments of percussion, one member ambitiously set himself the task of making a small and large drum. A triangle occasionally added its tinkle. In May, 1856, C. S. Joslyn, leader of the Community orchestra, arranged Blockley's air of "Love not" in eight parts. This was the group's first advance beyond three-part tunes of the instruction books. The effect of this complicated harmony was wonderfully stimulating to all the participants. Thereafter Mr. Joslyn was granted a portion of each day for the study of music and composition. Consequently, noon practice was occasionally enlivened by an original composition from this leader or a new arrangement of some old, familiar air.

By midsummer, 1857, the little orchestra was already beginning to attract attention from transient visitors to the Community. Gradually news of the regular noon practice spread across the surrounding countryside, and the orchestra found itself playing before large audiences. By the spring of 1859, the orchestra had grown to include twenty-five members. Compositions in its repertory numbered more than seventy, including marches, "quick-steps," ballads, and a few easy extracts from the operas. Their taste was eclectic, a bit undiscriminating, perhaps, but how energetic, how vital their interest!

We may regret that such enthusiasm could not have been guided by surer musical authority; but the Community musicians were no whit inferior to the prevailing musical taste of the American public. Whatever missteps they may have taken were more than compensated for by their touching achievement the following May. Then, under the direction of their ambitious leader, the full orchestra succeeded in a creditable performance of that entrancing, "perfect" overture with which Mozart entices us into the magic realm of his "*Noces de Figaro.*"

For the express purpose of improving his acquaintance with standard music, and studying orchestral organizations and effects, in the winter of 1860 Mr. Joslyn was sent to spend several weeks in New York. On his return, he brought with him piano copies of the overture to "*Le Calif de Bagdad*" by Boieldieu, an *andante* from "Sicilian Vespers" by Verdi, and Auber's overture to "Fra Diavolo."

No longer satisfied with self-taught methods of violin playing, some of the younger men now sent for copies of Hill's edition of Spohr, and resolutely went back, to ground themselves in foundations. By conscientious drilling they soon became competent soloists. Obtaining a hundred dollars by overtime work, one young man purchased with it a fine silver Boehm flute; but following professional advice he exchanged it for two silver-lined instruments.

One question always arose amongst these impassioned musicians: "Where shall we go to practice?" There were innumerable perplexities in a milieu so full of changes, and with so little room. Where could they all rehearse their music, so that every one of their Community audience should not know it by heart before the musicians were ready to perform in public? Where could they hide to scrape out those first lessons on the violin, to blare first brayings on the horn? Where could committees meet without disturbance? Where could they gather for this or that? The schoolroom was one favorite place. There desks could be piled at one end, leaving a space for rehearsals. The printing-office provided an occasional resort out of earshot.

Finally the "academy of music" found its favorite home in the dairy-house! Quartette clubs and amateur violinists gathered there, and "stage" performances were often rehearsed. In a pinch, some chilly dormitory was utilized. They contrived, after all, by dint of accommodation and organization and by the strategems of necessity, to find a place for all this musical activity.

In the summer of 1860, Felix Shelling, a Swiss music-teacher, came to the Community with his family, and remained nearly a year. His specialties were vocal music and the piano-forte. Felix Shelling did much to raise the musical standard in the Community; he gave serious attention to correctness of intonation, general artistic effect and technical niceties, which had previously, of necessity, been neglected. From this time the skill of the orchestra increased noticeably. Rapid improvement was made not only in the choice of compositions but in technical execution as well.

3

During the following years, Community musicians made profound advances in appreciation and education. Vocalists and instrumental soloists emerged; concerts became semi-professional entertainments. Indeed Community soloists occasionally developed an almost condescending attitude toward their audiences. But with these new attainments, much of the old spirit of coöperation vanished. In August, 1874, it became painfully apparent that some evil spirit, compounded of jealousy, envy, and egotism, was creeping into the minds of the young women of the musical sorority.

These symptoms were called to the attention of Noyes. In his attempt to diagnose the curious psychic ailment that had come over the musicians, he discovered that one girl had been, for a period of nearly a month, isolated and uncompanionable. Tactfully he sought to diagnose the young vocalist's case, finally asking if her feeling had not grown out of the failure she had made in singing. Lily admitted that it had. She confessed that since her failure she wished to stop singing altogether. Unless she could be acclaimed as the best singer in the Community, Lily did not want to sing at all. That was why she harbored hard feelings toward Marion–Lily confessed that she almost hated Marion at times, because the latter was recognized as the better singer.

Noyes decided to call the entire musical group together. The epidemic from which it suffered should be analyzed and remedied by the whole group, acting in unison. He called for general, candid, unreserved confession. Ann Hobart explained what was troubling Lily, and then added:

"Mr. Noyes thought that perhaps the other girls would have something to say, and I found they had. Lily not only felt hard toward Marion, but Marion felt so toward Lily. Although they seemed to be good friends aside from their music, the moment that subject was mentioned, they felt almost hatred toward each other. Marion would not buy a piece of music because she had heard Lily humming it. Lily could not bear the thought that Marion should excel her in singing, though she was willing Alice should. Edith also felt bad . . . because Carrie could play better on the piano than she could. She had not thought much yet of competing with Tirzah, but she was determined to be the best player in our own class. Carrie felt jealous of Edith, and thought that no one asked her to play anything but accompaniments, and then only because they could not get Tirzah or Edith. And Leonora has become disgusted because Edith and Carrie can do better than she can. They all say it is the meanest feeling they ever had, and they would rather give up music than to continue in this spirit."

"Mr. Noyes thought it would be a good thing for the older musicians to be as sincere as these girls have been," interjected one of the elder group; "perhaps the same rivalry has worked in them in the past, and does now to some extent. If we could get a spirit of sincerity that would cast that element out . . . we might enjoy music again."

A momentary silence fell. Then Noyes genially explained: "The essence of the evil seems to be, that music has evidently become a selfish, personal thing; they look on their talents, their reputation, ability and success in music as their own, and are quarreling in their hearts about the matter, just as the world quarrels about money and other selfish rights. Music in fact is uncommunized property. I thought that if the strife had become such a nuisance among those younger girls, it might be possible that the whole musical body is so affected by the same spirit."

"I had no temptation to rivalry in music until after my fifteenth year," one young woman confessed candidly. "I sang simply because I loved to sing; it was the greatest pleasure I knew. I was full of enthusiasm to study music, and sought every opportunity to improve myself. My first feeling of jealousy was toward Ann Eliza. We both sang alto; but at the time she was admitted into Mr. Burnham's quartette club, I was not so honored. I considered this as a personal slight. . . . One day I deliberately hid one of the books from which the club had practiced—putting those who sang to great inconvenience. In my eighteenth year Mrs. Harriet Noyes invited me to sing soprano in a cantata, adding that she considered my voice better adapted to that part than to alto singing. I soon discovered that she was right. A great ambition took possession of me to excel those with whom I was singing. A few years later, when Mr. Shelling came here, he made much of my voice; his praise fired me with a zeal to become a fine vocalist. I not only wanted to sing well, but I aspired to become the *best singer*, and the most ready at reading music. I was much of the time in an agony of jealousy lest some other would eclipse me. I made marked improvement as a vocalist, but I was not happy. I fell far short of the standard I had set for myself.

"When Alice made her début as a singer, I censured her style, for I had fallen into the professional way of criticizing every musician and singer that came into favor," she continued. "I liked to sing with Alice very much, though I tortured myself with comparisons; then I would feel discouraged and wish I had never tried to be a musician. When the proposition was made that she should go to New York to take singing lessons, it gave me a severe shock. Not that I objected to her going; but this had been for several years a pet idea of my own, and I was trying to summon the courage to ask leave to go to New York or Boston; and it seemed cruel and unkind that no one thought of me. No one knows the anguish I was in for weeks; it seemed the most unjust arrangement of Providence that could be made. I went through a severe struggle, in which I at last gave up my will to God concerning my voice, and felt not only reconciled but thankful to stay at home. I never had another pang about that matter, or about Alice's or any one else's singing. My pride in music was crucified. I gave up the idea of becoming a *musical artist*, and felt contented to sing well.... The old ambition to be first and best left me. The result was peace of mind.... I love music as well as ever, and feel a good deal of the old ambition for improvement, but I see how necessary it is to clear out this worldly spirit. It looks very mean and small."

"Eighteen or twenty years ago," queried one of the older musicians, "there were quite a number of persons practicing the violin, and now where are they? There is but one who plays the first violin."

"Don't you suppose that one great reason of the falling off from violin practice is owing to this spirit of jealousy and rivalry, which eats like a canker, and cannot bear to be second in anything?" asked Noyes.

"I presume it is," answered the first. "I have no doubt but that I should have kept up my violin practice until now, if I had not had some such temptations about it...."

"The natural tendency of this spirit is to bring the musical fraternity to a state in which, if a person cannot do the *best*, he cannot do anything," commented Noyes. "Then as a consequence of that step there would be but one player on each instrument, and one singer on each part. . . . The object of this meeting is to uncover the working of the spirit which is striving who shall be greatest. It seems to be the confession of quite a number of the . . . girls, that they are possessed with the spirit that is striving to be greatest. Though they hate it like poison, yet they find it difficult to get rid of it. If that spirit is essentially identified with music, we had better clear music out of the Community."

"I don't think it is," protested Theodore Noyes. "My observation is that the old band and some other organizations have been entirely free from it. I have never felt any of it, though I have always been in a secondary place in musical organizations, but on the contrary have had some of the most enjoyable fellowship in the practice of music. I think this spirit is more apt to make trouble in singing and solo-playing than in instrumental organizations."

"This selfish spirit which these girls have exposed, will work out in some other way, if they do not get rid of it in their music," continued Theodore. "I should go for giving up music, unless it can be separated from this spirit. If they do not rid themselves of it now, it will show itself in other forms, even if they drop music."

"I think so too," Frank now spoke. "I have practiced lately with Edith, and have not had the slightest suspicion of any such feeling working in her."

"It was quite a revelation to me," added John Noyes. "But I remember having quite a distinct intuition a while ago that there was some such jealousy. This new meanness has been nursed by our musicians having a great deal to do with outside music, and by performing before worldly audiences."

"That is so," agreed Theodore. "In those old times the family used to be our audience."

"Lately we have got our music altogether from the world, and have gone to New York for musical education, and we are suffering the consequences," concluded John Noyes.

"If we could separate music entirely from the idea of displaying ourselves to visitors," Theodore suggested, "and look on it as something for our own use, we might get back into the old feeling about it. We never before had a class of singers brought up on the stage and before the world as much as this class of girls has been."

The germ of their musical malady seemed now to be isolated and Noyes found a suitable name for it:

"They have been brought up on the stage, and have got the *prima donna fever*. There are always two sides in the matter of envying," he pointed out: "The one that is envied may be as much to blame as the one that envies. I wish criticism might reach that part of the game, if there is a glorying spirit at work in those who are higher up . . . a kind of *prima donna* air that sets envy going in others, you ought to have a searching time and clear it all out."

All now proffered suggestions for the eradication of the disease. All invited criticism. All vowed that in future they would live immune from jealousy, envy and carping. Noyes himself brought the conference to a conclusion: "After this astonishing disclosure in respect to the difficulties between these girls, I believe I have a sure diagnosis of the unhealthy condition of music in the Community. We doctors have long been trying to find out what is the matter, and after feeling pulses and looking at tongues all round, we find that it is the *prima donna fever!* I am going to doctor for that. If we can cure that, we shall have music back on its legs again. It is bedridden now and has been for a great while with the *prima donna fever!* That's what's the matter!"

4

In a note to C. S. Joslyn, long the musical director of the Community, Noyes once wrote: "As we assume that Christ is the soul of all the movements that constitute modern civilization, so we may be sure that the development of music has been his work, and that it has an important relation to the general movement in which he is engaged. If we settle this point we shall feel bound to study the *whole* development of music—'profane' music as well as religious. Our relation to the world of music will be similar to our relation to spiritualism. *It is a big thing, and I do not believe that there is any big thing in this world which has not Christ in the belly of it.* Music evidently has a close relation to religion. This is seen of course in all 'sacred' music. But has it not an equally close relation to sexual love? Is not the great mass of common 'profane' music an echo of the passions? If so, then music as a whole is the servant of love—'sacred' music serving the love of God and 'profane' music serving the love of the sexes. And as we are bringing these two kinds of love together, so we shall close up the gap between the two kinds of music, and abolish the distinction of 'sacred' and 'profane.'

"Such a theory as this would lead us to study the history of music, with an interesting purpose. Perhaps we shall get an appetite for reading on that subject. . . . My wish and hope are that you may take hold of music this time with a very serious purpose to become a *medium* not only of the musical genii that control the masters, but of the spirit of Christ that controls them; and that you will by example and lectures and practice lead the Community into the scientific, historical and spiritual mysteries of music, till it shall become a school of the harmonic art for the world."

Such grandiose aims, however, did not exclude their enjoyment of the lighter phases of music. At the period when Messrs. Gilbert and Sullivan's "H.M.S. Pinafore" was performed by every professional company in the country, the musicians and actors of the Community staged their own production in the great hall. They performed it not merely once, but night after night, before practically the same audience, made up of their comrades. (Community members may have felt themselves at home in the topsy-turvy world of W. S. Gilbert, a world in which all worldly pretensions were so savagely deflated.) Later, the Community singers and players gave performances in the neighboring towns, and cemented still further the good-will of the surrounding counties.

Chapter IX: STIRPICULTURE

> The existence of Noyes simplified the breeding problem for the Communists, the question of what sort of men they should strive to breed being settled at once by the obvious desirability of breeding another Noyes.
>
> —BERNARD SHAW.

I

HAD he been constituted like other men, John Noyes might have been ready, as his fifty-eighth birthday approached, to subside gradually into that retirement and retrospection that are the reward of the well-to-do sexagenarian. Prosperity had brought with it a certain degree of deference from the outside world. The Community factories were giving employment to hundreds—and that was an excellent thing for the shopkeepers, the banks, the business men of the surrounding towns. In nine years, the Community had earned something like two hundred thousand dollars over and above expenses, and its wealth was increasing every year. But Noyes had withstood the temptation to settle into the routine of the world, and now he withstood the temptation to fall into the routine of the elderly. Always he had refused to admit the validity of the claims of "old age." And now, in 1869, he inaugurated in the Community an experiment bound to unleash a new storm of protest from the exponents of traditional morality.

Certain men, we are told, are the instruments of "cosmic consciousness." Noyes seemed also to possess an unusual faculty of racial consciousness. The program of scientific breeding, to which he gave the name stirpiculture (from the Latin *stirps*, root, stock or strain), was no new concept that had sprung full grown out of Darwinian ideas of evolution. Noyes had long realized its importance, and as early as 1848, in his "Bible Communism," he wrote, long before Galton had invented the word "eugenics": "We are opposed to excessive, and of course oppressive procreation, which is almost universal. We are opposed to random procreation, which is unavoidable in the marriage system. But we are in favor of intelligent, well-ordered procreation. The physiologists say that the race cannot be raised from ruin till propagation is made a matter of science; but they point out no way of making it so. Procreation is controlled and reduced to a science in the case of valuable domestic brutes; but marriage and fashion forbid any such system among human beings. We believe the time will come when involuntary and random propagation will cease, and when scientific combination will be applied to human generation as freely and successfully as it is to that of other animals. The way will be open for this when amativeness can have its proper gratification without drawing after it procreation as a necessary sequence. And at all events, we believe that good sense and benevolence will very soon sanction and enforce the rule that women shall bear children only when they choose. They have the principal burdens of breeding to bear, and they rather than men should have their choice of time and circumstances, at least till science takes charge of the business."

In 1865, six years after the publication of "The Origin of Species," Charles Darwin's cousin, Francis Galton referred for the first time to the problem of human racial improvement; four years later, when he was nearly fifty, he published "Hereditary Genius, Its Laws and Consequences." It was not, however, until 1883 that in his book "Human Faculty," the word "eugenics" was first employed. Galton defined eugenics as the study of agencies under social control which may improve or impair the racial qualities of future generations either physically or mentally.

In the Sixties Noyes began to study Darwin and Galton and the problem of scientific breeding. He rebelled against the timidity of Galton: "When he comes to the point where it is necessary to look beyond his theory to the duties it suggests, he subsides into the meekest conservatism.... The commandment has come; we all acknowledge it and preach it and 'delight in it after the inward man, but we see another law in our members warring against the law of our minds.' Duty is plain; we say we ought to do it—we must do it; but we cannot. The law of God urges us on; but the law of society holds us back. This is a bad position. Either our convictions ought to become stronger and deeper till they break away into obedience, or we ought to be relieved of them altogether.

"The boldest course is the safest. Let us take an honest and steady look at the law. Let us march right up to this terrible analogy which has been so long troubling the world, and find out exactly what it is, and how far the obligation which it suggests is legitimate. What ought to be done can be done."

Noyes was not the man to refrain from putting innermost convictions into practice. As a laboratory of stirpicultural experiment the Community stood ready and waiting. It was obvious to Noyes that this experiment must begin with a pair, or, at most, with a small number of chosen volunteers, and must proceed by propagating exclusively, or nearly so, within its own circle. This process implied breeding in and in, mating between members of the same general *stock* related more or less closely. It would of necessity challenge all the most deeply rooted taboos of the race. It would bring a new storm of criticism on the Community. But animal breeders paid very little attention to the principles of the "law of incest" in any stage of their proceedings. It was even a matter of doubt and disputation among them whether there was any harm in the closest and longest breeding between related stock. Darwin and the best authorities among the breeders inclined to the opinion that long-continued mating of relatives and related stock, leads finally to weakness of constitution and infertility. But they all agreed that breeding in and in must be the general law for choice stocks.

The more he pondered over the problem, the more convinced Noyes became that if it were possible for men and women to be directed in their propagation by superior beings, as animals were, or by their own sincere enthusiasm for science, the results of suppressing the poorest and breeding from the best would be the same as in the development of thoroughbred cattle and sheep. If it were compatible with public morality and with the proper care of women and children to "give special privileges to the most exalted individuals in the perpetuation of the species," Noyes explained to those of his own circle, "the elevation of the human species would be as rapid as that of any of the lower races."

The younger men, already converts to the ideas of Darwin, were amazed at the leader's ready grasp of the implications of the doctrine of evolution. The older men warmed themselves at the fire of John Noyes's new enthusiasm. They, too, looked forward hopefully to the greater experiment of Stirpiculture. The Community had, Noyes went on to explain, cleared the way for the experiment. They had already abolished the institution of matrimony, which seemed an absolute bar to scientific propagation. For marriage pretended to no discrimination, gave no more liberty to the best than to the worst, even permitted the inferior classes to indulge in incessant procreation. The Community listened breathlessly as Noyes proclaimed: "Even common licentiousness, cursed as it is, is sometimes not without compensations in the light of the propagative law. It is very probable that the feudal custom which gave barons the first privilege of every marriage among their retainers, base and oppressive though it was, actually improved the blood of the lower classes. We see that Providence frequently allows very superior men to be also very attractive to women, and very licentious. Perhaps with all the immediate evil that they do to morals, they do some good to the blood of after generations. Who can say how much the present race of men in Connecticut owe to the numberless adulteries and fornications of Pierrepont Edwards?

Corrupt as he was, he must have distributed a good deal of the good blood of his noble father, Jonathan Edwards; and so we may hope the human race got a secret profit out of him. Such are the compensations of nature and Providence.

"Dare we now look beyond present institutions to the possibilities of the future? We may at least point out briefly the main boundaries of what is needed and must come. The institutions that shall at some future time supersede marriage and its accessories, whatever may be their details, must include certain essentials, negative and positive, which can be foreseen now with entire certainty.

"In the first place, they must not lessen human liberty. Here we touch the main point of the difference between the cases of animals and men, and the point of difficulty for our whole problem. . . . Man as a race has no visible superior. The fact declares that his destiny is self-government. . . . The liberty already won must not be diminished, but increased. If there is to be suppression, it must not be by castration and confinement, as in the case of animals, or even by law and public opinion, as men are now controlled, but by the free choice of those who love science well enough 'to make themselves eunuchs for the Kingdom of Heaven's sake.' If mating is to be brought about without regard to the sentimental specialties that now control it, this must be done only for those whose liberty consists in obeying rational laws, because they love truth more than sentimentalism."

2

For twenty years (1849-1869), the Community had deliberately refrained from bringing children into the world, increasing its number less than two a year in a population of some forty families. This policy, it was explained, was dictated by temporary expediency. Like all prudent parents, the Community awaited "responsible maturity and favorable circumstances." In entering its régime of scientific propagation, the Community claimed that it had reached its earliest marriage stage. Twenty years had tested the practicability of its sexual principles. The men from the original Putney group had no children in the so-called Children's House—with the exception of George W. Noyes, who was the father of a boy of seven. This was an intentional exception.

Early in 1869, they were ready to inaugurate their daring venture in planned, scientific procreation. They decided to name it Stirpiculture, because that word seemed to Noyes and his counselors to express the highest and most sacred art that humans could

(*From* Frank Leslie's Illustrated Newspaper, *April* 2, 1870)

AN EVENING SCENE IN THE COMMUNITY HALL

(From a wood engraving)

40 FRANK LESLIE'S ILLUSTRATED NEWSPAPER. [APRIL 2, 1870.

NEW YORK STATE.—THE BUSINESS OFFICE OF THE ONEIDA COMMUNITY OF FREE LOVERS—LADY BOOK-KEEPERS AT WORK.—FROM A SKETCH BY OUR SPECIAL ARTIST.—SEE PAGE 38.

NEW YORK STATE.—THE BAKERY OF THE ONEIDA COMMUNITY OF FREE LOVERS.—FROM A SKETCH BY OUR SPECIAL ARTIST.—SEE PAGE 38.

(*From* Frank Leslie's Illustrated Newspaper, *April* 2, 1870)

COMMUNITY WOMEN AT WORK

Above: in the business office.

Below: in the bakery.

cultivate. The idea the word expressed could never have originated in the minds of debauchees. It must have first been coined and brought into use where human offspring was most highly prized, where they received the most loving and intelligent culture.

As a result of these deliberations, fifty-three young women of the Oneida Community solemnly signed these resolutions:

"1. That we do not belong to ourselves in any respect, but that we do belong first to *God*, and second to Mr. Noyes as God's true representative.

"2. That we have no rights or personal feelings in regard to child-bearing which shall in the least degree oppose or embarrass him in his choice of scientific combinations.

"3. That we will put aside all envy, childishness and self-seeking, and rejoice with those who are chosen candidates; that we will, if necessary, become martyrs to science, and cheerfully resign all desire to become mothers, if for any reason Mr. Noyes deem us unfit material for propagation. Above all, we offer ourselves 'living sacrifices' to God and true Communism."

A corresponding statement, signed by thirty-eight young men of the Community, was addressed to Father Noyes:

"The undersigned desire you may feel that we most heartily sympathize with your purpose in regard to scientific propagation, and offer ourselves to be used in forming any combinations that may seem to you desirable. We claim no rights. We ask no privileges. We desire to be servants of the truth. With a prayer that the grace of God will help us in this resolution, we are your true soldiers."

3

This man in his sixties was destined to sire, during the next ten years, at least nine of the fifty-eight children born under the stirpicultural régime. The mothers were chosen from the ranks of the young women who had signed the pledge quoted above. Each felt honored at the privilege of having the patriarch as the father of her child. It might be a temptation here to call in romantic imagination, and to expatiate upon the possibly repellent aspects of these relationships. But evidence compels us to recognize that it is no unusual phenomenon for young women to be attracted, both spiritually and physically, to men in their sixties. Such attractions have furnished interesting chapters in the lives of great men. Henrik Ibsen takes this theme for "The Master Builder." At the Oneida Community there were a dozen *Hildas* and but one *Solness*.

One letter is preserved which gives a charming picture of the tender and touching esteem in which Noyes was held by a younger woman who was to become the mother of one of his children. She wrote:

"Last evening there was a call for volunteers to give a little extra help in the trap-shop, at putting together traps; and as I *used* to work at that, I thought I would volunteer.... My work—the noises and the odors of the shop,—everything around me—reminded me of old times; and when not looking up, I could almost imagine that you were standing at the bench with me. And so my thoughts went gliding down the gulf of time, and I saw myself at your side, heating springs for you to hammer out, a girl of fifteen just waking up to the idea that this world contained many things not dreamed of at the children's house. Then I found myself weighing steel for you, and could see your every attention to detail, and myself grown a little older, having just launched out in the great ship of experience, and met one or two icebergs; confiding in you for guidance, yet wayward and thoughtless. Again, the trap-shop was enlarged, and you and I were putting together traps with the greatest zest. I could see you screwing the posts so carefully, and inventing little improvements until we reached the maximum of speed. With every little improvement and incident in the trap-shop, my own life seemed intertwined; for thinking of one brought up the other; and at this stage, I could see myself wild with youthful excitement—having seen the end of several flirtations, but under new fascinations, and still clinging to you as my guide and refuge. And with this reminiscence, I was truly astonished at your patience with me. I cannot imagine what encouraged you to hold on to me, for I was indeed very wayward, but God alone put it into your heart.... My thoughts ran on. I passed through all the incidents previous to Ormond's birth, and saw that as I ended off my education in the trap-shop, I entered (how joyfully you know) upon a new sphere and a new series of lessons—the glad and sober experience of a mother. And by the time I had completed our work I realized, more than ever before, the great transition I then made from volatile girlhood to earnest womanhood.... After I graduated from the trap-shop, and God had given me a child, you weaned me off and sent me forth to take care of myself. Do not think of me as sentimental; but I had such a vivid sense of all the past, that I wanted to see you very much indeed, for a little while. So the next best was to write to you.... I confess my union with you in everything."

4

One year after the inauguration of the stirpicultural program, three children had been born, and five more were known to be on the way. This sudden expansion was accepted as proving at least two things: first, the general faithfulness of the men of the Community to male continence in the years past; secondly, that their virility had not been impaired by this practice. Fathers of four of these "stirpicults" were veterans of the first generation who had practiced male continence longest and most. The other four fathers were young men of the second generation, who had never known any other practice. These births also refuted the predictions of female sterility as a result of the Community's "social" practices.

The bold venture into scientific procreation, of which the Community made no secret whatever, was denounced by interested moralists as an attempt to introduce the "ethics of the barnyard" into a human group. But the experiment was widely discussed, even across the Atlantic. In an essay on "The Evolution of the Family," published in 1877, even Herbert Spencer referred to "Father" Noyes and stirpiculture.

The curiosity of outsiders now became even more insatiable. Certain visitors pried endlessly in their efforts to learn the names of the Community children, partly to satisfy themselves that each youngster actually possessed a name.

"Is it true that the children here really know who their parents are?" asked one lady.

"I suppose that they are in the same condition in that respect," answered her courteous guide, "as the children in ordinary society. They have to accept the testimony of their parents on that particular point."

One hundred men and women of the Community participated in the stirpicultural experiments, and eighty-one of these became parents. Fifty-eight live children were brought into the world; there were four still-births. During the earlier years, couples desiring to undertake a stirpicultural experiment applied to the cabinet of central members to decide upon their fitness. This meant that in reality John Noyes directed the mating, and in certain cases strictly forbade it. On January 25, 1875, a formal Stirpicultural Committee was appointed by the Community. This committee was composed of six men and six women. Two of its members were graduates of the Yale medical school and the rest were chosen for their exceptional experience and sagacity. However this committee functioned during a period of only fifteen months. After April 20, 1876, direction of the stirpicultural policy passed again into the hands of the central members of the Community. These changes of policy seem to indicate some inner disagreement.

Records of the Stirpicultural Committee indicate the general methods of selection. In the majority of cases, application to the Committee was made by couples desiring to become parents. After due consideration, the Committee either approved or vetoed the selection. If an application were disapproved, the Committee would always undertake to find other combinations satisfactory to all concerned, which it could approve. Occasionally the Committee itself took the initiative in bringing about combinations which, in its opinion, were specially "indicated."

Fathers of the stirpicultural infants averaged in age 12.2 years older than the mothers. This average was brought up, undoubtedly, by the mating of the leader members—the founder and leader taking the initiative in this respect—with the younger women. Quality of offspring, the central members were convinced, was more dependent upon selection among fathers than among mothers.

Out of fifty-one applications from men and women desiring to become parents, nine were vetoed on the ground of unfitness, and forty-two were approved. Care of the children was in accordance with the already established custom of the Community. During early infancy they remained in the care of their mothers. When able to walk, the child was admitted to the day nursery department of the Children's House, the mother continuing the night care. From the beginning of the play stage until adolescence the Children's House had complete charge, though parents visited their children and received visits from them. Much attention was given to diet, clothing, sanitation and profitable activity. Epidemic diseases common in outside society were vigilantly excluded; sickness among the children was rare. In case of illness good medical attendance and the best of nursing were immediately available. There were also facilities for quarantine, night watchers, and appliances for comfort and convenience, such as few private families could afford. During the forty years, 1841-1880 inclusive, in which a total of one hundred and ninety-three children were cared for, only five deaths occurred in the Children's House. At adolescence a young person graduated from the Children's House, and took his place in the general organization of the Community.

In the pioneer days of the Community, it has been estimated, approximately ten out of forty-four babies died before the end of the first five-year period. Out of the fifty-eight live births during the stirpicultural period, only six deaths had occurred in September, 1921, when the oldest "stirpicult" was fifty-two years of age and the youngest forty-two. According to actuarial computation based on the Elliott tables for 1870, the deaths of forty-five out of these fifty-eight would have been nearer normal. Selection of parents is not entirely accountable for this low death-rate. Other factors, such as exceptional care provided by the Community, and excellent hygienic conditions, decreased the infant mortality rate. Of the children of these stirpicults, out of a total of ninety-eight births, only three failed to survive the first twelve-month, and there were no still-births. One professional statistician has expressed the opinion that two-thirds fewer deaths occurred among this group than if typical rural conditions and customs had prevailed. Full credit must be given, of course, to the hardy New England stock represented in the stirpicultural matings, as well as to the exceptional intelligence applied to domestic and personal hygiene in the Community house. The results are said, by actuarial experts, to be unprecedented in the records of contemporary vital statistics.

5

A thin film of ice was beginning to glaze the surface of the pond at Willow Place. John Noyes stood naked at the edge and cried to the younger men:

> *"Dar'st thou, Cassius, now*
> *Leap in with me into this angry flood,*
> *And swim to yonder point?"*

The young men followed their leader into the icy water and were out as quickly. The whole jaunt took only fifteen minutes from fireside to fireside. A spontaneous gesture, it seemed to them all; its effect was to demonstrate to the younger generation that Father Noyes had not yet lost his virility or his daring. But there were other films of ice even more chilling through which he would be forced to break in the years to come. Winter was setting in, in more ways than one. They were beginning—the young men of the Community who had been sent away to Yale for their education, the medical students at Bellevue in New York—they were beginning to ask how far they might loose themselves from bondage to the letter of the Bible. The war between science and religion was raging, within and without the Community.

Most of the young men remained under the spell of Noyes's

radiant personality, warmed themselves at the still living fire of his enthusiasm. Yet these new ideas so brilliantly promulgated by Mr. Huxley and the rest of the "materialists" tended, in spite of all, to sweep away the old theology from young minds. They found themselves, as the Darwinian conflict spread through the middle Seventies, impelled to reject Father Noyes's theology. In vain he reiterated that the Bible was the best friend of those who sought to abolish traditions—that it was, itself, a revolutionary document—too revolutionary for many. He did not mean, Noyes explained to them, merely the Book—not the paper and ink nor the printed words, translated or mistranslated—nor even the theology in its pages, but the eternal Spirit that flowed through it and energized it.

"I have traveled far enough into the regions of free thinking to shake hands with the scouts of Positivism, and yet I have no thought of abandoning Bible religion.... I have followed Lyell into the geological ages, and Tyndall into the correlation of forces, and even Darwin into his endless genealogies; and yet I am as sure now that Christ is king of the world as I was before science began to swell into infidelity, which, indeed, is within my remembrance."

He had no quarrel with science, nor any idea of giving up religion because knowledge of physics was increasing. The mistake, he said, was in trying to import this quarrel into the United States and to make Americans take sides upon it. Voicing his Yankee opposition to "all imported systems," Noyes urged "the necessity of doing our own supreme thinking—which we shall do by and by." "We lose nothing," he said, "in giving up the old ideas of immateriality, if we still hold that matter is cunning enough to produce consciousness, thought, affection, and will. Names are of no consequence. If the latest thinkers choose to call the thing that manifests these phenomena 'nervous fluid' or 'ether' or 'force' or 'tissue' under the play and vibration of a combination of forces, I do not see in this language any danger of our losing our old-fashioned souls.

"It is true, the explanation of the mechanism of tissues and forces which produce consciousness... is not profoundly satisfactory, but sounds to me like the explanation of the motion of a steamboat addressed by a didactic father to his children, as they stood on the upper deck...: 'You see, my little dears, the thingumbob here hitches on to the crinkum-crankum, and the crinkum-crankum goes down and takes hold of the jigimoree; then the engineer turns the handle, and the captain gives the orders, and all hands shove, and so the boat goes ahead!' "

6

Father Noyes warned against permitting the impulses of immature men and women to govern in the matter of propagation, or to dictate the principles by which it should be regulated. Mature men should rule. "We do not have our laws made for us by beardless boys, or young men just graduated from college or seminary," he pointed out. "This is not the way in which railroads are built, stock companies formed, manufacturing and mercantile interests controlled. Such transactions are regulated by men of years, and the wisdom that comes of experience. But we allow this whole business of love, which is the most important of all, to fall into the hands of maidens of sweet sixteen, and youth of a few more years, but with scarcely more wisdom."

Youth was the season of impulse, the aging leader warned, forgetting his own rash course in his twenties. "Love, which is considered the special function of youth, is only a successsion of impulses, mostly blind, and often disastrous. We hold that the conduct of love between the sexes should be under the supervision of the best wisdom within our reach; that the whole theory of love should be reconstructed, and be brought under the dominion of reason and conscience. It should no longer be left a matter of unreasoning passion between immature youths of the opposite sex, but should be studied by thoughtful persons who have felt its emotions, and have obtained the mastery over their own passions."

In the years that followed, the façade of respect and reverence built up around the Community leaders became more imposing—it hid the heavy wall that separated the elders from the younger generation. No longer was there a sincere interchange of confidence. Among themselves, the young men spoke rebelliously of the old men who took advantage of the régime of stirpiculture to select the younger women as the mothers of their children. Some of them rebelled, likewise against the theory and practice of male continence—so that some of the children born during the period could not be registered as stirpicults. On paper—on the papers which the young devotees had signed—it was a glorious, a noble ideal. But in real life the practice of this "science" awakened, particularly among the more sensitive women, a resentment that smoldered long in secret and eventually burst into flames of anger. It made some of them feel like white mice in an experimental laboratory. In 1876, after Father Noyes's son Theodore had assumed his temporary leadership, there was particular resentment.

Theodore was kind and gentle, but he was lacking in the spiritual insight necessary to become a leader.

At last the dissension could no longer be ignored nor quieted, even by Noyes himself. The bitter internal struggle was one thing not recorded in the weekly paper—it was never brought out into the open. Deep, almost unanswerable questions, perplexed, perhaps for the first time, the mind of the patriarch, questions which brought with them the icy chill of doubt and defeat, questions that every aging man must eventually ask. How can wisdom, wisdom attained only through long suffering and laceration of the spirit, be transmitted to the next generation, so mutinous in receiving the stored-up wisdom of the race? Must this wall between the generations remain forever impenetrable? To the flesh of our flesh, the bone of our bone, we bequeath not one atom of the wisdom that we buy—at what a price—only as we are ready to depart from this earth. Impulsive, unreasoning, unteachable second and third generations push into the foreground, and refuse to accept the bitter lessons learnt by another. So all must plod along the same rough road, wresting, from life itself, torn fragments of wisdom only as they too are about to stumble into the grave.

How long, the aging man asked in vain, how long must we be born and grow up fools and only grow wise by suffering as our fathers did before us? "I can tell just when all this repeating of troubles is going to end. It will be when wisdom and righteousness are fixed in the blood, so that the lessons which the parents have learned by experience, the children will have in them when they are born. If you can tell when that will be, you can tell when the end of all these tribulations is coming, for it won't come until then. Lord hasten the day, is my prayer. We had better set the world to work in that direction for it is useless to seek for the millennium in any other.... It is a pleasant thing to hope for a time when people will not need to have trouble in order to be wise; when they will turn to the Lord and be good easily, without being criticized and worried and tormented all through their lives; and pleasant as it is to hope for, it is a practicable thing and is certainly before us in the natural, necessary course of evolution.... How soon it will come the Lord knows; but it is not at all likely that it will come until special and persistent attention is turned to the business of breeding human beings. Educating them is not going to do it, only as it helps the process of breeding. It is breeding that is going to finish the work."

PART THREE

RETREAT

Chapter I: HUE AND CRY

> Dullness is so much stronger than genius because there is so much more of it, and it is better organized and more naturally cohesive *inter se*. So the arctic volcano can do nothing against arctic ice.
>
> —SAMUEL BUTLER.

I

DURING the twenty-five years of struggle at Oneida, the outside world (or THE WORLD, as the Community children were taught to call it), had been more interested in the Community than the Community had in the world. There had been protests and persecutions, scandal and rumors of scandal, opposition in plenty and from almost every possible source. But it was not until 1873 that a crusade against this busy, self-respecting, self-contained group was finally organized; and plausibly enough, this crusade began with the clergy. It is doubtful, if, even then, the external pressure alone could have caused the debacle, the swift disintegration that followed. The real defeat came, not from outside opposition, but through dissension among Noyes's followers.

A new era of moral indignation and virtuous intolerance was emerging in the opening years of the Seventies. The spirit of John Robert McDowall seemed to be reincarnated in the person of young Anthony Comstock, as rabid a fanatic in his war against vice as the martyr of the Seventh Commandment had ever been. In 1872, at the age of twenty-eight, Comstock organized the New York Society for the Suppression of Vice, which was supported by the Young Men's Christian Association. In March, 1873, he persuaded the Congress to enact a Federal obscenity bill which classified all information concerning contraception as lewd, lascivious and obscene, and forbade the dissemination by the United States mails of all literature on the subject. This law was directly responsible for the cessation of all open discussion and private correspondence concerning the Community's doctrine of male continence. Comstock's adherents also discovered in the Oneidans an easy target for the arrows of their wrath.

Just after the War, newspapers in the vicinity of Schenectady had begun to publish articles bearing the signature of E. P. Freeman, who had an obsession against Noyes and the principles of the Oneida Community. Strangely enough, his son, upon reaching maturity, joined the Oneidans; and eventually the Community was called upon to help support its fiery antagonist in the declining years of his life. But this fact did not deter the old gentleman from doing everything within his senescent power to incite the public and the churches against Noyes. The mantle of Freeman's fanaticism fell upon Dr. Taylor Lewis, a professor in Union College, Schenectady. This adversary possessed more learning and ability than his predecessor, and his diatribes were frequently published by *The Independent*, a national weekly much read at that period by the clergy.

Into this crusade, about 1873, stepped Professor John W. Mears, of Hamilton College. Mears wrote to the newspapers, preached long Sunday sermons, and finally, in a sectarian paper, *The Watchword*, published at Ilion, New York, he sounded the call to arms. "Here in the heart of the Empire State," he trumpeted, "is an institution avowedly at war with the foundation principles of our domestic and civil order, a set of men banded together for the purpose of practicing shameful immoralities, and leading the young of both sexes who unfortunately happen to come under their care into impure and shocking practices.... The people of Illinois could not endure the immorality of the Mormons, but drove them from Nauvoo in 1846, and compelled them to take refuge in the Great Central basin, a thousand miles from the outskirts of civilization. Thus polygamy was treated; while the far more corrupt concubinage of the Oneida Community luxuriates at ease in the heart of New York State, enjoys the compliments of one portion of the newspaper press, and the silent acquiescence of another portion, uses the United States mails for the circulation of its poisonous literature, is visited by the throngs of the curious or the indifferent, by picnic parties organized for the purpose, and even by Sunday-School excursions."

Methodists and Presbyterians promptly responded to his call to arms. In August, 1873, an association of central New York Methodist ministers met at Perryville. Rev. R. C. Fox read an essay on the Oneida Community, and denounced the ethics of the Community as "free and licensed indulgence," "harlotry," and "the hideous thing that hides away from the light of day, and in dens and midnight hells revels in debauchery and shame." Noyes's influence was "corrupting the very fountains of social and domestic virtue ... to inaugurate a reign of license in place of Christian morality." More than twenty ministers and a large part of the congregation indorsed this Fox indictment, and were aroused to recommend the legal extirpation of the Community.

Moved by this action, the Synod of Presbyterians of central New York, meeting in Utica in October, 1873, appointed a committee of seven, including Professor Mears, "to consider further measures in the matter, and to report at its next meeting." The committee announced its intention "to confer with other religious bodies on the expediency of taking more action relative to the Oneida Community." At a session of the Presbyterian Synod at Oswego in October, 1874, this committee presented its report, obviously a Mears opus. The Mears committee admitted that the Community was well-organized, prosperous, and in cordial relationship with its neighbors; that for more than a quarter of a century it had maintained itself by the sterling virtues of its thrift and industry. The report conceded that the Community had vastly improved conditions in the neighborhood. Land there had become more valuable. The Community also gave employment to the poor, stimulated "stir and life" in an otherwise quiet region; did good work, and maintained an excellent business reputation. Moreover, the committee conceded, the Community had actually mobilized a large and influential circle of friends, almost a constituency, ready to do battle for Noyes. There were even respectable, religious people who opposed any interference. "One would not think there could be a Christian minister, a Christian man or woman, or a person of ordinary virtue, whatever his profession, but would be conscious of intense disgust and keen personal annoyance at the existence of such a moral defilement," the report fulminated. "Yet the frequent visits of large companies, and even the assembling of excursionists in crowds, not unfrequently of the young and of Sunday Schools . . . would go to prove that the existence of the Community is regarded as an accepted fact." The committee especially resented the attitude of many newspapers of the State with their apparent policy of profound silence, varied by favorable intimations concerning Noyes; certain dailies indeed had actively espoused the cause of the Community. The net result of the Mears report was the appointment of another committee to investigate these charges.

The general association of the Congregational Church of New York adopted resolutions denouncing the Community as a "pernicious institution, which rests substantially on a system of organized fanaticism and lust." In October, 1874, also, the Baptist State Convention, meeting at Hornellsville, appointed a committee to coöperate "in regard to suppressing the Oneida Community." Slowly, but steadily, the movement grew.

Professor Mears continued to denounce the Community as an "outgrowth of lust" and demanded its prompt suppression. Civilization, Christianity and monogamy were a trinity of agencies that should be recognized as indissoluble, he insisted. Attacks upon the family were attacks upon Christianity, upon the very life of the nation. The more delicacy and sanctity thrown around the relation of the sexes, the more personal honor would be secured to the women in wedlock; the more elevated, sweet and pure the life of the family, the sounder the very sources of the life of the nation.

Lust and religious fanaticism, he shouted, in unholy alliance had built up "this Utopia of obscenity." Did not Noyes and the central members of the Community discuss and print all details of the physical reaction of the sexes? Did they not print minute and analytical directions for managing these relations—instructions by no means inspired by "laudable Christian Asceticism"? Such publications, Mears protested, belong to "the nastiness of the Epicurean sty." Was not their purpose to show how nature's laws may be evaded without sacrifice of indulgence? Were they not precisely calculated to raise a race of Sybarites, "to imbrute and degrade to bestiality those following them?"

That Noyes was animated by any scientific interest, Professor Mears seemed incapable of believing. He dismissed disdainfully the possibility of the racial benefits which the Community's experiments might bestow if they could be carried out for two or three generations. That some astounding physical development might result, he did not doubt. Actually he foresaw something like Mrs. Shelley's Frankenstein.

Professor Mears called upon Comstock to suppress all Oneida publications. The Community had publicized its beliefs and practices as fast as they had advanced. The public had always been its confidant. Letters and documents were courageously published. This policy of outspokenness had secured the good conscience of honesty; and the fair-minded public paid respect to such frankness, even when they did not agree with the principles.

Facing the fury of the Mears crusade, Noyes and his advisors came to the decision that the Community's open secret should no longer be discussed in *The Circular* and that no further correspondence upon sexual problems be encouraged.

2

The newspapers of the immediate vicinity were on the whole inclined to fair play and tolerance. "A foul and corrupt fountain cannot send forth a stream so clean and thrifty, respectable and peaceful," the Fulton *Times* pointed out. "It is doubtless equally true that a prejudiced mind, even if it be in a Doctor of Divinity, cannot send forth a fair, consistent and strictly truthful report."

"To say that 'mischiefs' and 'glaring immoralities' and 'world-wide infamy' hide themselves beneath such disguises as these—consistently worn and regularly maintained for a quarter of a century and not detected by those who have known the Community best and longest, is to say that there is no frankness, no honesty, no conscience in the world. We ask—with not much faith that the question will be answered—Have Professor Mears and the Committee fairly observed the Golden Rule in their Report on the Oneida Community?"

The Utica *Herald* attributed the success of Noyes's experiment entirely to his Yankee shrewdness. "For the Oneida Community there is but one John Humphrey Noyes. It has reached the zenith of its prosperity under the impulse of his guiding mind and hand: its decay and distintegration will have begun when these are finally removed. It is the supremacy of the single intellect which makes such abnormal establishments possible. While human nature remains as it is, their healthy lives must be limited by the life of their ruling spirit. . . ." "His writings furnish no key to the real secret of the Oneida Community's success. Its peculiar religious tenets, its still more peculiar social tenets, have nothing to do with that success. It has held together, it has accumulated broad acres and a large bank account, it has built fine buildings and commanded ready markets for its goods and manufactures, not because of its religion, nor its Communism, but in spite of them. Remove the shrewd and practical administration, the strict discipline, the perfect obedience which the founder has been able to command, and the whole institution is delivered over to dry-rot. These cannot always remain; and the thirty years of prosperity which the Community boasts are no evidence of permanency, are no vindication of the theories that that prosperity has kept alive."

This comment was so incisive that it drew a reply from Noyes. He deprecated his own power and influence. The Community's success, he insisted, grew out of a great complexity of coöperating causes: the faithful help of a large body of men and women who would have been individually successful in ordinary professions; counsel and assistance of many good people and some eminent men in the region around the Community; the liberality and kindness accorded to the Community by the entire population of central New York, including the editors; above all "the astonishing 'good luck' which has hit the Community in every great emergency, till it has become proverbial. If any of these factors had failed, the Oneida Community would have failed and been forgotten long, long ago."

A reporter of the Chicago *Tribune* asked Noyes "how he got the moral courage to radically defy the usages of society as he did thirty years ago and still does." "I don't know," replied Noyes. "I don't think it was courage. I was always bashful and timid, and lacked confidence in myself. But, while lacking the courage, I could nevertheless do no otherwise than I did and have done, because I have always felt that I was right, and must go forward on the path of duty. You may call it fortune, luck or providence, but I call it religion, and duty, and the help of God."

The Providence *Journal* contrasted Noyes with Brigham Young: "Less famous, or infamous, than Brigham Young, his character presents some striking resemblances and differences.... Young is a man of coarser type, uneducated, and with that wider scope of his ambition which comes from ignorance of unsurmountable barriers." In contrast with Young, the *Journal* continued, Noyes had sought seclusion rather than exile; had sought toleration through good behavior, rather than defiant physical strength. "It is justice to Noyes and his disciples to say that they have had apparently no desire to disturb the world." "... Two such men as Noyes and Young are much rarer than great generals or statesmen," the article concluded; "It is singular that the United States in the nineteenth century should have been the home of two such remarkable movements, and the future Buckle may trace the cause either in our climate or in the mixture of our embryonic civilization and liberty: as the orthodox, if there are any orthodox in the next century, may ascribe them to the direct intervention of the devil. We may be thankful that neither will survive to perpetuate their shame, and whatever may be said of our country in the nineteenth century, it was not ready for a Mohammed or a prophet of Munster." In contrast to the judicial restraint of such newspapers, others joined ferociously in the hue and cry against the Community.

3

Had the original *afflatus* still flowed through the Community, this pressure from without could never have been a menace. But dissension within was now sapping the spiritual life of the group. To understand the elements of this dissension, we must retrace our steps.

On April 21, 1874, Noyes proudly announced at an evening meeting that the so-called "Cleveland family" had been accepted as members. In the matter of new memberships, Noyes explained, he was tired of absorbing bits and scraps "between meals." These twelve new members, survivors of a defunct Cleveland "free love" colony, would provide a "full meal" and test the Community's powers of assimilation. Incidentally, the newcomers would bring in a total of $14,000.

The Cleveland family, which presently appeared on the scene, came under the leadership of one James William Towner. Born in Willsboro, New York, fifty-one years before, Towner had studied theology as a young man, entered the Universalist ministry in 1849, had turned his attention to jurisprudence, and had been admitted to the Iowa bar ten years later. He was among the first to enlist with the Ninth Iowa Volunteer Infantry; he fought valiantly, and in the battle of Pea Ridge had suffered the loss of one eye. Taking only a few months leave of absence to recover, Towner was soon back on the field again. In 1863, however, he was so seriously disabled that he was forced to leave the service. Subsequently he resumed the practice of the law, and attaining no outstanding success in this field, had drifted into the Berlin Heights experiment in Ohio.

To Oneida he brought his wife Cinderella, two sons, Arthur and Frederick, aged twenty-three and eighteen, and his unmarried daughter, Lillian, aged twenty. With them came a married couple, the Reeves, and a few others related to the Towners by ties of marriage. With his legal background, his military bearing, his gentlemanly suavity, Towner seemed at first a valuable addition to the Community. Seven years earlier, he had proffered his services and counsel when Charles Guiteau had threatened blackmail and extortion. Now, he began to prepare for *The Circular* a lengthy, legal dissertation on "Community Contracts" designed to strengthen the Community's position in its relations with the outside world. Towner was shrewd, unctuous, worldly, distinguished on a provincial scale, and secretly ambitious to obtain control of the material affairs of the Community. His missing eye gave a certain sinister cast to his countenance, at least to those who found him unsympathetic. But the unsuspecting sought him out, soon after his arrival, for consolation and advice. It is easier, sometimes, to confide in new friends than in old. Some who nursed long-suppressed grievances unburdened their souls to this newcomer, who was adept in drawing out confessions of discontent.

Thus, gradually, James Towner became the center around which crystallized various elements of disaffection. The growing cleft which was dividing the house against itself was deepened by the inaccessibility of the founder. Noyes could not speak above a whisper, and deafness drew in like a slow curtain, so that he found it difficult to hear or to talk with the ordinary members who might have wished to come to him with their petty complaints or secret dissatisfactions. All that he discovered was written to him, or shouted at him by his ministers and ambassadors and wary messengers. And so the Community turned more and more to the man who was ready and willing to listen and to sympathize. Noyes became more and more dependent upon the members of his family cabinet and the elder statesmen of the Community, while the agents of division worked like mysterious chemicals.

We may at present only vaguely surmise that inner conflict: young men and women yearning to be "regular," to be respectable, reacting violently against the radicalism of parents and elders, suppressing their wrath to prevent open disaster, to protect their rights in the Community property and industries, yet focussing their resentment upon John Noyes, the only begetter of their unhappiness!

4

The Community *Circular* was converted into *The American Socialist*, the first number of which appeared on March 30, 1876. This step was taken, ostensibly, to "watch, report, and assist the evolution of the civilized world from an old and very defective social system to one adapted to the present needs of mankind, and to discuss the principles which should govern the transition." But the change of policy also permitted a shift of attention from the troubled internal affairs of the Community and its change of front.

In May, 1877, Noyes gave up the presidency of the Community. On May 24, *The American Socialist* published the announcement of his resignation. The announcement stated:

> The Editor-in-chief of this paper has the pleasure of announcing that he has resigned the Presidency of the Oneida Community, and will be free henceforth to devote himself wholly to editorial labor. There has been some incompatibility between the duty of the two offices, not only on account of the double labor imposed, but because THE AMERICAN SOCIALIST aspires to be the organ of Socialism in all its degrees, while the Oneida Community is the exponent of only one form of Communism.
>
> J. H. Noyes parts with the Community to which he has given thirty years of his life, in entire harmony, leaving his son, Dr. Theodore Richards Noyes, to be henceforth its responsible head.
>
> The *Socialist* will now be free to go its own way, and may ere long find a location more favorable to its circulation and influence.

Outside observers interpreted this announcement as indicating the first definite step in the disintegration of the Community.

5

The Community, like the nation, was plodding wearily through a period of depression. An epidemic of malarial fever remained unyielding in the vicinity of Wallingford. One after another of their most energetic workers was stricken by this elusive, persistent disease. It was the origin of George Noyes's illness, and had caused his death in 1870. In 1874 it struck at Charlotte Miller–the beloved "Mother" Miller of both communities–and carried her away. As soon as they became ill, Community victims were sent back to Oneida–but not all recovered. In exasperation Noyes cried: "We have tried both faith and the Turkish bath, we will now try quinine!"

Noyes's dream of a great "religio-educational publishing college" on the slopes of Mount Tom vanished. The epidemic seemed to doom also their water-power,–the "finest" on the banks of the Quinnipiac, into the construction of which they had sunk something like one hundred thousand dollars; it seemed, indeed, to mean the end of the whole Wallingford venture. That defeat was bitterly dramatized when the elder Noyes himself packed off the fever-stricken remnants to Oneida. They arrived, with chattering teeth and shivering limbs, stupefied by large doses of quinine–a "refuse lot" Noyes ruefully described them.

Dismal tales of returning victims acted as a challenge to Theodore Noyes. Confident in the power of science to defeat the mysterious epidemic, he went resolutely ahead with the construction of a new community dwelling at Wallingford, to replace the old Allen farmhouse. Charles Cragin, who had graduated as a mechanical engineer from the Sheffield Scientific School at Yale, proved invaluable. Together they completed the new house in 1876, at the very moment that all need for it was vanishing. The seventies were in an industrial depression; the water-power remained idle; and the printing plant, which had been manufacturing commercial labels after the removal of *The Circular* back to Oneida, was shut down. There was an annual loss of $5,000 in interest to be met.

Charles Cragin had inherited his mother's power of inspiring love. He was an extraordinarily handsome young man with chiseled features, and burning, widely-spaced eyes. He was not large, but his body was lithe, and well-coördinated. He was intelligent, ambitious, impetuous, and an insatiable zest for living animated his conversation, especially with women. Charles was a keen business man, searching always for new sources of income for the Community. Was it this "worldliness," his business ambition, or was it his popularity with the younger women at Oneida that led finally to his transference to Wallingford?

One thing was admitted—a "special," if not a completely "idolatrous" love existed between Charles Cragin and Edith Waters, the eighteen-year-old daughter of Louisa Tuttle and Hial Waters. In the eyes of Noyes, this was a sinful longing, a desire wholly selfish. But Edith was already in the incipient stages of consumption, and the very disease itself laid fuel on the fire that consumed her body.

Then as first lieutenant to the grandiose scheme of Dr. Theodore Noyes, Charles was sent to Wallingford. Edith saw him seldom after that. When he did return to the Community on occasional visits, his time was taken up in business consultations and their meetings were not only brief, but dampened by the chill disapproval of the central members.

Charles Cragin threw himself into the affairs of the Wallingford commune with the whole of his vast energy. One summer morning in 1877 he sat on the bridge abutment gazing down at the rush of water which they had raised to supply power to the Wallace Silverware factory, a quarter-mile below. He heard the crescendo of noise, as the daily toil of the distant factory began for the day. The muffled crash of the spoon "drops" punctuated the steady hum of polishing wheels. "Why can't we make spoons as well as the Wallace Company?" he asked himself suddenly. The power was there, the unused factory stood idle; and workers could be imported from the Oneida Community. He rushed up the hill, and ran into the office of Dr. Noyes. Theodore listened attentively. "Go ahead and find out what the machinery will cost, and the technical help, but keep mum about your plan," he said. Early in June, Charles Cragin completed his estimates. Dr. Noyes gave the order to go ahead, and by the middle of July the first spoon was cut—an ungraded tinned iron spoon!

Cragin was already a victim of Wallingford's mysterious fever and ague, and he refused to give way to the malady or to rest during the series of emergencies which accompanied the founding of the new spoon business. He saturated his system with quinine and kept going. By Christmas, 1877, this ardent young man collapsed and the day following the New Year, 1878, news of his death reached Oneida. It was a terrible blow to all, but it was fatal to Edith Waters. She survived her lover by a few months only. The tender, tragic love story of the Community awakened a warm sympathy in the breasts of even those reasoning members, who had been taught from childhood to despise worldly ideals of romantic love.

6

The inevitable, pitiless conflict of father and son was sharpening. The chasm between the generations was widening—though by present standards, Noyes was not senile. He was then in his middle sixties. But, shadows were lengthening; old companions were passing—the faithful, loyal disciples of Putney days. The younger generation—represented by his own son Theodore—was asserting itself and all its stubborn Darwinian ideas. Could Noyes surmise the strong undercurrent of this opposition to the old faith that once bound their little colony of Heaven invincibly together? Lip service they still paid to the patriarch. But the myth—that life-giving myth of the Kingdom—was disintegrating under his eyes.

Vexed at the struggle of beliefs in which so unwittingly and so unwillingly he found himself, once Theodore wrote his father in dismay: "The most horrible thing about this trouble is that it puts me in a position to be relieved by your death and I must get out of it some way!" The old man misunderstood—was Theodore only waiting for his death? Theodore made a lengthy apology and an explanation of his attempt to reconcile his scientific agnosticism with the tenets of the Community. "Sometimes in the anguish of our differences it has seemed as if we would be much happier to never see each other again, but yet, I always settle in the belief that you are really more liberal with me than the Community would be in your absence. I am not naturally very demonstrative in the way of family affection either toward my parents or my children and much hard experience has weaned me from some that I naturally have, but yet at the bottom I have a current of filial affection for you which under happier circumstances might make itself more seen and felt. It is my prayer that I may do it full justice and let it help as much as it can. It is our misfortune to belong to a mongrel race which probably abounds in such reversions to distant ancestors as is the case with me. We must recognize this and make the relation of father and son bridge over the space between us as far as is possible and this I mean to do." So Theodore wrote in January, 1878; but there was to be no bridging of the chasm that was deepening every day.

Rumors of Oneida's approaching collapse multiplied in the local and metropolitan press. Certain newspapers seemed to take malicious delight in reporting dissensions in the Community. The withdrawal of several prominent members was rumored—and the rumor proved to be true, although these withdrawals were by no means the most important elements in the conflict. Various reporters succeeded in interviewing Noyes, William Hinds, acting editor of *The American Socialist*, Theodore Noyes, and even Sewell Newhouse. Noyes resented this renewed invasion: he remained obstinately silent when they questioned him. Theodore, however, naïvely and unreservedly discussed the Community crisis.

Trained in the rigorous laws of natural and medical science, his outlook was fundamentally hostile to the mysticism of his father. Believing in evolution, Theodore had no faith in radical and isolated departures as a basis for new institutions. In April, 1878, he withdrew from the Community, migrated to New York City, and started in the printing business for himself. Subsequently, Theodore returned to the Community and placed himself upon probation for a few months. He was uncertain whether he could ever again bring himself to accept the doctrines of his father and the elder members, and his doubts exercised an undermining influence on many of the younger group. To this disintegrating effect were attributed many of the withdrawals. John Noyes's personal influence, once so potent, was now sinking like the setting sun. The new generation was absorbing the emergent spirit of doubt and skepticism. The elders were on the defensive. In vain had John Noyes introduced scientific terms, and talks on stirpiculture, altruism, scientific propagation, communal ties—the younger generation was convinced of the superficiality of such terms. Social science was superseding religion as the dominating force in the Community. The house of the Community was now in truth divided against itself.

The Townerites, as the faction opposing Father Noyes came openly to be named, were no longer content with holding secret meetings in an upper chamber of the New House (a wing completed in 1878), but were now openly, vociferously and menacingly expressing their disaffection, from the balcony of the hall at the evening meetings. Catastrophe was in the air. What could be done to save the women and children? They had heretofore been protected from the harsh realities of the outside world. The break-up would mean the separation of mothers, fathers and children. In many cases they could never be reunited. Instances were plentiful in which the father was not married to the mother of his children and never could be. The tragedy of the situation was intensified by the fact that gossip of the impending crash tended to hasten the inevitable.

It was a miniature revolution, and the mutiny was first and foremost against Noyes himself. There were whispers concerning his indiscretions and ugly threats of lodging against the elderly leader a complaint that might lead to his arrest and conviction on a statutory offense. Emanating from members of his own complex family, such charges alone, unsupported and factitious as they might be proven, would be ruinous to the patriarch upon whom the storm from without was already breaking.

7

Strangely enough, neither Professor Mears nor his cohorts became fully aware of the conflict within the Community until the changes were announced—the withdrawal and subsequent reinstatement of Noyes after the resignation and departure of Theodore in the middle of 1878, and the general blight of apathy and depression. Finally Mears decided that the time was ripe for a final offensive. On January 23, 1879, he issued a clarion call to his army of crusaders:

> Dear Sir: The great wrong done to society by the institution known as the "Oneida Community," from its deadly opposition to the principles of a Christian morality, appears to demand some united counsel and action on the part of teachers of the gospel and defendants of public and domestic virtue in this part of the country.
>
> After some informal consultation we, the undersigned, are encouraged to write you to attend a preliminary meeting at Syracuse, in the University building, on Friday the fourteenth day of February, at 2:30 o'clock P.M.
>
> Will you kindly inform the Rev. A. F. Beard, D.D., Syracuse, whether you may be expected to be present?

The conference was attended by forty-seven clergymen. Called on for a description of the Community, Professor Mears was obliged to admit that the members "were good citizens, orderly and cleanly in the manner in which they conduct their home." He charged that in the Community "men and women live in a state of concupiscence," that there was an "impure emanation" from it. Lawyers were called on for a remedy, and one of them suggested the insertion, in the New York statute against "disorderly persons," of the words "all persons living in concupiscence or adultery."

"What is 'living in concupiscence'?" taunted the New York *Nation.* "Concupiscence is a state of mind, and you cannot indict a man or woman for evil desires. Moreover, to prove adultery you must prove marriage, and the Oneida Community have no marriage. In fact, the subject is a most difficult one to deal with by legal penalties, and we think the clergy would do well not to attack it with the arm of flesh, lest they give the Communists the glory of martyrdom."

In the eyes of the press, the conference was a ridiculous failure. "It began the task of manufacturing public sentiment by excluding reporters," asserted the Utica *Herald.* "It is needless to say that any body of men which is afraid of the reporters and the publicity that follows their presence is not capable of inaugurating any great movement. It appeared subsequently that the conference had no plan of action, and simply appointed a committee to report at a future meeting. It is more than probable that the future meeting will never be held."

The weekly *Puck*, then savagely anti-clerical and edited by the genial H. C. Bunner, published a cartoon of Joseph Keppler showing a group of hypocritical clergymen gazing at the Community. The caption read: "O, dreadful! They dwell in peace and harmony, and have no church scandals. They must be wiped out." Not that *Puck* wished to champion Noyes. The incident merely provided ammuntion to aim at snooping, hypocritical parsons who were the object of its ire. "We have in the northern part of this State a little community of theorists who are banded together to carry out certain principles of their own," *Puck* wrote editorially: "Their peculiar characteristic is their adherence to some ideas, rather odd in the eyes of outsiders, concerning the creation, preservation, and all the blessings of this life.... Whether these ideas are right or wrong, this people has seen fit to carry them out in a quiet, orderly, decent and law-abiding way. It has flourished, and waxed strong, and done no one wrong, and wise men have been satisfied to leave it in peace. But we have all over the land a vast tribe of gentlemen in white chokers, who, entertaining the same idea, prefer to carry it out in secret and unavowedly. And this is the bare and simple statement why the gentlemen in the white choker regards the Oneida Community as a Blot and Blotch and Festering Sore and an Ulcer and a Canker and all sorts of things upon the civilization of America."

Special target for this type of a stinging denunciation, Professor Mears's indignation now cooled off most precipitately. Under the criticism of the liberal press, he decided to revise his

OUT OF THE FOLD

"Oh, dreadful! They dwell in peace and harmony, and have no church scandals. They must be wiped out."

(*Courtesy of Oneida Community, Ltd.*)

MUSIC IN THE GREAT HALL

This drawing was made by Milford Newhouse, son of Sewell Newhouse.

tactics. The complete extermination of the Community was not necessary—only its "scandalous social customs" should be extirpated. He would be content if John Noyes could be driven out. From Hamilton College, Mears renewed his attacks. In a communication to *The Independent* (April 10, 1879) he cried anew: "If polygamy is a great evil and immorality, the organized concubinage of the Oneida Community is a still greater. If the Oneida Community were upon so large a scale as the Mormon settlement, it would fill the public eye and create more profound and widespread indignation than Utah has ever done."

District Attorney Smith of Madison County stated that he had not yet been consulted concerning any arrest or indictment of Noyes. Although Noyes was a resident of that county, no complaint had been made against him. Circulation of alleged obscene writings five years previously could not now be an indictable offense, in the eyes of a Madison County Grand Jury. This District Attorney confessed that he had never heard of any cruel or brutal treatment on the part of the Community toward any of its members. Not only had the Community violated no laws, he declared, but it had always seemed desirous of obeying laws. Its members were industrious, frugal, hospitable, honest.

"For the life of me," similarly exclaimed District Attorney Barnett of Oneida County, in Utica, "I don't see how they can ever get a legal hold on those people.... They are planted as firm as a rock. People may theorize about them, you know, and it is easy enough to reason out that their social habits are wrong because they don't conform with ours—that is, with what we say ours are—but if indictments could be procured on the ground of general immorality, who wouldn't be liable? I don't believe they can ever be indicted for their belief, in this State. What the United States Court might do I don't know. A charge of circulation of obscene literature would naturally go to it. Not a word has been said to me about prosecuting them or about an arrest. I feel safe to predict that none will occur. They are good citizens, mind their business, have the respect of their neighbors and the confidence of their customers all over the country, own a large property and valuable industries, furnish employment to hundreds of people at good wages, and are altogether too serviceable to warrant either county in doing anything to risk their displeasure without very good cause."

Confronted with a total lack of moral fervor on the part of the District Attorneys, Professor Mears came to the bitter realization that the popularity of the Community was solidly rooted.

Mears was the butt of stinging rebukes, pestered by newspaper reporters from New York, trapped into contradictions and inconsistencies which were duly printed and reprinted. He was met with glacial courtesy by most of the sound pillars of business and industry between Syracuse and Utica. Nor did legislative action, aimed at John Noyes, seem a feasible step. Among Mears's adversaries, it was rumored that agents acting with his approval had attempted to have a special bill pass the Legislature, and that the Assemblymen to whom the bill was taken had asked the applicants why they didn't present the bill through members from Oneida or Madison County. The reply was that it was useless to broach such a distasteful subject to them. When a reporter from the New York *World* by relentless cross-examination drove Professor Mears into contradiction and evasion, the badgered moralist protested that the matter was disagreeable enough at any rate, and the committee was not disposed to thrust it prematurely upon the public.

Fortunately for Noyes, his enemies outside the gates of the Community were unable to join forces with his adversaries within. But should a complaint be lodged with the District Attorney of Madison County, and an indictment returned charging Noyes with a statutory offense based upon the testimony given by members of the Community itself, the direst consequences might be expected.

This danger of a complaint from within seemed quite within the realm of possibility to Myron Kinsley, who had remained, these thirty-one years since his coming to the Community as a boy of twelve, unquestioning and unswerving in his devotion to Noyes.

Myron told his fears to the leaders of the loyal group. There was but one solution, he declared: that was to place Noyes, as swiftly and as secretly as possible, outside the jurisdiction of the State of New York.

Noyes consented at last. All plans were so carefully made that the suspicions of the Townerites were never aroused. In the middle of the night of June 19-20, 1879, Myron Kinsley escorted Noyes from his room in the south tower out of the darkened house. At some distance old Mr. Kellogg and Theodore Pitt waited with a team of horses. In the early hours of the morning, they drove across the country to a distant railroad station. From there Noyes took a train in the direction of the Canadian border.

Perhaps he laughed once more as he had laughed after his arrest in Putney. This time he might have been amused by the fact that, as he was escaping like a thief in the night, "Uncle

Ruddy's boy" was sleeping soundly and virtuously in the President's bed in the White House. But if he laughed, the angels must have wept at the differing destinies of these two grandsons of old Rutherford Hayes–mediocrity in the White House, genius on its way to exile.

Chapter II: BREAK-UP

Socrates: By what Gods will you now swear? For in the first place, Gods are not a current coin with us.

—ARISTOPHANES.

I

ON August 20, 1879, the acting heads of the Community received from its exiled leader a message advocating a peaceful retreat from its social policies. On August 26, all adult members, gravely conscious of the crisis which confronted them, gathered in the hall to listen to the reading of this communication and to consider the proposals it contained. Many did not know where Noyes had gone; even his departure was as yet unknown outside the Community. All listened intently as his letter was read.

"I hardly need remind the Community that we have always claimed freedom of conscience to change our social practices, and have repeatedly offered to abandon the offensive part of our system of communism if so required by public opinion," began the momentous message. "We have lately pledged ourselves in our publications to obey any new legislation which may be instituted against us. Many of you will remember that I have frequently said, within the last year, that I did not consider our present social arrangements essential parts of our profession as Christian communists, and that we should probably have to recede from them sooner or later. I think the time has come for us to act on these principles of freedom, and I offer for your consideration the following modifications of our practical platform:

"I propose—

"1. That we give up the practice of Complex Marriage, not as renouncing belief in the principles and prospective finality of that institution, but in deference to the public sentiment which is evidently rising against it;

"2. That we place ourselves, not on the platform of the Shakers, on the one hand, nor of the world, on the other, but on Paul's platform, which allows marriage but prefers celibacy....

"If you accept these modifications the Community will consist of two distinct classes—the married and the celibates—both legitimate, but the last preferred.

"What will remain of our Communism after these modifications may be defined thus:

"1. We shall hold our property and businesses in common, as now;

"2. We shall live together in a common household and eat at a common table, as now;

"3. We shall have a common children's department, as now;

"4. We shall have our daily evening meetings, and all of our present means of moral and spiritual improvement.

"Surely, here is Communism enough to hold us together and inspire us with heroism for a new career. With the breeze of general good-will in our favor, which even Professor Mears has promised us on the condition of our giving up the 'immoral features' of our system, what new wonders of success may we not hope for in the years to come!

"For my part, I think we have a great reason to be thankful for the toleration which has so long been accorded to our audacious experiment. Especially are we indebted to the authorities and people of our immediate neighborhood for kindness and protection. It will be a good and graceful thing for us to relieve them at last from the burden of our unpopularity, and show the world that Christian communism has self-control and flexibility enough to live and flourish without Complex Marriage."

With no dissenting voice, the Community accepted Noyes's proposals. Professor Mears was left a crusader without a cause, a falcon deprived of its prey. "I see his signature there, and yet I can scarcely credit my senses!" one Syracuse clerical crusader exclaimed.

The consensus of opinion was that Noyes had proved himself a more adroit tactician than his antagonists, and had adopted a graceful and entirely Christian method of putting his enemies to rout.

2

However, this mere announcement was not enough, insisted Professor Mears. The Professor wanted to inspect marriage licenses with his own eyes. Cheated of the spoils of his long-anticipated victory, Mears presented a sanctimonious façade of extreme pleasure. Would the ministers' association continue its crusade? he was asked. "I can only give my own view," he answered. "As a member of the committee, I can say unreservedly that if the Community faithfully conforms to the principles it is here declared to have adopted, it seems to me our occupation is gone. A mistaken idea is abroad that our purpose is to crush the Oneida Community. That is wrong. Our efforts and intent have been against its immoral features—the same that the Community now abandons. There is, as I now see, nothing for us to do....

Personally, I wish the Oneida Community well in all that pertains to its best interests and the best interests of the community at large. I desire to accord it full credit for honesty of purpose in this new and welcome departure."

Nevertheless, all Community marriages should be made public, Professor Mears insisted. "I do not intend to express or harbor distrust. But . . . still more satisfactory would be the announcement in the columns of *The American Socialist*, or of the Utica *Herald*, or other public journals, in the usual form, of the names of those parties who now propose, or may hereafter propose, to live together in the sacred relation of husband and wife."

Announcement of the Community's surrender brought reporters flocking to the doors of the Community. The change was *bona fide*, they were assured. The Community had always held itself in readiness to recede from its social practices when public opinion might make such recession expedient. William Hinds, who as a boy of fourteen had aided in that night flight of George and Mary Cragin from Putney, acted as spokesman. Mr. Hinds was extremely conciliatory with these gentlemen of the press. The whole transition was accomplished in an atmosphere of respectability, if not indeed of uninspired dullness. No one seemed to comment on the unexplained absence of John Noyes.

Most of the members completed arrangements for a recession into matrimony. An unfounded legend persists that Noyes himself lined men and women up opposite each other in the upper hall, and arbitrarily paired them off in the manner of a parlor game, thus expressing his disdain of the institution of marriage. There is no element of truth or half-truth in it. Noyes was absent; and the marriages were carefully and seriously solemnized. Marriage offered the only protection for the children and their mothers. Pitiful indeed was the lot of the unmarried mothers for whom no husbands were available; but there were only a few of these. In several cases the men were unable to marry the mothers of their children, because these mothers were married to others. So, too, certain women graciously and unselfishly relinquished all claim upon the fathers of their children.

Within three months following the abandonment of the complex marriage system, a large number of marriages took place in the Community. Father Noyes *in absentia* was advised of them, and his counsel in unraveling the tangle of relationships was sought by letter. Certain of the younger women asked him to choose husbands for them. With those mothers of his own children who chose husbands from the ranks of the dissentients, the bonds of sympathy were forever severed.

Some members celebrated their return to monogamy with elaborate ceremonies and festivities. So they heralded to the world their jubilant reëntry into the ranks of the respectable. But those who remained most loyal to Community ideals contented themselves with quiet marriage by contract, as provided by the laws of the State of New York. Many stirpicultural children were given the names of their step-fathers.

3

The Community soon became a hotbed of dissension. The recession from the complex marriage system brought with it, inevitably, a desire to return to private property and all the institutions of the world. Meanwhile the little colony of Heaven remained without a shepherd. It had become an armed camp of two bitterly opposed factions. The immediate need was for a "provisional government" to tide the Community over the difficult days until an agreement could be reached on the eventual dispersal of members and goods. Myron Kinsley acted as messenger to Noyes in his unnamed hiding place, and returned with a list of twenty names selected as council of governors. These candidates were divided between the Townerites and Noyesites, with the latter predominant in number. On December 9, 1879, this "commission" was appointed.

For most of the following year, plans for reorganization were threshed out in the evening meetings. Not until September 1, 1880, was the program completed in satisfactory form. On that day an "Agreement to Divide and Reorganize" was signed by two hundred and ten adult members of the Community.

Sewell Newhouse remained alone in his obstinate refusal.

In its abundance of technically legal terms, that covenant reveals the Towner influence. The members agreed to divide; but the method of division was not yet determined. This preliminary document signified only the consent of the adult members to recede from communism in property to some form of joint-stock corporation. They agreed to a reorganization not only of business but of domestic affairs. Each adult member, it was agreed, should hold a certain number of shares in a joint-stock company—a number to be subsequently determined. The spoon business was to be removed to Niagara Falls, and a power-site to be acquired there. The four "property owners" were to remain in control until reorganization was effected. Whatever plans of property division were eventually proposed must win the approval of no less than nine-tenths of the members. That approval must be accepted as unanimous. If agreement proved impossible, the problem should be solved by "outside" arbitrators to be selected by the Commission.

Furthermore, it was agreed by the signers, wages paid to officers, superintendents, agents and other employees of the new company should be kept as low as could be found consistent with efficient management, in order to make the dividends of the new company "as large as possible." This suggests the specter in the background of officers who might be inclined to loot the treasury—and foreshadows the current view of the equitable rewards of capital and labor.

Instead of stock in the new company, the option of a life guarantee of support was offered to the aged and invalid. Support and education of every child of the Community under the age of sixteen was provided in another section. And, possibly in justice to Father Noyes and other absentee members of his group, it was definitely specified that those absent during the reorganization might vote by proxy. Between the lines of this unprecedented document, one detects the influence of strong, intelligent leadership and full confidence in the "four property holders."

This agreement had been signed on September 1; two weeks later, on September 15, the "Plan of Division" was presented to the members, and adopted. The main provisions of this plan were that: (1) One-half the value of the property brought in should be returned in shares of stock, to those who brought it. (2) All persons who had passed the age of sixteen since joining the Community should receive a bonus of $200.00; that all children born in the Community should receive a similar bonus upon attaining the age of sixteen—these sums to be issued in stock to all who will have reached the age of sixteen before January 1, 1882 (after that date in cash, payable to parents and guardians) from the earnings of the Company. (3) After satisfying the provisions named above, the remainder of the capital was to be divided amongst all members above the age of sixteen, in proportion to the period of membership above the age of sixteen. (4) The education of the children would be undertaken until the age of sixteen. (5) Widowers were to have two-thirds and widows one-third of the amount brought in by themselves and their deceased partners, as a credit subject to the same rule of division as other property brought in.

Despite sharp difference of opinion, this plan to unscramble the eggs of communal living and industry received the necessary nine-tenths vote. There was no resultant litigation, nor even the threat of a lawsuit by any actual members.

The appraisal committee soon brought in its report: All the property owned by the Community was estimated at $517,179.00. Good-will of the trap, fruit, tableware, silk and chain businesses brought the amount to be divided to the round total of $600,000. Undoubtedly there had been a little juggling, or retouching of values, to attain this exact figure. But it was finally accepted. On the basis of the amount of property brought in by members, the allotted total amounted to $64,269.42. On the basis of the time of membership, the total was $535,730.58. Membership must have been estimated in terms of days and weeks—for the calculations resulted in all kinds of odd figures. Finally it was agreed that these figures should be "tied up" to the amount nearest divisible by $25.00, the par value of a share of stock. Thus if one member's allotment amounted to $987.51, he received $1,000.00 in stock—but if it tallied to $987.41, he received only $975.00.

Allotments were made to 225 members, 210 of whom were adults, and 15 of whom were minors between the ages of 16 and 21 years of age. Of the allotments to the 210 adult members, one received as little as $475.00; eleven received between $675.00 and $1,000.00; forty-nine between $1,000.00 and $2,000.00; eighty-four, sums varying between $2,000.00 and $3,500.00; sixty, between $3,500.00 and $5,000.00; and only five received more than $5,000.00 in shares. The largest allotment was $13,475.00. Noyes's individual allotment amounted to less than he had contributed more than thirty years previous.

At the meeting on November 10, members agreed that no stockholder in the new company should sell his stock during the ensuing three years, to any except present stockholders, without a two-thirds vote of the directors; nor after that until the proposed sale had been advertised for a period of sixty days, thus giving actual shareholders an opportunity to buy.

For purposes of convenience there was some assigning of rights, and consolidation of family allotments. Two aged members chose a guarantee of life support; and one member accepted a small cash settlement and went on his way to find another community to join.

The one dissenting and uncompromising protestant was Sewell Newhouse. That canny Yankee woodsman, now seventy-four years old, remained adamant in his conviction that as the inventor of the Newhouse trap he had laid the foundations of the Community's most profitable industry, and was therefore entitled to a larger share. But, it was pointed out, he had been bankrupt at the time of joining, and the Community had paid his debts. On the other hand, he had contributed his invaluable technical knowledge in the development of the trap business. By common consent, old Mr. Newhouse's allotment was assigned to Charles Otis Kellogg until it was either definitely accepted or rejected; and five years later, as he approached his eightieth year, Newhouse finally acquiesced.

4

Meanwhile, step by step, the separation of "Church and State" was painfully and bitterly effected. On November 27, 1880, the stock subscribers of the new Oneida Community, Ltd., elected the first board of nine directors. Dr. Theodore Noyes, acceptable to both factions, received the largest number of votes, and James Towner and George D. Allen the smallest. The following month, Towner introduced a resolution that salaries should be based upon the condition that the company should be able to declare at least a ten per cent dividend to its stockholders; but this resolution was voted down at a subsequent meeting.

Bitter incidents marked this transition period. About the middle of November, 1881, a number of small fires in the buildings of the Community—two in the canning factory, and one in the Mansion House—indicated the presence of an incendiary criminal. Three nights later these attempts culminated in the complete destruction of the Community's horse barn, including some twenty horses. The constable was called in, rewards were offered, and the culprit apprehended. James Vail, a former member of the Community, slightly deranged because of fancied wrongs, was convicted after a sensational trial, and sentenced to the full penal period.

The Towner influence in the business of the Oneida Community, Ltd., waned steadily until 1882, when, with a considerable contingent, the ex-soldier and lawyer retired and migrated to Santa Ana, in southern California. There, eventually, he became a judge in the Superior Court of Orange County. All social connection with the notorious Community was severed; and directions to forward yearly dividends in plain unmarked envelopes were given by certain ex-members.

Following the defeat and retirement of the Townerites, a new schism divided the leaderless flock at Oneida. When men have decided to disagree, some subject of disagreement is readily found. Despite the influence still exercised by the leader, his followers were floundering about in a maze of new religious excesses. Spiritualism was sweeping the country, with its mediums and trances and table-tapping and communication with departed spirits. It was a cult to which many of the Oneidans were predisposed since it was difficult for them to return to ordinary denominations; and most of them craved some substitute for the faith that had been so rudely shattered. Spiritualism divided the Community into two new conflicting factions—each determined to win control of the Board of Directors. Business ability had nothing to do with a member's fitness to serve; the sole consideration became whether he subscribed to the dogma of Spiritualism or not.

The Community sank step by step into its own Dark Ages. The reaction against Communism continued. It was said that each individual counted his pins; and that it was almost impossible to borrow a hammer from one's next-door neighbor. The energy, the idealism, the current of vitality seemed to be ebbing away in petty antagonisms. For a time, that "complex family" tree seemed to be permanently blighted. But occasionally, from a tree that has seemed dead, springs up a growth that eventually, in size, beauty and vigor, equals the original tree. The old Community was dead forever; but the human fabric created by John Noyes remained indestructible. It was his heritage of indomitable courage, of ability to face the world unashamed, of energy that translates conviction into action, that enabled the younger generation of the Community's complex family to rescue the new body from defeat and oblivion.

In 1881 the original Oneida Community had not merely changed its form. It had dissolved, and the revolution from Community to Corporation was no more thorough than the shifting of personal ambition from general to private welfare. By April, 1886, little was left of the old Community but the name—now become the Oneida Community, Limited. The last vestige of the communistic spirit passed, and an arid commercialism seemed to supplant it. Instead of the democratic business board which had sat in the south sitting room, and the interesting family discussions of finance and policy; instead of "bees" of music and manual labor; instead of religion and humble manual tasks, a bitter factional contest over the election of the board of directors was arising, with endless discussions of dividends and the salaries of officers and employees. The reaction from communism in living and working ran an unchecked course for the next ten years, and it appeared increasingly apparent that no coöperative or socialistic ideals would ever again be tolerated.

Chapter III: STONE COTTAGE

I was a stricken deer, that left the herd
Long since; with many an arrow deep infixt
My panting side was charg'd, when I withdrew
To seek a tranquil death in distant shades....
Since then, with few associates, in remote
And silent woods I wander, far from those
My former partners of the peopled scene;...
I see that all are wand'rers, gone astray
Each in his own delusions....

—William Cowper.

I

Noyes's destination, following his secret departure from the Community, was the farm of Walter Brett, an outside disciple. The Bretts even hoped that their homestead, located at Strathroy, near Caradoc township in western Ontario, might become the center of a new community composed of faithful disciples. They were waiting at the lonely little station, some twenty miles west of London, Ontario, when the exile and his faithful "guard," Theodore Pitt, descended from the train. Across the country, tame and monotonous and dispiriting after the rolling lawns and green trees of Oneida, Walter Brett's team of horses carried them at last to the primitive homestead.

The eight Brett children gazed in awestruck wonder at these visitors, who, with their inexplicable vocabulary, might have dropped in on them from another age. They seemed like prophets out of the Old Testament, or kings in exile—for both were tall, majestic, commanding, and their language was tinctured with the flavor of the King James version. Despite his deafness, Noyes soon became a favorite with the older boys. His gray eyes still snapped with fire, and beamed with kindness and humor. Instinctively the young people flocked about him, followed him into the woods to shoot squirrels, and listened to his secrets of woodcraft.

Without delay he plunged into correspondence with his lieutenants at the Community. Each day he drove with young Harry Brett into Strathroy to meet the incoming mail, laughing with unrestrained amusement at the youth's awkward handling of the reins.

"There's a fine spirit here!" he cried to Theodore Pitt. But all his outward gayety was but a mask to conceal the desolation in the exile's heart. Some of the letters he wrote to his closest intimates at the Community carried the burden of his despair. The monotony of the landscape alone would have been sufficient to depress—there was so little to see, so little to do. But the drabness of the days was increased by an unending sameness of diet, for in that poverty-stricken farmhouse they lived almost exclusively on potatoes. To make matters worse, the grandmother was dying, and when death released her at last they carried her body a little distance from the house and committed it to the barren soil.

Manual labor, Noyes knew, was the surest anodyne for the mental anguish during his Gethsemane. When the news sent by Myron Kinsley from Oneida became unbearably disappointing, Noyes sought solace in the woodyard behind the farmhouse. There, with torso bared, he armed himself with a cross-cut saw and attacked logs three feet in diameter, sawing until the task was finished and the sweat was pouring from his body.

For a time it seemed that his enemies in the Community would be completely victorious, and that he could expect nothing more from that quarter. He must look for support elsewhere. There were loyal disciples outside the Community; and to enlist their aid he sent Theodore Pitt as his emissary to the Middle West. The results of that mission were disappointing. To sympathize is one thing; to convert that sympathy into active support is another. Mr. Pitt met with coolness and indifference—it may be that rumors of the war at the Community were already circulating among the scattered groups of disciples. One outstanding exception was the loyalty of William and Mary Findlay, of Tamarack, Illinois. Mary made a love-offering of one hundred dollars, and her husband gave fifty. With these funds, Theodore Pitt returned reluctantly to the lonely farm of the Bretts.

So months passed in monotonous exile. The message advising retreat from the "social principles" did nothing to bring peace in the warring Community. Reaction from the old communism there was steadily gaining in momentum. Toward the end of the year, Noyes resolved that he himself should go to Chicago to rally the interest of his Middle Western disciples. Theodore Pitt should accompany him as companion and guide.

The two old men registered at the Palmer House—strange, unworldly figures set down in the midst of the turmoil and bustle of Chicago in 1879! They had sent out appeals to the men and women who had been faithful subscribers to *The Circular* for years. They announced that on a certain day a conference of the friends of J. H. Noyes would be held, to consider the advisability of organizing a new community of Perfectionists somewhere in the Middle West.

The appointed day and hour for the conference arrived, and with it only the faithful William Findlay put in an appearance.

There was nothing for the two exiles to do except to return once more to Walter Brett's home at Strathroy. We can glimpse these two old men on the lonely little station platform in midwinter, as the young Bretts came to meet them, driving their sled through the blinding snow which swept down from the north. There is something in the picture that suggests Lear on the Heath.

But it was not in Noyes's constitution to surrender to despair, nor to admit defeat. He remained incorrigibly hopeful, looking always to the future. He had not lost his power of laughing at misfortune; he was sure that the dice were always loaded in his favor. He left a note for future historians of his experiment, pointing out that they must not neglect the comic aspects of this bold adventure. To himself, in retrospect, it seemed at times like the ride of John Gilpin, who had gone farther than he intended but had come safe home again—

> *"So like an arrow he flew*
> *Shot by an archer strong. . . ."*

In December, 1879, Noyes sent his recommendation for the appointment of a commission of twenty men and women to guide the course of the Community back to "normal" customs of society. Three months later, after considerable discussion, this Commission decided to award the absent leader one hundred and fifty dollars a month for his living expenses, and to provide a home for the members of his group near Niagara Falls, where the Community's tableware factory was to be established.

Following the death of Charles Cragin, on January 2, 1878, Myron H. Kinsley had been appointed director of the spoon industry at Wallingford. During the years 1878 and 1879 large quantities of iron spoons were manufactured for the Meriden Britannia Company. In 1880 after some preliminary negotiation an offer came from the Niagara Falls Hydraulic Power Company of a 300-horsepower site on the very brink of the gorge at Niagara, at a purely nominal cost. On September 9, 1880 an agreement was signed, and the new Oneida Community, Ltd., leased land, power and factory buildings a short distance below the upper Suspension Bridge. Charles Cragin's iron spoon was thus destined to save the Community from financial ruin. The steel-chain business, an adjunct of the steel-trap industry, was also established at

Niagara, though its factory was started on the Canadian side of the river.

Niagara thus became instrumental as a solution to the conflict and controversy at Oneida. The tableware factory and the chain industry formed the nucleus of an informal community, composed mainly of loyal Noyesites who established homes on both sides of the river. On the American side lived Myron H. Kinsley and his wife, George Noyes Miller, Edwin C. Burnham, J. Homer Barron, Daniel M. Kelly and their families; on the Canadian side, Erastus Hamilton, Henry W. Thayer, John F. Sears, William Kelly, Stephen Leonard, and the faithful Theodore Pitt.

So the eight months of exile at Strathroy came to an end. Gazing into the tear-stained faces, as the Bretts gathered about him in farewell, Noyes exclaimed: "These have been the happiest eight months of my life!"

2

A new life began—a life remote from the strife and the attacks of his enemies and the ridicule of the world. His providential good luck remained with him still, for the purchase of the Stone Cottage was speedily effected on easy terms. Noyes was reunited with the "Josephine" of his youth, the ever-faithful Mother Noyes, and with his sister Harriet Skinner, and a little family of followers.

The Stone Cottage was on the brow of the hill overlooking the Falls. It had been erected during the earlier decades of the century by some romantic Briton who had evidently a keen appreciation of the beauty of its site. From the unrailed veranda one could look down at the American Falls, the suspension bridge, and even glimpse the swirling "green marble" waters of the Niagara river. It was a cottage in name only, for the low rambling structure was far more commodious than the word implies. Five spacious rooms were spread out on its first floor, and there were seven bedrooms upstairs under the "Gothic" roof. There were two pantries, a kitchen and a summer kitchen. A great woodshed linked the house itself with the barn and stables behind. In that woodshed was soon installed a Turkish bath; and eventually its low attic was to be converted into a dormitory for the boys who were sent from Oneida.

In the parlor an old-fashioned piano was placed, and a special armchair for Noyes. He passed from this corner room into the long dining room, with its table always ready for a dozen or more, a table which on occasion was stretched out to accommodate twenty diners. Mother Noyes usually sat at the head of this table, and Noyes at her left. In the dining room between meals, Mother Noyes and Aunt Harriet Skinner used to work industriously at the making of fish-scale flowers, with a single bowl placed between their rocking-chairs.

Noyes chose as his bedroom the chamber located directly above the parlor. Through its diamond-paned windows he could gaze down at the tumbling, foaming cataracts of the Horseshoe Falls. Incessantly the panes of the windows vibrated in response to the roar of the plunging waters. There, often, as if lulled by the roar that never stopped, he fell into an old man's revery of the past and the future. Sometimes he would be found resting in his chair, with his eyes closed and both arms folded across his body. He seemed almost asleep, wandering dream-like in his thoughts. But the intruder discovered that both thumbs and index fingers moved in a sort of shuttle-like rubbing of the lower seams of his waistcoat. This habit became so inveterate that finally two patches of stout leather were sewed on as a protection against this strange reflex; it had worn out the fabric of certain garments! The heavy head, surmounted by its crown of unkempt locks, sank deep in the chair; his face wore an expression of ineffable serenity.

Under the supervision of Aunt Harriet Skinner, life at the Stone Cottage was efficiently and democratically organized. Miss Jane Kinsley presided in the kitchen, with Mrs. Ellen Miller second-in-command there. The gentle, self-effacing Mother Noyes chose as her daily task the washing of the dishes. Miss Chloe Seymour, in her prim gray and white gowns, was keeper of the linen, mender of clothes and seamstress-in-chief. The gardens outside were under the care of her brother Henry Seymour. At first Theodore Pitt acted as Noyes's prime minister and man Friday; but he was later superseded by James Burton Herrick.

They lived on terms of formal, old-fashioned courtesy with their neighbors, exchanging gifts of flowers and fruits with those living closest. The neighbors and the other townsfolk might well have asked what enigmatic past held together this picturesque group of eccentric characters. Somehow, some one began to circulate rumors that they were "free lovers"; but the appearance of those elderly ladies, so prim, so gentle, so innocent of the ways of the world, completely disarmed criticism.

Quaintest of them all, and most unworldly, was Aunt Harriet Skinner. After the incredible adventure life had held for her the past forty years, Harriet Skinner remained to the end as unspoiled and as deliciously naïve as a little girl. Daily her eyesight grew dimmer and dimmer—so that she armed herself with reading glasses, finer reading glasses, house-work glasses and far-seeing glasses, which were always lost or left behind. Clad in dresses which she cut and sewed herself, Harriet presented a curiously unworldly appearance. Especially on those occasions when she departed to visit her nephew Charles Ransom at Kalamazoo or the Charles Meads in New York, and came back with amusingly incongruous tales of horse-races and great dinner parties.

Harriet threw herself into all her appointed tasks with the absorption of a little girl, but she was more in her element as amanuensis for John than in the kitchen preparing Graham mush. The children who eventually became members of the household were never to forget how jealously Aunt Harriet guarded Mother Noyes's privilege of pouring first from the pitcher of heavy cream at the dining-table! In striking contrast stood Henry Seymour, dictator and magician of the orchard and garden, an uncouth, rustic Franciscan friar, reveling, when not actually wallowing, in his life-giving manures and mucks. "I am as happy as ten thousand kings!" exclaimed Henry one frosty morning at five as he broke the ice in the tub. His crude manners at the table might affront his prim sister Miss Chloe Seymour; but no one could deny Henry's uncanny powers of persuasion over all growing things. The size of his strawberries was phenomenal—one of them measured nine inches in circumference. "When I go *over* I'm going full of projects!"

On the other hand, Mr. James Burton Herrick introduced into the family at the Stone Cottage a note of urbanity, of sophistication, of humor. He had been a young minister who had preached to a fashionable New York City congregation. Some deep undercurrent of mysticism had drawn him into the orbit of Noyes; had drawn him so completely that he had given up his wife and children to join the Community. Impressed at the presence of this aristocrat, a curious visitor had once asked him what office he held. "I am the rinser of dishes," James Herrick gravely replied. Despite his suffering at the self-inflicted separation from the wife and children he loved, Herrick remained a passionate Noyes disciple, and was delighted to share the exile's life at the Stone Cottage.

3

On Sundays, regular meetings were held in the parlor. Across the suspension bridge, up the hill came all those loyal members of the old Community who now lived at Niagara Falls. Ensconced in his great chair, surrounded by members of his reunited family, Father Noyes continued his home talks. His words were recorded with even greater care than before. His message was the same: Your destiny is proportioned, not to your own greatness but to the greatness to which you are joined, the greatness that has taken possession of you and flows through you. He advised them not to be poisoned by discord; to forget resentments of the past; to forgive and forget; to turn their hearts toward the center, which is Christ.... "The one who has the largest heart and the best faculty of forgiving and uniting will get the lead among us."

The voice, as always, could scarcely rise above a whisper. Sometimes he was only faintly aware of their loving presence. Always he seemed to return, almost as though speaking to himself, to his one central thought: I am one; we are all; the great labor of salvation is to melt the one into the all, the *I* into the *we:* individuality will blossom into infinitely greater productivity and splendor when it is attached to the *all*, than when it is working by itself.

After the home talk, they stayed, the members from across the river, to partake of an informal communion of wine; to exchange reminiscences; and to report the growth and progress of the Community children, since the dispersal. Some of these children were now reaching the age when something must be done concerning their education.

4

Noyes's nine younger boys and girls were now his special consideration. At the time of the "break-up," however, the mothers of some of these children became affiliated with the dissentients, and subsequently married outside the circle of loyalists. The mothers of other children remained unmarried.

To all of his children Noyes wrote from the Stone Cottage offering them, each, his support, his home, his parental protection. This letter is said to be a remarkable and touching document. Noyes's letter to his children received serious consideration. The mothers of two or three were indeed definitely alienated;

and some of the children had been given the family names of their step-fathers.

But three of these sons presently arrived—all stalwart, well brought-up lads. One or two of the daughters came too, and a nephew, his brother George's son. More than a little awed in the presence of this aged patriarch who was indeed their father, the boys felt more comradeship with Mr. Herrick, who initiated them into the fun of lacrosse, fishing, and picnics at Brock's Monument, led them in the battles against skunks under the barn, or introduced them to the cow Cushie and her calf, and Oldie and Youngie, the roosters. The youngsters exulted in the new sense of liberation at Niagara, for they had suffered during their childhood from the taunts and jibes of the hoodlums of "Turkey Street" and had been more or less successfully isolated from outside contacts.

So many young folk of Community parentage were living now at Niagara Falls—on both sides of the river—that the organization of a school became imperative. Teachers could be drawn from their own members. Of prime importance, Noyes insisted, were their spiritual attainments. The subjects to be taught were chosen according to what the teachers had to offer rather than according to the worldly needs of the young pupils. Thus he himself would teach them Hebrew, Aunt Harriet Skinner could impart the elements of Greek, and the urbane Mr. Herrick, with his city background, could teach them dancing as well as mathematics. That school made the neighbors whisper, so thoroughly did it dispense with routine discipline. The hours of its sessions varied—classes were usually held only in the morning and vacations were dispensed with except upon the vote of the students. The school was assembled first in the "blue house" back in the village of Clifton, where Mr. Kelly lived. Later it moved to the North Cottage, a house straight back through the trees from the Stone Cottage; finally, in 1885, to the "new house" built by the Kellys. Greek and Hebrew were studied around the dining-room table in the Stone Cottage itself. There were long excursions into the woods, and geological surveys of the whole Niagara region.

The young people were assigned to definite tasks and household chores. The boys helped in the care of the horse, the cow, the chickens and the barn; they chopped wood and carried coal into the house to feed the eight hungry stoves in the various rooms upstairs and down.

Every summer, in a grove over the hill across the railway

tracks to the west, a camp meeting was held, and the boys and girls attended every evening. At least the boys were supposed to attend. But they entered a conspiracy to evade this boresome duty. They drew straws and one was elected to go and report the goings-on, so that the rest could answer questions intelligibly at breakfast. The lucky were thus freed to "spark the outside girls" those long summer evenings.

One evening the zealous evangelist created something of a sensation and shocked his listeners by a curious slip of the tongue. Fervently he had begun to lead the singing of a hymn:

"*Free love* and grace everlasting
Free love and grace everlasting–"

The singer became conscious of the expressions of shocked surprise that swept over his listeners—but it was too late to correct himself, and he continued:

"Free love and grace everlasting
Reigning in the New Jerusalem–"

But the devout corrected him in taking up the chorus–

"Free *grace* and *love* everlasting
Reigning in the New Jerusalem!"

They reported this *contretemps* to Father Noyes at the breakfast table next morning. His silent, wheezing laugh set them off into gales of merriment; he explained that it was a practical joke of the angels.

5

At the end of August, 1885, an epidemic of colds and grippe broke out in the Stone Cottage. Almost every member of the family was laid low. Noyes himself was stricken on September 5; and by the last of September, he remained in so weakened a condition that Dr. George Cragin was summoned from Oneida. The old man protested that he did not want to consult doctors, but felt strengthened after the visit of Dr. Cragin. He decided to move over to the New House, which had just been completed across the garden—he wanted a change, he explained. He regained some of his vitality, but by the first week of November he showed symptoms of a general breakdown, and his son Theodore was summoned from New York. Dr. Clark, a physician from across the river, was called in consultation, and gave little hope for Father Noyes's recovery.

By January, 1886, however, he announced himself much better. Some of his old brightness returned; he felt happier than he had been in months. Less than a week later, however, he asked: "How long does it take to die?" and seemingly resigned himself to that tiresome ordeal. From then until early in April he rallied and grew weak, improved and relapsed by turns. At last, however, began the final decline, and the end became a question of days. They watched over him in relays. They held prayer meetings in the New House and the Stone Cottage. Across the bridge one by one came the disciples, the children, to make their silent farewells. The heavy white head lay immobile on its pillow, its bony structure accentuated by the lamplight. On April 8, Mother Noyes wrote once more for Theodore to hasten back from New York. The following day a telegram was dispatched to him; when this son of the faithful Harriet arrived, the dying man's face lighted with pleasure, but it was too late for words; only the tightened clasp of their hands could express the love that had survived so many bitter differences. After that, consciousness of all worldly things ebbed away like an outgoing tide. Noyes stopped breathing April 13, 1886, half an hour before noon.

Closest to the supine body, remained Harriet Holton Noyes, who had accompanied him for nearly half a century on his uncharted path. There, too, knelt Harriet Noyes Skinner. Theodore was at the bedside too, and his nephew George, a youth of sixteen. And completing the background with figures of the utmost purity and naïveté, were Miss Chloe Seymour, Miss Jane Kinsley, and Emily Otis Kelly, who had followed this outlaw saint into exile.

Burial, the little group decided, would be in Clifton, Ontario. They were not certain that those in control of the Oneida Community, Ltd., would receive the remains of the exiled leader. The next morning, however, a telegram was received from the Community, urging that the remains of the founder be buried on the hillside with the rest of the companions who slept there. So the body was placed on the train that left Niagara Falls at three that afternoon. The elders departed on the same train—Mother Noyes, Aunt Harriet Skinner, Theodore, Erastus Hamilton, Mr. and Mrs. George Miller, Myron Kinsley and his wife, and Jane Kinsley. The younger children—boys and girls—were left at the Stone Cottage; and one of them, seeking refuge in her diary, jotted down: "Aunt Harriet and Mother Noyes left in good spirits and I heard Auntie say that it didn't seem a bit like a funeral."

On the hillside they buried the body of John Noyes. True to the spirit of the Community, no conspicuous spot was selected for

Noyes's grave, no towering monument erected above it. His resting place was among the ranks of the little army he had led in his raid upon the world from the Kingdom of God. The gravestone merely gives his name and the dates of his birth and death.

6

For years following the death of Noyes, the survivors of the Community drifted further and further away from the solidarity of spirit he had once evoked among them. They ran after new beliefs, were blown willy-nilly by the winds of many new doctrines. Spiritualism, which had already attracted many of them, now split the joint-stock company into two rival factions. The whole venture seemed at that time to belong only to the past.

In the world at large, John Humphrey Noyes was forgotten until the popularization of Socialism of the Fabian and Marxian schools. Then the Oneida Community was studied as an example of industrial coöperation and communistic organization, but with a note of condescension, because of its religious origin. George Bernard Shaw went to the British Museum to read what he could about the Community; most of his reading was, perforce, the unreliable accounts of Hepworth Dixon. But Mr. Shaw, with his flair for character, recognized the superman qualities in Noyes; so that when finally he came to write the "Revolutionist's Handbook" as a supplement to "Man and Superman" he paid an eloquent tribute to the genius of Noyes. But even Mr. Shaw did not awaken serious interest in the significance of this "mighty shepherd."

Some twenty years after the death of Noyes, Herbert George Wells paid his first visit to America. Mr. Wells made a pilgrimage to the shrine of pre-Marxian communism. Instead of decay he found new life throbbing in the old Community. The red bricks of the old home were mellowing and covered with green vines. It stood in the midst of green lawns and the trees now towered above the rambling house vaguely suggesting an English country house. On the verandas he found the survivors of that unprecedented adventure—serene old ladies and gentlemen to whom the inquisitive Briton yearned to ask the most personal questions—questions which, for all his radicalism and modernity, he did not quite dare to express. But there were others, too, not quite so old, and more willing to talk. They were of the generation which had rebelled. Mr. Wells was escorted to the upper sitting room and permitted to scrutinize daguerreotypes and stereopticon views of the past—the preposterous, incredible, fantastic past which betrayed not an inkling of its secret in those photographs of gentlemen in frock coats; in the decorous gentility of the ladies, for all their short skirts and short hair! For Mr. Wells, there remained an ineradicable quality of New England about it all. It seemed to him a secret gone forever, which could not be divulged—any more than the fragrance could return to a pressed flower fluttering out of the pages of an old book. Touched by profane hands, it would crumble into powder.

But the factories of the Oneida Community, Ltd., Mr. Wells found buzzing with new industry. A new generation was coming into power—the generation of the "stirpicults," the stalwart sons of John Noyes, and the descendants of the Yankee founders. Proud of its heritage, this rising generation was asserting its inalienable right to work out its own destiny on its own terms. The fabric of lives John Noyes had so closely woven created a bond of close fraternity between the boys and girls born during the final decade of the Community. In 1895, Pierrepont B. Noyes, while still in his twenties, was already exhibiting the vigor and determination of his father. He, too, was inspired by a vision, neither religious nor mystical, but one of industrial justice. He and his half-brothers and comrades threw their youthful energies into the creation of an organization in which there would exist no one too rich, no one too poor.

The spoon business, inaugurated almost by chance upon the suggestion of Charles Cragin, developed into a tableware industry of international scope. On the farmlands of the old Community a city of homes gradually grew up; today it is the city of Sherrill. Employed laborers shared in the profits and were encouraged to own their own homes. While communistic equality was not attempted, the new company rewarded, with overmeasure, as the elder Noyes had in the beginning, those outside the group of descendants. The second and third generations have remained members of a ramified family group, working and playing together, identifying the one in the whole, respecting individual creeds and opinions, and bound by a tacit law of family agreement.

Time could not destroy the unique tapestry he wove out of those lives. A sort of dynasty was created—a dynasty re-inforced by the other families of the Community—the Kinsleys, the Cragins, the Allens, and others. In certain aspects, this dynasty reminds us of those great family trees of the Renaissance and after—the Negroli of Milan, the Pénicauds of Limoges, the Hannongs of

Strasbourg. The founders left them no special craft, it is true; their heritage was a combination of valor and vision, of Yankee practicality and a disdain for worldly ostentation, qualities conspicuously dramatized in Noyes's own life.

EPILOGUE

EPILOGUE

Ideas must be lived, not merely entertained.
—André Malraux.

Was he a saint or a madman?

Academic theologians have dismissed John Noyes as the crack-brained leader of a misguided sect, and have relegated him to eternal oblivion. Havelock Ellis has written that he considers Noyes "one of the noblest pioneers America has produced.... His solution may not be suitable for general adoption, but his insight foresaw the problems which we today are encountering."

If there remain readers who are shocked by this chronicle, who feel that no good purpose is served by reviving this long-buried chapter in the social history of America, they may be reminded that in the eyes of their contemporaries and even afterward the saints and mystics and liberators have always seemed mad. Let us not, therefore, be misled by the absurdities, the naïvetés, the jewels of unconscious humor and inverted wisdom we have here unearthed. For through the ages the "saints"—not merely of the church but all who have led reborn consecrated lives—have appeared ridiculous, obsessed, monomaniacal. They have defied tradition and social habits; they have been eternally reckless in declaring their independence of the world and the church. Their *euphoria* in proclaiming the Kingdom of God on earth has been denounced as a symptom of their insanity. The outpouring of the inner energy that flows from them has been destructive, a menace to the existing order. But if their energies are tumultuous and torrential, their heresies flare up like incendiary flames, and the moralists rush to extinguish them. It has been the purpose of this book to show that John Humphrey Noyes is entitled to a place among these divine madmen.

Asceticism seems the accepted *sine qua non* of the saint; here is a man who dared to establish a régime of sexual communism in the very heart of Puritan New England; who managed to maintain it, in the center of New York State, for a period of thirty years. How can such a man be described as a "saint"?

The Christian saint or mystic has been characterized by Henri Bergson, in his luminous crowning work,* as one whose spiritual energy is transformed into "action, creation, love." The Oriental stops at the stage of contemplation; for the Christian, faith can not remain in the realm of passivity, nor seek ultimate expression in mere words. The force of that inner energy drives him onward

* See Bibliography.

into external activity, into the realization of his conviction. He lives out his ideas. Such sainthood refuses to be discouraged by practical obstacles, refuses to retreat into renunciations, or to dissipate itself in occult ecstasy. Its drive is relentlessly forward. For Bergson, such men incarnate the *élan vital.* They "break the dike" for a humanity in bondage to the rigidity of external, static morality.

This saintliness has little to do with sanctimoniousness. The true saint is an organizer, a statesman, a leader of men. He is rich in the power to inspire allegiance; ardent in driving his disciples onward in the creation of new patterns of living. In addition, Bergson writes, the authentic mystic experiences an imperious desire to impregnate the world with the germ of his truth, to broadcast his good news to humanity at large. This urge drives him on, to use Bergson's expression, *comme un élan d'amour.* It is a passion. The hope for the human race becomes an all-compelling motive for saints of this order, a love they are certain will lift man into a new dimension, a new heaven.

Bergson's dramatic portrayal of the character of the mystic's life might have been written with John Humphrey Noyes specifically in mind. His life was no mere matter of visions, transports, ecstasies. In a forbidding, even grim, social environment, rigidly prescribed by custom and clerical authority, he deliberately violated the sacrosanct taboos. For nearly half a century he fought to release physical love from the inferno into which it had been relegated by New England Puritanism. He sought to integrate this fountainhead of human activity with the life of the spirit, to reclaim a basic factor of life that had been crushed, thwarted, and denied. His aim was not the pallid, academic recognition of sexual activity as mere "facts of life." Rather it was the elevation of erotic expression into ordered sacrament, a rite lifted above individual desire; for in it Noyes found the symbol of all spiritual community, the allegory of the unity of man and God.

No account of these sexual innovations should overshadow Noyes's eminence as a statesman in the true sense of that misunderstood word. He initiated experiments in every phase of social and industrial life; and, in the face of ridicule, castigation, and persecution, he carried these experiments through to mature fruition. To cultivate and maintain a régime of communal living through four decades of the nineteenth century in the midst of a period of change and chaos, remains in itself a monumental achievement in American history. Let us value it as an expression of a steadfast intensity of purpose all too rare in the annals of humanity.

It may be objected that he went too far, that he should have reminded himself that while all things are lawful, all things are not expedient. But he was of that type of man for whom there can be no sharp dividing line between inner conviction and external conduct. An old legend narrates that when Genius was born, all the gifts lavished upon it were marred by one unkind fairy who withheld the power of knowing when to stop. That is why, Samuel Butler suggests, genius seems so immoral, for "it is even more immoral for a man to be too far in front as to lag too far behind. The only absolute morality is complete stagnation."

However obvious his defects remain, John Noyes possessed the attributes of genius. With swiftness and direction he gave purposive expression to his faith; with heroic courage he tested his truth in the crucible of experience; with supreme indifference to threats and coercion he pursued, without deviation, his chosen course. Allied to genius also was that power of his to persuade men and women to unflinching allegiance, and his gift of arousing them from lethargy and inertia, to follow him to heaven or to hell.

Because of these qualities, a true estimate of Noyes entitles him to a place among those pioneers whose lives William James has compared to the crest of some great wave. They seem to embody humanity's thrust forward into the unknown. They are the seekers for complete, God-like liberty. The crest breaks, the wave recedes; but something has been gained forever—a new liberty. In the case of Noyes, it was the freedom to think anew on old problems, the freedom to experiment, and to speak aloud on physical love without hypocrisy.

Such a life has seemed far more worthy of commemoration than many of those more celebrated, more honored by the nation and the world, yet who never dared, as Noyes did, to translate ideals into the reality of living.

ACKNOWLEDGMENTS

It is impossible to name all who have helped me to gather the information which forms the foundation of this book. My first and outstanding debt is to Mr. George Wallingford Noyes, who has consecrated his life to the task of preserving and protecting all the records of the Oneida experiment. Without constant reference to his book "John Humphrey Noyes: The Putney Community" a clear insight into that period could never have been gained. To the sons and daughters of John Humphrey Noyes, who have at all times answered my questions with honesty, courage, and generosity, I am scarcely less indebted. For permission to read unpublished manuscripts I am indebted to Pierrepont Noyes, Holton Van Velzer Noyes, Mrs. Wilber Earl, Mrs. Gertrude Noyes, and Mrs. Jessie Kinsley. For information concerning the stirpicultural experiment, I express my thanks to Dr. Hilda Herrick Noyes and George Wallingford Noyes; information concerning Noyes's sojourn in Strathroy has been generously contributed by Mr. Harry Brett of Niagara Falls.

In the final task of compressing the manuscript to a length which would permit its publication in a single volume, and in the revision of much of its material, the conscientious and steadfast assistance of my wife, Jessie Daves Parker, can be acknowledged as nothing less than collaboration.

R.A.P.

New York,
July 17, 1935

BIBLIOGRAPHY

BIBLIOGRAPHY

Berdiaeff, Nicolas. "*Esprit et liberté; essai de philosophie chrétienne.*" Paris: *Société commercial d'édition et de librairie.* 1933.

Bergson, Henri. "*Les deux sources de la morale et de la religion.*" Paris: Librairie Felix Alcan, 1932.

Billot, Cardinal Louis, S.J. "*La Parousie.*" Paris: Gabriel Beauchesne. 1920.

Dartmouth, The. Hanover: New Hampshire. Vol. III, No. 2-4.

Dickinson, Robert Latou and Louise Stevens Bryant. "Control of Conception." Baltimore: The Williams and Wilkins Co. 1932.

Dixon, William Hepworth. "New America"; with illustrations from original photographs. Philadelphia: J. B. Lippincott & Co. 1867. "Spiritual Wives." London: Hurst, 2 v.

Eastlake, Allan (Abel Easton). "The Oneida Community." London: Redway, 1900.

Eastman, Hubbard. "Noyesism Unveiled; a History of the Sect Self-styled Perfectionists, with a Summary View of Their Leading Doctrines." Brattleboro, Vt.: The author. 1849.

Edson, C. P. (Pseud. of C. E. Robinson). "Communism: Oneida Community." (*Manufacturer and Builder, N. Y.*, vols. 25, 26, 1893-94.)

Ellis, Havelock. "Studies in the Psychology of Sex." Vol. vi. Philadelphia: F. A. Davis Company. 1911.

Frankland, Frederick William. "Thoughts on Ultimate Problems; being a series of short studies on theological and metaphysical subjects." London: D. Nutt, 1911.

"Garrison, William Lloyd (1805-1879): The Story of His Life Told by His Children." 4 v. New York: The Century Co. 1885.

Haskett, William J. (formerly of the Society of Shakers). "Shakerism Unmasked, or the History of the Shakers." Pittsfield: Published by the author. 1828.

Hinds, William Alfred. "American Communities; brief sketches of Economy, Zora, Bethel, Aurora, Amana, Icaria, the Shakers, Oneida, Wallingford, and the Brotherhood of the New Life." Oneida, N. Y. 1878.

Howells, William Dean. "Sketch of the Life and Character of R. B. Hayes." New York. 1876.

James, William. "The Varieties of Religious Experience; a study in human nature." New York: Longmans, Green. 1902.

Knowlton, Charles. "Fruits of philosophy. A treatise on the population problem." Boston. 1833.

McGee, Anita Newcomb. "An Experiment in Human Stirpiculture." (Reprint, *American Anthropologist*, Oct. 1891.)

Montefiore, Leonard. Letter to London *Times*, Aug. 16, 1879.

Nation. N. Y. Feb. 20, 1879. No. 712; p. 128.

Newhouse, Sewell, and others. "The Trapper's Guide; a manual of instruction for capturing all kinds of fur-bearing animals." Edited by John Humphrey Noyes. Kenwood, N. Y., 1893.

Nordhoff, Charles. "The Communistic Societies of the United States." New York. 1875.

Noyes, George Wallingford. "Religious Experience of John Humphrey Noyes, founder of the Oneida Community"; with seventeen illustrations, compiled and edited by George Wallingford Noyes. New York: Macmillan. 1923.

"John Humphrey Noyes, the Putney Community"; compiled and edited by George Wallingford Noyes; with twenty-four illustrations. Oneida, N. Y. 1931.

Noyes, Hilda Herrick, and George Wallingford Noyes. "The Oneida Community Experiment in Stirpiculture." (Reprint, *Eugenics, Genetics and the Family*, vol. 1, pp. 374-386. 1923.)

Noyes, John. An Oration, delivered in Brattleborough, July 4, 1811. Brattleborough, Vt. Printed by William Fessenden, 1811.

Noyes, John Humphrey. "The Berean: a manual for the help of those who seek the faith of the primitive church." Putney, Vt.: Office of *Spiritual Magazine*. 1847.

Noyes, John Humphrey. "A Treatise on the Second Coming of Christ." Putney, Vt. 1840.

Noyes, John Humphrey. "Bible Communism." Oneida, N. Y. 1848

Noyes, John Humphrey. "Dixon and His Copyists. A criticism of the accounts of the Oneida Community in 'New America,' 'Spiritual Wives,' and kindred publications." Wallingford, Conn.: Wallingford Printing Company. 1874.

Noyes, John Humphrey. "Essay on Scientific Propagation," with an appendix containing a health report of the Oneida Community, by Theodore R. Noyes. Oneida, N. Y., Oneida Community. 1875(?).

Noyes, John Humphrey. "Home-talks." Edited by A. Barron and G. N. Miller. Oneida, N. Y. The Community. 1875.

Noyes, John Humphrey. "Male Continence." Oneida, N. Y. Office of *The American Socialist*. 1873.

Noyes, John Humphrey. "Salvation from Sin, the End of Christian Faith." Oneida, N. Y.: Oneida Community. 1876.

Noyes, Theodore R. "Report on the Health of Children in the Oneida Community." Oneida, N. Y. 1878.

Noyes, Theodore R. "The Oneida Community's Change of Base." (Letter to *Nation*, Sept. 11, 1879. No. 741, p. 173.)

Oneida Community Publications (Periodicals)

The Witness, 2 vols., 1837-1843. Ithaca, N. Y., and Putney, Vt.

The Spiritual Magazine, 2 vols. 1846-1850. Putney, Va., and Oneida, N. Y.

The Perfectionist and Theocratic Watchman, 3 vols, 1843-Feb. 14, 1846. Putney, Vt.

The Perfectionist, vol. 1-2, 1834-1836. New Haven, Conn.

The Free Church Circular. A weekly journal of home science and general intelligence. 12 vols, Nov. 6, 1851-Feb. 22, 1864 (old series). Brooklyn, N. Y., and Oneida, N. Y.

The Circular, 13 vols., March 21, 1864-March 9, 1876 (new series). Wallingford, Conn. and Oneida, N. Y.

The American Socialist, 4 vols., March 30, 1876-Dec. 25, 1879. Oneida, N. Y.

The Community Quadrangle, 1908-1913; 1926-1930.

Oneida Community. Annual report of the Oneida Association. Oneida Reserve, Leonard & Company, Printers. 1849-1851. 3 vols. Full title, First report: Annual report of the Oneida Association: exhibiting its history, principles, and transactions to Jan. 1, 1849.

Oneida Community. "Handbook of the Oneida Community; with a sketch of its founder, and an outline of its constitution and doctrine." Wallingford, Conn: 1867, 1871, 1875. 3 vols.

Oneida Community. "Mutual criticism." Oneida, N. Y.: Office of *The American Socialist*. 1876.

"Oneida Community, The: a familiar exposition of its ideas and practical life, in a conversation with a visitor." Wallingford Circular office. 1865.

"Oneida Community Cooking; or, A dinner without meat"; by Harriet H. Skinner. Oneida, N. Y.: 1873.

Owen, Robert Dale. "The moral physiology; a treatise on popular questions, or means devised to check pregnancy. By a physician." New York, printed for the author. 1836.

Pratt, James Bissett. "The Religious Consciousness." New York: Macmillan. 1920.

Realf, Richard. "Poems by Richard Realf, Poet, Soldier, Workman." With a Memoir by Richard J. Hinton. New York and London: Funk & Wagnalls. 1898.

Reed, Isaac G., Jr. "The Oneida Community of Free Lovers: what they think, what they do, and what they are." (*Frank Leslie's Illustrated Newspaper*. N. Y., April, 1870.)

Russell, J. Stuart. "The Parousia; a critical inquiry into the New Testament doctrine of our Lord's Second Coming." London: T. Fisher Unwin. 1887.

Sellers, Charles Coleman. "Theophilus, the Battle-Axe; a history of the lives and adventures of Theophilus Ransom Gates and the Battle-axes." Philadelphia: Press of Patterson and White Company. 1930.

Shaw, George Bernard. "Man and Superman." New York: Brentano's. 1912.

Strachey, Rachel Conn. "Religious Fanaticism." Extracts from the Papers of Hannah Whitall Smith. Edited with an Introduction by Ray Strachey. London: Faber & Gwyer, Ltd. 1928.

Tricoche, George Nestler. "*Le Communisme en Action: études des communistic societies aux Etats Unis.*" (*Journal des Economistes*, Paris. March 15, 1896.)

Warfield, Benjamin Breckinridge. "Perfectionism." 2 vols. New York and London: Oxford University Press. 1931.

Wayland-Smith, F. "Heaven on Earth: A Realistic Tale." (By Gerald Thorne.) New York: Lovell Brothers & Company. 1896.

Wells, H. G. "The Future in America: A Search after Realities." New York and London: Harper & Brothers. 1906.

INDEX

INDEX